PROPERTY OF
RIVERWOOD COMMUNITY MENTAL HEALTH

THE PSYCHOLOGIST
AS EXPERT WITNESS

THE PSYCHOLOGIST AS EXPERT WITNESS

THEODORE H. BLAU

A Wiley-Interscience Publication

JOHN WILEY & SONS

New York / Chichester / Brisbane / Toronto / Singapore

Copyright © 1984 by John Wiley & Sons, Inc.

All rights reserved. Published simultaneously in Canada.

Reproduction or translation of any part of this work
beyond that permitted by Section 107 or 108 of the
1976 United States Copyright Act without the permission
of the copyright owner is unlawful. Requests for
permission or further information should be addressed to
the Permissions Department, John Wiley & Sons, Inc.

Library of Congress Cataloging in Publication Data:

Blau, Theodore H.
    The psychologist as expert witness.

    (Wiley series on health psychology/behavioral medicine)
    "A Wiley-Interscience publication."
    Bibliography: p.
    Includes index.
    1. Evidence, Expert—United States.   2. Psychology,
Forensic.   I. Title.   II. Series.   [DNLM: 1. Expert
Testimony.   2. Psychology.   3. Professional Practice.
BF 75 B645p]
KF8965.B37   1984   347.73'66   84-7512
ISBN 0-471-87129-X   347.30766

Printed in the United States of America

10 9 8 7 6 5 4 3

Series Preface

This series is addressed to clinicians and scientists who are interested in human behavior relevant to the promotion and maintenance of health and the prevention and treatment of illness. *Health psychology* and *behavioral medicine* are terms that refer to both the scientific investigation and interdisciplinary integration of behavioral and biomedical knowledge and technology to prevention, diagnosis, treatment, and rehabilitation.

The major and purposely somewhat general areas of both health psychology and behavioral medicine which will receive greatest emphasis in this series are: theoretical issues of bio-psycho-social function, diagnosis, treatment, and maintenance; issues of organizational impact on human performance and an individual's impact on organizational functioning; development and implementation of technology for understanding, enhancing, or remediating human behavior and its impact on health and function; and clinical considerations with children and adults, alone, in groups, or in families that contribute to the scientific and practical/clinical knowledge of those charged with the care of patients.

The series encompasses considerations as intellectually broad as psychology and as numerous as the multitude of areas of evaluation treatment and prevention and maintenance that make up the field of medicine. It is the aim of the series to provide a vehicle which will focus attention on both the breadth and the interrelated nature of the sciences and practices making up health psychology and behavioral medicine.

THOMAS J. BOLL

The University of Alabama in Birmingham
Birmingham, Alabama

Preface

A burgeoning interest by psychologists in the application of psychological principles and practice to the field of jurisprudence seems to have occurred during the past decade. I use the term *seems* advisedly. Efforts to make psychology available to the bar and the bench go back 100 years. Although in the present era most of the contact between psychology and the law is between those professionals in psychology who apply the science and those attorneys and judges who wish the benefit of professional psychology, the origins of the interface between psychology and the law rest firmly with the academicians and experimentalists.

Some psychologists see their role in relationship to the courts as that of ancillary psychiatrists or alienists. Issues of sanity and competence, however, represent a rather small portion of psychology's potential to promote human welfare through the American system of jurisprudence.

There were few guidelines for the use of psychology in the courts. As a result, psychology and law "just grew." It is doubtful that any one individual can define the field. The purpose of this book is to make an attempt at defining psychologists' current and future potential as expert witnesses. An attempt will be made to delineate the ways in which psychology has come into contact with the court, where we have done well, and where we have done badly. Primary emphasis will be on standards for practice and practical training in providing expert testimony to the courts.

In no way can this book be considered definitive. Psychologists who intend to make themselves available to the bar and the bench should understand that the law is much more dynamic and changing than psychology. By the time this book goes to press, many of the citations will have been replaced, enhanced, or challenged in various jurisdictions. This is the nature of the law. Lawyers accept it, and if psychologists are to practice within the framework of the American court system, it behooves us to understand and to accept this dynamic system.

The interaction between psychology and the law can have a salutary effect on the quality of psychological concepts and services. The burden of proof always lies with the expert witness. As psychologists function in the role of expert more frequently, there will be a tendency to emphasize quality of supporting data in terms of traditional reliability and validity.

Clinical and professional psychologists may find it difficult to adapt to the extremely open adversary system practiced in our courts. In a sense, academic and experimental psychologists are likely to fare better than clinicians because they are accustomed to being challenged, and to supporting their conclusions with precedent and relatively substantial data. Clinicians and professionals, however, are likely to do better in the practical requirements of the courtroom since they are more practiced in rendering opinions, within reasonable psychological probability, in their everyday clinical work.

I will venture to risk the statement that there is a place in the court system for almost anyone in psychology. I would certainly hope that more psychologists will prepare themselves and invest their skills and talents in helping to forward the purposes and goals of American jurisprudence. One need only travel to other countries to come to understand the fairness and openness of the American system of jurisprudence.

This system is in dire trouble insofar as court dockets are concerned. It is extremely difficult to apply the constitutional guarantee of early trial and early justice when there simply are not enough places on the docket for the number of cases that require attention. Psychologists will find that when they are retained by attorneys or the court as expert witness, in civil or criminal matters, adversary issues tend to become clarified, settlement or plea bargaining occurs, and the case is frequently removed from the docket. If psychologists, by being available to the courts, are able to do anything to help clear the crowded dockets, psychology will have made a significant contribution to the promotion of human welfare.

A wide range of situations in which psychologists have appeared as expert witnesses is addressed in this book. In those areas where psychologists are likely to be called frequently and/or where there are current controversies, details of the law, procedures, and samples of testimony will be more extensive than in areas where psychologists are not so involved. Where pertinent reference works are available, efforts have been made to refer the reader to appropriate sources. In areas where the average attorney may be somewhat unsure about the appropriate use of psychological experts, case law is cited so that the psychological expert can make reference to the appropriate precedent. Common legal terms are introduced and defined throughout the text. A glossary is provided to define most legal terms that the psychologist is likely to find in functioning as an expert witness.

This volume is more of a cookbook than a learned treatise. The objectives are to introduce psychologists to the world of the psychologist in the courtroom, identify current and emerging areas of application, and prepare the psychologist to function credibly as an expert witness.

Acknowledgments are in order at this point. My colleagues in psychology who were helpful and generous with ideas, critique, manuscript evaluation, and encouragement include Linda Coleman, James Crumbley, L. G. Daugherty, Sheldon Freud, F. Girsh, D. Grossman, Blaze Harkey, Florence Kaslow, Elizabeth Loftus, Paul Lipsitt, Robert Leark, Orin McEuen, Maria Martinroe, Maurice Pavlow, Elliott Rapoport, Edwin Shneidman, Sherry Skidmore, R. Bob Smith, and Gretchen White.

Members of the bar whose ideas, guidance, suggestions, and influence have contributed to the tone and content of this book include C. Richard Baker, Charles Baldonado, Donald Bradshaw, Bernard H. Dempsey, Jr., Frank Glinn, J. Bert Grandoff, Mark Horwitz, Bennie Lazzara, Mark Luttier, Ed Ratiner, Robert Scott, Patrick Sirridge, Harrison T. Slaughter, Jr., Tom Tweedy, and Dewey Villareal.

Special recognition and immeasurable thanks are due Jeffrey Alan Blau, Esq., and Richard Michael Blau, Esq., for their generous help in defining points of law, procedure, and in obtaining legal citations.

Ms. Ann Dimity and Ms. Susan Davenport were extremely helpful in the preparation of this manuscript.

Dr. Lili R. Blau deserves special recognition for loss of consortium during the preparation of this manuscript.

Finally, to all the colleagues and students who have attended my classes and workshops on the psychologist as expert witness, for their support and continuing feedback, many thanks.

THEODORE H. BLAU

Tampa, Florida
August 1984

Contents

1

Coming of Age

The psychologist as expert witness is not a new topic. It has been over three-quarters of a century since lively debate began in scientific journals and law reviews all over the world on the psychology of testimony and the value of psychology to the judicial process (Goldofski, 1904; Jaffe, 1903; Lobsien, 1904).

Munsterberg brought together a number of essays on psychology and crime, initially publishing these in the *Times* magazine and then as the book *On the Witness Stand* (1908). In his enthusiasm Munsterberg stated:

> The lawyer and the judge and the juryman are sure that they do not need the experimental psychologist. They do not wish to see that in this field pre-eminently applied experimental psychology has made strong strides, led by Binet, Stern, Lipmann, Jung, Wertheimer, Gross, Sommer, Aschaffenburg and other scholars. They go on thinking that their legal instinct and their common sense supplies them with all that is needed and somewhat more; and if the time is ever to come when even the jurist is to show some concession to the spirit of modern psychology, public opinion will have to exert some pressure. Just in the line of the law it therefore seems necessary not to rely simply on the technical statements of scholarly treatises, but to carry the discussion in the most popular form possible before the wider tribunal of the general reader.

Munsterberg then goes on to state:

> [M]y only purpose is to turn attention of serious men to an absurdly ne-glected field which demands the full attention of the social community.

Following this, Munsterberg presented a series of essays on illusions, the memory of witnesses, the detection of crime, untrue confessions, hypno-tism and crime, and the prevention of crime.

Munsterberg's effort was interesting, very enthusiastic, and predictive of things to come for psychology and law. It was, unfortunately, somewhat premature. Munsterberg's work did not go unnoticed. John H. Wigmore, professor of the law of evidence at Northwestern University, wrote a scath-

1

ing parody about *On the Witness Stand* that was published in the *Illinois Law Review* in 1909. The critique took the form of a report of a mythical suit filed in the city of "Windyville, Illiania" against Munsterberg for having "caused to be printed, published, and circulated in Illiania and throughout the country . . . which said book contained . . . certain assertations, erroneous, incorrect and untrue concerning the said plaintiffs, in their capacity as members of the bar."

Wigmore went on to present a mock trial in which Munsterberg's allegations that "the lawyer alone is obdurate" formed the basis of a mythical civil suit brought by several lawyers against Munsterberg. In his parody, Wigmore confronts Munsterberg on the lack of published evidence to support the claim that the law is ready for psychology. (In truth Munsterberg cited no references in his pioneer text.) The article cites 127 learned treatises to justify the proceedings. The mock trial ended with a finding against Munsterberg with the jury assessing damages at one dollar.

Wigmore's attack was telling. Few references to psychologists as expert witnesses appeared for a quarter of a century.

In 1931, Lewis M. Terman, then professor of psychology at Stanford, appeared before the Los Angeles Bar Association to present the address "Psychology and the Law." Terman took pains to refer to Munsterberg's *On the Witness Stand* and Wigmore's scathing response. He suggested that Munsterberg's error was in exaggerating the importance of psychology's contributions based on research then at hand. He went on to suggest that in light of significant scientific advances the ultimate significance of psychology for the legal profession could not be overstated. Terman emphasized the value of experimental psychology in clarifying errors of testimony. He ranged broadly in his presentation suggesting that psychology might be helpful, among other things, in lie detection, evaluation of eyewitness accounts, and clarification of the vagaries of the insanity pleading and jury selection. Terman ended his presentation with a critique similar to that presented by Hugo Munsterberg a quarter of a century before: "Our laws, like our proverbs and adages, are the product of folk-thinking and like those they are a mixture of shrewd wisdom, childish error, superstition, and folly" (1935).

By this time, Wigmore's *On Evidence* was considered the definitive work being used and cited by attorneys and judges in America. Psychology's bitterest critic in the law modified his position in the last edition of his master work (1937), just before his death. In this Wigmore opined:

> Nevertheless, within the limitations of these special judicial rules (pertaining to partisan presentation of evidence in an adversary proceeding), judicial practice is entitled and bound to resort to all truths of human nature established by science, and to employ all methods recognized by scientists for applying those truths in the analysis of testimonial credit. Already, in long tradition, judicial practice is based on the implicit recognition . . . of a num-

ber of principles of testimonial psychology, empirically discovered and accepted. In so far as science from time to time revises them, or adds new ones, the law can and should recognize them. Indeed, it may be asserted that the Courts are ready to learn and to use, whenever the psychologists produce it, any method which the latter themselves are agreed is sound, accurate and practical. If there is any reproach, it does not belong to the Courts or the law. A legal practice which has admitted the evidential use of the telephone, the phonograph, the dictograph, and the vacuum-ray, within the past decades, cannot be charged with lagging behind science. But where are these practical psychological tests, which will detect specifically the memory-failure and the lie on the witness stand? There must first be proof of general scientific recognition that they are valid and feasible. The vacuum-ray photographic method, for example, was accepted by scientists the world over, within a few months after its promulgation. If there is ever devised a psychological test for the valuation of witnesses, the law will run to meet it. Both law and practice permit the calling of any expert scientist whose method is acknowledged in his science to be a sound and trustworthy one. Whenever the Psychologist is ready for the Courts, the Courts are ready for him.[1]

Clearly, Wigmore was demonstrating the flexibility, awareness, and practicality psychologists are likely to find among lawyers and judges when presented with psychological data, techniques, and methods generally accepted by colleagues and concordant with the standards of the profession.

One of the earliest reviews of the legal and psychological literature regarding the psychologist as expert witness was published by Louisell in 1955. An appendix to this article presented the testimony of Kenneth E. Clark in the case of *Robinsdale Amusement Co. v. Warner Bros. Pictures Distributing Corp. et al.*[2] Dr. Clark was qualified as an expert in public opinion techniques and so testified.

During the 1950s psychologists were sometimes qualified as experts and sometimes dismissed by the judge. In 1954 Dr. Michael H. P. Finn, then chief psychologist at the Springfield State Hospital, appeared in *Hidden v. Mutual Life Insurance of New York.*[3] The judge refused to allow Dr. Finn to testify. On appeal, the U.S. court of appeals reversed on the grounds that Dr. Finn was qualified to give expert testimony.

In the earliest formal text on private practice in clinical psychology, Blau (1959) included a chapter titled "The Clinical Psychologist and the Legal Profession." Blau suggested that psychologists would do well to prepare themselves to be competent expert witnesses within their field. Court transcripts were included to illustrate direct examination and cross-examination of psychologists in a personal injury suit and a matter of competence.

The role of the psychologist as expert witness in matters of mental disease or defect was spelled out in considerable detail in the landmark

[1] 3 J. H. Wigmore, Wigmore on Evidence, 367–368 (3rd ed. 1940).
[2] Civil #4584 (4th Division, Minneapolis).
[3] *Hidden v. Mutual Life Insurance Co.*, 217 F.2d 818, 821 (4th Cir. 1954).

Jenkins v. United States in 1962.[4] Jenkins, after indictment, was committed to the District General Hospital, Washington, D.C., for a mental examination on September 4, 1959, to determine his competence to stand trial and his mental condition at the time of the alleged offense of housebreaking with intent to commit an assault, assault with intent to rape, and assault with a dangerous weapon. Jenkins was given a series of psychological tests by staff psychologists under the supervision of Bernard I. Levy, Ph.D. Jenkins was also examined by several psychiatrists, who informed the district court that Jenkins was incompetent. He was then committed to St. Elizabeth's Hospital until mentally competent to stand trial. At St. Elizabeth's, he was tested extensively by Lawrence Tirnauer, Ph.D., who concluded Jenkins was schizophrenic. Two psychiatrists found no evidence of mental disease or defect. Margaret Ives, Ph.D., administered additional tests and concluded that Dr. Tirnauer's diagnosis was correct. The trial court, *sua sponte* (on its own motion), instructed the jury to disregard the testimony of the three defense psychologists that the defendant had a mental disease when he committed the crimes charged.

On appeal, Bazelon, circuit judge of the U.S. Court of Appeals, District of Columbia Circuit, held that the lower court erred on several points, including the rejection of qualified psychologists as experts on the presence or absence of mental disease. This decision was rendered in spite of an amicus curiae brief submitted by the American Psychiatric Association urging the court not to allow psychologists to qualify as experts. Judge Bazelon's scholarly opinion defined the fully trained psychologist. In a rare concurrence, Judge Burger (now chief justice, U.S. Supreme Court) agreed with Bazelon (see Appendix 1).

The court thus affirmed that titles or degrees are insufficient to qualify a witness as an expert. Quoting eminent authority, the court underscored the conditions under which experts are qualified:

> An observer is qualified to testify because he has firsthand knowledge which the jury does not have of the situation or transaction at issue. The expert has something different to contribute. This is a power to draw inferences from the facts which a jury would not be competent to draw. To warrant the use of expert testimony, then, two elements are required. First, the subject of the inference must be so distinctively related to some science, profession, business or occupation as to be beyond the ken of the average layman, and second, the witness must have such skill, knowledge or experience in that field or calling as to make it appear that his opinion or inference will probably aid the trier in his search for truth. The knowledge may in some fields be derived from reading alone, in some from practice alone, or as is more commonly the case, from both.[5]

[4] *Jenkins v. United States*, 307 F.2d 637 (D.C. Cir. 1962).
[5] C. McCormick, *Law of Evidence* §13 (1954).

Since the *Jenkins* decision, the rejection of psychologists by the court as experts in their field of specialization has been considered to be trial error.

It is important to understand that all psychologists are not likely to be accepted by the court as expert witnesses in all areas of psychology. The psychological expert must first be qualified before the court in the matter about which he or she will testify. The rules of jurisprudence are specific: An expert is one who is so qualified by study or experience that he can form a definite opinion of his own respecting a division of science, branch of art, or department of trade concerning which persons having no particular training or special study are incapable of forming accurate opinions or of deducing correct conclusions.[6]

The second issue determining qualification by the presiding judge concerns the expert's ability to render an opinion that will assist the jury: Expert opinion may be or may not be admissible, depending on whether or not the subject matter is within common experience or whether it is a special field where the opinion of one of special skill and experience will assist and be of greater validity than that of the ordinary juryman.[7]

As legal scholars have pointed out, the issue must be such that the expert may answer by giving an opinion that is a reasonable probability, rather than conjecture or speculation (Ladd, 1952).

The credibility of any expert's testimony in many jurisdictions follows the admonition delineated in *Frye v. United States* where the court opined:

> Just when a scientific principle or discovery crosses the line between the experimental and demonstrable stages is difficult to define. Somewhere in this twilight zone the evidential force of the principle must be recognized, and while courts will go a long way in admitting expert testimony deduced from a well-recognized scientific principle or discovery, the thing from which the deduction is made must be sufficiently established to have gained general acceptance in the particular field in which it belongs.[8]

The American Psychological Association, in principle 4g of *Ethical Principles of Psychologists* (1981), requires concordant standards for all its members: "Psychologists present the science of psychology and offer their services, products, and publications fairly and accurately, avoiding misrepresentation through sensationalism, exaggeration, or superficiality. Psychologists are guided by the primary obligation to aid the public in developing informed judgements, opinions, and choices."

Since the *Jenkins* decision, psychologists have appeared more frequently in the courts as experts. Most published reports of psychologists as expert witnesses have to do with competency, evaluation, and the insanity plead-

[6] 31 American Jurisprudence 2d *Expert and Opinion Evidence* §1 (1967).
[7] *Id.* at §16.
[8] *Frye v. United States*, 293 F. 1013 (D.C. Cir. 1923).

ing. In this narrow area of expert testimony, psychologists have invaded the province of psychiatry. Although there is some tendency for psychologists to regard themselves as "second-rate" experts in these areas, the data suggest that psychologists as expert witnesses in matters of competence and sanity are successful and well regarded. Perlin (1980) reports three studies comparing the thoroughness and quality of psychologists' performance at a forensic center. Serving as judges, a prosecuting attorney and a law school professor evaluated reports and testimony of psychologists, psychiatrists, and social workers. Ratings of quality of report and of trial testimony indicated that the work of psychologists was consistently rated equal to or better than that of psychiatrists.

Judges are becoming increasingly aware of the potential psychologists have for the courts. Recently, Patricia McGowan Wald (1982), circuit judge for the U.S. Court of Appeals, District of Columbia, stated: "I find that after a decade or more of increasing awareness among psychologists and lawyers about what litigation can and cannot accomplish, the era of their most productive relationships built on mutual respect and realistic idealism may be only just beginning."

The psychologist who functions as an expert witness should be competent. Many who testify are not. There is a growing movement to set standards, and the California State Psychological Association (1980) has proposed requirements for expert witnesses. Such standards tend to be pedantic and somewhat rigid and should be viewed as preliminary efforts, likely to change as more psychologists begin to bring a variety of psychological data to the courts (see Chapter 2).

Few graduate schools at this time prepare psychologists to function as expert witnesses in the courts. Psychologists who expect to function in this role must acquire education, training, and experience ad lib or from continuing education at the postdoctoral level. Interest in this area is burgeoning, and it seems likely that doctoral students in professional training programs in the future will have a greater opportunity for preparation as experts in the courts. Within the last decade, joint Ph.D-J.D. programs have emerged for psychologists who want roles in policy development. Such programs produce psychologist-lawyers who, it is hoped, will bridge the gap of knowledge between the two professions (Wolinsky, 1982).

At this writing, then, psychologists must take the initiative to become aware of the many areas in which expert testimony can be offered and must engineer their own study and training programs to become competent, effective, ethical expert witnesses. The following chapters will present guidelines and information to help achieve such goals.

2

Present and Future Roles of the Psychologist

Psychologists have served in a variety of roles as expert witnesses, especially during the past three decades. Until now, the courts have used a minute part of the information that the science of psychology has generated. The scarcity of psychologists willing and competent to serve as expert witnesses to present this knowledge to judges and jurors has been a barrier to providing useful information that would be helpful during court proceedings.

As psychologists become more aware of the opportunities and, thus, more available as experts, a broadened involvement between psychology and the law can be expected. The increase in numbers of psychologists who have served as experts in a judicial setting and the wide variety of consultations between psychologists and attorneys which have developed in the past decade suggest that the anticipated burgeoning of interaction between psychology and the law has started (Kerr & Bray, 1982; Saks & Hastie, 1978; Sales, 1981).

The purpose of this chapter is to present a brief overview of some roles psychologists have served as expert witnesses and to describe testimony or testimonial strategy that has been used rarely or is yet to be used with psychologists as experts. Later chapters will explore some of these roles to illustrate the ways and means by which psychologists may serve effectively, ethically, and professionally as experts.

TRADITIONAL ROLES

Competence to Stand Trial

A defendant is guaranteed the right to a fair trial via a variety of constitutional safeguards. Essentially, the law requires that a defendant must be able to understand the nature of charges against him or her, must be able

7

to understand the proceedings and the participants in the trial, and must be able to cooperate with his or her attorney to a reasonable degree. When the court is in doubt about a defendant's competency in any of these areas, expert opinion is sought to aid the court in deciding whether to postpone the proceedings until the defendant is found competent. Traditionally, psychiatrists have conducted relatively brief examinations at the request of the court and reported their findings to the judge, who then decides to proceed or postpone.

Most recently, psychologists have been appointed by the court, or privately retained by counsel (usually for the defense), to conduct psychological evaluation in order to render a report or an opinion to the presiding judge as to the defendant's psychological capacities under the competency criteria in the jurisdiction where the issue occurs. Again, the judge makes the final decision, accepting or rejecting the report of the expert witness.

The Insanity Pleading

During the past 30 years, again, following psychiatry in the courtroom, psychologists have been called upon to render expert opinion as to the sanity of the defendant. Previous to that time, psychiatrists, physicians, examiners (called *alienists*), and lay witnesses had been used to help the triers of fact (judge and jury) decide whether a defendant should be excused from a criminal act either because he or she lacked the ability to understand that the act was wrong or because some defect or illness rendered the defendant unable to act in an expected or lawful manner. Sometimes the burden falls to the defense to prove by *preponderance of evidence* (something better than chance) that the defendant was insane at the time of the offense. In other states, the law is such that when a plea of innocent by reason of insanity is filed by the defense, it becomes the burden of the prosecution to prove *beyond reasonable doubt* (90% or better) that the defendant was sane at the time of the crime. Weights of evidence and other technical considerations will be presented in greater detail in Chapters 5 and 6. Contrary to the prevailing belief among the lay public, very few defendants plead innocent by reason of insanity, and few of those who so plead are exculpated of guilt. There is much public concern as to the practicality and fairness of this small but important aspect of American jurisprudence (Leo, 1982). In the past decade, psychologists have served more and more frequently to help clarify issues involving insanity (Perline, 1980).

Competence to Manage One's Own Affairs

Because of innate deficiencies, illness, injury, or deterioration due to age, some people become unable to adequately deal with the normal demands of daily living. When this happens, relatives, associates, friends, or even interested citizens may file a civil petition for the court to appoint a guardian or conservator to protect the defendant from his or her own incompetence. It is usually the burden of the plaintiff to prove *beyond reasonable doubt* that the incompetence exists since the courts are reluctant to deprive anyone of constitutional rights without considerable evidence that this is in the defendant's best interests. Psychologists, often using standardized tests to measure cognition, reasoning, planning ability, and personality integration, have begun to appear more frequently in conservator or guardian hearings to testify as experts in the matter of the defendant's competence to govern his or her own life.

Involuntary Commitment

People sometimes become so emotionally disturbed because of disease or psychological dysfunction that the courts must decide if it is in the person's best interests to undergo treatment or custodial care whether the individual agrees to this or not. The essential rule of law focuses on the question of whether the individual is a danger to himself or herself or to others. In spite of research evidence which suggests that prediction of dangerousness is quite unreliable, the courts are required to act on such petitions while bending every effort to guarantee the defendant due process and the least restrictive environment. Psychologists testify at initial pleadings where the issue is first brought before the court. In this phase, the judge decides whether to dismiss the petition or to remand the defendant to a mental health facility for a specific period of time, usually not exceeding 30 days, so that experts can observe and evaluate the defendant and decide whether to recommend involuntary commitment. Most states give the defendant the right to hire independent mental health professionals to perform the examination and report the results to the judge, who will then decide for or against commitment. Many psychologists work in mental health facilities where such evaluations are conducted while private evaluations requested by the defendant's attorney are likely to be conducted by psychologists in independent practice.

Dangerousness and Treatment Potential

During the past quarter-century, psychologists have frequently served as experts in determining how convicted felons should be classified in terms of placement in minimum-, medium-, or maximum-security facilities, as well as potential for rehabilitation, and appropriate treatment procedures while the prisoner serves his or her sentence. In those states where capital crimes are dealt with in bifurcated procedures (a guilt-determination trial followed by a penalty trial if convicted), psychologists together with other mental health professionals have been called upon to give evidence as experts to help the triers of fact determine whether rehabilitation is a likely expectation or whether the death penalty should be invoked.

Psychologists who serve as experts in these settings are often part of a *forensic evaluation team* ordinarily set up under state jurisdiction as a special diagnostic clinic or as part of a broader mental health facility.

MIDCENTURY DEVELOPMENTS

As professional psychology emerged following World War II, opportunities to serve as expert witnesses in a wide range of civil, regulatory, and legislative settings grew. The law had been ready for psychology for some time, and with the enormous growth of research findings in behavioral science, training, and involvement in applied areas, psychologists began to appear as experts, testifying to a wider variety of issues than ever before. Psychologists began leaving the psychiatric model to appear as experts in the science of psychology, providing testimony to the triers of fact about widely varying issues involving human behavior (Louisell, 1955).

Product Liability

Civil suits claiming injury, deficit, or death as a result of insufficiencies or defects of various products represent a common type of litigation. Sometimes liability hinges on how the consumer sees a product, interprets directions for its use, or responds to its feature description or advertised qualities. Psychologists have been called upon to testify as experts in advertising, perception of products, evaluation of the merit of research findings concerning a product, and other matters. Sometimes psychologists testify before governmental committees as experts in matters of product liability.[1]

Personal Injury and Wrongful Death

When a person is injured or dies as a result of negligence on the part of an individual or corporate body, the law provides the opportunity for remedies or compensation through civil litigation. As part of the legal proceedings (see Chapter 10) experts may be called on behalf of the plaintiff (the one who seeks remedy) or for the defendant (the party accused of negligence) to testify as to the psychological factors in either the negligent act or the results of negligence. Most frequently, such testimony has been about psychological deficits following physical injury. Psychologists have a wide range of knowledge and instruments to evaluate a person's intellectual, neuropsychological, and emotional status as well as potential for recovery and rehabilitation. In personal injury matters psychologists are

[1] *See Smoking Prevention Education Act: Hearing on H.R. 1824 Before the Subcomm. on Health and the Environment of the House Comm. on Energy and Commerce, 98th Cong., 1st. Sess. 76, 76–78 (1983).*

often asked to render their expert opinion as to an individual's current psychological status in comparison with estimates of functional levels previous to the injurious event and the individual's rehabilitative future.

Labor Relations, Workers' Compensation, and Equal Opportunity Issues

Civil suits, regulatory hearings, and administrative judgments may require presentation of evidence about such issues as tests and their proper and fair application, skills required for certain positions, performance criteria, and individual vocational capability. Psychologists are frequently called upon during such proceedings to submit reports or give testimony concerning the results of psychological evaluations, the nature and quality of psychological tests, and the likelihood that an individual is able or unable to perform safely and effectively in certain vocational settings. Procedures for this type of testimony are usually mandated in some detail, including types of tests and procedures psychologists are permitted to use.[2]

Patent and Trademark Infringement

A civil suit may be filed accusing a defendant of using a process, a logo, or a descriptive phrase that has been registered by someone else and who, by dint of patent and trademark laws, "owns" the process, the device, or the written or illustrated material. During the judicial deliberations, evidence is usually presented to support the plaintiffs' claims that their rights have been infringed upon, while defendants seek to convince the triers of fact that the claims have no merit. Testimony by psychologists—concerning the impact of trademarks, logos, advertising, and such on the general public or the similarity of devices or materials and other matters that can be measured scientifically through consumer surveys and laboratory experiments—has become relatively well accepted.[3,4]

Child Custody Issues

It is generally agreed that divorce is bad for children. In 85% of divorce cases the child is awarded to the mother without contest by the father as a result of a century-old tradition known as the *tender years doctrine*. This unspecific shibboleth (judge's rule) suggests "the child of young and tender years belongs with the mother" (Weitzman & Dixon, 1979). More re-

[2] 6 Mental Disability L. Rep. 438 (1982).

[3] Rogers, *An Account of Some Psychological Experiments on the Subject of Trademark Infringement*. 18 Mich. L. Rev. 75, 99 (1919).

[4] *Robinsdale Amusement Co. v. Warner Bros. Pictures Distributing Corp. et al.*, Civil #4584 (4th Division, Minneapolis).

cently, fathers have been successful in gaining sole custody of the child or children in contested custody issues (Orthmer & Lewis, 1979). In traditional adversary custodial issues psychologists, together with other mental health professionals, are usually called upon by the judge and/or the adversary parties to conduct psychological evaluations of the children, the parents, and even the custodial home setting in order to testify as experts on how the best interests of the children and the parents may be served.

Currently, most states have rejected the tender years doctrine and mandated instead that the divorcing parents attempt to share custody and/or responsibility for the children in ways that will best serve the needs of the children. In cases where conflict arises, the judge will usually order professional mediation, which frequently involves a psychologist. If mediation fails, the psychologist is likely to be required by the court to serve as an expert witness to aid the judge in making the Solomonic decision in awarding sole custody to one parent. Chapter 8 will present a review of expert psychological testimony in issues of family law.

RECENT AND EMERGING ROLES

A keynote for the increasing use of experts was sounded by Melvin Belli, past president of the American Trial Lawyer's Association. He suggests that experts can be found in the most esoteric fields, and although their cost may be high, the cost may well be higher *not* to employ experts appropriately. He admonishes trial lawyers to understand that choosing to proceed without an expert may be "flirting with malpractice" (Belli, 1982). This attitude seems to be increasing among trial lawyers, and psychologists are being summoned as experts in an ever-broadening range of issues.

Some of the newer areas of expert testimony have resulted in the appearance of academic and research psychologists as experts. This, in a sense, is a recapitulation of origins since the first psychologist "experts" were academicians and researchers (Loftus & Monahan, 1980).

Eyewitness Testimony

The weight of credibility which has traditionally been given to the testimony of individuals who say they saw or heard something or someone is unparalleled in the legal field of evidence. "He is the one who did it!" is perhaps the most powerful statement a witness can make. Although triers of fact have always had the right and responsibility to evaluate the credibility of eyewitnesses, the focus of concern has been on the witness's personal background, style, and degree of certainty about the testimony. Research now casts serious doubts on many aspects of eyewitness testimony (Loftus, 1979; Buckout, 1974). Experts in matters of eyewitness identification are usually psychologists who have conducted research in memory and cognition or are very familiar with such research. They generally have a strong academic and research background. Testimony generally focuses on research that demonstrates that various environmental conditions influence reliability and validity of the testimonial statements of witnesses. Experts also testify (which in a sense means "lecture the jury") about personal characteristics of humans which influence accuracy of recall. Such testimony is usually arranged by the defense in criminal cases for the purpose of increasing the probability that the triers of fact will evaluate eyewitness testimony of the prosecution's witness with increased caution and sophistication.

The quality of eyewitness research is generally considered quite good, but the courts have been reluctant to allow such testimony.[5] Appellate review may result in changes in this exclusionary response if lower-court decisions are reversed.

Penalty Phase Testimony

In many states, capital offenses may be tried vià *bifurcated trial*. In this type of trial, the issue of the defendant's guilt or innocence is first decided by a jury. If the defendant is found "guilty," then a second trial may be held to decide whether the death penalty should be imposed. Often the same jury which considered the evidence and rendered a verdict in the first trial, or guilt phase of the proceedings, will hear further pleadings and evidence in order to recommend the death penalty or a lesser alternative. During this second trial, attorneys for the defense usually present evidence that the death penalty will amount to cruel and unusual punishment and is contrary to constitutional safeguards.[6] They may also argue that the defendant, though guilty, is not dangerous, has suffered sufficiently to deserve a lesser punishment, or is capable of rehabilitation. Psychologists may be called as experts to render an opinion about the defendant's psychological state of repentence, potential for dangerousness, or potential to lead a reasonably stable life in prison and possibly in society after a period of incarceration. Different states allow widely divergent degrees of leeway in the kind and extent of testimony allowed in presenting mitigating circumstances during the penalty phase of a trial.

Behavioral scientists may also be retained by the prosecution to testify in penalty phase trials. As part of the prosecution's attempt to convince judge and jury that the defendant is not only guilty but should pay the supreme penalty, behavioral scientists may be called to present opinions, as experts, that the defendant is unrepentent, without conscience, and likely to be a danger to others not only in society at large but within the prison system. Given the very subjective nature of testimony about dangerousness, psy-

---

[5] *Dyas v. United States*, 376 A.2d. 827 (D.C. 1977).
[6] U.S. Const. Amend. VIII.

chiatrists are more frequently found in this testimonial role than psychologists (Tierney, 1982). Until such time as dangerousness can be more thoroughly understood and more accurately predicted, psychologists are likelier to appear in court to testify about dangerousness and its predictability as witnesses for the defense.

Composition Challenges

The Constitution guarantees each defendant the right to a fair and impartial trial.[7] If there is reason to believe that an impaneled jury does not meet this important criteria, an attorney may challenge the composition of the jury. Arguments and sometimes evidence are presented to the presiding judge after which the judge rules on the attorney's motion (usually to dismiss). Psychologists have served as expert witnesses where the *composition,* or makeup, of the jury is at issue. Most frequently, this occurs when a jury is "death qualified."

A death-qualified jury is one in which no member of the panel has stated any serious reservations about voting for capital punishment. In *Witherspoon v. State of Illinois,* the Supreme Court ruled that disqualifying a juror for this reason is acceptable during the *guilt* phase of the trial and is not an abrogation of Sixth Amendment rights to an impartial jury but that such disqualification is unacceptable during the *sentencing* phase of the trial.[8] Thus the Supreme Court decided that a jury from which all those on the original venue or panel who are generally opposed to the death penalty have been challenged and excluded is acceptable in the initial phase of a dual, or bifurcated, trial where the guilt or innocence of a defendant is determined. To exclude those philosophically opposed to the death penalty for any reason or with any degree of personal conviction results in a jury more prone to recommend the death penalty. This, according to the *Witherspoon* ruling, deprives the defendant of fundamental constitutional guarantees to an impartial jury. In reaching these conclusions, the court considered as part of the petitioner's brief the research findings of W. C. Wilson, F. J. Girsch, and H. Zeisel whose studies suggested that jurors who have no concerns against the death penalty are likely to be more prosecution prone than jurors who object to the death penalty. During the original trial, Wilson, Girsch, and Zeisel testified as experts in this matter.[9] Since then, psychologists have been called as experts in similar matters.[10] This kind of testimony by social scientists reflects the growing interest in

[7] U.S. Const. Amend. VI.
[8] 391 U.S. 510, 20 L. Ed. 776, 88 S. Ct. 1770 (1968).
[9] 36 Ill.2d 471, 224 N.E.2d 259 (1967).
[10] *Hovey v. Superior Court of Alameda County,* 616 P.2d 1301, 28 Cal.3d 1, 168 Cal.Rptr. 128 (1980).

social science research as one frame of reference from which judicial decisions can be made objectively and fairly. Research in this area has recently been reviewed (Haney, 1984).

Prison-Conditions Defense

There is a deep and pervading concern about the purpose, usefulness, and potential danger of the prison system in the United States. To be in prison is rarely an experience likely to rehabilitate. Certainly, prison is a punishing, cruel, and dehumanizing experience in most instances. Much crime is commited in prisons, including murder. When prisoners commit crimes, they are culpable under the extant laws of the land and must be brought to trial (Anderson, 1982).

In recent years, psychologists have testified as experts in the trials of prisoner-defendants about the effects of prison conditions on human behavior. In such matters, the psychologist or sociologist, testifying for the defense, (usually) opines that the conditions which exist in most prisons can make people deeply disturbed and thus not responsible for their acts of violence.

Evaluation Testimony

Evaluation concerns itself with the *assessment of merit*. Since all research is subject to a variety of interpretations, evaluation scientists attempt to act as objective evaluators of research findings and identify the degree of confidence one can place on research findings. Evaluation science has been a growing area of research and practice during the past two decades. Participants include psychologists, biostatisticians, mathematicians, and social scientists from a variety of disciplines. In the legal setting, evaluation scientists may serve as educators, bringing to judge and jury information and concepts which may help them weigh and judge the quality of findings placed before them by other experts. Thus, following a psychologist's testimony based on test results, an evaluation scientist might be called as a *rebuttal witness* to discuss the standards and limits which are ordinarily applied to the test instruments under consideration.

Psychologists who qualify as evaluation scientists may testify as experts before juries making decisions in civil and criminal matters or in regulatory and legislative hearings where the interpretation of research data is a significant aspect of the process. As lawyers and judges become more aware of the extensive research done in the behavioral sciences, it is likely that psychologists trained and experienced in evaluation science will be sought to provide triers of fact with help in the interpretation of complex data.

FUTURE ROLES

The acceleration in the use of psychologists by attorneys is likely to continue if the work of such experts is useful in forwarding the purposes of American jurisprudence. Behavioral research and its expert interpretation are of growing significance in criminal, civil, and regulatory decision making. Psychologists have a very good record to date. The limits as well as the potential for psychological testimony will be determined by the content and quality of research in the behavioral sciences.

3

The American
Court System

In no way will an extensive treatise on the development and function of the American court system help an expert witness. A warning in this regard is in order: Do not become an attorney by association. Those psychologists who become so involved in learning the lawyer's tradecraft can become impediments to the judicial process. The psychologist as expert must be a psychological expert.

A general knowledge of the system within which expert testimony plays a significant role can be helpful as well as reassuring. To know the framework within which one must operate will tend to enhance the psychologist's skill as an expert.

The American system of jurisprudence has developed from over 5000 years of human experience in the search for justice and equity. Elements of the Hammurabi Code, Talmudic principles, Roman law, Judaic and Christian philosophy, Anglo-Saxon jurisprudence, and, finally, the U.S. Constitution, with its articles and amendments, form the base for justice in the United States (Sales, 1981; Kerr & Bray, 1982).

The bureaucratic system, within which rules, mandates, principles, decision making, and remedy operate, is dynamic and tends to change with changing times. The rules may change by legislative action at either the state or federal level or by appeals to higher courts on points of law that one side or another in an adversary issue considers to be in error.

Courts are formal settings where issues of law are debated and settled. Judges are elected or appointed to arbitrate adversary issues in the legal arena; the gladiators are the attorneys, who are officers of the court. Decisions are made by the judge or by a jury (or venire) of 6 or 12 members who listen to all evidence in an issue and then render a decision called a *verdict*. (A glossary is provided at the end of this book to provide the reader with a more complete definition of some of the terms employed by the members of the legal profession.)

17

Courts may be sponsored by the state or the federal government. Many of the procedures and rules are shared by both, while some procedures are unique to federal courts and some to the courts of individual states.

A civil case may be brought to the courts (or *filed*) by an attorney representing a client with a grievance (the *plaintiff*) against a person or body of persons (the *defendant*). In domestic court, essentially a civil court, a parent (the *petitioner*) may seek custody of a child from the defendant (a custodial parent or the *custodian of record*). In criminal court, a state attorney, or prosecuting attorney, or a *grand jury* may decide there is sufficient evidence to charge a person with a major crime (*felony*) and may present a formal charge to a judge (*indictment*) requesting that the defendant be kept in custody until the trial. A defendant who the judge is convinced will not abscond before trial may be released without bond (*on his or her own recognizance*) or may be required to post a sum of money (*bail*) to ensure an appearance at trial. The judge may believe the defendant unreliable or dangerous and may, instead of setting bail, require detention at a local jail until the time of the trial.

Lower courts (*municipal* or *magistrate courts*) are more informal and deal with minor infractions of the law (*misdemeanors*), such as vehicular violations, disorderly conduct, and so on, or minor civil matters (*small claims* or *people's courts*). No jury is present at these lower-court hearings, all decisions being made by the presiding magistrate. If the issue is of major proportion, the presiding judge may move the case to a higher court for adjudication. A person whose case comes before a judge in a lower court may request a jury trial, which requires that the judge move the case to the jurisdiction of a higher court (the case is "bound over"). Figure 3.1 shows the various state and federal courts in the U.S. judicial system.

It is unlikely that a psychologist will be called as an expert witness in a magistrate or lower court. If the case becomes that complex, it is usually bound over to a circuit or district court. It is conceivable that a psychologist would testify at traffic court, but it is highly unlikely. The same is true in federal magistrate courts where initial charges are brought (the defendant is *arraigned*) and a decision is made as to whether there is sufficient evidence to move the case to a grand jury for further consideration or to a higher court for trial. Except in the rarest of instances, psychologists will appear in circuit or district courts to give evidence.

Appellate courts are the places in the judicial system that consider appeals after a decision has been rendered by a lower court. Not every request for a rehearing is granted. The judges of the various appellate courts must be convinced that there is some reasonable doubt that the decision of the lower courts was entirely fair and properly arrived at. Errors of fact, conduct, and procedure by attorneys, witnesses, jurors, or the judge may be grounds for appeal.

Witnesses occasionally appear before higher courts, usually to present evidence as experts. More frequently, the results of research are presented

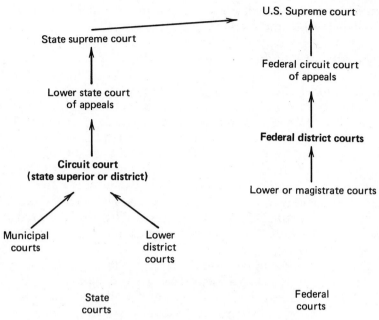

FIGURE 3.1.   State and federal court systems.

to the appeal judges by attorneys for either side in the adversary process or as a brief of *amicus curiae* (friend of the court) by interested third parties. (The American Psychological Association has supported or prepared briefs as *amicus curiae* in a number of landmark Supreme Court decisions.[1,2] Experts usually participate in the preparation of such briefs and may testify on occasion, usually in special hearings before federal judges.

Chapter 10 outlines the details of a legal case moving through the court. The procedures are formal and differ from the handling of both civil and criminal cases in other parts of the world. In keeping with basic principles of democracy and fair play, the American system of jurisprudence is extremely humanistic by world standards. Constitutional safeguards for the individual are very extensive; standards for the nature and quality of evidence that may be presented are high and designed to protect the accused who is deemed innocent until proven guilty. Varying weights of evidence are required to ensure equity and justice.

Certain aspects of the philosophy, rules, and standards of the American jurisprudence system must be understood if a psychologist expects to be regarded as a credible expert witness. In no way does the following cover all the issues involved in the presentation of evidence. The psychologist

[1] *Addington v. Texas.* No. 77-5992. Brief for the Appellant. S.C. October Term, 1978.
[2] *Parham v. J.L.* No. 75-1690. Brief for the Appellant. S.C. October Term, 1977.

who understands these issues will have a firm base upon which to become more knowledgeable and credible in performance.

The Adversary Model

The legal model and consequent procedures for the discovery of facts and the administration of justice may puzzle and even disturb some psychologists when they first serve as expert witnesses. This is likely to be more a reflection of the psychologist's naïveté than the law's inadequacy. Most scientists and professionals work on the basis of an Aristotelian model of cause and effect; they make empirical observations and collect or aggregate data in a variety of standard ways using field and laboratory research methodology; and they attempt to discover meaningful relationships which, when sufficiently clear and replicable, allow for prediction to a greater degree of statistical accuracy. The probability model is the essence of psychological data.

The adversary model of fact seeking begins with the assumption on the part of the judge and jury (the triers of fact) that no crime or civil inequity exists. The prosecutor in criminal cases and the plaintiff's attorney in civil cases vigorously present information to suggest as strongly as possible that the defendant is guilty of a crime or liable for damages or remedy. Defense counsel, with equal intensity and vigor, will argue that the criminal defendant is innocent of the charges as drawn or that the civil defendant is without liability in the issue at hand. Each side "takes turns" in making presentations of arguments and witnesses. It is obvious that each side is "out to win" at almost any cost. Tempers flare, and accusations, recriminations, and heated debates are common. The intensity of the presentation may reach such a point that the presiding judge may admonish an attorney who has become too loud, too abusive in his or her language, or too leading or manipulative with a witness. If the judge's admonishment is not heeded, the judge may recess the trial and bring the attorneys for both sides to his or her chambers to deliver a more severe admonishment to the offending attorney. Should an attorney continue to act in a manner deemed inappropriate to the proceedings, a judge may fine or even jail the offender for *contempt of court*. The degree of the judge's control of the interchange may vary from judge to judge, but the judge's power in the courtroom is close to absolute.

Unless a psychologist serving as expert witness is fairly experienced, each trial brings new experiences with the adversary model. Psychologists who are serious about becoming competent expert witnesses would do well to attend a number of civil and criminal trials early in their career in order to better understand the process. The psychologist may not agree with the adversary system as a philosophical concept, but certainly any psychologist who intends to serve as an expert witness must understand the mechanics and logic of the process. The expert witness is part of the process.

A general review of the terms in the glossary of this book will give the aspiring expert witness a view of some of the concepts and terms likely to be encountered in dealing with the court system.

In addition, there are certain concepts which require clear understanding on the part of those who expect to perform credibly as experts giving testimony in judicial settings. These concepts significantly influence the style and language of the experienced expert's testimony as well as his or her method of collecting and examining information. An expert who does not understand these ground rules may be prevented, on technical legal points, from doing a proper and credible job. Some of the most important and more frequently encountered concepts that should be understood by experts giving testimony include the following.

Hearsay Evidence.   Frequently encountered in TV and movie presentations of testimony, this concept refers to the exclusion of information that comes to the witness via another person. Should a police officer testify, "Mr. Jones told me he had seen the stolen vehicle in Mr. Smith's garage," opposing counsel would rise to object on the grounds the testimony was "hearsay" and not admissible. The judge would sustain the objection, cause the testimony to be stricken from the record, instruct the jury to ignore the officer's remarks, and caution the witness to testify only about those matters in his or her own experience.

If an expert in behavioral sciences is the witness, the rules of hearsay are somewhat less stringent. As long as the expert indicates clearly that "secondhand" information is necessary to come to a conclusion concerning a person or event, the court will usually allow it. This includes information gathered from a defendant's friends, family, employer, hospital records, police reports, school records, the statements of survey participants, and so forth. The witness can be challenged on these matters and can expect to be questioned closely about the degree of reliability, validity, and acceptance of such methods in usual and customary professional practice (Ziskin, 1981). The judge may refer specifically to the use of such quasi-hearsay issues while instructing the jury at the end of the trial or may provide a more general caution to jurors, such as, "You may accept or reject the opinion expressed by experts in this case, using your own judgment as to the worth and quality of the information upon which the expert's opinion is based." Once again, *Frye v. United States* is a sound and conservative test an expert may use in presenting information leading to the opinion.[3] Professionals whose testimony is based on a generally accepted set of procedures and explanatory theories and whose testimony

---

[3] *Frye v. United States*, 293 F. 1013 (D.C. Cir. 1923).

Apprisal of Rights

Name of Examinee _____ Date of Exam _____

This psychological examination to be conducted by _____
was scheduled at the request of

_____

_____

This agency retained _____ for this
examination.

The examination will consist of questions and psychological tests. These will be used by
_____ to write a psychologist report for the agency requesting this examination. The information in this report may be used against me. The report and the tests will be
available to my attorney(s).

This statement has been read to me and I understand it. I understand I have the right to
consult with my attorney if I have any question about this.

Signed _____

Examiner _____

Witness _____

FIGURE 3.2.   Apprisal of rights form to be used with a defendant before conducting an
evaluation.

concerns a proper subject matter in the case can usually feel assured that
they are functioning within the proper framework of judicial rules for
expert witnesses.[4] The issue of hearsay evidence should be discussed with
the retaining attorney during the pretrial conference, after the expert's
report has been submitted. In short, hearsay evidence is information obtained from another person and is considered secondhand evidence unless
the expert can justify its use as reliable, valid, and customary practice.

Exclusionary Rule.   Sustained by the U.S. Supreme Court in *Miranda v.
Arizona*, no information obtained against a defendant may be admitted as
evidence unless at the time the information was obtained, the defendant
was made aware of his or her rights to remain silent, to have counsel, and
that any information revealed could be used against the defendant in
court.[5] Failure to read the defendant his or her rights is now a common
basis for excluding a defendant's admissions and confessions from the trial
process or reversing the decision of a court that convicts after allowing
such evidence to be admitted during trial.

Recently, the Supreme Court has ruled that information obtained during
a standard mental health examination comes under the exclusionary rule.

---

[4] *United States v. Amaral*, 488 F.2d. 1148 (9th Cir. 1973).
[5] *Miranda v. Arizona*, 394 U.S. 436 (1966).

Aviso de Derechos

Nombre del Examinado _____ Fecha del Examen _____

Este examen psicologico, el cual sera conducido por _____
fue fijado a peticion de

_____

_____

Esta agencia empleo _____ para conducir este
examen.

El examen consistira a la vez de preguntas y pruebas psicologicas. Basandose en estos datos
_____ escribira un informe psicologico para la agencia que ha pedido este
examen. Los conocimientos contenidos en este informe podran ser usados en contra mia. El
informe y las pruebas seran puestas a la disposicion de mi abogado(s).

Me han leido esta declaracion y yo la comprendo. Si tengo alguna duda acerca de esto,
entiendo que yo tengo el derecho de consultar con mi abogado.

Firmado _____

Examinador _____

Testigo _____

FIGURE 3.3.   Apprisal of rights rendered in Spanish.

In *Estelle v. Smith* the Court opined that unless the defendant was informed
of the purposes to which examination results might be put, the testimony
of the expert is to be considered inadmissible.[6] Figure 3.2 shows a written
form useful in ensuring that the expert's opinion will not be excluded on
the grounds that the defendant was deprived of constitutional safeguards
against self-incrimination. Figure 3.3 presents the same "rights" material
in Spanish. It is the responsibility of the examiner not only to read such
rights but to ensure that they are understood by the examinee.

Since few attorneys provide experts with both the information and the
forms to ensure that the examination of a defendant is not excluded from
evidentiary consideration, it is important that experts be aware of this
important issue and be prepared to protect the viability of their examination and anticipated testimony.

Some mental health experts suggest that their evaluation will be a step
in obtaining professional help for the defendant with his or her problems.
In a well-meaning effort to establish rapport, a mental health expert may
suggest that he or she can try to obtain other professional services for the
defendant. Even a promise of trying to get help for a defendant with
emotional problems can result in evidence being excluded.[7] The expert

[6] *Estelle v. Smith*, 451 U.S. 454, 101 S.Ct. 1866, 68 L.Ed.2d 359 (1981).
[7] *People v. Hogan*, 647 P.2d 93 (Cal. 1982).

must be very clear as to the purposes of the examination and to whom the report will be sent. No effort should be made to disguise or avoid the potentially negative adversary nature of the expert's examination.

Weights of Evidence.   Almost every intelligent layperson is familiar with the phrase "beyond a reasonable doubt." Few are familiar with the concept "weight of evidence" and how this forms a cornerstone of American jurisprudence.

Although decisions of small and large import are made by judges and juries, such decisions are not accidental or loosely developed. Among the structures and concepts which guide, shape, or restrict decision making in the courts is the *quality* or *weight* of the evidence relating to the decision to be made. The more serious the consequences to the defendant, whether in criminal or civil issues, the more stringent are the rules for weighing the quality of the evidence. The benefit of the doubt almost always falls to the defendant, especially in criminal cases, to ensure the fairness of the proceedings for the accused.

The lowest or weakest quality or weight of evidence is called *preponderance of evidence*. Although concepts of "weight" are not defined with mathematical precision, most jurists seem to accept the probability concept of "slightly better than chance," or "about 55% sure," as the defining parameter of preponderance of evidence. Although this parameter is rarely used against a defendant, a judge will decide or instruct a jury to decide if the weight of evidence is better than chance in such matters as whether the defendant was insane at the time of an alleged crime. Thus as much benefit of the doubt as possible is given the defendant.

A somewhat heavier weight of evidence is called *clear and convincing evidence*. In this instance the statutes require that the judge and/or jury decide that the evidence is quite clear-cut in the direction of their decision. Some jurists are informally willing to define clear and convincing evidence as "75–80% sure." Again, numbers are seldom, if ever, used in defining this weight of evidence. In civil commitment hearings, such as whether an individual is considered incompetent to handle everyday affairs or a danger to self or others, the standard for weight of evidence sufficient for a judicial commitment is now considered "clear and convincing evidence."[8]

The better-known *beyond reasonable doubt* represents the most stringent test of the quality of evidence. Evidence that is deemed of sufficient weight or validity so as to be virtually certain falls in this category. Some jurists are willing to say that beyond reasonable doubt means that the facts supported by evidence are "90–95% sure." Some judges instruct juries in such a way as to suggest that *any* doubt is reasonable doubt.

In some jurisdictions, a defense plea of innocent by reason of insanity places the burden on the state to prove, beyond reasonable doubt, that the

[8] *Addington v. Texas.* 441 U.S. 418, 99 S.Ct. 1804, 60 L.Ed.2d. 323 (1979).

defendant was sane at the time of the alleged crime. This is considered a more conservative requirement, increasing the probabilities of acquittal over the situation where the defense must prove the existence of insanity by the preponderance of evidence (Leo, 1982). This will be explored in greater detail in Chapter 5.

The Decision-Making Process.   Experts do not make judicial decisions. At no time is the expert witness to render an opinion as to the guilt, innocence, or liability of a defendant. When an expert does render an opinion regarding the key issue of guilt or liability, he or she is "testifying to the ultimate question." Although this is allowed in some jurisdictions, it is strongly advised that expert witnesses avoid rendering such opinions. These decisions belong to the triers of fact. The judge and the jury deliberate and decide.

Juries are impaneled to hear cases, weigh evidence with the guidance and instructions of the presiding judge, and render a decision in the matter at hand. At bench trials, judicial hearings, and appellate reviews, judges render decisions and opinions.

Research suggests that most decisions by judges and juries are based on the quality of evidence (Kalven & Zeisel, 1966), although many tangential factors may influence decisions, such as the judge's bias, community standards and expectations, and individual prejudice among jurors. Since the quality and clarity of the evidence are the most powerful variables behind the decision-making process, the expert witness is in a key position to enhance the decision-making process through the most careful, substantial, clear, and appropriate testimony.

4

Preparing to Serve as an Expert Witness

As has been noted in Chapter 2, psychologists are called upon to play a wide variety of roles as experts in the courts. Procedures, techniques, and professional styles are bound to vary. The following recommended procedures will be appropriate for most situations in which the psychologist is asked to serve as an expert witness. Variations will undoubtedly occur, but they should stand the tests of being in the client's best interests and falling well within the expectancies and constraints of professional ethics, the law, and standards for the delivery of professional services. Although the expert may review literature, write a learned treatise, and serve as a rebuttal witness to attest to known and/or accepted scientific principles, the usual role of the expert is to perform a professional or scientific study or evaluation and render an opinion as to the meaning of the results. The procedures outlined in this chapter should fit virtually all situations in which psychologists are asked to serve as expert witnesses.

GETTING STARTED

Sources of referral vary considerably, but a psychologist is most likely to be sought out by an attorney who has heard of or observed the psychologist's performance as an expert witness in another case. This means that getting started as an expert witness may be somewhat of a problem for a psychologist who has never served in this role. Experience as a member of a forensic center staff, juvenile or family court, or community agency where staff are called upon to conduct forensic evaluations is helpful. An expert should have appropriate education and training in forensic matters through courses, workshops, and internship experience. An apprenticeship served as an assistant to an experienced forensic psychologist is probably going to be the modus operandi of entrance into a forensic practice in the future.

Psychologists who have attained significant status and recognition in neuropsychology, behavioral medicine, child clinical psychology, marketing research, evaluation science, and other professional subspecialties are often approached to serve as experts by attorneys seeking a professional or scientist whose work and publications are related to significant issues in a particular case. It is easier for a psychologist who has achieved a measure of status and recognition in his or her subspecialty to become known as an "expert witness" than it is for an entrance-level psychologist, recently finished with education and training and anxious to enter the field of forensic psychology. Although entrance-level psychologists may be qualified to render expert opinion in their special area of professional skill or knowledge, attorneys tend to be drawn to known and/or "tested" experts.

The young, aspiring forensic psychologist need not be excluded. After acquiring the fundamental professional skills and postdoctoral training in forensic psychology, which is available through continuing education workshops and postdoctoral training institutes, the neophyte expert can increase his or her visibility in a number of ways.

Becoming a part of the forensic psychology establishment will put the psychologist in touch with colleagues who can serve as mentors, sponsors, and sources of referral. Such opportunities include the Division of Psychology and the Law of the American Psychological Association and the Psychology-Law Society. Many state psychological associations have formed sections on psychology and the law. The professional psychologist who wishes to receive referrals for work with the courts must make his or her interest known to colleagues, attorneys, and the courts. A professional card sent out to announce one's interest and qualification can be helpful. Such announcements should be accurate and conservative. Figure 4.1 illustrates a general announcement that might be sent to selected colleagues, lawyers, and judges by a psychologist trained and prepared to offer forensic services.

Each community has a variety of legal organizations (often referred to as the "criminal bar" or the "matrimonial bar"); these meet regularly, and an educational program is usually presented at each meeting. The forensic

JANE W. DOE, Ph.D.
takes pleasure in announcing the addition of
FORENSIC CONSULTATION
to her practice of clinical and child psychology

Custodial evaluations	*Marital dissolution mediation*
Competency evaluation	*Assessment of psychological deficit*

24 Oak Ridge Parkway   Hours by appointment
Suite 127
[Phone number]

FIGURE 4.1.   An announcement of forensic services by a professional psychologist.

psychologist seeking recognition and referrals from the legal community can enhance visibility and offer a professional service to the various bars by offering to make presentations about psychology and the law to these groups. Where appropriate, groups of forensic psychologists may announce or describe services by way of a descriptive brochure, which is in good taste within the ethical requirements of the profession.

Work which is carefully, ethically, and professionally done is the best source of referral and continuing respect from colleagues and the legal profession.

Academic psychologists generally become expert witnesses in the courts as a result of their being known as specialists in an area of behavioral science that attorneys have found to be useful in clarifying evidence. Academic psychologists are sought as experts in such areas as eyewitness identification; visual perception; and evaluation of the merit of research, memory, and opinion surveys. Publication and collegial respect are the usual routes by which lawyers seek out academic psychologists.

STARTING A CASE

The Initial Interview

The initial contact in a forensic case is usually made by telephone. The attorney who wishes to retain the psychologist will ordinarily make a telephone call to discuss the facts of the case and to determine whether the psychologist is able and willing to participate as an expert witness. Occasionally, the telephone call is made by the attorney's paralegal assistant or secretary. In most cases, however, the psychologist can expect to hear directly from the attorney. If the psychologist is too busy to talk at some length (usually 15 to 30 minutes), the psychologist should ask for the opportunity to call the attorney back to discuss the case when sufficient time permits the psychologist to make an informed judgment as to whether he or she will take the case. If this is the way it is handled, the psychologist should be sure to set a specific time to call the attorney, the same day if possible. Whether the psychologist participates or not should be settled early on as a courtesy to the attorney.

During the initial portion of the telephone contact, the attorney ordinarily gives the psychologist a brief synopsis of the litigation in the form of "the facts of the case." This is legal terminology for the bare essentials that would be required to understand the source of the litigation and the remedies sought. It is important that the psychologist determine a number of things during this initial interview, in order to accept or reject the consultation. The following represents an outline of such information:

1. *The Facts of the Case.*   Psychologists will be pleased to find that most attorneys are quite expert at summarizing the essential facts of the case. If this does not occur during the initial phase of the telephone interview, the

psychologist need only ask, "Could you please tell me the facts of the case, counselor?" In response to this, the attorney will ordinarily tell the psychologist the situation under which the case came about; whether the attorney represents the plaintiff or the defendant; the essential issues of the case; and the kind of information, testimony, facts, or opinions that the attorney seeks in order to support the litigation effort. Exact details are usually unnecessary at this stage, since if the expert is willing to serve, volumes of material will be provided to help the expert understand the facts of the case in detail. During the initial interview, the expert must have sufficient information to decide whether his or her unique scientific or professional skills can be appropriately applied.

2. *The Anticipated Court Date.*   Depending on the kind of case involved, considerable time may be required for the psychologist to make appointments to conduct an examination, review literature, prepare learned theses, or do a variety of other things. Some attorneys are not aware of this and may call upon their experts one or two weeks before the anticipated trial date. Some attorneys exert a good deal of pressure to convince the potential expert that his or her help is unique and very much needed. The psychologist should politely but firmly reject any efforts that would result in hurried evaluative procedures or the cutting of corners in any respect. Each expert must develop his or her own sense of how much time is necessary to "work up" a case. It is far better to err on the long side than the short side in requiring time to prepare properly. The expert should remember that it is usually necessary to consult with the attorney one or two times before a trial, and some time must be available for depositions to be taken by opposing attorneys. This should be discussed and clarified at the time of the initial interview.

3. *The Hypothetical Questions.*   When a professional or scientific expert is retained by an attorney, no matter what the expert's skills or talents may be, the result planned by the retaining attorney will be the presentation of testimony by the expert that concludes with an opinion. The opinion is elicited by one or more *hypothetical questions* presented by the attorney. The hypothetical question brings together and focuses all the issues in which the expert is involved so that a simple, straightforward opinion or conclusion may be presented to the jury. Attorneys cannot tell exactly what their hypothetical questions will be before they have completed preparing their case, but they can certainly present some general statement that will help the expert understand the focus of the information the expert is to provide. The reason for discussing this during the initial contact with the attorney is to ensure that the expert knows approximately what is expected. This allows the expert to determine whether to participate in the case. Examples of hypothetical questions might include: "Doctor, given all the facts of the case, as you know them and as they have been presented to the jury, within reasonable psychological probability is the defendant, Ms. Jones, suffering neuropsychological deficit?" "Given all the information

that is available, and calling upon your own background and research, doctor, is it your opinion that the witness, Mr. Smith, could make a clear, reliable eyewitness identification in this case?" "Given the information that has been provided you, doctor, as well as your own extensive examination, is it your opinion as a professional psychologist that Mr. Green is able to understand the nature of the charges against him and the consequences that will accrue to him if convicted?" The purpose of asking for anticipated hypotheticals early on is to ensure that the psychologist understands what is expected and can state the likelihood of being in a position to render an opinion in the matters at hand.

4. *The Condition and Availability of the Plaintiff.*   In the event that a psychological examination of a plaintiff or a defendant is required, the psychologist should determine from the retaining attorney whether there will be any difficulty having the individual come to the expert's offices for examination. At times, the attorney may require the psychologist to conduct the examination elsewhere. The place may not be conducive to a proper examination under standardized conditions. In some cases a judge may have limited the number of hours that a plaintiff or defendant is available for evaluation, restricting the psychologist's opportunity to perform in an ethical, professional manner. Any such limitation should be known at the beginning of the consultation to ensure that a thorough and professional job can be done. If the proper conditions cannot be arranged, the professional should refuse the consultation.

5. *Retrieval of Records.*   The opinion of the expert in any matter of litigation is but a small part of the entire process. Considerable information will have been collected by the time the psychologist is asked to consult. Although the expert will take a history in most instances, the analysis of records can form an important part of the process of coming to an opinion. Whether the matter involves a personal injury suit, product liability litigation, or exculpation because of mental status, background is important. Hospital charts, school records, work records, evaluations, and military records can be helpful in the evaluation process. During the initial interview the psychologist should ask the attorney to obtain and forward such records. A letter from an attorney is much likelier to bring forth records from a bureaucratic organization than a request from a psychologist. The psychologist should encourage the attorney to pursue this promptly, so that the records are available as quickly as possible. It is helpful if lawyers know where to retrieve certain records. Current military service records can be obtained from:

> Commander
> Reserve Components Administration Center
> Attention: PAE-E
> 9700 Paige Boulevard
> St. Louis, MO 63132
> Telephone: (314) 263-3901

For those who have been in the military, and have received service from the Veterans Administration, these records can be obtained from:

> Records Processing Center
> P.O. Box 5020
> St. Louis, MO 63115
> Telephone: (314) 263-3772

If the litigation involves examination by other behavioral scientists, the lawyers should be encouraged to make the reports of these examinations available, particularly in respect to when they occurred. If testing is to be done, the expert must be sure that sufficient time has elapsed to avoid test–retest problems.

Figure 4.2 presents the Forensic Intake form, which has been found to be useful for taking down significant information during the initial telephone interview and will allow the expert to have basic facts about the case readily available in the case folder. During the course of the initial interview, the psychologist should ask the attorney whether she or he wishes to be called at home in the evening in the event some question arises or should the expert come to some conclusion during the course of the evaluation. Many attorneys devote themselves intensely to their cases and have no objection to this.

Date _____

Attorney _____ Telephone _____

Address _____ Home _____

_____ Intake by _____

Case _____ _____ Plaintiff
                                                  _____ Defendant
Facts of the Case: _____ Amicus curiae
                                                  _____ Court-appointed

Hypothetical Questions:

Anticipated Trial Date _____ _____ Request initial letter
                                                         Designate as consultant
Judge _____   Fees on 30-day basis

Court _____   _____ Suggest retrieval of records
                                                         and information
Secretary to Attorney _____

Additional: _____ Discuss fee structure

                                                  _____ Discuss pretrial meeting

                                                  _____ Confirming letter

                                                  _____ First appointment

FIGURE 4.2.   Forensic intake form.

Knowing the judge who will try the case and the jurisdiction of the litigation may be helpful in determining the kind of setting in which the litigation will take place. Judges are extremely individualistic, and as one becomes experienced as an expert witness, one comes to understand that each judge conducts the courtroom in his or her own particular way. Part of being a very competent expert involves understanding the expectancies of the court in terms of such matters as dress, decor, and style of presentation. This will be explored in some detail in Chapter 10.

Most lawyers depend on a secretary or a paralegal assistant. During the course of the case, the expert may want to know all kinds of information about the case that is more readily available from the lawyer's assistant than from the attorney. Knowing who the secretary is can be quite helpful. Ordinarily, the lawyer's secretary is quite aware of changes in court dates, availability of witnesses, and unusual aspects of the case and is the person with whom the expert can establish a working relationship that in some instances is extremely helpful in clarifying issues and avoiding misunderstandings. If arrangements must be made for examination of litigants, the attorney's secretary will often be the person that the psychologist or the psychologist's secretary will contact. All kinds of minutiae arise during litigation, and a close working relationship between the psychologist's office and the attorney's immediate assistant can be a very helpful liaison.

6. *Fee Arrangements.*   It is important that fee arrangements be discussed during the initial telephone interview. The expert should be sure that the retaining attorney understands the kinds of fees the psychologist will be charging and that the financial arrangements required by the expert are agreeable. During this interview the expert should indicate his or her hourly fee for work to be done during the case. This may include research, constructing reports, conducting examinations, appearing at depositions, pretrial meetings, and the trial itself. Where the expert uses assistants, such as psychometricians or research associates, the fees for such services should be indicated. It is strongly recommended that the psychologist charge the same fee for forensic work that is charged for any kind of clinical or professional work. During the course of a cross-examination, in open court, the opposing counsel would be very happy to find that the psychologist charges more for forensic work than for ordinary professional work. This issue would probably be brought to the attention of the judge and jury, with intimations that the psychologist's presence is less a matter of objective, professional opinion than of an opportunity to increase his or her fees. By charging the same amount as for usual professional work, a psychologist can avoid this situation.

Any objections to the expert's fee structure should be stated at once by the attorney. Some attorneys work on a contingency basis and are reluctant to pay professional fees before the case is finished. This could take three or four years and places the psychologist under a considerable financial bur-

Jones, Farnham, Abercrombie, and Zilch
Attorneys at Law
Post Office Drawer 1276
Waukegan, Illinois 47209

Re: *Mulligan v. Consolidated Box Corp.*

Dear Doctor Jones:

Pursuant to our telephone conversation of June 7th, our firm would like to retain you as consultant in clinical psychology in the above-captioned matter. We represent the defendant in this case. Please send all invoices to this firm, and they will be honored within thirty (30) days of receipt.

Pursuant to our further discussion, copies of medical records, psychological reports, hospital records, and military records will be forwarded as they are received.

Thank you for agreeing to assist in this matter.

Very truly yours,
Albert B. Abercrombie

FIGURE 4.3.   Example of attorney's letter retaining a psychologist as expert witness.

den. To avoid this, once the fee arrangements are found to be acceptable, the psychologist should ask the attorney to forward a letter stating that the psychologist is retained as a consultant and that "all invoices forwarded by the expert will be honored on a 30-day basis."

The expert should beware of such reassurances as "Don't worry," "I will protect your fee," or "You will be paid promptly." Telephone agreement is insufficient. In order to avoid building large accounts receivable with various attorneys, forensic psychologists must insist upon such a letter. If a lawyer is unwilling to do this, the psychologist should withdraw from the case. Figure 4.3 presents an attorney's retaining letter.

During the initial telephone conversation, it is wise to mention to the attorney that after the report is submitted, a pretrial meeting is required before going to court. Although the attorney may have great confidence in the expert, it is extremely important that the kind of direct examination to be conducted should be thoroughly discussed before it takes place. The reasons for this are presented in detail in Chapter 10.

PREPARING THE CASE FOLDER

Psychologists who are unfamiliar with the forensic area may begin their practice by setting up clinical folders similar to those they have used in their professional work. They will soon find that this will not do in forensic work. Attorneys produce large quantities of documents and frequently send copies to the expert, who must classify and file them.

Attorneys use $8\frac{1}{2}$-by-14-inch (legal-size) sheets in their work. It is hopeless to attempt to fit such documents into a standard clinical folder. The

PROPERTY OF
RIVERWOOD COMMUNITY MENTAL HEALTH

psychologist who intends to become a practicing forensic expert is urged to begin setting up legal files to ensure efficiency and accuracy. Attorneys have developed all kinds of helpful filing materials and equipment. It is strongly urged that psychologists activate a legal case folder after the initial telephone call has been completed and the case has been accepted.

A recommended type of case folder is called a legal-size, two-partition, hardboard folder, as shown in Figure 4.4. As can be seen, this large folder

FIGURE 4.4.   Legal case folder.

has two inner partitions. The front cover, the back cover, and both sides of the two partitions have metal clips to hold paper that is punched at the top. This allows the psychologist to sort and classify the large variety of materials received during the course of a legal consultation. During the depositions and at the court trial, the psychologist will be grateful for the time spent classifying and organizing the folders. It is quite embarrassing to search through a folder of loose papers when a specific question is asked. Preparing such a folder from the beginning will ensure that the expert can find and review materials about any aspect of the case at any time.

Setting up classifications within the case folder is a matter of individual taste. For a professional clinical psychologist, the tabs might be:

1. Tests, working notes, and final report
2. Initiating documents and letters from retaining attorney

Theodore H. Blau, Ph.D., P.A.
213 E. Main St.
Tampa, Fla. 33808
Fed. ID No. 00-0000000
Charge Schedule

Case _____ No. _____

Date	Staff Person	Function	Time	Amount

FIGURE 4.5.   Charge sheet for recording and summarizing fees.

3.   Reports and records from other sources
4.   Depositions and conference notes
5.   Subpoenas, case chronology and material delivery, and other corre-
     spondence
6.   Fees and miscellaneous matters

Figure 4.5 shows a charge schedule that has been found to be useful. Experts should understand that lawyers keep such a charge sheet and understand it thoroughly. By submitting a copy of such a charge sheet with invoices, the expert provides the lawyer with a clear picture of exactly what the expert did and how much time was spent on each task. It should be noted that the federal identification number is included since some firms have checks issued by insurance companies which require such a number. Providing it on the charge sheet avoids a lot of correspondence and delay in payment.

Psychologists ordinarily do not charge for telephone time. In forensic matters, the expert will find that lawyers often consult by telephone since it is convenient and practical. When such consultations take place, it is perfectly legitimate to place a charge on the charge sheet based on the amount of time actually utilized. Attorneys do this, and they expect it of their consultants.

Useful Forms

There are no standards, as such, for the forms and procedures to be used by the psychologist in preparing to serve as expert witness. The forms recommended here were designed to ensure an orderly preparation of materials and procedures as the consultation develops. They are products of experience, both positive and negative. The psychologist who intends to perform at a high level of professional skill, competence, and efficiency should be aware that, when consulting with attorneys or working within the court system, a much greater degree of detail and supportive documentation is likely to be necessary than in the conduct of professional practice. Lawyers and judges are usually very concerned about when things happened, what was said, who said it, and where it happened. The expert-aspirant is well advised to err in the direction of excessive detail at the beginning, later developing forms, procedures, and systems dictated by personal experience.

As a rule, all contacts relating to the litigation should be noted, dated, and initialed by the person who made the contact, whether it be the psychologist, secretary, psychometrician, or receptionist. There is no way of predicting just what information will be required of the expert when he or she is finally called upon to be deposed or to testify at the trial, so it is wise to have all this information available.

Case Chronology Form.   Once the initial lawyer–psychologist contact is made, there are various styles in which a case develops. Each consultation is somewhat different. The expert can expect to be called upon, by either the retaining attorney or the attorney for the opposition, to specify how the expert was retained and by whom. Questions are commonly asked during trial about when the expert did things, received information, or forwarded reports. Figure 4.6 presents a form which has been found to be useful in keeping a record of the chronology of events in a case.

Beginning with the intake call, all telephone calls, conferences, examinations, receipt of materials from the retaining attorney, examination sessions, report writing, and report forwarding (including letters) should be noted as each event occurs. The psychologist should record how much time was spent during those contacts in which any work was done on the case or any discussion with the attorney or key figures took place. Again, it is a matter of personal style, experience, and judgment as to the detail recorded on this form.

Case Material Delivery.   In a complex case or one that extends over a period of time, the psychologist may wish to abstract from the case chronology a sequential list of materials received and forwarded. Hospital records, academic transcripts, professional reports, and legal citations are commonly forwarded to experts by legal counsel. The psychologist may

Case Chronology

Case _____   Number _____

Date	Contact	Time

FIGURE 4.6.   A form to record all significant events as the case develops.

return some of these, send research reprints, or other learned treatise material and reports to the retaining attorney.

Copies of material may be sent to the adversary attorney (in response to a subpoena). These exchanges should be noted for quick reference if the information is required during a deposition or the trial. Figure 4.7 presents a case material delivery log or record. Parenthetically, all important material, such as reports, should be sent by certified mail, with a return receipt requested.

Pretrial Checklist.   As a forensic case develops, the psychologist may find that while the trial date approaches, important preparatory steps can be forgotten. In a complex case, preparing for trial can be a busy and demanding experience. To ensure that the psychologist is indeed prepared to perform as an expert, a checklist of necessary procedures and preparations can be helpful. Finding oneself on the witness stand looking for something that was not done or was not prepared is a disconcerting experience. Such embarrassing moments are viewed by most attorneys as evidence of poor professional competence. Figure 4.8 presents a checklist that covers most of the important tasks in preparing to testify as an expert and is useful in reviewing the status of the case.

The nature and purpose of items that seem unfamiliar at this point will become clear as they are addressed in subsequent chapters.

Case Material Delivery

Date	Material	Sent by or Received by

FIGURE 4.7. A case material delivery form.

Pretrial Checklist

Preliminary
____ Referral letter from attorney received.
____ Hypothetical questions.
____ Curriculum Vita sent to attorney.
____ Vita annotated for this case.
____ All appointments checked and verified.
____ Case chronology form started.

Process
____ Reports and records annotated and indexed.
____ All interviews and examinations completed.
____ All background material reviewed.
____ Observation notes complete.
____ All materials dated and initialed.
____ Preliminary report to retaining attorney.
____ All test scoring double-checked.
____ Report written and forwarded.
____ Conference with retaining attorney to review findings.

Preparation for Court—Preliminary
____ Review all materials.
____ Review own deposition.
____ Prepare special items for cue book (test reviews, learned treatise support).
____ Prepare charts and illustrations (rough).
____ Prepare qualifying questions for attorney.

Preparation for court—final
____ Prepare charts and illustrations (final).
____ Final conference with retaining attorney.
____ Prepare direct-examination questions for retaining attorney.
____ Location of courtroom and time expected.
____ Last-minute check with attorney's assistant to ensure case has not been settled or postponed.

FIGURE 4.8. A pretrial checklist.

COLLECTING PRELIMINARY DATA FOR DECISION MAKING

The psychologist retained by an attorney to function as an expert is expected to produce an opinion. The most credible expert opinions are usually the result of a process in which the expert collects extensive materials, conducts necessary evaluations under properly controlled conditions, and prepares, with great care, a document stating opinions or findings in a thorough, reasonable, and supportable manner. The findings may not always be to the retaining attorney's liking. When the expert's findings are not supportive of the attorney's case, the retaining attorney will thank the psychologist and tell him or her that the findings and opinion will not be used. This is proper and ethical. The decision as to whether the psychologist's findings will be used lies entirely in the hands of the attorney who is in charge of the case. This in no way should influence how thoroughly the psychologist prepares. All legal consultations should be conducted with the expectancy that the psychologist will be prepared to render an expert opinion based on his or her best professional knowledge and skills.

Psychological evaluations prepared properly for court are frequently more extensive and detailed than customary psychological assessments. Time constraints are usually less stringent in forensic work than in professional practice. Extensive background data and materials are often available to the forensic psychologist, which would be difficult, impossible, or unnecessary to obtain during the course of a usual psychological assessment. Often, but not invariably, financial resources are available for sophisticated or unusual procedures (a full battery of vocational aptitude tests, sequential repetitions of neuropsychological assessments, preliminary rehabilitation procedures, or retrieval of military or school records). Much of this may have little to do with the assessment process but is necessary to ensure that the expert can respond to even tangential questions by an adversary attorney during trial.

Facts of the Case

Although the psychologist has been given a summary of the facts of the case by the attorney, an array of materials can be expected from the attorney which will provide details of the circumstances that led to the civil or criminal action. The materials may include a detailed patent or copyright search in a trademark suit, police and emergency room reports in a personal injury case, or officer and detective reports in a criminal case. The more thoroughly a psychologist understands the facts of the case and the issues to be resolved in the litigation, the more effective he or she can be as an expert witness. Some attorneys forward legal citations, rules of evidence, judge's instructions, and other materials to help the expert witness understand more clearly the facts of the case and the legal issues involved. If such material is not forthcoming, it is always appropriate to ask the attorney who retains the psychologist to forward such material as is likely to be helpful.

After reviewing the records associated with the facts of the case, it is suggested that the psychologist write an abstract of these facts to ensure that the expert's services are being utilized with appropriate understanding and focus. The following illustrates such an abstract.

FACTS OF THE CASE

Wright v. Alameda Power Co.

James Wright, age 12 at the time, climbed a tree in his backyard to retrieve a lost kite. While reaching for the kite, his arm touched a high-voltage electric line. The electrical jolt which followed threw Jim from the tree. He dropped approximately 25 feet to the ground, unconscious from the electrical shock. His friend, who watched these events, called Jimmy's mother. They put the dazed boy in the family car and drove him to the emergency room of the local hospital. Though conscious on admission, Jim was in severe shock. Burns to his right arm were so extensive that the surgical team at the hospital amputated the arm just above the elbow. Jim seemed to recover well from the trauma and the surgery.

Jimmy is now 15 years of age. During the two years subsequent to the accident, Jimmy's family reports that he had become a very aggressive behavior problem. He bullies younger children. He is passing none of his school subjects. He seems to have memory loss and confusion at times. The family says he is "very changed" since the accident.

The firm of Sloane and Witty, representing James Wright and his parents, has filed suit against the Alameda Power Company for substantial sums claiming Jim is irreparably brain damaged and severely disturbed emotionally as a result of this accident.

It is sometimes helpful to check the summary with the retaining attorney to ensure that the details are accurate and complete. When the expert's final report is written, this statement can serve as an introduction to the report.

Records

In many instances, particularly personal injury cases, when the expert is asked for an opinion, it is in reference to a plaintiff's or defendant's previous status. In the facts of the case presented above, the plaintiff's attorneys claim that James Wright is brain damaged and emotionally disturbed as a result of his accident. This assumes that these conditions did not exist before the accident. School records, records of guidance counselors, family physicians, and other sources may shed light on premorbid status. Treatment records before and after the accident, reports of neurological and psychological examinations, and standardized school tests—before and after the accident—can be of value in determining psychological status at different times in a subject's life.

The psychologist may wish to retrieve consumer survey reports in a trademark infringement suit or sunset tables in an eyewitness identification issue where the relation of visual acuity to ambient illumination is important. In the insanity defense, police records; statements of friends, relatives, and casual observers; treatment records; and other behavioral records of the defendant's activities and demeanor before, during, and after the crime are vital to the expert seeking to give an opinion as to a person's probable mental state. The more objective, or replicated, the records or observations, the more useful they tend to be. All available records that are associated with the facts of the case should be retrieved, reviewed, and analyzed.

As with the facts of the case, records may be summarized to advantage and may serve as part of the final report. Such a summary of records was made for the case of *Wright v. Alameda Power Company*.

SUMMARY OF RECORDS

Wright v. Alameda Power Co.

Medical Records.   Jimmy Wright was brought to the emergency room of Alameda Community Hospital at 2:40 P.M. on June 29, 1977. Emergency room records indicate that he was conscious but dazed and apparently in shock. A very severe electrical burn of the right arm extending from the wrist to above the elbow was treated by the triage team, and the boy was immediately sent to surgery. James E. Watts, M.D., orthopedic surgeon, headed the team which amputated Jimmy's right arm. Postoperative course was indicated as normal, and the physicians' notes state that Jimmy "tolerated the procedure well and recovered with no unusual sequelae." Postoperative visits with Dr. Watts note good progress.

Reports from rehabilitation services indicate that Jimmy has been resistant to learning to use a prosthesis. Consultants urged no pressure in this issue in view of Jimmy's rapid physical growth during the past two years.

At present, medical reports indicate that Jimmy is a healthy 15-year-old, ready to be fitted with a prosthesis for his right arm. He seems more interested in this now than last year and plans are proceeding to arrange for fitting and training.

Academic Records.   School records from the Alameda School District, the McFarlane School, are quite complete. Jimmy started the first grade at age seven. He did poorly and was referred to the school psychologist for evaluation. A WISC-R at age eight years, one month, dated November, 16, 1973, was reported as follows:

Factor	Deviation IQ	Percentile
Verbal scale	77	7th
Performance scale	81	10th
Full scale	77	7th

In the second grade, Jimmy was placed in a class for slow learners. Notations on the school records indicate that his teachers saw him as aggressive, unsociable, and bullying. The school psychologist notes "family problems." He failed and repeated the third grade.

Jimmy was returned to regular classes in the fourth grade. He repeated the fourth grade and entered the fifth grade at age 12. Standardized Metropolitan Achievement Tests reported on the school record during the fifth grade showed the following:

Factor	Grade Equivalent
Reading comprehension	2.6
Arithmetic	2.7
Language	2.2

After he entered the sixth grade at 13, three months after his accident, his record shows "satisfactory" progress. He entered the seventh grade, moving to LaBrea Junior High School. A referral to the school counselor for aggressive behavior in the classroom was followed by an assessment by the school psychologist. A WISC-R dated November 14, 1982, when Jimmy was 14 years, 1 month, of age was reported as follows:

Factor	Deviation IQ	Percentile
Verbal scale	81	10th
Performance scale	87	20th
Full scale	83	14th

The record shows that Jimmy passed shop, physical education, and American history. He failed functional math and English.

Psychological Records. Jimmy was examined by Arnold W. Pallac, Ph.D., at the request of Jimmy's attorneys during spring 1983. His psychological report includes the following results of a WISC-R:

Factor	Deviation IQ	Percentile
Verbal scale	84	16th
Performance scale	88	21st
Full scale	85	18th

Dr. Pallac also indicates that a Halstead Reitan Neuropsychological Battery (partial) indicates "signs of significant brain disorder." No Impairment Index was reported. Wide Range Achievement Test results were as follows:

Factor	Grade Equivalent
Reading	5.8
Arithmetic	5.6
Spelling	5.1

Dr. Pallac administered an MMPI as well as Draw-a-Person and Sentence Completion tests. He reports that Jimmy is depressed, withdrawn, and "suffering a severe posttraumatic depression." Dr. Pallac makes no mention in his report of having examined previous school records or other data. Dr. Pallac opined that all of these defects resulted from the accident and that Jimmy was of "at least normal intelligence before his accident."

These summaries make it quite clear that a careful review of academic and psychological records can be critical to a proper professional evaluation. Dr. Pallac's omission became the source of considerable embarrassment when he was cross-examined in court.

Literature Review. The psychologist who intends to act as an expert witness will be expected to be reasonably familiar with the scientific literature associated with the case at hand. Guesses, vague recall, and evasions are unacceptable. The reliabilities and validities of all test instruments which make their appearance in the case should be known. A photocopy of the *Mental Measurements Yearbook* (Buros, 1933–1978) citation of each test given in the case should be made part of the case folder for reference at the trial. The psychologist will be put forth as an expert at court and must make every effort to meet this expectation. In the case of *Wright v. Alameda Power Company*, the psychologist retained by counsel for the plaintiff claimed that Jimmy's condition is best described as that of a "brain-disordered youngster suffering a chronic posttraumatic neurosis." As either a collaborating or opposing witness, one would be remiss not to review the DSM-III descriptions of these conditions (American Psychiatric Association, 1981) and the more recent research concerning these diagnostic categories.

THE NEEDS-ASSESSMENT

Given the information and materials which have been collected, the psychologist should be able to formulate a needs-assessment of his or her role in the case. This "gap analysis" (Kaufman & English, 1979) identifies the scope of the assessment task. The general basis of the needs-assessment is found in the retaining attorney's original request for consultation, which, in turn, should be made clearer by the hypothetical questions the attorney suggests during the initial contact. The needs-assessment is a formal or informal process whereby the psychologist determines the gap between currently available information and the information that will be necessary before an expert opinion on the matter at hand can be rendered. The strategies chosen to fill the gap represent the psychologist's skill and expertise. They also will represent the basis and justification for the expert's opinion.

The needs-assessment may result in a relatively simple gap in a disability determination, such as, "Is there objective evidence that the plaintiff is mentally retarded?" Complex gaps are more the rule than the exception and can include various issues, such as in the case of the insanity defense (Chapter 7), "At the time of the crime, was the defendant able to appreciate that what he did was unlawful?" or in change of venue issues (Chapter 11), "Is community awareness and prejudice such that the defendant may not be assured of a fair and impartial jury?"

The character, quality, and extent of the opinions, which the psychologist is expected to render in court, should be as clear as possible before deciding on and implementing strategies to reach those opinions.

STRATEGY SELECTION AND IMPLEMENTATION

It is here that solid psychological background and assessment skills are required. There is rarely "one and only one" approach to psychological assessment or evaluation. The experienced, competent professional psychologist will be prepared to review all strategies and select those most appropriate and available for the task at hand. Whether the strategic options involve testing procedures to be used in determining the presence or absence of psychological deficit in a personal injury case (Chapter 9) or the kinds of interviews, evaluations, and record review required for an opinion in a child custody matter (Chapter 7), certain guidelines are helpful in selecting the strategies to be implemented:

1. **Are the Strategies Available?** In a jury evaluation project the psychologist may recommend a sophisticated procedure, such as a base-rate demographic study of the voters' registration list in a community; however, if the local laws forbid using that list, the strategy may not be used.

2. **Are the Strategies Ethical?** The psychologist must be sure that any procedure, test, evaluation, or assessment done is well within the American Psychological Association (APA) code of ethics (APA, 1981) and the APA standards for the delivery of psychological services (APA, 1977). (For details, see Chapters 5 and 12.)

3. **Are the Strategies Professionally Acceptable?** Anything that the psychologist chooses to do in order to come to an opinion will be reviewed and possibly challenged during a deposition or at the trial. All procedures should be such that they have general acceptance in the profession and represent acceptable practice and procedures.

4. **Are the Strategies Practical?** Such factors as cost, personal agreeability to all parties, and time constraints must be taken into consid-

eration. In some cases the psychologist may feel certain procedures are vital to support an expert opinion, whereas the attorney or the attorney's clients may see them as unacceptable. In such cases the psychologist should ordinarily withdraw from the case. An example of this would be when a psychologist is asked to render an expert opinion on prison conditions and the attorneys for the state are unwilling to agree to a series of on-site visits and interviews with dissident inmates.

No set of procedures can create or replace training, experience, and good judgment. Guidelines presented here must be used or adapted intelligently by the psychologist, choosing among various strategies and techniques to gather sufficient information to support an expert opinion. The competent professional will avoid redundant or unnecessary strategies. In choosing a strategy, the psychologist must always keep in mind the question of how the information resulting from the procedure will relate to the requirements for the expert's opinions at court in the matter at hand.

Implementation

Once the psychologist has decided on the test battery, the evaluation study, or whatever procedure will constitute the data collection phase of the preparation, it is essential that these be carried out in such a way that the procedures cannot be reasonably assailed by an opposing attorney. Tests should be administered in standardized style in appropriate settings. During the implementation stage of the psychologist's work, preliminary results should be analyzed and, where appropriate, communicated to the retaining attorney. In some instances, interim or formative results may suggest additional strategies. In some cases early results may suggest that the expert's opinion will *not* add support to the retaining attorney's case. The decision whether to continue lies with the retaining attorney. Some experts become indignant when an attorney decides the expert's services and opinion will not be used when the initial or final results indicate information adverse to the case at hand. A clearer understanding of the adversary process in American jurisprudence would be helpful for psychologists who react in this manner. The expert's job is to provide an attorney with an opinion on some psychological matter related to the case at hand. If that opinion is not supportive of the attorney's legal efforts on behalf of the client, the attorney is duty bound not to use the psychological expert.

OUTCOMES

Whatever the type of case for which a psychologist is retained as an expert witness, there must be an outcome or a product. In a forensic consultation the outcome is presented in the expert's testimony in a court of law. At that time the psychologist identifies himself or herself, states what he or she has done, and renders an opinion in response to hypothetical questions. Before this happens, the psychologist will ordinarily finish a series of psychological tests, examine documents, review research, or conduct research or evaluative studies. The psychologist will come to conclusions and form opinions. A report of all of this constitutes the outcome of the expert's work.

As soon as the outcomes, carefully checked and reviewed, are available, the psychologist should call the attorney and discuss the findings. This preliminary report should be rendered as early as possible so that the attorney who retained the psychologist can begin to consider the most appropriate trial strategy for using the psychologist's information. Many personal injury suits are settled once the expert's opinions are available.

Following the preliminary report, in clinical assessments a written report is mandatory. Some attorneys may ask the psychologist not to write a report until late in the judicial proceedings. This strategy is questionable, and the psychologist should simply tell the attorney who suggests it that the report must be written as part of the psychologist's professional standards and ethics. Certain guidelines for such reports may be helpful:

1. **Focus.**   The introduction, procedures, and conclusions of the report must focus on the issues of the case.
2. **Clarity.**   Jargon, obscure terms, and erudition should be avoided.
3. **Validity.**   The psychologist must put nothing in a forensic report that cannot be substantiated and supported in a relatively objective way.
4. **Opinion.**   The forensic report must conclude with an opinion or opinions based on the information in the report and responsive to the hypothetical questions posed at the beginning of the case by the attorney retaining the psychologist.

Because of the many areas of knowledge and professional activity in psychology, there is a consequent variety of needs-assessments, strategies, and outcomes to deal with the expectations of lawyers and judges in the rapidly developing relationship between psychology and the law. Basic principles will apply but an ever-widening range of forensic applications of psychological knowledge and practice can be expected.

5

Psychological Tests in the Courtroom

After the development of testing instruments used for officer selection in World War I, psychology built the art and science of testing on a foundation of scientific research. Lewis Terman (1931) resurrected Munsterberg's position after almost a quarter of a century and suggested that the use of psychology in the courts be reconsidered in light of developments in the science of psychology since the publication of *On the Witness Stand* (Munsterberg, 1908). His work came to the attention of the legal profession (Terman, 1935).

There is no question that many psychologists qualify as experts in American courts (Perline, 1980). At issue is the scientific quality of the testimony and the degree to which it is accepted in the scientific community. In this matter, guidance is clearly given within the framework of *Frye v. United States*.[1] Although the *Frye* test does not inquire into the essence of the merit of scientific evidence—the internal and external validity of that evidence—it states clearly that to be admissible, the evidence should be generally accepted by the scientific community of which the expert claims membership. Under this test, a technique, a procedure, or a finding must have been available for a fairly long period of time in order to have a history of general acceptance or utilization (Suggs, 1979). It has been suggested that *Frye* is most applicable if a device or standardized methodology is being considered and if the average juror would view the results of a "test" as fairly infallible when so purported by a qualified expert.[2] Although the various standards of admissibility of scientific evidence are relatively vague, psychological tests, when presented as a basis for expert opinion, may have to withstand cross-examination based on constraints within *Frye v. United States*.

As psychologists began to appear on the witness stands of America, frequently using psychological tests to explain or justify their opinions,

---

* An early version of this chapter appeared as (1984) Psychological tests in the courtroom. *Professional Psychology: Research and Practice, 15*, (2), pp. 176–186.
[1] *Frye v. United States*, 293 F. 1013 (D.C. Cir. 1923).
[2] 29 Stan. L. Rev. 969, 1017 (1977).

opportunities for lawyers to learn to probe the credibility of such testimony began to appear (Blau, 1959; Poythress, 1980; Ziskin, 1981). Psychologists who represented themselves as experts and used psychological tests to justify their opinions were asked to delineate the merit and limitations of such tests.

TESTIMONY INVOLVING PSYCHOLOGICAL TESTS

Where psychologists have testified as expert witnesses in a wide range of civil and criminal issues, psychological tests, inventories, or surveys have often formed an integral part of their testimony. If the test instrument is specifically constructed or adapted to the issue or questions concerning the psychologist's testimony, challenge as to the appropriateness of the instrument tends to be minimal. This kind of acceptance occurs most frequently in patent, trademark, and other cases where opinion surveys are conducted and reported as part of the expert's testimony.[3] Most testimony supported by psychological tests focuses on the psychological state of an individual who is either plaintiff or defendant in a civil or criminal matter at issue. The range of psychological instruments that have become available in the past 75 years is considerable, as is the range of quality and applicability of those instruments (Buros, 1933–1978). Testimony by psychologists about tests and test construction, as such, has been fairly narrow. Such testimony usually focuses on civil rights issues in which the courts become arbiters of testing practice in schools, agencies, and employment practices (Bersoff, 1981).

Use of Tests in Predicting Violence

The courts have traditionally vested almost unlimited power in psychiatry to aid in judicial decision making by identifying or certifying those likely to act in violent ways toward themselves or others. The judicial issues generally involve involuntary commitment, and psychological tests have been frequently used to support such predictions (Robitscher, 1980). The deficiencies of psychological tests in these matters have been well documented (Slovenko, 1973; Ziskin, 1981). Ziskin (1981a) suggests that failure of research to support any method of predicting violent behavior should deter sensible psychologists from responding to the demands for opinions in this matter. Some have suggested that "the past is a prologue" and that dangerousness can be best predicted from a history of violence (Wenke, Robison, & Smith, 1972; Monahan, 1981). Recent evaluation of the violent history paradigm does not support this concept. It is suggested that

---

[3] *Robinsdale Amusement Co. v. Warner Bros. Pictures Distributing Corp. et al.*, Civil #4584 (4th Division, Minneapolis).

violence is frequently due to transitory psychological state that emerge in response to atypical circumstances and is a fairly poor indicator of future violence (Holland, Holt, & Beckett, 1982).

In practice, testimony concerning potential dangerousness is generally accepted by judges and jurors if opposing counsel is insufficiently versed in challenging the merit of the research and its methodology and is unable to conduct a rigorous cross-examination (Suggs, 1979). The degree to which unsupported opinions concerning "dangerousness" can become a travesty of justice has been recently chronicled (Tierney, 1982). All studies to date that relate psychological measuring methods or instruments to violent behavior are subject to a variety of methodological critiques. The most important problem preventing accurate predictions of dangerousness remains the issue of stable, acceptable, measurable, and uncontaminated criteria by which to assess the strength of the predictors. If a model of accurate prediction of dangerousness is to be developed, long-range studies of experimental subjects in natural settings using stable and valid behavioral measures are necessary. On careful evaluation or replication, most currently available instruments fail in prediction. Projective techniques, objectively utilized, show some promise as predictors of violence (Mullen & Dudley, 1981).

Hypothetically, psychological tests could be useful in providing the court with probabilities concerning the future occurrence of dangerous acts by individuals. Considerable longitudinal research, with large samples, adequate designs, and careful replication would be the first step in bringing the use of psychological tests in the prediction of dangerousness to a level acceptable to the requirements of *Frye v. United States*. Although much general psychological information may be admissible without meeting the stringencies of the *Frye* test, the specificity of the concept of dangerousness carries it beyond McCormick's assertions that for some expert opinion a lower standard of admissibility, such as "general scientific acceptance," is sufficient.[4]

Competence to Stand Trial

Competency statutes represent one of the safeguards for protecting the constitutional rights of a defendant to a fair trial. The U.S. Supreme Court in 1960 ruled:

> [I]t is not enough for the district judge to find that the defendant is oriented in time and place and has some recollection of events but that the test must be whether he has sufficient present ability to consult with his lawyer with a reasonable degree of rational understanding—and whether he has a rational as well as factual understanding of the proceedings against him.[5]

[4] C. McCormick, *Law of Evidence* §13 (1954).
[5] *Duskey v. United States,* 362 U.S. 402 (1960).

Common-law criteria for competency include an ability to cooperate with one's attorney in one's own defense, an awareness and understanding of the nature and objectives of the proceedings, and an understanding of the consequences of the legal proceedings. If a defendant does not meet the criteria of competence, the speedy trial rule is laid aside and the proceedings are postponed until the defendant is found to be competent.

Thus if a defendant lacks minimal effective and cognitive resources to assume the role of defendant, he or she is deprived of the due-process right to testify in his or her own defense, to confront adversary witnesses, and to maintain an effective psychological presence in the courtroom beyond mere physical presence. The issue is legal, not psychological or psychiatric. Mental health professionals are sought as experts to *assist* judges and juries in settling competency issues. Psychologists, psychiatrists, and lay witnesses may present informed or expert opinion—they do not make the competency determination. This remains a formal judicial procedure (Lipsitt, Lelos, & McGarry, 1971).

Psychiatrists tend to view psychotic patients and mentally retarded individuals as incompetent to stand trial. Rarely are objective tests or criteria used to assess the validity of the psychiatric opinion (Roesch, 1979). Psychologists have developed a variety of competency screening instruments to supplement standardized tests of intelligence, brain dysfunction, and personality for determining competence to stand trial. Promising replication and validation have been reported (Nottingham & Mattson, 1981).

Each state specifies, with a greater or lesser degree of exactness, what is required in the way of an opinion or a report from an expert appointed to advise the court on the competency of a witness to stand trial. The Florida Rules of Criminal Procedure, for instance, are quite explicit:

(1) In considering the issue of competence to stand trial, the examining experts should consider and include in their report, but are not limited to, an analysis of the mental condition of the defendant as it affects each of the following factors:
    (i) Defendant's appreciation of the charges;
    (ii) Defendant's appreciation of the range and nature of possible penalties;
    (iii) Defendant's understanding of the adversary nature of the legal process;
    (iv) Defendant's capacity to disclose to attorney pertinent facts surrounding the alleged offense;
    (v) Defendant's ability to relate to attorney;
    (vi) Defendant's ability to assist attorney in planning defense;
    (vii) Defendant's capacity to realistically challenge prosecution witnesses;
    (viii) Defendant's ability to manifest appropriate courtroom behavior;
    (ix) Defendant's capacity to testify relevantly;

(x)   Defendant's motivation to help himself in the legal process;

(xi) Defendant's capacity to cope with the stress of incarceration prior to trial.[6]

Should the presiding judge decide a defendant is incompetent to stand trial, the proceedings will be delayed and appropriate treatment mandated by the judge. A specific time will be set for reexamination to determine whether the defendant has become competent to stand trial.

Standard psychological tests of intelligence, neuropsychological function, and personality offer an opportunity to measure a wide range of responses and capabilities that could address the issue of an individual defendant's competence to stand trial.

Not Guilty by Reason of Insanity

The insanity issue has an entrenched place in Anglo-Saxon law and probably dates back to prebiblical codes of conduct. Since the fourteenth century, English common law has excused offenders mentally unable to control their conduct. In 1843 a psychotic Scot, Daniel M'Naghten, murdered Edward Drummond, secretary to the prime minister of England, Sir Robert Peel, who was the real object of M'Naghten's homicidal and delusional impulses. M'Naghten was acquitted, touching off a national furor similar to that which recently developed when John Hinckley, who attempted to assassinate President Ronald Reagan, was acquitted by reason of insanity. Following M'Naghten's case, Queen Victoria commanded all 15 high judges of England to appear before the House of Lords in an effort to clarify the confusion around this issue. The legal guidelines which emerged have been known as the *M'Naghten Rule* ever since. The rule states: "It must be clearly proved that, at the time of the committing of the act, the party accused was laboring under such a defect of reason, from disease of the mind, as not to know the nature and quality of the act he was doing; or, if he did know it, that he did not know he was doing what was wrong."[7]

During the 1950s jurists began to believe that psychiatry could provide clear guidelines regarding the limits of responsibility in criminal matters. As a result, broader tests of responsibility or its lack developed. The major alternative to the M'Naghten Rule, developed in the mid-1960s, is the test proposed in the Model Code of the American Law Institute (ALI) which states: "A person is not responsible for criminal conduct if at the time of such conduct as a result of mental disease or defect he lacks substantial capacity either to appreciate the criminality (wrongfulness) of his conduct or to conform his conduct to the requirements of the law."[8]

[6] Fla. R. Crim. P. 3.2111.
[7] M'Naghten's Case, 10 C. & F. 200, 8 Eng. Rep. 718 (H.L. 1843).
[8] Model Penal Code §4.01(1) (1961).

The M'Naghten Rule is a "right–wrong" test to which the ALI Model Code adds volitional elements. The M'Naghten Rule recognizes no degree of incapacity, while the ALI Code permits consideration of a wide range of mental impairments. At this writing, 26 states use a version of the ALI "substantial capacity" rule; 22 states adhere to the M'Naghten Rule; and Idaho and Montana have abolished the insanity plea.

Despite the general familiarity with the term, the plea of not guilty by reason of insanity is only invoked in 1 of a 1000 trials. The issue becomes one of general concern when famous people are involved, as in the *Hinckley* case. In 1835, Richard Lawrence, a house painter, was acquitted of attempted murder for shooting Andrew Jackson, as was John Schrank for shooting Theodore Roosevelt in 1912, after an insanity pleading. Each "famous" case is usually followed by a public outcry demanding elimination of this pleading (Leo, 1982). In all likelihood the plea of innocent by reason of insanity will remain a small but important aspect (and problem) of American jurisprudence.

Psychiatrists generally seem willing to render opinion as to the legal, mental, and/or moral status of defendants at the time of a criminal act. As a group, psychologists are less willing to speculate on a person's mental state at a time other than when they examine an individual. Some join psychiatric colleagues in using imprecise science to make absolute moral judgments (Tierney, 1982).

It has been proposed that there are no valid diagnostic tests of "insanity" and that both psychiatric and psychological testimonies on issues of sanity are questionable since neither distinguishes between a defendant "unable" and one "unwilling" to control unacceptable impulses (Ziskin & Coleman, 1981). It is suggested that it is "risky" to make a statement as to a defendant's psychological state at the time of a crime (Ziskin, 1981b).

Neuropsychological assessments may, in the future, provide objective, valid data to help the courts decide the merits of an insanity defense. Recent court rulings, appealed and sustained, affirm that expert neuropsychological testimony stating that minimal brain dysfunction destroyed a defendant's capability to choose right and refrain from wrong does establish a connection between defect and behavior.[9,10]

Personal Injury Issues

Attorneys representing clients who are suing for injuries or attorneys representing estates or survivors in cases of wrongful death frequently seek psychological testimony to substantiate claims by the plaintiff. Defense attorneys use psychologists to challenge such claims. In both instances testimony using psychological tests may form a substantial seg-

[9] *People v. Wright*, 648 P.2d 665 (Colo. 1982).
[10] *Hendershott v. People*, 653 P.2d. 385 (Colo. 1982).

ment of the psychologist's testimony. Traumatic cerebral damage is a frequent issue as are questions of posttraumatic stress. Psychologists testify as to the significance of the plaintiff's performance on tests of intelligence, memory, neuropsychological functioning, aptitude, rehabilitation potential, marital adjustment, and personality. Psychologists are frequently asked to render opinions as to the future status or potential of the defendant. In some instances, psychologists are asked to testify as to the status of dead persons using techniques of psychological autopsy;[11] expert testimony about the results of psychological tests is frequently used as evidence in social security benefit determination; and specific test instruments are sometimes required by statute.[12]

Custody Issues

Psychologists, together with other mental health professionals, have testified in matters of child custody for decades. The issue may involve the interests of the child or the suitability of the parents. Testimony based on psychological tests frequently represents the psychologist's contribution to the proceedings. Whereas psychological tests are helpful in understanding children's developmental progress and needs (Blau, 1979), they are of unproven value in helping a judge make the Solomonic decision required in awarding custody to the most appropriate parent (Blau, 1982).

Judges traditionally call for expert testimony to aid them in making custody decisions. In spite of frequent involvement of mental health professionals in custodial cases, Lowery (1981) reports that the advice of professionals is ranked at a relatively low level by jurists who are asked what factors they use to form their opinions and make their decisions.

Developmental psychology research and a wide range of testing instruments to measure children's intellect, achievement, social adjustment, neuropsychological status, and personality are uniquely helpful in implementing the recent trend toward *joint custody*, or *shared responsibility*. Recognizing the potential trauma of marital fracture to minor children, more jurisdictions are mandating *shared responsibility* for minors as part of marriage dissolution proceedings. Although the judge may determine that the primary physical residence for the child will be with one parent, most of the child's needs are to be jointly considered by the divorced parents. These statutes often specify mediation or conciliation procedures where psychological testing and testimony become integral aspects of the process.[13]

[11] *Diagnosing the Dead*, 18 Am. Crim. L. Rev. 617 (1982).
[12] 6 Mental Disability L. Rep. 438 (1982).
[13] Fla. Stat. §61.13 (1982).

STANDARDS FOR THE USE OF TESTS IN COURT

As the tradecraft of psychologists becomes more generally known to the legal profession, requests for broader application of psychological measurement to adversary issues may be exercised.

Testing is, in a sense, psychology's birthright. The development, standardization, and use of psychological tests is, as much as anything, characteristic of psychology's long and productive history of scientific exploration of behavior, its origins, and its consequences (Anastasi, 1981).

Since 1954, the APA has formally recognized the importance of scientific standards in the development and application of test instruments. Joining with the American Educational Research Association and the National Council on Measurement in Education in 1955, the APA published *Standards for Educational and Psychological Tests and Manuals*. As issues become more complex, the APA established the Committee on Psychological Tests to study the issues and prepare a revision of the earlier work. The result appeared as *Standards for Educational and Psychological Tests* (APA, 1974).

Although the 1974 edition makes no specific mention of the interpretation of psychological tests in judicial settings, the recommendations, guidelines, and constraints it contains are cogent. In essence, the standards recommend, in considerable detail, the qualifications of test users, methods of choosing tests for specific purposes, administration and scoring standards to be followed, and acceptable procedures and limitations for the interpretation of psychological tests. The latter is particularly applicable to testimony based on test results.

The APA Committee to Develop Joint Technical Standards for Educational and Psychological Testing completed a first draft of the new *Standards* in 1982. For the first time, studied concern for the way in which the *Standards* will be interpreted by the legal profession has been a part of the committee's deliberation (Committee, 1982).

Psychologists who testify about the meaning of psychological test scores and results should realize that their opinions will be subjected to minute scrutiny by competent opposing counsel. Reports and depositions in which the psychologist renders opinions about tests and test results are likely to be reviewed by psychologists retained for the specific purpose of identifying errors, distortions, improprieties, and inaccuracies. The psychologist who testifies about psychological tests or their meanings must adhere to the highest standards in order to service his or her client properly, minimize courtroom assailability and embarrassment, and protect the good name of psychology.

Clear-cut guidelines for the use of psychological tests are available to psychologists. The *Standards* published in 1974 are being revised and will be published in 1985 (Committee, 1982). The *Standards* are intended as a statement of technical requirements for sound professional practice. As new systems and procedures develop, additional standards can be expected. Given the current state of the art, psychologists who testify on the basis of psychological tests should consider the following as the current guidelines for forensic practice.[14]

General Testing Knowledge

The psychologist who uses tests as a basis for expert testimony in court should possess the education, training, and credentials appropriate to the content of the testimony and the instruments used. The test user should have a substantial general knowledge of testing principles, the relevant literature and the tests being used, and the general limitations of test interpretations. The test user is responsible for knowing the limitations as well as the values of tests used.

Test Selection

The forensic psychologist must scrupulously avoid bias in selection. A periodic review of the appropriateness of often-used tests is critical. The test user should consider more than one variable for assessment and more than one test for each variable being considered. This is particularly important if tests are used to support expert opinion in matters of law where broad-range decisions are being considered.

The test user should be able to relate the history of research and development behind the intended application of the test in order to justify its choice for the legal issues being considered. Characteristics of the examinee, such as age, cultural background, or handicaps, should be carefully evaluated in all test-selection situations.

Administration and Scoring

The test user should follow standardized administration and scoring procedures described in the test manual. Desirable testing conditions should be provided to enable the examinee to do his or her best. Any modification of standard procedures must be noted and documented. When ethnic or linguistic minorities are to be tested, efforts should be made to include staff with similar background during the testing procedures. Any factors interfering with optimum performance should be documented and noted when results are reported. The test user is accountable for accuracy in scoring and recording test results.

The purpose of the testing must be clearly explained to the examinee. In criminal matters, examinees must be apprised of their rights, as mandated by *Estelle v. Smith*.[15] The examiner must ensure the defendant understands

---

[14] These recommended standards rely heavily on the 1974 *Standards* as well as elements of the 1982 *Committee* revisions.

[15] *Estelle v. Smith*, 451 U.S. 454, 101 S.Ct.1866, 68 L.Ed.2d 359 (1981).

which attorney or judge has requested the examination, that the defendant has the right to have his or her attorney present, that he or she has the right to refuse to participate in the examination, and that the results may be used against the defendant in court.

Interpretation of Tests

If specific cutting scores are to be used as a basis for decisions, the psychologist must be prepared to justify or explain the adopted cutoff score during direct examination or cross-examination.

Test scores should be explained or interpreted as an *estimate* of performance under a given set of circumstances and should not be interpreted or put forth as an *absolute* characteristic of the examinee. Test results should not be interpreted as permanent or generally applicable to all circumstances. It is the forensic psychologist's responsibility to ensure that attorneys and triers of fact, unsophisticated in the matter of tests and testing, be provided with careful, justifiable, generally acceptable explanations of the test results sufficient for the recipients of the interpretations to view them with clarity and understanding.

On completion of testing, the forensic psychologist should render a written report of the testing that communicates scores, interpretations, conclusions, and opinions.

If relying on computer-based test interpretations, the forensic psychologist should be familiar with the rationale and validity of the interpretations and be prepared to justify their use in the judicial matter at hand.

If test scores are interpreted in relation to normative references, the user should be prepared to demonstrate that the norms of reference are appropriate to both the examinee and the judicial matter under consideration.

The test user should always consider alternative interpretations of a specific test score. Great care must be taken when generalizing test validity from one situation to another. Value judgments involved in the use of test scores in prediction must be explicitly and rationally explained.

In comparing clinical versus statistical interpretations of psychological tests, psychologists must be candid and accurate regarding current research and be more supportive of statistically derived interpretations. If nonstatistically based interpretations are given, the test user should be prepared to justify interpretations in a manner consistent with the *Frye* test.

The guidelines discussed here must be enhanced by the psychologist's continuing efforts to be aware of new developments in tests and testing, current research regarding the testing instruments and procedures being used, and current standards for ethical and appropriate use of tests and test results.

6

Competency to Stand Trial

It has been noted previously and it will be explored extensively in the next chapter that the insanity defense rarely appears in criminal trials. However, the question of competency occurs with some frequency in the early stages of arraignment if there is any reason to suspect that the defendant lacks *mens rea*. If the judge, the prosecutor, or the attorney for the defense suspects that the defendant is not able to perceive his or her situation realistically, expert opinion is usually sought to determine whether the defendant is competent to stand trial. If the judge decides that the preponderance of evidence suggests such incompetency, no trial is scheduled. This tends to abort many pleas of innocent by reason of insanity. Frequently, by the time the defendant is found to be competent to stand trial, some arrangement to deal with the charges has been negotiated. Thus the issue of competence to stand trial should precede any plea of innocent by reason of insanity.

THE LAW

Constitutional Issues

The Sixth Amendment to the U.S. Constitution, handed down in 1791, states:

> In all criminal prosecutions, the accused shall enjoy the right to a speedy and public trial, by an impartial jury of the state and district wherein the crime shall have been committed, which district shall have previously been ascertained by law, and to be informed of the nature and cause of the accusation; to be confronted with the witnesses against him; to have compulsory process for obtaining witnesses in his favor, and to have the Assistance of Counsel for his defense.[1]

[1] U.S. Const. Amend. VI.

Thus the defendant has the absolute right to know the nature of the charges, know the kind of evidence or allegations that led to the charges, be allowed to confront and challenge witnesses, demand that witnesses or evidence be introduced in an effort to demonstrate innocence, and participate with a knowledgeable officer of the court in constructing the best-possible defense against the charges. These rights form a keystone of the American system of jurisprudence. If for any reason the defendant is not able to exercise these constitutional rights, a proper legal proceeding cannot take place. To take an extreme case, if the defendant were in a coma, the trial could not proceed. Having no ability to exercise receptive or expressive communication deprives a comatose defendant of constitutional rights to a fair trial. Such a defendant would be considered incompetent to stand trial.

Federal Rules

Specific issues of mental or psychological incompetency before trial are addressed in the U.S. code. In part it states:

> Whenever after arrest and prior to the imposition of sentence or prior to the expiration of any period of probation the United States Attorney has reasonable cause to believe that a person charged with an offense against the United States may be presently insane or otherwise so mentally incompetent as to be unable to understand the proceedings against him or properly to assist in his own defense, he shall file a motion for a judicial determination of such mental competency of the accused, setting forth the ground for such belief with the trial court in which proceedings are pending.[2]

A motion for judicial order for examination may be made by the prosecution or the defense on behalf of the accused. Receiving such a motion, the judge, after evaluating the facts on which the request is based, has the discretion of ordering an examination of the defendant to determine whether he or she is competent to stand trial. Should the report of the examination indicate to the satisfaction of the presiding judge that the accused is incompetent, the judge may then order the defendant to a treatment facility until such time as subsequent examination or examinations indicate that the accused is competent to stand trial. The examination's sole purpose is to guide the judge in the issue of whether the trial should be postponed.[3]

The federal standard of competence to stand trial is the accused's ability to understand the nature of the charges against him or her and whether the defendant has sufficient mental capacity to consult with attorneys with a reasonable degree of rational understanding. Furthermore, the defendant

---

[2] 18 U.S.C. 4244.
[3] *United States v. Davis*, 481 F.2d 425 (4th Cir. 1973).

must have a rational as well as factual understanding of the proceedings against him or her.[4] The landmark decision in this issue was *Duskey v. United States;* the Supreme Court held:

> [I]t is not enough for the district judge to find that "the defendant is oriented to time and place and has some recollection of events" but that the test must be whether he has sufficient present ability to consult with his lawyer with a reasonable degree of rational understanding—and whether he has a rational as well as factual understanding of the proceedings against him.[5]

To be adjudicated as mentally incompetent to stand trial, in federal jurisdictions, the defendant must be shown by the preponderance of evidence to have a mental defect, illness, or condition that would result in some loss of the right to a fair trial. The federal statutes are clear that incompetency to stand trial is not defined in terms of mental illness. A defendant may be competent to stand trial while mentally ill, but a defendant may be incompetent to stand trial without being mentally ill. Conditions of "synthetic incompetence" as a result of using prescribed drugs are not grounds for a finding of incompetency to stand trial.[5] Examinations by mental health experts serve only as recommendations to the court. The judge always makes the final determination of competence to stand trial.[6,7]

State Courts

Although a state court cannot use any statute that would deprive a defendant of his or her constitutional rights, each state develops specific definitions and procedures regarding the issue of competency to stand trial.[8] The rules, examination procedures, and statutory language differ considerably from state to state. In Florida, details concerning the examination and report in the matter of competence to stand trial are quite elaborate:

> Upon appointment by the court, the experts, shall, prior to the hearing, examine the defendant with respect to the issue of competency to stand trial, and shall report to the court, in writing, at such time as shall be specified by the court, with copies to attorneys for the State and the defense, setting forth the results of such examination. If the court determines that there is reason to believe that the defendant may require involuntary hospitalization the court shall also order the experts to include in their report a report on issues of involuntary hospitalization. The experts shall consider the following issues

[4] *Riccardi v. United States,* 428 F. Supp. 1059 (D.C. N.Y. 1977), *aff'd* 573 F. 2d 1294 (2nd Cir. 1977).

[5] *Dusky v. United States,* 362 U.S. 402 (1960).

[6] *United States v. Zooluck,* 425 F. Supp. 719 (D.C. N.Y. 1977).

[7] *United States v. Horowitz,* 360 F. Supp. 772 (D.C. Pa. 1973).

[8] Fed. R. Evid. 601

each of which shall be specifically addressed in the report:

(a).   Whether the defendant meets the statutory criteria for incompetence to stand trial, that is, whether the defendant has sufficient present ability to consult with his lawyer with a reasonable degree of rational understanding and whether he has a rational, as well as factual, understanding of the proceedings against him.[9]

It will be noted that in addition to an awareness of the proceedings and the capacity to cooperate with the defense attorney, the defendant must be able to present a psychological presence in the courtroom. This is stated explicitly in some states, such as California: ". . . giving the accused the right to appear and defend in person and requiring him to be personally present at trial for felony, the accused must be both physically and mentally present at every stage of a felony prosecution, and mere physical presence is insufficient."[10]

THE EXAMINATION FOR COMPETENCY TO STAND TRIAL

When the defendant's ability to participate in the trial process seems questionable, the presiding judge may order an examination by a mental health expert to aid the court. The decision of competency rests with the judge, and the mental health expert's report is only one factor considered in the decision process. The competency evaluation, in general, should address the issues of whether the defendant is capable of understanding and perceiving the nature of the judicial process to a reasonable degree (note that it is not the experts role to define *reasonable*). The accused must understand how and why he or she is being charged, the pretrial and trial procedures which will occur, what will happen if convicted, and the accused's constitutional rights and privileges to participate in the process. In addition, the expert must determine if the defendant has any mental defects or conditions that would prevent a reasonable degree of cooperation with the attorney in pursuing a good representation and a fair trial. Finally, the expert should be prepared to address the issue of whether the accused has any mental defect or disease that would preclude making a reasonable self-presentation, in his or her own best interests, during the trial proceedings.

As in many criminal issues, the psychologist as expert follows to the witness stand a long tradition established by medicine and psychiatry in matters of competency to stand trial. Traditional psychiatric examination

---

[9] Fla. R. Crim. P. 3.211 (1982). Further details of competency are presented in the section "Competence to Stand Trial," Chapter 5 (pp. 51–52).

[10] *People v. Williams* 15 Cal.Rptr. 191, 194 Cal. App.2d 523 (1961).

tends to relate issues of competency to psychiatric symptomatology and diagnoses. There is no data to support such assumptions, and the reliability and validity of psychiatric opinion in the competency issue are in doubt. The presiding judge will frequently remand the accused to a restrictive psychiatric institution where a stay of as much as 60 days is necessary before an opinion as to competency is forthcoming. There is no evidence that lengthy institutional evaluations are necessary in determining the accused's mental fitness to stand trial. Evaluating a defendant's competency to stand trial in a sheltered, restraining institutional setting may have no validity in respect to the mental state of the accused in the courtroom setting. Evaluations done in the community, at the time of the trial, with reference to the statutory definitions of incompetence are likely to be more realistic (Roesch, 1979).

Psychological Procedures

Whereas some psychologists may imitate their psychiatric colleagues in conducting competency evaluations emphasizing the Mental Status Exam, results of such examinations are rarely followed in the courts' final decision (Roesch & Golding, 1978). Legal definitions of competency are not directly addressed by traditional mental health nosology or classification (Shah, 1969).

A request for a psychological evaluation of a defendant's competence to stand trial may come from the prosecutor, the defense attorney, or the court. The psychologist is asked to render an expert opinion as to the mental condition of the accused. If the defendant is mentally incompetent to stand trial, it is the psychologist's responsibility to identify, delineate, and report the incompetence in terms consonant with current standards for psychological services and ethical constraints. The report must, however, in every reasonable way, relate to the questions being asked relative to the legal definitions of incompetency to stand trial. Assessment of the accused's cognitive, affective, and behavioral capabilities and deficits should form the basis for the report. Although the referral for examination for competency to stand trial frequently includes a request for evaluation of sanity at the time of the felony, the evaluation and report of competency to stand trial must be an entirely separate, segmented issue. The psychological evaluation for issues of insanity is much more complex and will be discussed in depth in the next chapter. The psychological examination for competency to stand trial should include the following elements.

History and Interview.   The psychologist should determine how the defendant views his or her present situation. Direct questions should include:

1.   Why is the defendant in jail?
2.   What are the charges against the accused?

3. What are the procedures faced by the defendant?
4. Who represents the defendant, and how well are they relating?
5. What will happen if the defendant is found guilty?

Should the initial interview indicate clearly that the defendant is competent to stand trial in respect to the statutes of the jurisdiction in which the trial will take place, the psychologist may conclude the examination at this point. This is more likely to be the exception rather than the rule since few intact, stable defendants are referred for competency evaluation.

In an effort to formalize the competency evaluation, Lipsitt, Lelos, and McGarry (1971) from the Harvard Medical School developed a screening instrument to evaluate competency for trial. Consisting of 22 incomplete sentences, the instrument requires that the defendant finish the sentence stems with the best answer he or she can. The sentence stems focus on courtroom procedure and defendants. Figure 6.1 presents the items of the *Competency Screening Test*.

The responses are scored according to a 3-point scale (0, 1, or 2). Poor responses receive a score of 0, responses that are borderline but not clearly appropriate receive a score of 1, and clearly appropriate responses are

1. The lawyer told Bill that _____
2. When I go to court, the lawyer will _____
3. Jack felt that the judge _____
4. When Phil was accused of the crime, he _____
5. When I prepare to go to court with my lawyer _____
6. If the jury finds me guilty, I _____
7. The way a court trial is decided _____
8. When the evidence in George's case was presented to the jury _____
9. When the lawyer questioned his client in court, the client said _____
10. If Jack had to try his own case, he _____
11. Each time the D.A. asked me a question, I _____
12. While listening to the witnesses testify against me, I _____
13. When the witness testifying against Harry gave incorrect evidence, he _____
14. When Bob disagreed with his lawyer on his defense, he _____
15. When I was formally accused of the crime, I thought to myself _____
16. If Ed's lawyer suggests that he plead guilty, he _____
17. What concerns Fred most about his lawyer _____
18. When they say a man is innocent until proven guilty _____
19. When I think of being sent to prison, I _____
20. When Phil thinks of what he is accused of, he _____
21. When the jury hears my case, they will _____
22. If I had a chance to speak to the judge, I _____

FIGURE 6.1. The Competency Screening Test. (*Source:* Reprinted with permission from Paul D. Lipsitt, *Competency Screening Test* [Boston: Competency to Stand Trial and Mental Illness Project, 1970]. © 1970 Paul D. Lipsitt and David Lelos.)

scored 2. Scoring standards are provided; Figure 6.2 presents several examples from the scoring handbook (Lipsitt, 1970).

The original standardization of this screening instrument was based on a comparison of the test with the psychiatric and psychological evaluation of 380 people accused of felonies. These defendants were sent to a state

---

1. The lawyer told Bill that
   (a) Legal criteria: ability to cooperate in own defense, communicate, relate
   (b) Psychological criteria: ability to relate or trust
     Score 2:   includes obtaining and/or accepting advice or guidance
       Examples: "he should plead not guilty"
                   "he was free"
                   "he should plead nolo"
                   "he should plead guilty"
                   "he would take his case"
                   "he would need to know all the facts concerning the case"
                   "he should turn himself in"
                   "the outlook was good"
                   "he will try to help him"
     Score 1:
       Examples: "he is innocent"
                   "everything is all right"
                   "be truthful"
                   "he will be going to court soon"
                   "he is competent to stand trial"
                   "it will be filed"
     Score 0: includes regarding lawyer as accusing or judgmental
       Examples: "he was wrong in doing what he did"
                   "he is guilty"
                   "he is going to be put away"
                   "no comment"
2. When I go to court the lawyer will
   (a) Legal criteria: ability to cooperate in own defense, communicate, relate.
   (b) Psychological criteria: ability to relate or trust
     Score 2:
       Examples: "defend me"
                   "be there to help me"
                   "do his best to get me off with a light sentence"
                   "represent me"
                   "present my case"
     Score 1:
       Examples: "be there"
                   "ask for a postponement"
                   "ask me to take the stand"
     Score 0:
       Examples: "put me away"
                   "keep his mouth shut"
                   "prosecute me"

FIGURE 6.2.   Examples of scoring standards for the Competency Screening Test. (*Source:* Reprinted with permission from Paul D. Lipsitt, *Competency Screening Test* [Boston: Competency to Stand Trial and Mental Illness Project, 1970]. © 1970 Paul D. Lipsitt and David Lelos.)

institution to be evaluated for competency to stand trial, and 43 of the sample were found to suffer serious mental pathology. Comparing their performance with five other groups (students, nonadjudicated patients, defendants not suspected of mental disorder, civilly committed patients, and a noninstitutional group), the screening instrument appeared to be relatively efficient and successful in identifying those likely to be found not competent to stand trial.

In a cross-validation of the Competency Screening Test (CST), Nottingham and Mattson (1981) used the performance of 50 male residents of a state forensic unit to predict competency to stand trial. The criterion against which CST scores were compared was the full forensic staff decision as to whether the defendant was competent to stand trial. The CST did not predict any false negatives (competent) but did predict nine false positives (incompetent).

Although at the present time there is no competency screening test that can substitute for a full psychological evaluation, the development of specific instruments is a worthy objective, and it is anticipated that further research will enhance the use of such instruments.

The extensiveness of the psychological assessment battery will depend on a number of style and situational factors. Should the psychologist, after examining all records and conducting a clinical interview with the defendant, believe that there is no question about the accused's competence, this may be reported to the court without further evaluation. Any sign of mental defect or disturbance, either observed or reported, requires that a full evaluation be conducted. Assuming the psychologist proceeds beyond a history and clinical interview with the defendant, the procedures used should provide information about the following:

1. The defendant's intellectual capacities and deficiencies
2. The defendant's neuropsychological status
3. The defendant's personality
4. The validity of the examination

At the present time there is no standard or prescribed series of examination procedures. Some traditions and precedents are now being developed based simply on the experience of psychologists in both institutional and independent settings who have been called upon to evaluate defendants' competency to stand trial. Variability is common in selection of test instruments and other procedures. The psychological expert should keep in mind that any procedure selected should stand the *Frye v. United States* test in order to be acceptable to the court.[11]

The Interview.   There is, at present, no "standard interview" for matters of competency although questions concerning the defendant's current

---

[11] *Frye v. United States*, 293 F. 1013 (D.C. Cir. 1923).

perception of his or her status with the criminal system are mandatory. Most psychologists who work as experts in the forensic field prefer to take a full background history since most examinations require the psychologist to render opinions not only about competency to stand trial but also regarding the issues of insanity, mitigating circumstances, treatment potential, qualification of the defendant as a mentally disordered sex offender, and so forth. In respect to the issue of competency to stand trial, the following should be inquired:

1. The defendant's perception of why he or she is in the adjudication situation
2. The defendant's opinion of his or her attorney and what they will be doing together
3. The role of judge and jury in the anticipated court proceedings
4. The defendant's understanding of the concept of "plea bargaining"
5. The defendant's awareness of the consequences should a verdict of "guilty" be rendered by the judge or the jury
6. The defendant's status and adjustment to jail if he or she is not out on bond
7. The defendant's perception of his or her probable response to a prison term should this be an outcome of the court proceedings

Much of the above will be validated to a degree by the defendant's responses on a competency screening instrument should such a device be used during the evaluation.

Most experts prefer to avoid asking defendants whether they are innocent or guilty. This is a very difficult matter when the expert must render an opinion in respect to issues of insanity. The defendant's description of "what happened" is vital in determining mental status at the time a crime was committed. Should the defendant discuss his or her involvement in a criminal act, it raises serious procedural questions regarding the defendant's Fifth Amendment rights to protection against self-incrimination. The privilege against self-incrimination is one that may not be violated. Some courts have ruled, however, that certain practices, including history taking by qualified experts, are securing "real" evidence (such as X rays, blood tests, and observation of behavior), as opposed to "testimonial" evidence (such as the defendant's statements about himself or herself). In the classic *Murphy v. Waterfront Commission*, the Supreme Court emphasized the importance of the privilege against self-incrimination:

> [O]ur unwillingness to subject those suspected of crime to the cruel trilemma of self-accusation, contempt, or perjury; our preference for an accusatorial rather than an inquisitorial system of criminal justice; our fear that self-incriminating statements will be elicited by inhuman treatment and abuses;

our sense of fair play which dictates "a fair state–individual balance . . . by requiring the government in its contest with the individual to shoulder the entire load . . ."; our respect for the inviolability of the human personality and of the right of each individual "to a private enclave where he may lead a private life," *United States v. Grunewald*, 233 F.2d. 556, 581–582 (2nd Cir. 1956) (Frank dissenting); our distrust of self-deprecatory statements; and our realization that the privilege, while sometimes "a shelter to the guilty," is often a "protection to the innocent."[12]

While tests, including projective techniques, are midway between real and testimonial evidence,[13] the interview can represent a significant threat to Fifth Amendment values, requiring the psychologist to apprise the defendant of his or her rights before conducting any interview or history taking.[14] Procedures for ensuring the qualification and acceptability of an interview are described in detail in Chapter 4.

The psychologist is well advised *not* to probe innocence or guilt during history taking. Needless to say, very accurate note taking is required during an interview. Recording the interview is permissible if the defendant is informed and agrees. The recordings, as well as all handwritten materials, may be subpoenaed by opposing counsel. Whether material obtained during an interview by mental health experts should be admissible as part of an expert's opinion which is detrimental to the defendant's case is still a matter of judicial concern and discussion.[15] In most instances, such material as notes and test forms or profiles is "discoverable," or subject to inspection by opposing counsel during deposition (see Chapter 10). When a psychologist has any question concerning the propriety of an examination procedure, a call to the attorney or judge who requested the evaluation is indicated.

Intellectual Deficiencies and Capabilities.   The instruments available to psychologists to evaluate intelligence are many, with varying degrees of validity and reliability. Different tests measure different factors. Most psychologists today depend on the Wechsler scales—for the broadest view of intellectual functioning. Other procedures or revisions of current tests are expected in the future and will probably be more effective than current instrumentation. At this writing, the age-appropriate Wechsler scale (either the Wechsler Adult Intelligence Scale–Revised, or WAIS-R, or Wechsler Intelligence Scale for Children–Revised, or WISC-R) is most frequently chosen by forensic clinical psychologists for the evaluation of a broad spectrum of intellectual function.

---

[12] *Murphy v. Waterfront Comm'n*, 378 U.S. 52, 55 (1963).
[13] 5 Mental Disability L. Rep. 269 (1981).
[14] *Estelle v. Smith*, 101 S.Ct. 1866 (1981).
[15] *United States v. Byers* No 78-1451 (D.C. Cir. 1980).

The law is not clearly instructive as to the issue of intellectual competence. In issues of credibility of witnesses, the courts generally consider children below seven as of questionable credibility although some accredit younger witnesses; children between 7 and 14 years are usually considered potentially credible, subject to *voir dire* (questioning) by the court preliminary to testimony; and those over 14 years of age are usually considered credible. This is a very rough guideline for psychologists, and results of intellectual evaluations should include the appropriate calculated mental age of the defendant to aid the court in determining competence. The following is abstracted from a psychological report of a defendant who was later found incompetent to stand trial.

Intellectual Factors

Objective results of the Wechsler Adult Intelligence Scale–Revised (11 subtests) were as follows:

Factor	Deviation IQ	Percentile (Ages 25–34)
Verbal scale	46	<1st
Performance scale	63	1st
Full scale	52	<1st

The above results suggest that Mr. A falls in the Moderate range of mental retardation. None of his subscale scores exceeded the first percentile for his age group. Mr. A's ability to understand, comprehend, and respond is equal to a child of approximately six years of age or less. Some of Mr. A's intellectual capacities fell below the scoring standards, so these results should be considered somewhat of an *over*estimate of his functional intellectual skills.

The results of the Peabody Picture Vocabulary Test (Form M) indicated a mental age of four years and three months for Mr. A. This would place him below the first percentile for adults and suggests his retardation is Moderate to Profound. In practical terms this means that Mr. A cannot comprehend most adult language where more than three sequential words are involved. He cannot add two single-digit numbers. He cannot repeat a two-digit number. In short, Mr. A is not able to cooperate, participate, or even be realistically responsive to any but the simplest interactional activities.

Although a complete evaluation was done in this case, the above was sufficient to convince the judge that Mr. A was not competent to stand trial.

This was a very clear-cut case, without areas of variable intellectual capability to cloud the issue. If considerable variability in the Wechsler subscales occurs, the issue is more complex. The following portion of a report illustrates a situation in which a psychologist's report of intellectual functioning included a "normal" full-scale intelligence quotient but resulted in a finding of incompetent to stand trial by the court. Subscale scores as well as summative scores must be evaluated in rendering information as to whether an individual is competent to stand trial.

Intellectual Factors

Objective results of the Wechsler Adult Intelligence Scale–Revised (11 subtests) were as follows:

Factor	Deviation IQ	Percentile (Ages 55–64)
Verbal scales	100	50th
Performance scale	86	18th
Full scale	93	32nd

The above results suggest that Mr. B functions in the Low–Average range of intellectual ability. Examination of subscale variability, as follows, suggests otherwise:

WAIS-R Subscale	Percentile (Ages 55–64)
Information	95th
Digit Span	<1st
Vocabulary	91st
Arithmetic	2nd
Comprehension	63rd
Similarities	75th
Picture Completion	37th
Picture Arrangement	<1st
Block Design	2nd
Object Assembly	84th
Digit Symbol	2nd

The above suggests that Mr. B is intellectually disabled to a very severe degree. Significantly lowered subscale scores indicate severe distractibility, difficulties in concentration, social ineptness, impulsivity, great difficulties in accurately attributing causation to his own behavior and that of others, and poor social judgment. These results are consistent with severe neuropsychological deficit.

Later segments of the report detail the neuropsychological deficits underlying the scattered intellectual capacity noted above, as well as the effects on personality. These results of a massive stroke involving the middle cerebral artery rendered the defendant psychologically dysfunctional in a variety of areas, and the court ruled that Mr. B was incompetent to stand trial. The psychologist reports to the court whether a defendant is intellectually competent. The expert may render opinions as to the quality of a defendant's intellectual processes, which may result in the judge's deciding that the defendant should not stand trial. The report should not contain a legal opinion (a response to the "ultimate question") unless requested by the judge or the statutes.

Neuropsychological Status.   Whenever there are indications of neurological incidents or neuropathic behavior in the background history or crime report, a neuropsychological evaluation is indicated. Neuropsychological testing is also important if the defendant reports persistent or debilitating difficulties with speech, hearing, vision, memory, or other modalities commonly associated with neurological dysfunction. If the results of the intellectual evaluation suggest the presence of neuropsychological deficit, a full neuropsychological evaluation is indicated.

Most psychologists include a neuropsychological screening test with most or all of their assessment batteries. Some prefer individual visual–motor screening instruments, such as the Benton, the Bender Visual-Motor Gestalt Test, the Graham-Kendall Memory for Designs, the Wechsler Memory Scale, the Reitan-Indiana Screening Short Form (cards numbers 1, 2, 3, and 27 of the Halstead-Reitan Aphasia Screening Booklet), or other relatively simple tests that, together with the subscale pattern of the Wechsler scales, may suggest the defendant suffers neuropsychological deficit.

Even mild to moderate signs of deficit warrant a full neuropsychological battery. The preferred instruments at this writing are the Halstead-Reitan Test Battery or the Luria-Nebraska Neuropsychological Batteries. The latter has the advantage of being available in several forms in the event retesting is necessary with a short interest time interval. This is sometimes necessary for adversary purposes (both the prosecution and defense may request separate examinations). Also, alternate forms allow the psychologist to explore questions of competency under the influence of drugs; one administration of the test serves as a baseline under nontoxic conditions, whereas the other reflects function while influenced by the drug. Occasionally, two administrations of a test may be indicated to clarify questions of malingering or "faking bad." Neuropsychological batteries with alternate forms are quite useful in forensic practice.

The following illustrates the neuropsychological section of a psychological report that influenced a judge to declare the defendant incompetent to stand trial.

Neuropsychological Factors

Variability in WAIS-R subtests suggests that Mr. C may suffer neuropsychological deficit.

The history section of this report indicates that while awaiting adjudication, Mr. C dropped a barbell on himself while exercising. A frontal contusion was treated, with minimal apparent aftereffects. This occurred approximately three weeks before this examination. Since that time Mr. C's behavior has been "strange" as noted in the Referral section of this report.

Neuropsychological screening using the Reitan-Indiana Short-Form (square, cross, triangle, key) indicates moderate impairment, probably in the left hemisphere.

As a result of this, the Luria-Nebraska Neuropsychological Battery— Form A—was administered to Mr. C.

Scales which exceeded Mr. C's critical level included Expressive Speech, Motor, Receptive Speech, Intellectual Processes, and the Pathognomonic Scale. These results suggest that the primary sources of the deficits are likely to be in the left frontal and right frontal lobes. This is supported by significant elevations on the Right Frontal and Left Frontal Scales of the Brain Lesion Localization Scales.

Mr. C shows his greatest deficits in his inability to grasp verbal relationships and what the verbal relationships mean for tasks of a practical nature. He has considerable trouble comprehending even simple logical grammatical relations. He has trouble remembering and repeating both simple and complex words. Concentration and attention to auditory material are very poor. Memory is exceedingly deficient.

These deficits are characteristic of the type of injury Mr. C has suffered and are likely to interfere significantly with his ability to understand, to remember, and to cooperate.

These neuropsychological deficits were extensive enough for the court to send Mr. C to a treatment facility until such time as his neurological deficits subsided sufficiently for him to be considered competent to stand trial.

Personality Evaluation.   The sequence from screening to full battery can provide an efficient approach to personality testing in issues of competency to stand trial. Where severe disturbance is suggested by police reports, interviews, or attorney's observations of behavior characteristic of well-known personality dysfunctions, a full battery of personality tests may not be indicated. If screening is the appropriate choice, most clinical psychologists prefer the Minnesota Multiphasic Personality Inventory (MMPI) although, recently, forensic reports are beginning to include the 16 PF (16 Personality Factors), the Clinical Analysis Questionnaire, and the Million Clinical Multiaxial Inventory (Millon, 1982). The value of these types of instruments clearly lies in the substantial body of research available to support opinions based on their results (Ziskin, 1981b). Forensic clinical psychologists would be wise to include a screening test for reading comprehension to ensure that the defendant has sufficient reading skill to make a valid representation on the tests that require functional reading. Should the defendant read below the 5.5 grade level, it would probably be wise to have the items of the personality test read and the defendant's oral responses recorded.

Once the forensic psychologist decides on the administration of a full battery of personality tests (more likely in issues of the insanity pleading), there are no hard-and-fast rules. As long as the tests applied are usual and customary to the profession and the expert is willing and able to explain the development, standardization, utilization, and validity of conclusions based on the instrument, a wide range of test instruments has been found admissible. Testimony based solely on such seldom taught or used projective techniques as the Michigan Picture Story Test and the Szondi Test has been admitted.[16]

The report of a personality evaluation that did not result in the judge's ruling that the defendant was incompetent to stand trial follows.

Personality Factors

Mr. D was able to complete the MMPI and the Rorschach Examination. He was unwilling to complete the Thematic Apperception Test or any of the projective drawing tasks. He refused to do the Sentence Completion Test.

The MMPI profile was characterized by extremely high elevations on the 6 and 8 (paranoia, schizophrenia) scales. Both exceeded T-scores of 80. This profile suggests a serious thinking disorder and strong paranoid mentation. Mr. D is generally nervous, anxious, and depressed. His reaction to any stress will be pervasively hostile and suspicious. Mr. D suffers a severe

---

[16] *Jenkins v. United States,* 307 F.2d 637 (D.C. Cir. 1962). (See Appendix 1 for details.)

thinking disorder characterized by bizarre ideas, disorganization, and suspicion. It is the profile of a deeply disturbed psychotic person.

The Rorschach was a disturbing experience for Mr. D. He rejected Cards IV, VI, and IX. He claimed to have seen "things too dangerous to talk about." His responses to the remaining seven cards were characterized by disorganization, original responses, contaminations, and confabulations. Some truly creative original responses were spoiled by extended, confabulated ideas. Many responses indicated explosiveness.

Mr. D suffers a severe and debilitating psychosis and should be receiving intensive inpatient treatment at this time.

The expert is again cautioned to choose evaluation instruments and techniques that fall within the conservative constraints of *Frye v. United States.*[17]

The Validity of the Examination. It is generally preferable, from the defendant's point of view, to be found incompetent to stand trial (or innocent by reason of insanity) rather than to undergo a trial that ends in conviction and sentencing. This can be a life-or-death issue for a defendant charged with a capital offense. All experts in matters of competency to stand trial, the insanity pleading, mitigating circumstances, penalty phase trials, and evaluation for classification of mentally disordered sex offenders must be aware of the potential for malingering, or faking bad.

Although statements as to the validity of the testing circumstances and the response of the accused are considered of some value by judges, more objective measures of factitious potential in defendants are likely to be given greater credibility.

The F-K ratio of the MMPI has long been considered one indicator of an individual's tendency to "fake bad" (Anthony, 1971). Other scales of malingering have been developed using the MMPI (Cofer, Chance, & Judson, 1949; Dahlstrom, Gough, 1954; Welsh, & Dahlstrom, 1975).

A simple test which has shown merit in identifying those seeking a self-serving goal through poor performance is the 15-item test, developed by Rey (1941). The subject is shown a card (Figure 6.3) with 15 figures illustrated. It will be noted that although there are 15 figures, they are arranged in five sets of three figures, each systematically related to each other. Because of the grouping, only a profoundly brain-disordered person or orthopedically dysfunctional person could not reproduce these figures with only a brief exposure to the stimulus card.

The subject is told he or she will be asked to perform a difficult task involving the memorization of 15 different figures, with an emphasis on *difficult* and *different*. The stimulus card is then exposed for 10 seconds. The card is removed, and the subject is told to draw as many of the 15 figures as

[17] *Frye v. United States,* 293 F. 1013 (D.C. Cir. 1923).

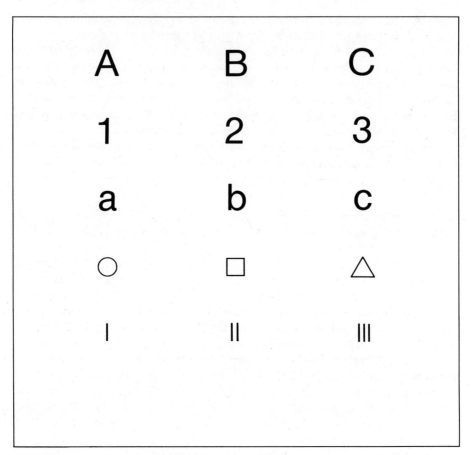

FIGURE 6.3.   The 15-items test.

he or she can recall. Unless there is significant dysfunction in the neuropsychological or peripheral systems, adult subjects of normal intelligence
should be able to reproduce at least three of the five sets accurately (Lezak,
1976).

REPORT OF FINDINGS

The style of the report that is submitted will vary among jurisdictions,
depending on the requirements of the statutes. In some jurisdictions, a
simple three-part report containing the referral data, current mental status,
and legal opinion is acceptable (Petrella & Poythress, 1983). In other jurisdictions, an elaborate set of statements relating the psychological test findings and interviews to specific criteria may be required.

A report of psychological evaluation of competence to stand trial may be as simple as a letter to the judge stating the psychologist's opinion. More often, the question of competence to stand trial is part of a series of questions posed by the referring attorney or judge. The following case illustrates this point.

PSYCHOLOGICAL REPORT

July 29, 1981

NAME: Jones, David Charles

DATE OF EXAMINATION: 6/26, 6/30, 7/8, 7/16/81 (9 hours total)

ADDRESS: Central Booking—County Jail

TELEPHONE: 000-0000

BIRTHDATE: 4/17/50   AGE: 31–2

OCCUPATION: Unemployed

EDUCATION: 10

Referral

Joseph Smith, refers Mr. Jones for evaluation. Mr. Smith has been appointed as a public defender for Mr. Jones who is charged with several counts of armed robbery. Mr. Smith would like Mr. Jones evaluated for competency to stand trial, capacity to waive his rights, current emotional status and their implications, and an estimate of Mr. Jones's sanity at the time of the offense.

History for Mr. Jones

Mr. Jones is charged with armed robbery and armed burglary. He feels that the maximum penalty he may receive for this is life imprisonment. He states that he is pleased that Mr. Smith is his attorney. Mr. Jones states that he has been arrested before for possession of drugs, drunkenness, and escape from a police station. Four robberies are involved in this series of charges. He states that he was sitting in a bar drinking, and some men started talking, and the first time it happened he simply "went along for the ride." After that, they came to his house and sought him out for participation. He states that at the time of the interview he felt mixed up and depressed. He has little hope that anything good will happen to him. His only wish is to get back to his first wife.

He was asked about his confession, and he indicated that he doesn't remember a good part of this. He drank a lot of alcohol the day before and had been drinking every day. In the prison situation, he has withdrawn from alcohol, and although this was difficult at first, he now feels somewhat better.

He states that he was born in Hoopers Island, Maryland. His mother is living, but he doesn't know whether or not she is well. She is a housewife. She is in her 60s. The father is living and well, 66, and retired. He has had odd jobs, but he hasn't talked to the father in several years. There is a brother, 27, and sisters, 25 and 23. He grew up in Cambridge, Maryland. He quit high school in the 10th grade at the age of 17. At that point he enlisted in the Army (RA123456789). His course in the military included basic training at Fort Bragg, and advanced training at Fort McClelland, Alabama. MOS-11 Bravo. He went to Fort Benning and attended Jump School and graduated. At Fort Dix he was given orders for the 101st Division. He was shipped to Vietnam where he became a replacement in the First Infantry Division. He spent 45 days short of two years in Vietnam, signing up for a second tour of duty. His first year he served as an infantryman and during the second year as a door gunner on a helicopter. He had several R and R's. His basic weapons included the M-16 and M-60. He was wounded with shrapnel in his leg. His decorations included his Jump Wings, CIB, Bronze Star, and various theater ribbons. The Bronze Star was with V. He rose as high as E-5, but was "busted." He states this was because he fell asleep. He tried to get stationed somewhere near to his home and couldn't. He went AWOL. He turned himself in as sick.

During the service he took a great many drugs in Vietnam. He also drank heavily. He received a discharge in 1970 at Fort Meade, Maryland, which he claims was a medical discharge. He states that he saw psychiatrists there and feels that perhaps he had a nervous breakdown.

He had an automobile accident with unconsciousness at age 20. He had a barbiturate overdose at age 20. He was unconscious for five days as a result of his accident. He has never been in a VA hospital. He has been in the state hospital and has attended with various psychiatrists.

In talking about his military career, he is bland and flat. When asked what his job was in the military in Vietnam, he said, "My essential job was to kill people." There was a great deal of drinking, use of marijuana and other drugs. He undertook a second tour in Vietnam because he was promised that he could get out of his enlistment several months early if he finished the second tour with less than 150 days of duty left. By the end of his tour he just wanted to get out under any circumstances.

Following his discharge he thought about Vietnam for a while. He had bad dreams, and his first wife told him he would wake up screaming and shaking. Now he sometimes talks about it when he is drinking. He feels that he would do it again if he had to. He dislikes discussing it when sober.

He married at age 20 while he was still in the service. The wife was 17 at the time. She still lives in Maryland. She is a housewife on welfare. There are daughters, 9 and 7 years of age. He talks to her whenever he can now.

She says she would like to have him back. They were divorced in 1974 because of his drinking and doing drugs.

Background Information

Mr. Smith provided police records of the offense, deposition of codefendant Morgan, summary of treatments at the Eastern Shore State Hospital, Cambridge, Md., therapy notes from Doctor Smithers, and military records from his enlistment through his discharge.

From these records it was learned that Mr. Jones did not live with his parents until he was five or six, being raised by his grandmother. The father was a heavy drinker. The mother and the father were generally in conflict and argumentative. The mother was running around with other men. The mother and sister have had Grand Mal Seizures. Mr. Jones has been suspected of this, and at one time he was on rather heavy anticonvulsant medication. Mr. Jones has had some suicidal attempts. He has been deeply depressed. He has been drinking heavily for a good part of his adult life. He considered suicide when he returned from the service. He had much difficulty in the Army, and was eventually discharged after court martial. He waived his rights at the time of this court martial. He enlisted at the time when the military was taking people of questionable emotional and intellectual status. His tests indicate that he was of Low Average intellect at the time he was enlisted. In spite of this he did his duty in a satisfactory manner. In an evaluation dated September 12, 1970, an Army psychiatrist, Dr. Rheingold certified that Mr. Jones is "severely depressed and in need of psychiatric treatment." In spite of this he was not given a psychiatric discharge, nor recommended for veterans' benefits. This is certainly a very poor recommendation of the military of that era and their treatment of those who served honorably in combat theaters.

Following his discharge, his emotional condition apparently worsened, and he received a variety of psychiatric treatments in Maryland, both inpatient and outpatient. He was diagnosed as having Alcohol Addiction, a Depressive Neurosis, and an Explosive Personality Disorder (Eastern Shore State Hospital, January 7, 1971).

The history is that of an individual who was raised under very poor family conditions, who did very poorly academically, left school, joined the service, received a considerable amount of combat training, performed well under extremely stressful combat circumstances, but began to "crack" while in the service. Drugs, and various emotional reactions, including getting into difficulty with the authorities, allowed him to complete his term in the military, but not before he became acutely disturbed and was discharged. He was not given proper treatment by the military or the Veterans Administration. He continued to drift and became worse. He became addicted to alcohol, continued to have considerable family and interpersonal problems, and continued downward until he has reached his present circumstance.

Examination Procedures

Wechsler Adult Intelligence Scale–Revised, Wechsler Memory Scale, Torque Test, Indiana-Reitan Neuropsychological Short Form, Competency Evaluation, Luria-Nebraska Neuropsychological Investigation, Thematic Apperception Test, Minnesota Multiphasic Personality Inventory, House-Tree Test, FIRO-B, History, Observation, and Interview. (All examinations took place at Central Booking, except the Luria-Nebraska Neuropsychological Examination which was conducted at 213 East Davis Boulevard, Tampa, Fla.)

Response to Evaluation

Mr. Jones is a short, brown-haired man with a touch of gray. He has long eyelashes. He wears a mustache. His speech is crackly and deep. He speaks low with moderate verbal skills. Motor behavior is controlled, and hearing seems within normal limits.

Clinical Observations

Mr. Jones shows little emotional affect. He listens intensely and concentrates sometimes well and sometimes poorly. In general he is somber.

Results of Examination

A. *Intellectual Factors*

Objective results of 10 subscales of the WAIS-R were as follows:

Factor	Deviation IQ	Percentile
Verbal scale	88	21st
Performance scale	96	40th
Full scale	90	25th

The above scores represent Low Average intellectual capacity. No unusual scatter is noted, and it certainly confirms the estimate made based on Army records.

B. *Neuropsychological Factors*

No evidence of mixed cerebral dominance is found. The Wechsler Memory Scale, Form 1, resulted in a Memory Quotient of 92 which correlates with his intelligence quotient as expected. The Indiana-Reitan Neuropsychological Short Form suggests the presence of minimal signs of cerebral disturbance, the quality of which is primarily in the left hemisphere. A complete Luria-Nebraska Neuropsychological Battery resulted in the Rhythm Scale exceeding the critical level, with the Pathognomonic Scale fairly low. This suggests that there is some old pathology of long-standing. The primary location of his difficulties would be in the left frontal area and in the right sensory motor strip.

Analysis of the Deficit Scale indicates that Mr. Jones is brain-disordered in such a manner that he will have special difficulty in translating verbal relationships into action. The pattern is that which would be associated with anterior damage, most probably in the frontal lobes.

C. Competence to Stand Trial

Mr. Jones in general knew that he was in a difficult situation, and that he could receive a long jail sentence. He was depressed and discouraged. At the time he was given the Lipsitt Competence Screening Test, he scored a total of 25 points which would be called "borderline competent." This means that at times he would be competent to understand the charges against him and to assist his attorney. At other times he might not. The results of the neuropsychological examinations certainly suggest that at times he understands the implications of verbal instructions, and explanations, and at other times he does not.

D. Personality Factors

(1) *Interpersonal Activity.*   This is a man who is a "loner." A dependent, concrete-thinking person, he is often unable to understand the nature of situations and the implications of his behavior. He is very dependent. He thinks simplistically. He has episodes in which he is disorganized, confused, and suffers bizarre thought processes. At times his behavior is totally unpredictable. In general he tends to be nervous, anxious, and depressed. At other times he is quite apathetic and listless. He has great difficulty in concentrating, or formulating any reasonable kinds of plans or goals. Socially he is a shy, inhibited person whose behavior is quite unpredictable. His decision making is inappropriate.

(2) *Early Identifications.*   The personality tests suggest that this man had extremely poor modeling from both the mother and the father. There are indications that the parents were not available. The picture of the mother is that of a disturbed, depressed, volatile person, while the father is seen as a rigid, harsh, stubborn, inadequate model.

(3) *Anxiety Structure.*   Life to Mr. Jones is confusion. The expression of emotion is a grave danger, and he tends to avoid it. He is unable to deal with stress or conflict. His coping mechanisms are almost nil. He suffers a severe dominance/submission conflict, and he never really knows when to

act, when to withdraw, when to stand up for himself, and when to comply with others. His perception of life is confused, alternating with terror and hopelessness.

(4)   *Defense Mechanisms and Coping Capability.*   Mr. Jones suffers a serious thinking disorder. He could be properly classified as suffering from paranoid schizophrenia. His intellectual defenses are limited to being hostile, suspicious, keeping people at a distance, moodiness, dependent gullibility, and a tendency to be drawn to aggressive male leadership. His less intellectual defenses include turning rage inward and suffering considerable depression, the release of anxiety through the excessive use of alcohol and drugs, and the explosion of inappropriate behavior while drinking. He is unable to be efficient in vocational activity. His defense mechanisms are very poor, and this is a man who simply cannot govern his own behavior. Although he has periods of clarity, he is frequently in a psychotic state.

Summary and Conclusions

Psychological evaluation of Mr. David Jones finds him to be a man of Low Average intellectual capacity, probably suffering from a variety of brain disorders both in terms of electrical disturbance and damaged brain tissue. The personality structure is that of an individual unable to accommodate himself to life. He experiences frequent psychotic episodes, and there are times when he explodes with no control or appropriateness in the behavior. He is drawn to drinking and to drugs to relieve his terror and anxiety, but these in turn lead to acting out aggressive impulses. He adjusted poorly in his childhood, had a short period of adjustment during training in the service, but began to break down during combat. At the end of his service career he was experiencing very severe psychiatric symptoms, and although these were identified, they weren't treated. He was discharged, faced the stress of civilian life and marital difficulties, and moved deeper into psychotic behavior. He was treated rather poorly in several psychiatric sessions, and became worse. He suffers a post-Vietnam stress syndrome, which is a special form of Post-Traumatic Stress Disorder, Delayed and Chronic (309.81). Because of the organic personality disorders, he must be considered as suffering an Organic Syndrome (310.10), in addition to the above.

In the past several years we have seen the emergence of stress disorders among Vietnam veterans (Figley, 1978). A common characteristic of the trauma of combat in this particular setting is the delayed onset of symptoms either in their development or their recognition (DeFazio, 1975). In this situation, individuals avoid psychosis or severe depression by "psychically closing off" (Krystal, 1968). People such as Mr. Jones have been found to become lower in coping abilities, particularly if they had early stressful parental relationships and had a tendency to use alcohol and drugs (Struen & Solberg, 1972). Such veterans show severe adjustment problems including disorientation, violent acting out, hopelessness, and apathy (Strayer & Ellenhorn, 1978). Such cases often show a severe depression 8 to 12 months after returning from Vietnam (Helzer, Robins, and Davis, 1974). About 35 percent of those who served in combat were found to have clinically depressed personalities on return to the United States (Beck, 1967). A large proportion of these broke down in the service and received fairly severe discipline and even court martials when they returned from Vietnam (Beck, 1967). Researchers generally agree that the Vietnam-related experiences tend to result in numerous psychiatric problems, but the emergence of these severe problems tends to be delayed until after removal from the combat setting and until the time the person returns to the United States or joins the civilian environment (Lifton, 1973; Solomon et al., 1971). It is common to find moral crises, readjustment problems, drug and alcohol addiction, and unemployment among such veterans. One of the syndromes that is often found has been called the "numbed guilt" reaction. This includes psychic numbing, depression, anxiety, nightmares, insomnia, denial, suppression, confusion, disillusionment, uncontrollable hostility, wanton violence, drug and alcohol addiction, unemployment, lack of goal-oriented motivation, and inability to adapt to civilian life (Bourne, 1972; Fox, 1972). Hostile impulses, angry episodes, alienation, interpersonal conflict, and tyrannical behavior can be expected. Fully one-third of Vietnam veterans use some kind of illicit drug, as well as alcohol.

There is no question that those who had family problems before they entered the service were much more likely to suffer the most severe kinds of reactions (Worthington, 1976). One can conclude from the above that Mr. Jones certainly has followed the pathways noted above. At the time of our examination, it is questionable whether he is competent to stand trial most of the time, although he tends to be "in and out." He is certainly very disturbed, experiences fragmented psychotic episodes, and within reasonable psychological probability, while using drugs or alcohol, based on the settled condition he suffers, is unable to understand the nature of his acts or their consequences. He, especially during such times of stress and alcohol or drug abuse, is unable to form intent. Mr. Jones is desperately in need of long-range psychiatric custody and treatment.

References

Beck, A. T. (1967). *Depression.* New York: Harper & Row.

Bourne, P. G. (Ed.) (1969). *The psychology and physiology of stress.* New York: Academic Press.

DeFazio, V. J. (1975). The Vietnam era veteran. *Journal of Contemporary Psychotherapy, 7* (1), 9–15.

Figley, C. R. (Ed.) (1978). *Stress disorders among Vietnam veterans.* New York: Brunner/Mazel.

Fox, R. P. (1972). Post-combat adaptational problems. *Comprehensive Psychiatry, 13,* 435–443.

Heltzer, J. E., Robins, L. N., & Davis, D. H. (1974). Depressive disorders in Vietnam return-ees. Unpublished Manuscript, Washington University.

Krystal, H. (Ed.) (1968). *Massive psychic trauma.* New York: International Universities Press.

Lifton, R. J. (1973). *Home from the war.* New York: Simon & Schuster.

Solomon, G. F., Zarcone, V. P., Yoerg, R., Scott, N. R., & Maurer, R. G. (1971). Three psychiatric casualties from Vietnam. *Archives of General Psychiatry, 25,* 522–524.

Strayer, R. & Ellenhorn, L. (1975). Vietnam veterans: A study exploring adjustment patterns and attitudes. *Journal of Social Issues, 31,* 81–94.

Struen, M. R. & Solberg, K. B. (1972). The Vietnam veteran: Characteristics and needs. In L. J. Sherman & E. M. Caffey (Eds.) *The Vietnam veteran in contemporary society.* Washington, D.C.: Veterans' Administration.

Worthington, E. R. (1976). The Vietnam era veteran. *Military Medicine, 141,* 169–170.

Becoming an expert witness in the matter of competence to stand trial requires diagnostic skill and experience, a knowledge of the statutory criteria and expectancies in the jurisdiction of record in the case, and the ability to communicate clearly to the points at issue.

7

The Insanity Defense

In the eyes of the law it is insufficient to be guilty of an act of criminality, or *actus rea*. The defendant must also be found to have the capacity to understand the wrongness of the act and to choose behavior other than the criminal act. This concept of *mens rea* means knowing what one does is wrong or impermissible. As Glueck (1925) wrote: "The *mens rea* of criminal behavior includes the volitional-inhibitory as well as cognitive modes of mental life and a disease of either of these constitutes one of the legally recognized factors of the guilty mind that is the *sine qua non* to responsibility." For almost 2000 years civilized societies have codified exculpability, or blamelessness, for those whose mental condition renders them without the ability to know right from wrong (Howell, 1982). Historically referring to "moral blame worthiness," in the twentieth century *mens rea* has come to refer to the specific state of mind, including intent and malice, required for conviction of particular criminal offenses (ABA Standing Committee, 1983).

The purpose of the plea of "not guilty by reason of insanity" is to allow triers of fact to consider excusing criminal behavior in those they find to be without *mens rea*, without awareness or cognition that their act is illegal, unacceptable, forbidden, or subject to society's judgment and punishment. The insanity defense has an entrenched place in Anglo-Saxon law and morality. The acts of deranged persons are not to be judged in the same way as the acts of rational persons (Leo, 1982; Slovenko, 1973).

Public concern and consequent legislative action tend to occur in dramatic instances where the insanity defense becomes a matter of public debate. In 1843 Daniel M'Naghten, in attempting to shoot Robert Peel, the prime minister of England, killed Peel's secretary. At the trial, defense counsel convinced the jury that M'Naghten was laboring under such a defect of reason resulting from a disease of the mind that he did not know the nature and quality of the act he was doing and did not know that what he did was wrong. The jury found the defendant innocent by reason of insanity. A public hue and outcry followed. A royal commission was appointed to study the issue. After much deliberation, and considerable dependence on early nineteenth-century psychiatric thinking, the commission established what has been since that time known as the *M'Naghten Rule*.[1]

Sometimes designated the "all-or-none rule," the M'Naghten Rule is based on an archaic and unsubstantiated psychiatric concept that an "insane" person suffers a disease rendering the cognition and volition of the individual clearly defective. This should not be surprising considering what was known about human personality 150 years ago when the M'Naghten Rule was developed and accepted. The M'Naghten test states: "To establish a defense on the ground of insanity, it must be clearly proved that, at the time of the committing of the act, the party accused was laboring under such a defect of reason, from disease of the mind, as not to know the nature and quality of the act he was doing; or if he did know it, that he did not know what he was doing was wrong." This represented a narrow, cognitive definition of insanity based on the limited and often incorrect assumption in the early nineteenth century as to the nature and cause of psychiatric conditions.

In 1961, a new definition of insanity was adopted as part of the Model Penal Code of the American Law Institute (ALI): "A person is not responsible for criminal conduct if at the time of such conduct as a result of mental disease or defect he lacks substantial capacity either to appreciate the criminality of his conduct or to conform his conduct to the requirements of the law."[2] The ALI insanity definition broadened the M'Naghten concept by asking whether defendants understood the criminal nature of their act and whether they were able to conform their conduct to what was required by law.

Two alternatives to the insanity defense have been proposed in order to do away with the concept that a mentally disturbed person is in some way exculpated from usual standards of guilt. The first, often referred to as "guilty but mentally ill," is a standard first legislated in Michigan in the mid-1970s. "Guilty but mentally ill" allows a jury to find that although the defendant is not insane, and as a result is guilty of the offense of which he or she is charged, the mental illness demonstrated during the trial must be taken into consideration. Procedure requires that the judge sentence the defendant to a prison where meaningful mental health care is available. An opportunity to find a defendant guilty but mentally ill allows a jury an alternative to acquitting a defendant by reason of insanity.[3] At this writing, nine states have enacted a version of the alternative of guilty but mentally ill (Alaska, Connecticut, Delaware, Georgia, Illinois, Indiana, Kentucky, New Mexico, and Michigan).[4]

While 22 states use the M'Naghten Rule, 26 states use a version of the ALI Model Code definition of insanity. Two states—Idaho and Montana—

---

[1] M'Naghten's Case, 10 C. & F. 200, 8 Eng. Rep. 718 (H.L. 1843).
[2] Model Penal Code, §4.01 (1961).
[3] 6 Mental Disability L. Rep. 363 (1982).
[4] 6 Mental Disability L. Rep. 219 (1982).

TABLE 7.1. CURRENT TESTS FOR INSANITY FOR FEDERAL AND STATE JURISDICTIONS

Jurisdiction	Insanity Test Used	Allocation of Burden	Quantum of Proof
Federal			
All Circuits	ALI**	Government	Beyond reasonable doubt
States			
Alabama[0]	ALI**	Defendant	Reasonable satisfaction of jury
Alaska*	ALI modified	State	Beyond reasonable doubt
Arizona[0]	M'Naghten	State	Beyond reasonable doubt
Arkansas	ALI	Defendant	Preponderance of evidence
California[0]	ALI (§1)	Defendant	Preponderance of evidence
Colorado[0]	M'Naghten/irresistible impulse	State	Beyond reasonable doubt
Connecticut[0]	ALI	State	Beyond reasonable doubt
Delaware*	ALI/irresistible impulse	Defendant	Preponderance of evidence
District of Columbia	ALI	Defendant	Preponderance of evidence
Florida[0]	M'Naghten	State	Beyond reasonable doubt
Georgia*	M'Naghten	Defendant	Preponderance of evidence
Hawaii[0]	ALI modified	Defendant	Preponderance of evidence
Idaho	No affirmative defense— "Mens rea" only (1982)	State	Beyond reasonable doubt
Illinois*	ALI	State	Beyond reasonable doubt
Indiana*	ALI	Defendant	Preponderance of evidence
Iowa[0]	M'Naghten	State	Beyond reasonable doubt
Kansas[0]	M'Naghten	State	Beyond reasonable doubt
Kentucky*	ALI	Defendant	Preponderance of evidence
Louisiana	M'Naghten modified	Defendant	Preponderance of evidence
Maine	ALI modified	Defendant	Preponderance of evidence
Maryland	ALI modified	Defendant	Beyond reasonable doubt
Massachusetts	ALI (§1)	State	Beyond reasonable doubt
Michigan*	ALI modified	State	Beyond reasonable doubt
Minnesota	M'Naghten	Defendant	Preponderance of evidence
Mississippi	M'Naghten	State	Beyond reasonable doubt
Missouri[0]	ALI modified	Defendant	Preponderance or greater weight of evidence
Montana	Limited defense (1979)***	Defendant	Preponderance of evidence
Nebraska[0]	M'Naghten	State	Beyond reasonable doubt
Nevada	M'Naghten	Defendant	Preponderance of evidence
New Hampshire[0]	Unique	Defendant	Preponderance of evidence
New Jersey[0]	M'Naghten	Defendant	Preponderance of evidence
New Mexico*	M'Naghten/irresistible impulse	Defendant	Preponderance of evidence
New York	M'Naghten modified	State	Beyond reasonable doubt
North Carolina	M'Naghten	Defendant	Satisfaction of jury
North Dakota	Unique	State	Beyond reasonable doubt
Ohio	ALI (§1)	Defendant	Preponderance of evidence
Oklahoma	M'Naghten	State	Beyond reasonable doubt

TABLE 7.1.   (*Continued*)

Jurisdiction	Insanity Test Used	Allocation of Burden	Quantum of Proof
Oregon[0]	ALI	Defendant	Preponderance of evidence
Pennsylvania[0]	M'Naghten	Defendant	Preponderance of evidence
Rhode Island	ALI modified	Defendant	Preponderance of evidence
South Carolina	M'Naghten modified	Defendant	Preponderance of evidence
South Dakota	M'Naghten modified	State	Beyond reasonable doubt
Tennessee[0]	ALI	State	Beyond reasonable doubt
Texas[0]	ALI	State	Preponderance of evidence
Utah	ALI	State	Beyond reasonable doubt
Vermont	ALI modified	State	Beyond reasonable doubt
Virginia[0]	M'Naghten/irresistible impulse	State	Beyond reasonable doubt
Washington[0]	M'Naghten	Defendant	Preponderance of evidence
West Virginia	ALI	State	Beyond reasonable doubt
Wisconsin[0]	ALI	Defendant	Reasonable certainty by greater weight of credible evidence
Wyoming[0]	ALI	State	Beyond reasonable doubt

Source: Reprinted from 7 *Mental Disabilities Law Reporter* 140 (1983) by permission.

[0] States where insanity defense revisions received consideration during 1981 and 1982.

* States which also have "guilty but mentally ill" verdict.

** 1982 Alabama Legislature's "crime package" abolished the defense. Governor signed bill but Court of Criminal Appeals held legislation null and void for executive's failure to file with secretary of state as required by law. Matter now on *cert.* to Alabama Superior Court (Nov. 1982).

*** No psychiatric testimony at trial unless necessary to show that defendant was so insane that mens rea not possible.

have eliminated the plea of innocent by reason of insanity. Although eliminating the insanity pleading, such legislation does allow expert testimony on the issue of *mens rea* or any state of mind that is an element of the crime in question. Such testimony is not admissible if it focuses on "insanity" or "diminished responsibility." The testimony on mental disability must strictly focus on *mens rea*. How broadly the courts will interpret *mens rea*, as defined by evidence of mental disability, is yet to be seen. Likewise, what expert testimony will be ruled admissible to show an absence of *mens rea* is unknown at this time.[5] Table 7.1 presents current tests for insanity, by state and for federal jurisdictions.[6]

[5] 6 Mental Disability L. Rep. 364 (1982).
[6] 6 Mental Disability L. Rep. 140 (1983).

TRIAL STRATEGY

The insanity pleading is invoked in less than 1 in every 1000 criminal cases. Only 4–5% of such pleadings result in a finding of innocent by reason of insanity. Thus only 1 in 25,000 criminal cases ends with a verdict of innocent by reason of insanity (Howell, 1982). In determining trial strategy, an attorney must weigh the possible advantage of the insanity defense against losing all the options available when pleading "not guilty." By notifying the court of intent to plead the defendant innocent by reason of insanity, so that the court may order the necessary mental examinations prescribed by statute, the attorney, in essence, pleads the defendant guilty of the crime but claims excusal on the basis of insanity. Many attorneys are reluctant to use the insanity defense because there is no going back to a plea of "not guilty" and all its consequent options.

BURDEN OF PROOF

The initial burden of proof for the insanity defense falls on the defendant. The attorneys who intend to use the insanity defense must go forward and introduce some evidence that counters the assumption that the defendant is sane. Once this evidence is placed before the court, the burden of proof may fall on the prosecution or the defense. In approximately one-half of the states, the defense must prove, by *a preponderance of the evidence*, that the defendant was legally insane at the time the offense was committed. In the other half of the states and in the federal jurisdiction, the prosecution must prove *beyond reasonable doubt* that the defendant was legally sane at the time the crime was committed. Thus the defendant's rights are protected by requiring the lowest burden of proof when the defense must convince a jury that the defendant was insane. In those jurisdictions where the burden of proof falls on the prosecution, the defendant must be proved sane at the highest weight of evidence. In order to accomplish the latter, the prosecution must present evidence and witnesses to demonstrate unequivocally that the defendant was without disease or defect of mind at the time the crime was committed.

To this end, the judge's instructions charge the jury with the responsibility of deciding the issue. The following pattern jury instruction is currently used by judges in federal courts:

There is an issue in this case concerning the sanity of the defendant at the time of the acts or events alleged in the indictment.

The sanity of the defendant at the time of an alleged offense must be established by the government beyond a reasonable doubt because willful intent, as you have been instructed, is an essential element of the offense charged, and a person who is insane is not capable of forming such intent.

A person is insane within the meaning of these instructions and is not responsible for criminal conduct if, at the time of such conduct, as a result of mental disease or defect, he lacks substantial capacity either to appreciate the wrongfulness of his conduct or to conform his conduct to the requirements of the law.

The term "mental disease or defect" does not include an abnormality manifested only by repeated criminal or otherwise antisocial conduct.

If, after consideration of all the evidence in the case, you have a reasonable doubt as to whether the defendant was sane at the time of the alleged offense, you must find him not guilty.

Responsive to the considerable scholarly, legislative, and public interest in the insanity defense, the American Bar Association (ABA) has proposed new standards of nonresponsibility for crime. The proposed new test of insanity identifies the defendant's appreciation of the wrongfulness of his or her conduct alone as a basis of exculpation and rejects the volitional element of the ALI Penal Code test for insanity. The ABA further opposes the enactment of statutes which supplant or supplement a verdict of not guilty by reason of insanity with a verdict of guilty but mentally ill. The proposed standard (7-6.1) states:

(a) A person is not responsible for criminal conduct if, at the time of such conduct, and as a result of mental disease or defect, that person was unable to appreciate the wrongfulness of such conduct.

(b) When used as a legal term in this standard, "mental disease or defect" refers to either:
 (i) impairments of mind, whether enduring or transitory; or
 (ii) mental retardation,
 Which substantially affected the mental or emotional processes of the defendant at the time of the alleged offense. [ABA Standing Committee on Association Standards for Criminal Justice, 1983]

It is anticipated that these proposed standards will influence legislative modifications of the insanity defense in the foreseeable future.

TESTIMONY OF EXPERTS QUESTIONED

Experts are sharply divided on the issue of whether the existing statutes are fair or practical in respect to the testimony of experts. In the aftermath of the attempted assassination of President Ronald Reagan by John Hinckley in 1982, the defendant was found innocent by reason of insanity. Wide media coverage indicated that the jury was in considerable conflict about its decision (Isaacson, 1982). Various experts debated the issues. At one extreme it was suggested that in the future psychiatrists and psychologists must confine their testimony to experimental findings and statistical facts, devoid of opinions and theoretical notions (Robinson, 1982). Some experts have long advocated the legislative banishment of all psychological and psychiatric testimony, making such statements as, "There is absolutely no scientific or medical criteria for determining the presence or absence of mental capacities" (CSPA, 1981). At the other extreme some noted psychiatrists believed that the abolition of the existing system would lead to unfairness and danger to the mentally ill (Bockman, 1982).

In 1983 the American Psychiatric Association urged a tightening up of standards and procedures to protect the public against premature release of potentially dangerous individuals but recommended that the insanity defense be retained. The association opposed any form of the plea "guilty but mentally ill." The position expressed by the American Psychiatric Association is that there is a lack of clear, objective methods of ascertaining mental states with a high degree of accuracy (Boffey, 1983). Both the American Bar Association and the American Psychiatric Association Committee on Legal Issues have recommended reforms (Melton, 1983).

CURRENT ROLE OF EXPERTS

The courts are guided by statutory provisions in the matter of expert testimony. Judges will generally follow the *Federal Rules of Evidence*, which advises: "If scientific, technical, or other specialized knowledge will assist the trier of fact to understand the evidence or to determine a fact in issue, a witness qualified as an expert by knowledge, skill, experience, training or education may testify thereto in the form of an opinion or otherwise."[7] In the matter of insanity, the court may allow a variety of professional and lay witnesses. Traditionally, physicians—most frequently, psychiatrists—have testified as to the defendant's mental state at the time of the felony. More recently, psychologists have testified in the matter of insanity.

The role of the expert is to provide the judge and jury with information and opinions that the average jury member could not deduce from the evidence. These opinions are to be based on the special skill, knowledge, and experience the expert uses when examining the facts of the case and the defendant. The decision as to whether a defendant is innocent by reason of insanity lies with the triers of fact. *The expert is not brought to court to render an opinion as to whether the defendant is innocent.*

The behavioral scientist as an expert witness in a case involving the insanity defense is in a difficult position. The court is seeking information concerning the defendant's capacity to exercise free will, while the behav-

---

[7] Fed. R. Evid. 702.

ioral scientist is a nonjudgmental professional. Testimony as to the defendant's background, personality, intellect, reality contact, or cognitive skills is only of importance if it leads to an opinion on the part of the expert as to the defendant's ability to understand the criminal nature of his or her act at the time it occurred or, in those jurisdictions following the ALI Model Code, if the defendant had substantial capacity to understand the wrongfulness of an act or to conform his or her behavior to the requirements of the law.

Whereas a psychiatrist generally depends on the facts of the case and a psychiatric examination of the defendant as the basis for the opinion that will be rendered in court, psychologists often focus their testimony on the results of psychological tests.

PSYCHOLOGICAL EXAMINATION OF DEFENDANTS

In preparing to examine a defendant who has filed a plea of innocent by reason of insanity, the psychologist should consider what factors may indicate or suggest an absence of criminal intent or an inability to conform to the expectancies of the law. No psychological test is standardized adequately for this specific purpose. Tests and other materials serve as aids in helping the psychologist, as an expert in human behavior, to form an opinion based on *reasonable psychological probability* (more likely to be so than not) as to the state of mind of the defendant at the time of the felony.

The issue is convoluted. There are many instances where the psychologists may find insufficient information on which to base an opinion. Behavior of the defendant on psychological examination is only rarely sufficient for the expert to render an opinion concerning a previous event. A substantial approach to the psychological evaluation of a defendant who has pleaded innocent by reason of insanity requires the following:

1. *Events and Observations concerning the Crime.* The psychologist has a responsibility to collect a complete dossier on the facts of the crime. This includes the police and witness reports. The psychologist must be careful not to use any statements or reports from unsworn witnesses, since such material may be ruled hearsay and could result in the psychologist's testimony being excluded during the trial. From all the material available, the psychologist must construct as objective a picture as possible of what actually happened. No exploration of the *mens rea* can occur until there is an accurate picture of the *actus rea*.

2. *The Defendant's Recall.* There should be available to the psychologist a transcript of the defendant's description of the events leading up to the crime, the act itself, and the defendant's behavior following the act, usually in the form of police reports or statements. The facts of the crime as the defendant relates them should also be part of the history taken by the

psychologist. The way in which the defendant perceives and recalls his or her involvement in the crime will be an important element of the psychologist's formulation of an opinion as to whether the defendant possessed *mens rea* at the time the crime was committed. In some instances, the defendant will claim total or partial amnesia for the events that occurred before, during, or after the crime. This, of course, could be significant in the appraisal of the probability of the presence of a mental disease or defect at the time of the criminal act.

3. *Ancillary Sources.*   In most instances, it is possible to obtain information from witnesses and bystanders about events immediately preceding the crime, the crime itself, and the behavior of the defendant immediately following the crime. In order to be able to assess the mental state of the defendant at a time and place where no direct observation was made by the psychologist, the use of techniques developed in psychological autopsy are necessary (Shneidman, 1976). It may even be possible to retrieve information of value concerning the victim or victims of the crime to determine what influence this may have had on the behavior and cognition of the defendant. Such evidence has been ruled admissible in some jurisdictions (Lichter, 1981). It is important that the psychologist make known during the initial contact with the attorney who requested consultation that these materials will be required. They are best obtained by the attorney's investigative staff.

4. *Psychological Evaluation.*   It is recommended that a standard, complete, psychological evaluation be the keystone of every consultation involving the insanity defense. Since questions concerning a defendant's mental status include competence to stand trial, the evaluation should include the instruments and procedures necessary to answer questions relating to both sanity and competence to stand trial. The psychological test battery should include:

  a. *A History from the Defendant.*   This should include background, previous treatment experience, and recall of circumstances surrounding the crime.
  b. *A History from the Family of the Defendant.*
  c. *Intellectual Evaluation.*   The psychologist should use a multiscale, well-standardized battery of intelligence tests that assesses verbal and nonverbal factors.
  d. *Neuropsychological Factors.*   Even if no neuropsychological deficit is suspected from either history or behavior, a screening evaluation should be done. Any anomalies of significance found on the screening test will require proceeding to a full neuropsychological evaluation.
  e. *Competency Evaluation.*   An evaluation of the defendant's competency to stand trial should be included, as noted previously. Procedures and instruments are reviewed in Chapter 6.

f. *Reading Skills.*   A well-standardized test of reading skills is necessary to ensure that the defendant can be given test materials requiring a variety of reading capabilities (vocabulary, comprehension, speed). This is particularly important should there be
questions, regarding the defendant's intellectual capacity, reality
contact, confusion, or bilingualism, to be considered and evaluated when the psychologist is called upon to render opinions
based on the defendant's test performance.

g. *Personality.*   Although the other areas of assessment will contribute to the psychologist's final opinion as to *mens rea*, it is the
personality evaluation that is likely to define the defendant's perception of the world, cognitive style, response capabilities, and
limitations. The choice of tests, projective and objective, must be
made with a view to the psychologist's ability to justify and defend these instruments as reliable and valid. Psychologists with
extensive background and experience rarely have difficulty in explaining and justifying projective techniques. Some have suggested using only a single, standardized, objective personality test
as a strategic move to avoid challenge of projective methods by
opposing counsel (Ziskin, 1981b). In choosing personality-mea-
suring procedures, the psychologist would be well advised to conform to the expectancies of *Frye v. United States,* which was addressed in detail in Chapter 1.

h. *Measures of Faking or Malingering.*   Although current methods
leave much to be desired, every effort should be made to measure
the presence or absence of these factors.

5. *The Report of Findings and Opinion.*   In all cases, the psychologist should
prepare a report that integrates all the information, material, and examination findings noted above. The report should include the following areas or
subsections:

a. The process by which the psychologist was retained.

b. The facts of the case and their sources.

c. The defendant's recollection of events surrounding the crime.

d. Observations of the defendant's behavior by friends, relatives,
witnesses, and enforcement personnel.

e. Family history and events of significance in the defendant's life.

f. Tests and procedures used. Dates and time spent with the defendant.

g. Clinical observations during testing. A statement as to competence at this time is appropriate here.

h. Test results.

i. A summary statement of the defendant's psychological state at
the time of the examination, including any diagnosis or categori-

zation of this state which may be appropriate. Comments concerning the validity of the procedures and/or indications that the defendant attempted to fake bad should appear here.

j. An evaluation of the degree of "fit" or absence of such concordance of the facts of the case with the history, observations of behavior, and the defendant's psychological state and recollections.

k. A statement of the psychologist's opinion as to effect on the defendant's *mens rea* of any mental defect or disease and whether the events described in the facts of the case suggest, within reasonable psychological probability, that the defendant was unable to understand the acts he or she committed were unlawful or wrong. If there is reasonable evidence to support an opinion that the defendant may be capable of understanding the act was wrong but, because of a defect or disease influencing the defendant at the time of the crime, was unable to conform his or her behavior to those standards, it should appear as an opinion. This is best done in the written report, as answers to a series of questions posed by the retaining attorney.

There are frequent instances in which the psychologist may finish an extensive evaluation and be unable to state an opinion with certainty, in respect to the statutory definition of insanity in the jurisdiction where the defendant is being tried. When this happens, it must be stated straightforwardly to the attorney retaining the psychologist at the earliest time possible. Every expert should realize that his or her opinion is a part of the retaining attorney's trial strategy and the earliest notification of the expert's findings and opinion is not only proper professional courtesy but essential to the attorney's representation of the case.

Mental health experts with much experience in examining for purposes of testifying regarding insanity find that a small number of defendants easily meet the legal criteria of being without *mens rea*, a modest number clearly had *mens rea*, and the largest number consists of complex, difficult cases where opinions are likely to be equivocal and varied. Some of this reflects the inexactness of all the behavioral sciences. Much of the difficulty arises, however, in attempting to reconcile the analysis of an individual by a mental health professional using classification systems derived from medicine, Aristotelian logic, and the empirical data and norms of behavioral science with the requirement of jurisprudence that a moral judgment must be made. The reconciliation is possible, but the route is tortuous and fraught with opportunities for the psychologist to slip into the role of trier of fact, rather than the proper stance as an expert presenting opinions based on material from the expert's field of science.

The psychologist as expert in an insanity pleading would be well advised to avoid exotic or complex analyses of data. In all probability, a defendant likely to be found innocent by reason of insanity will suffer from one of the following diseases or defects which are known to affect *mens rea:*

1. *Mental Deficiency.*   A severely or profoundly retarded individual may simply lack the cognitive capacity to understand his or her participation in an illegal act. The exculpation of young children also falls in this category. A person with a mental age of three or four years is unlikely to be held to have *mens rea,* whether the individual is 3 or 33 years of age chronologically. Intelligence tests provide clear support for an expert opinion of "not able to understand the nature of the act." The issue becomes hazier as the mental age of the individual passes five years and will depend on a variety of factors and circumstances in addition to the limited intellectual capacity.

2. *Neuropsychological Dysfunction or Defect.*   The rapid development of neuropsychological research and the development of sophisticated neuropsychological examination techniques over the past decade have provided the instrumentation and the data base to enable psychologists to render opinions as to defects in cognition, awareness, and judgment based on clearly defined and generally accepted neuropsychological deficits. Individuals suffering focal conditions, such as temporal and frontal lobe lesions, and more diffuse tissue disturbance or convulsive pathology are known to have periods in which judgment, planning, or awareness disappear or are seriously diminished. Such objective findings lend significant weight to the opinion of a neuropsychologist testifying that under the conditions surrounding the defendant's crime, it was probable that the defendant was not in possession of the capacity to control or understand his or her own behavior.

A recent decision by the Colorado Supreme Court sustained the use by a psychologist of neuropsychological assessment to support expert testimony that a defendant in a murder trial suffered minimal brain dysfunction and thus had poor impulse control. The defendant was acquitted of the charge of murder, by reason of insanity.[8] This suggests that, as Wigmore predicted, "the courts are ready for psychology when psychology is ready for the courts" (Louisell, 1955).

3. *Emotional Disturbance.*   Although in common parlance severe emotional disturbance (or "psychosis") is viewed as synonymous with insanity, this equivalence is not accepted by the courts. No matter how severe the emotional disturbance, it is irrelevant to the issue of insanity unless the condition results in such a state of mind that the individuals are without an understanding of the criminality of their act or, as a result of their condition, are unable to exert their "will" to conform to the expectancies of society and the law.

The analysis of all the data available, including personality tests, may indicate that the defendant is the product of a very inadequate develop-

---

[8] *People v. Wright,* 648 P.2d 665 (Colo. 1982).

mental experience, has suffered numerous psychiatric hospitalizations, and is subject to episodes of psychosis. Such findings indicate deep emotional disturbance but are insufficient for a jury to find such an individual innocent by reason of insanity. Expert testimony is likely to be seen as credible in this setting only if the psychologist can demonstrate that the emotional disturbance is such that the defendant's *mens rea* is cast in doubt for the time the crime was committed.

In evaluating the emotional status of a defendant pleading innocent by reason of insanity, the psychologist should be able to clearly relate the defendant's current test results and descriptive diagnosis to the events and observation concerning the crime, the defendant's recall of the events and his or her perceptions, and the data concerning the defendant's behavior from ancillary sources. Unless a clear, logical, and consistent pattern of behavior indicates that the defendant's emotional disturbance was responsible for an absence of awareness and/or will, the psychological expert has nothing to say that will be viewed by the triers of fact as salient to the issue of insanity.

The psychologist is placed under a considerable judgmental burden in testifying about the mental state of a person at a point in time often far removed from the time the psychological evaluation is conducted. At the time of the examination, the defendant's emotional or neuropsychological condition may be in remission. By the same token, the patient may be in worse condition during the psychological examination than at the time of the crime. The psychologist must never omit the possibility that the defendant may attempt to present a factitious disorder since the secondary gains that could accrue from convincing an expert that he or she is "crazy" are considerable.

Being an expert witness in an issue involving the insanity pleading often places the psychologist in a difficult and vulnerable position. The expert will be pressed to make moral rather than scientific judgments, and the issues and data are so variable that a gaggle of opposing witnesses is more the rule than the exception. It is important that the psychologist make as early a determination as possible as to whether the facts of the case warrant the thorough, expensive, and time-consuming procedures necessary for competent psychological opinion on the issue of insanity. This is in the best interests of the defendant, the attorney, and the expert. It is usually best to be able to opine "I don't know" early on, instead of pursuing an extensive exploration where there are few indications that the defendant lacked *mens rea*.

The case illustration that follows presents a psychological examination conducted in an effort to determine whether a defendant was insane at the time he planned and executed a bank robbery. The case was being retried after the defendant had already been convicted and was serving a sentence in prison. The issue of insanity had not been raised by the defendant's counsel during the original trial even though the defendant was legally incompetent at the time of the trial.

While the defendant was in prison, it became apparent to the prison's psychological counselor that the defendant had not been properly represented by counsel during the trial. A *writ of habeas corpus* was filed on behalf of the defendant, and a new trial was mandated by the courts. New counsel was appointed, and in preparation for the trial, a psychologist was retained to evaluate the defendant as part of a defense of innocent by reason of insanity. In the report, which follows, the psychologist addresses specific questions posed by the attorneys for the defendant in an effort to determine whether there was any possibility that the defendant was insane at the time of the bank robbery. The case jurisdiction was in federal court, so it was the defense counsel's responsibility to raise the issue of insanity. The prosecution would then bear the burden of proof to demonstrate beyond reasonable doubt that Browne was sane at the time of the robbery.

PSYCHOLOGICAL REPORT

August 8, 1983

NAME: BROWNE, Albert S.

DATE OF EXAMINATION: 8/3/83, 8/4/83, 8/6/83

ADDRESS: 106 Evergreen Street, Winter Haven, Florida 30000

TELEPHONE: 000-0000

BIRTHDATE: 2/12/46   AGE   37–6

OCCUPATION: Disabled

EDUCATION: Grade 6 + GED

Referral

Mr. Browne was convicted of bank robbery in 1977. He has been in jail until recently. A Writ of *Habeas Corpus* was filed on his behalf, indicating that his lawyer during his original trial did not make the insanity pleading even though Mr. Browne was at that time still legally insane.

The courts have overturned his original conviction and have mandated a new trial. The courts have appointed Messrs. Gregg Thomas and Michael Piscitelli of the firm of Holland and Knight as his attorneys.

Attorneys Thomas and Piscitelli request psychological evaluation to determine answers to the following questions:

1.   Does Mr. Browne suffer mental disease or defect?
2.   Is it likely that he suffered a mental disease or defect at the time that he committed the bank robbery in 1977?

3. If indeed he does suffer a mental defect, is it one that results in a lack of substantial capacity to appreciate the wrongfulness of his conduct?

4. If Mr. Browne suffers a mental disease or defect, is it such that it results in periods of time when he is unable to conform his conduct to the requirements of the law?

5. If indeed he suffers a mental disease or defect, is it an abnormality manifested only by repeated criminal behavior or antisocial conduct?

6. If Mr. Browne suffers and has suffered a mental disease or defect, and it is your opinion that he suffered it at the time of the bank robbery, is it your opinion that he was either unable to appreciate the wrongfulness of his conduct or unable to conform his conduct to the requirements of the law at that time?

Interview with Mr. Browne

Mr. Browne was seen for psychological evaluation on August 3, August 4, and August 6, 1983. Interviews and tests covered a total of seven and three-quarter hours of time. On August 6, an extensive history was taken from Mr. Browne. Mr. Browne was first informed of the purpose of the examination and that the material would be provided to his attorneys. He agreed to all aspects of the examination. He states that Messrs. Thomas and Piscitelli were appointed as his attorneys in 1982. Mr. Browne states that he was in the Avon Park Correctional Institution, convicted of bank robbery. The bank robbery took place on September 13, 1976. It took place at the Barnett Bank in Cypress Gardens. He and his partner, Jimmy Roberts, pulled up to the back of the bank as the manager was transferring night deposits. Mr. Browne was armed with a pistol. He does not remember what kind. He was apprehended after this act because of a cigarette lighter he left, with his CB "handle" on it. They traced the name to him.

His attorney at that time was Jim T. Crowley. Mr. Browne tried to get Mr. Crowley to use the defense of insanity. He states that Mr. Crowley knew that he had been declared insane. Mr. Browne says that he was having visions and talking with his dead father.

Mr. Browne feels he is now competent to stand trial. He likes his attorneys and understands what they are trying to do for him. He has no hallucinations at the present time. He states that things seem more crystal clear to him than he ever remembers in his entire life. He states that while in prison he was a "loner" and "did my own time." He states that during the last couple of years in prison he got involved with the church and studied the Bible. He feels it took "root" in him, and is helping him to work out things in himself which were wrong. He goes to church two or three times a week.

Mr. Browne says that he was born in Myrtle Beach, South Carolina, where he lived until 18 years of age. His mother, living, 60 years of age, still is in Myrtle Beach. She is a housewife. He describes her as a person who "survives." His recollections of her are that of a cruel person who seemed to be more cruel to him than the other children. The father, who died in 1974, was 58 years of age at the time. Cause of death was a stroke with complications. He had been a farmer. He was a person who "was a terror to be around." He never gave Mr. Browne any love or affection. He drank and became violent. He beat Mr. Browne unconscious on several occasions when Mr. Browne was a child.

There are six brothers and five sisters. Two brothers have been in mental institutions. Several of his siblings are ambidextrous, and can write with both hands.

He recalls his grandmother trying to drown him in the ocean when he was small. His brothers also tried to kill him in a similar way. The family thought he was "slow." He remembers that at age 10 or 11 his brothers tied him to a tree and forced him to have oral sex with them and with some of their friends. Mr. Browne remembers trying to tell his mother and father about this, but they "slapped me down." They accused him of lying. He ran away from home on a number of occasions, living in the woods, until the family would find him and bring him home. It would then start all over. He feels his family tried to get rid of him.

He attended Myrtle Beach Elementary School through the sixth grade. He left at age 12, running away from home. He lived in the streets and in the alleys and sheds of the community. He was always terrified of his family. He hid from them. He stayed with friends occasionally but also slept in alleys and in boxes and in sheds. Between 14 and 15, he was picked up by the police and sent to reform school for petty larceny. They tried to get him to work on a farm. He was forced to drive a tractor against his wishes, and he cut down 12 acres of corn. They put him into seclusion, where he stayed until he was almost 16. He was picked up at school by his mother and his brothers. The same thing happened—his father became drunk and violent. Mr. Browne was picked up by the police for stealing saws from a construction job. He spent 18 months on the chain gang for that. He went in at 17 and came out when he was about 19. He decided he could not stand Myrtle Beach and came to Florida in 1966. His cousin got him a job, but he could not keep the job. He drank, and when he was not drinking, he would just walk off in a daze or a trance. He felt people were following him, and he tried to run them over. They were all imaginary. He tried to shoot them with a gun, and the Sheriff picked him up and put him in jail. His wife and his cousin asked for a doctor to examine him. He was committed to Arcadia in 1967. He was there six to eight months and his wife signed him out. He attended Hillsborough County Guidance Center on an outpatient basis after that. He was taking heavy medication. He went back to the county hospital about 1968. He was in and out of the county hospital because he was not taking his medicine as he was supposed to. Some truck drivers gave him some pills, and he also drank whiskey, and he just "ran around like crazy." In 1970, he was picked up for Breaking and Entering and charged with Grand Larceny. They found him insane and committed him to Chattahoochee. He was there three months and then was released to the courts. They sent him on an outpatient basis to the Hillsborough County Guidance Center. He stayed there until August or September of 1971. He got into bad shape with drinking, and he began to scare everyone, accusing his wife of all sorts of things. He heard someone calling him. He left Hillsborough County, left his family, and went to Winter Haven. He did not know anyone. He met a woman and eventually married her.

She is now his wife. He took her to Georgia in order to get married. He was still married and told her nothing about this. She found out he was married and forced him to get a divorce, and then later they remarried, in 1973. He went off his medication, was drinking, and had lots of problems in 1973. He did not tell his wife anything about his background. He covered up his whole life. In May of 1974, their house burned down. He thought he saw figures standing in the fire. People tried to calm him down. They tried to give him liquor to calm him, and this made him worse. He called home to tell them that his house burned down, and shortly after that his father had a stroke from which he never recovered. (At this point, Mr. Browne cried softly.) He says he did not know how he got to the hospital. He got a call from his baby brother, "Daddy is dead." He walked out, left his wife, and headed for South Carolina. He does not know how he got there.

He states he loved his father, but never had a relationship with him. After Mr. Browne married his second wife, he feels his father started to like him. He remembers standing at the grave of his father saying, "I won't let you die." His father replied to him, "I am not dead—I'm within you." Mr. Browne says he talked to his father a lot. The father told him that he wanted a farm. (Mr. Browne cries volubly at this point.) He says that the father told him he loved him and that Mr. Browne should go out and get a farm. He started out stealing things and selling them and collecting the money. The burglaries got larger and larger. He would see people carrying money or cashing checks, and he would just go and take it. He says that his father would pat him on the back and say, "Everything will be O.K., son." He says that the voice of his father told him he loved him very much.

He is not clear about all aspects of the bank robbery. The purpose of the robbery was to continue to get money for the farm. He says that he wanted his father to love him. He feels that his father finally did start to love him. He then died. When asked his memory about the bank robbery, he says that he remembers getting up in the morning, and that his father put his arm around him and talked to him and told him to wake Jimmy up and "Go get the money." He says that his father's voice said, "Go get the money—tell that man to give us the money." When asked how he knew about the bank manager taking the money out of the bank, he says that he thinks that a week or a month or so before that, he saw the transaction at the bank—with the bank manager walking across the parking lot with the bank bag. When asked how he convinced Jimmy to go along with him, he does not recall convincing Jimmy of anything—it just happened. They went back home, and he was still talking with his father. He put the money in a jar and buried it with the other money. The police found them out. He got an attorney—Jim T. Crowley. He told his story to Mr. Crowley. Mr. Browne says that Mr. Crowley told him to go and get the money and bring it to him. They dug up the money and gave him all of the money. It was in excess of $40,000.

He says that the authorities never believed him when he told them that. Mr. Crowley denied receiving it. He has only one receipt for $1,500. Mr. Browne says that he remembers piling the money on the lawyer's desk.

Mr. Browne did not testify at his own trial even though he wanted to. He was not allowed to take the stand. He was convicted and sentenced to 10 years in prison.

The Writ of *Habeas Corpus* resulted from a filing by a fellow prisoner who worked in the library. He also feels that he was helped by a psychological counselor, Norman Payne, who took an interest in him. When Mr. Payne found out that Mr. Browne was 100 percent disabled and still registered as insane and legally incompetent since 1970, he helped with the Writ. Mr. Browne served 5 years, 6 months, and 21 days in prison. Two cases were involved. While he was out on bond in the first bank robbery, awaiting appeal, the same lawyer told him to "listen to your father and get more money—and buy the farm." Mr. Browne was picked up on another robbery, a store down the road from his own place, where people knew him. They sent him to Doctor Darbey in Polk County in December of 1978. He was still talking to his father. They put him on three or four different medications. Over several months, he seemed to improve. He has been in jail between 1977 and the present time when he was released.

Mr. Browne is under the medical care of Arturo Perez, M.D. He receives counseling from Roy Mercer, a psychologist at the Winter Haven Hospital Mental Health Clinic. Mr. Browne takes Stelazine, 2 milligrams, twice a day, and Elavil, 5 milligrams, at bedtime for sleep.

He remembers no severe accident. His only unconsciousness remembered is when his father beat him several times. Mr. Browne chews tobacco, but uses no alcohol. His activity includes shooting pool with his wife one night a week, cutting yards, landscaping yards, doing some woodwork, and jogging. He is beginning a citrus nursery and hopes that this will lead to something permanent.

He first married at age 21 to a woman who was 11 years his senior. There was one son to that union, who is now 12 years of age. Mr. Browne began to write to him when he was in prison, and he sees him occasionally. The current marriage to Judith still exists. The wife is 42 years of age, a secretary. There are two stepchildren of her former marriage, and Mr. Browne says, "I've become their Daddy."

Records Reviewed

Order adjudging Mr. Browne incompetent, dated 6/27/67, signed by Judge Brooker, indicating that Mr. Browne suffered a Schizophrenic Reaction, Paranoid Type. He was said to have Homicidal and Suicidal Ideas, Threatening and Uncontrolled Behavior, Potential Violence, Inappropriate Mood with Flattened Affect, Persecutory Feelings, Emotional Lability, and Low Frustration Tolerance. *Order Adjudging Restoration,* dated 9/26/67, indicating competency was restored. *A Committee Finding of Incompetency,* dated 6/26/67. *A Commitment to State Hospital,* dated August 10, 1970. After a charge of Breaking and Entering to commit a felony, it was stated in this order that Mr. Browne "is deranged at the present time, did not know right from wrong." He was sent to the State Mental Institution in Chattahoochee. *Report,* signed by G. W. Barnard, M.D., and Gustave Newman, M.D., stating that Mr. Browne was incompetent, unable to stand trial, and insane. Evaluation, dated July 16, 1970. *Report* of Charles DeMinico, M.D. *Psychiatric evaluation,* dated August 31, 1971, diagnosing Mr. Browne as Schizophrenia—Paranoid Type, Chronic, Active. *Note* indicating that Mr. Browne was seen by Doctors R. H. Coffer and A. Gonzalez, Psychiatrists. They agreed on a diagnosis of Schizophrenic Reaction, Paranoid Type. *Report of A. DenBreeijen M.D., Psychiatrist,* dated April 13, 1973. Diagnosis: Schizophrenic Reaction, Paranoid Type. Delusions, hallucinations, fears. It was found that Mr. Browne could not deal effectively with others. Prognosis poor. *Report* of J. R. Price, Ed.D., Psychologist at Community Mental Health Center, indicating a diagnosis of Schizophrenia, Chronic, Undifferentiated Type. *Report* of November 18, 1982, by Peter Holden, M.D., Psychiatrist at the Federal Correctional Institute, Camp Butner, North Carolina. Paranoid Schizophrenia, In Remission. Axis II Anti-Social Personality Disorder. Axis III Mild Hypertension. 100 percent disability pension. *Report* by William P. Reevy, Ph.D., Psychologist at the Butner Federal Correction Institution, dated October 13, 1982. I Schizophrenia, Paranoid Type, In Remission. II Anti-Social Personality. *Deposition* by Mr. U. Richardville, dated 3/19/82. Mr. Richardville states he has been a neighbor of Mr. Browne for eight years. He reports Mr. Browne discharging firearms on many occasions, with no apparent purpose. He was beaten up by Mr. Browne. He described Mr. Browne as "schizo." A person given to sudden emotional outbursts. At times Mr. Browne would shoot his weapon at cattle several miles away. *Deposition* of Judith Browne, dated 3/19/82. She describes her husband's odd, impulsive behavior from time to time since they were married. At one time, she asked him to try some mashed potatoes, shortly after they were married, and he left, and drove off in the car, leaving her. Sometime after they were married, he suddenly pulled out some pictures at a social gathering and began showing his children and his ex-wife to her friends. Mrs. Browne claimed that the bizarre behavior was interspersed with kind and loving behavior. He would sometimes pull a gun and threaten her life. He pursued a voice that he heard on the CB. He would suddenly decide to drive 600 miles to go to visit his father's grave. He would sometimes insist that Mrs. Browne go with him while he talked to his dead father. She reports many incidents of bizarre, changeable, psychotic behavior. He would suddenly shift from awareness and good reality contact to bizarre, driven, unaware behavior that showed obvious lack of reality contact. This behavior was typical of a schizophrenic, with paranoid and delusional systems, hallucinations, and sudden dangerous behavior. *The testimony and proceedings before Honorable William B. Hand,* District Judge, in the matter of the United States of America versus Albert Browne on May 30, 1977. Mr. Jim T. Crowley for the defendant and Honorable Anthony J. LaSpada, Assistant U.S. Attorney for the United States.

Summary and Analysis of Records

The records show that Mr. Browne has a long-standing psychotic condition, which has been generally labeled Schizophrenia, Paranoid Type. This very severe mental disease and its consequent and resulting defects are well in keeping with the history reported by Mr. Browne relating to his family and his treatment therein. There is no question that at times he is actively psychotic, experiencing persecutory feelings, hallucinations, and delusions. There is no question that at times his conduct has been such that he cannot appreciate the wrongfulness of such conduct, nor can be conform his conduct to the requirements of the law or of society. He was found legally incompetent in June of 1967. In 1970, he was found to be insane, and committed to a state mental institution on this basis. There is little or no disagreement among the various professional persons who have examined him in the past as to his severe mental condition. It is a mental disease or defect which is sometimes subject to the ameliorating effects of medication, and sometimes appears to be in remission. Thus, the person can at times appear to be perfectly rational, with substantial capacity to deal reasonably in a seemingly normal manner, as long as there are no stressful conditions in the environment, both internal and external.

Examination Procedures

Wechsler Adult Intelligence Scale–Revised, Luria-Nebraska Neuropsychological Battery, Gates-MacGinitie Reading Tests—Survey D—Form 1, Thematic Apperception Test, Minnesota Multiphasic Personality Inventory, Draw-a-Person Series, House-Tree Test, History, Interview, and Clinical Observations.

Response to Evaluation

Mr. Browne is a man of somewhat above middle height, with dark-brown hair and dark-brown eyes. He wears a moustache. He states that he has high blood pressure and is taking medication for it. He speaks in a deep, soft, intense manner. He is very serious. Motor behavior is controlled. He cooperates well and seems to have good confidence. He talks a great deal about his poor background, his time in prison, and his tendency to be several different people at different times.

He claims that prison has given him a new perspective on life. He talks of enjoying history and expresses pride in the heritage of America. He claims descendancy from American Indians. He has tried to share his problems and experiences with other people who have problems, but he is frustrated in finding "they don't understand." He feels himself to be a changed person today. He is fearful of the label "chronic" because he wants to feel that he can change.

Results of Examination

A. Intellectual Factors

Ten subtests of the Wechsler Adult Intelligence Scale–Revised were administered with the following results:

Factor	Deviation IQ	Percentile
Verbal scale	99	47th
Performance scale	93	33rd
Full scale	96	40th

The above results place Mr. Browne in the Average range of intellectual capacity. No significant scatter. These results are in keeping with previous estimates of intellectual capacity.

B. Neuropsychological Factors

The results of the Luria-Nebraska Neuropsychological Battery indicate no signs of central nervous system damage.

C. Reading Skills

The results of the Gates-MacGinitie Reading Test—Survey D—indicate that Mr. Browne is a functional reader and has very good vocabulary and comprehension. His responses to the written tests can be considered entirely valid.

D. Personality Factors

(1) *Interpersonal Activity.* The profile presented by Mr. Browne is that of a serious thinking disorder. About 2 percent of males in psychiatric populations show this profile. His thinking and behavior is frequently marked by confusion and misunderstanding. Thinking is markedly unconventional. His thoughts tend to be fragmented and tangential. He will be seen as frequently making impulsive, unrealistic decisions that show emotional unpredictability. His behavior is often hostile and suspicious, showing the Distress Syndrome (nervousness, anxiety, and depression). His ideas tend to be scattered, confused, and contaminated. His associations are often autistic and bizarre. People who know him will report sudden outbursts of unfriendliness and anger for no apparent reason. His choices and decisions are disorganized and represent behavior regression. The pattern is entirely in keeping with the history reported by the patient and the behavior reported by those who have seen him in his daily life.

(2) *Early Identifications.* His projective techniques, interviews, and personality tests suggest that the parental models were vague, disturbed, and without real substance. The mother and father were apparently frequently in conflict. Although the mother was the primary figure in his life, Mr. Browne has always been fearful of losing her love. She was apparently quite rejecting. The father was an unknown, frightening figure who became a "monster" when he drank. Mr. Browne fantasizes some sort of integration with the father figure into his life, in a delusional way.

(3) *Anxiety Structure.* Mr. Browne has no real feeling about the integrity of his body or his mind. He has no inner identity. He feels no ties to the past. He has very severe mixed feelings of repulsion and attraction in respect to his father. He experiences terror when he feels he will lose female support. He has no idea of the appropriate sexual role he should play in terms of capacity, skill, responsibility, or acceptability. His sexual identification is superficial and fragmented.

(4) *Outlets and Defenses.* Intellectual defenses abound but are of extremely poor quality. His ego is seldom of any strength. He behaves in an antisocial manner, megalomaniacal, sometimes sadistic and punishing. He can be extremely self-righteous without any realistic basis for it. He deals with new situations with suspicion, without any relation to reality. He is ruminative and overideational.

He suffers a severe psychosis. His defenses are quite deteriorated, and when there is any kind of stress or lack of chemical control, his basic schizophrenic personality structure will emerge. It is characterized by paranoia and delusional systems. He can be suicidal, and in the future, there is a potential for homicidal behavior.

Summary and Conclusions

Analysis of the records of Mr. Albert Browne, his previous professional evaluations, his history, and the current psychological evaluation indicates that he is a man of Average intellectual capacity, suffering a very severe mental illness with concomitant social disorders. Although at the time of our evaluation, Mr. Browne was under control and not experiencing florid psychotic behavior, the psychosis was clearly found to be present. In answer to the questions posed at the beginning of this assessment, the following can be said on the basis of all the previously noted material:

1. Mr. Browne suffers a fixed, long-term mental disease with concomitant defects. It is agreed among all professionals who have examined him that this defect is Schizophrenia, Paranoid Type (DSM III 295.3x).

2. Mr. Browne has suffered this condition for most, if not all, of his adult life.

3. There are times, during the florid aspects of this condition, where Mr. Browne lacks substantial capacity to appreciate the wrongfulness of his conduct (marrying a woman while he was still married to a first woman, stealing money to fulfill the wishes and demands of a dead father with whom he has consulted in his hallucinations, threatening his wife with imminent death).

4. During florid episodes of his psychosis, Mr. Browne has been unable to conform his conduct to the requirements of the law (note the above, plus driving at reckless rates of speed for 600 miles to speak with his dead father at the grave, as a result of his delusional system, attempting to "run over" or to shoot delusional figures that he thought were after him, and so forth).

5. Although Mr. Browne has acted in an antisocial manner, this has been a minute part of the manifestation of his condition.

Mr. Browne seems to do well when under medication and under little stress. His potential for dangerousness to himself and to others is quite high without proper supervision and treatment.

In the psychological report, no effort was made to determine whether Browne was insane or sane at the time of the bank robbery. The psychologist was prepared to testify, as an expert in such matters, that Browne suffered a well-known mental disease with consequent mental defects most of his adult life. Furthermore, the psychologist was prepared to testify that Browne, as a result of defects of perception and volition, was subject to florid psychotic episodes and that during such episodes Browne was more likely to be driven or governed by his delusions and hallucinations than by rational thought, usual societal controls, and legal standards. Browne's claim that he was finally winning his dead father's love and approval by stealing money to buy the farm that his father wanted was in keeping with Browne's circumscribed delusions about communicating with the dead father.

Whether Mr. Browne was sane, beyond reasonable doubt, at the time he robbed the bank is a decision to be reached by the jurors. The psychologist's role, as expert, in matters of insanity, is *not* to testify as to the ultimate issue but is to provide the jury with an opinion as to the defendant's psychological condition and potential for episodes of behavior that meet the legal criteria of insanity.

8

Domestic Issues: Marriage, Dissolution, and Custody

The right to marry and create a family is held to be fundamental in almost all societies. Very little beyond being of legal age and having the capacity to make a contract is required for a marriage (Clark, 1974). Although there may be legal matters at the time of marriage, such as prenuptial agreements, contracts, and property transfer arrangements, issues of law tend to occur after the marriage or living arrangement of an unmarried couple has existed for some time.

The practice of family law has been considered to be of low status in the legal profession until recently. Issues such as divorce mediation, wrongful birth, adoption of babies of surrogate mothers, and postdivorce disputes of various types have received increasing attention from the courts. Family issues are the most likely reason for a person in American society today to be exposed to the court system; for instance, 60% of people with postdivorce problems go to court, as against 20% for accidents. The practice of family law has burgeoned into a broad and open field of practice. In the four years from 1980 to 1983, the membership in the American Bar Association's Family Law Section has grown from 6000 to 14,500. The most frequent and major issues in family law are property rights and child custody (Dullea, 1983). Divorcing is simpler than ever before with 48 of 50 states having "no-fault" laws. For every two marriages today, there is one divorce. This may make divorce easier for marital partners, but it places almost impossible burdens on the courts, to say nothing of the children of the broken marriages (Press, 1983).

In some jurisdictions, the same courts handle conflicts relating to marriage, divorce, juvenile misbehavior, abuse, battery, and custody, whereas in others, judges are designated as "juvenile," "domestic relations," or "family" judges. A judicial circuit is likely to have certain judges who hear all family matters. In a sense, such judges represent mergers of court structure with social services. Conflicts over jurisdiction, consistency, and the quality of social services are found in these settings. Efforts to organize and standardize family court procedures have resulted in the promulgation of standards (Institute of Judicial Administration, 1977). Some critics have expressed concern that organization of family court systems has attended too much to the efficiency of the judicial process at the expense of issues of effectiveness and outcome (Scanlon & Weingarten, 1963).

Merging the court system and its responsibility for family matters with social science has resulted in the development of a variety of assumptions about family dynamics, child growth and development, juvenile behavior, and appropriate treatment of family problems. The judiciary has a tendency to assign simplistic and frequently inappropriate causation and solutions to family conflict or dysfunction. The family court's treatment philosophy can sometimes disrupt the family system rather than provide helpful guidance or constraints. The courts have a poor record of diagnostic prediction concerning such questions as: Who should have child custody? Which children or parents may be dangerous? What are the effects of foster care? and Which parent is best able to enhance the child's development? (Mulvey, 1982) With the ever-mounting divorce rate, issues of custody and the child's adjustment to a one-parent family have risen. In 1970, the proportion of children living in one-parent families was 12%; by 1980, it had become 20%. In 1970, there were 47 divorced persons per 1000 married persons, while in 1980, the ratio had risen to 109 per 1000. In 1981, approximately 12.6 million children lived with one parent, according to the 1981 population survey of the Census Bureau (Strout, 1982).

CUSTODIAL ISSUES

Current Perspectives

In about 85% of all divorces or dissolutions, custody of the children is awarded to the mother without contest from the father (Weitzman & Dixon, 1979). Even when the divorce is contested, the court has usually awarded custody of the children to the mother (Freed & Foster, 1981). In recent years the frequency of naming fathers the custodial parent has increased (Molinoff, 1977). Even unmarried fathers have been deemed to have custodial rights.[1]

The contemporary style of custodial award is joint custody (sometimes labeled "shared responsibility"). This rests on the concept that children have the right to keep alive their relationship with both parents. It allows divorced fathers to have more say in their children's everyday lives and is designed to ease the pressures of single parenthood.

Until 1839, children of divorce were automatically awarded to the father

---

[1] *Rothstein v. Lutheran Social Services,* 59 Wis.2d 1, 207 N.W.2d 826 (1973).

as a form of "property." From the midnineteenth to the midtwentieth centuries, the awarding of children in custody matters depended heavily on the "tender years doctrine." Known as a "judge's shibboleth," or informal rule, this doctrine suggested that mothers are able to provide better and more loving, "natural" care than fathers. During the past two decades, this doctrine has been seriously questioned. The Uniform Marriage and Divorce Act (National Conference of Commissioners, 1971) recommends:

> The court shall determine custody in accordance with the best interests of the child. The court shall consider all relevant factors including: (1) the wishes of the child's parent or parents as to his custody; (2) the wishes of the child as to his custodian; (3) the interaction and interrelationship of the child with his parents, his siblings, and any other person who may significantly affect the child's best interests; (4) the child's adjustment to his home, school, and community; and (5) the mental and physical health of all individuals involved. The court shall not consider conduct of a proposed custodian that does not affect his relationship to the child.

In spite of these recommendations, many courts continue to depend on subjective judgment and traditional concepts (Ruback, 1982).

Current research casts question on the traditional concepts of the importance of early bonding with the mother (Ainsworth, 1973; Brody, 1983). Many fathers have been found to be competent primary caretakers. Their children seem to do as well as or better than children in sole custody of the mother (Santruck & Warshak, 1979).

Joint Custody

At this writing, 28 states permit or give priority to joint custody of children following marriage dissolution. Each state has a different set of guidelines and generally spells out the details of the concept and delineates the judge's responsibilities. An example of a recent joint-custody law, enacted in Florida, follows:

Be It Enacted by the Legislature of the State of Florida:

Section 1. Subsection (3) and paragraph (b) of subsection (2) of section 61.13, Florida Statutes, are amended to read:

61.13 Custody and support of children, etc., power of court in making orders.—

(2)

(b)1. The court shall determine all matters relating to custody of each minor child of the parties as a part of any proceeding under this chapter in accordance with the best interests of the child and in accordance with the Uniform Child Custody Jurisdiction Act. It is the public policy of this state to assure each minor child frequent and continuing contact with both parents after the parents have separated or dissolved their marriage and to encourage parents to share the rights and responsibilities of child-rearing. Upon considering all relevant factors, the father of the child shall be given the same consideration as the mother in determining custody regardless of the age of the child.

2. The court shall order that the parental responsibility for a minor child shall be shared by both parents unless the court finds that shared parental responsibility would be detrimental to the child. If the court determines that shared parental responsibility would be detrimental to the child, the court may order sole parental responsibility.

a. "Shared parental responsibility means that both parents retain full parental rights and responsibilities with respect to their child, and requires both parents to confer so that major decisions affecting the welfare of the child will be determined jointly. In ordering shared parental responsibility, the court may consider the expressed desires of the parents and may grant to one party the ultimate responsibility over specific aspects of the child's welfare or the court may divide those aspects between the parties on the basis of the best interests of the child. Where it appears to the court to be in the best interests of the child, the court may order or the parties may agree how any such responsibility will be divided. Such areas of responsibility may include primary physical residence, education, medical and dental care, and any other responsibilities which the court finds unique to a particular family and/or in the best interests of the child.

b. "Sole parental responsibility" means responsibility of the minor child shall be given to one parent by the court, with or without rights of visitation to the other parent.

c. The court may award the grandparents visitation rights of a minor child if it is deemed by the court to be in the child's best interest. Grandparents shall have legal standing to seek judicial enforcement of such an award. Nothing in this section shall be construed to require that grandparents be made parties or given notice of dissolution pleadings or proceedings, nor shall such grandparents have legal standing as "contestants" as defined in §61.1306. No court shall order that a child be kept within the state or jurisdiction of the court solely for the purpose of permitting visitation by the grandparents.

3. Access to records and information pertaining to a minor child, including but not limited to medical, dental, and school records, shall not be denied to a parent because such parent is not the child's primary residential parent.

(3) For purposes of shared parental responsibility and primary physical residence, the best interests of the child shall be determined by the court's consideration and evaluation of all factors affecting the best welfare and interests of the child, including, but not limited to:

(a) The parent who is more likely to allow the child frequent and continuing contact with the nonresidential parent.

(b) The love, affection, and other emotional ties existing between the parents and the child.

(c) The capacity and disposition of the parents to provide the child with food, clothing, medical care or other remedial care recognized and permitted under the laws of this state in lieu of medical care, and other material needs.

(d) The length of time the child has lived in a stable, satisfactory environment and the desirability of maintaining continuity.

(e) The permanence, as a family unit, of the existing or proposed custodial home.

(f) The moral fitness of the parents.

(g) The mental and physical health of the parents.

(h) The home, school, and community record of the child.

(i) The reasonable preference of the child, if the court deems the child to be of sufficient intelligence, understanding, and experience to express a preference.

(j) Any other factor considered by the court to be relevant to a particular child custody dispute.[2]

Many marriage dissolutions result in a more informal "joint custody" and never come before the court. When a court mandates joint custody, or shared responsibility, there is usually some conflict regarding custody. Some attorneys are quite skeptical about whether these new procedures will result in significant lessening of custodial conflict. An appellate court has stated: "But despite our belief that joint custody will be a preferred disposition in some matrimonial actions, we decline to establish a presumption in its favor or in favor of any particular custody determination."[3]

The court opined that for joint custody to be workable and in the child's best interests, the parents must show a potential for cooperation in matters of child rearing. Some judges find that joint custody eases their conflicts in the Solomonic issue of "splitting the child." The facts involved in some custodial issues are mind-boggling. The joint-custody concept relieves the judge of the responsibility of dealing with these vague, tangential, and often convoluted issues.

Early research in joint custody suggests that it is not as simple a solution as it may appear. Parents tend to find the arrangement more convenient than the children. A large proportion of the children are overburdened by the demands of being part of two families in two homes (Steinman, 1981).

Divorce can be quite disturbing for children. The immediate results can be disruptions of school, play, and social relationships in preschool children (Hetherington, Cox, & Cox, 1979). There is reason to believe that the distress one sees in children two and more years following divorce is the result of parental instability, anxiety, and stress. The more relaxed and less

[2] Fla. Stat. §61.13 (1982).
[3] *Beck v. Beck*, 86 N.J. 480 (1981).

guilty the parent, the more likely the child will be spared extreme psychological reactions to the divorce (Luepnitz, 1978).

The myth that joint custody will prevent divorce from changing children's lives should not be encouraged. The reality is that no court can "order" joint custody and make it work. The parents must be able to suspend their own hostility, anxiety, guilt, and personal animosity. These are often long-standing and may be what led to the breakdown of the marriage in the first place. When joint custody is ordered for a family in spite of obvious personal antagonisms, it is a sham (Span & Cantor, 1983). Appellate courts are beginning to recognize that an order for joint custody is inappropriate where the parents have little potential for cooperation.[4] Research on the effects of various life-cycle changes, parenting styles, and home environments on joint-custody outcomes is sorely needed (Clingempeel & Reppucci, 1982).

In some instances, joint custody seems to work well. Some early research suggests that factors leading to success in joint custody include commitment to the arrangement, mutual support between the divorced parents, a flexible sharing of responsibility, and agreement on the implicit rules of the sharing system. Even with these positive factors, structural impediments may diminish success or satisfaction in a joint-custody arrangement. Structural factors include lack of geographic proximity, children getting older and insisting on more control of the arrangement, children insisting on one-home continuity, and stresses caused by a parent living with a new partner, creating blended families in one or both of the homes (Abarbanel, 1979).

There are some indications that fathers who participate in a joint-custody arrangement have a higher degree of involvement with their children than fathers who are granted visitation rights with children in sole custody of the mother (Greif, 1979). Although research about joint custody has been quite limited, with rather loose experimental designs, the consistency of a variety of reports suggests that some broken families are able to retain important bonds. About 30% of the couples who have joint-custody arrangements maintain a friendly, caring interaction, compared to 20% of a matched, single-custodian (mother) sample. Even when joint custody seems to work, it is likely that the formerly married partners are not "co-parenting" but are "parallel parenting," where each parent operates as a self-contained unit (Collins, 1982).

Parental Fitness

The court is likely to evaluate a wide range of factors in determining parental fitness. These include both the mental and the physical health of the proposed custodian.[5]

---

[4] *Mastropole v. Mastropole*, 181 N.J. Super. 130 (App. Div. 1981).
[5] *Atwood v. Atwood*, 550 S.W.2d 465 (Ky. 1976).

Although each state defines fitness in a variety of ways, judges are prone to consider such issues as the wishes of the child, the parents' desires, the sex of the child, adjustment to siblings, biological relationships, length of the custodial relationship, age of the child, age of the parents, school and community status, parents' moral character, financial sufficiency, and the stability of the home. Psychological testimony is appropriate for some of these matters but not for others. The psychological expert is again warned not to go beyond the boundaries of recognized competence in testifying as to parental fitness. This will be addressed in the section "The Psychologist's Roles." (Table 8.1, which appears later in this chapter, presents the factors most influential in judge's decisions concerning parental fitness.)

Change of Custody

Petitions to modify custody are seldom granted. The initial custody decision is frequently challenged, and the issue is usually heard and decided by the same judge who mandated the original custody decision. Once custody is granted, a change is warranted only if it can be shown that the child will be placed in immediate jeopardy, emotional or physical, by continuation of the custodial arrangement.[6,7] Thus in order to effect a change in a previously agreed-upon and mandated custodial arrangement, the petitioner must demonstrate to the court's satisfaction that the child is likely to suffer a fairly immediate danger to growth and development if the existing arrangement is continued. In this instance, the best interests of the child are very narrowly defined as imminent danger to his or her physical or emotional state. This is the essential reason why a relatively small number of petitions for change of custody are granted. A noncustodial parent would be well advised to proceed cautiously in petitioning for a change of custody when the reasons do not meet the criteria of immediate danger to the child's physical or mental health.

Visitation

The courts usually mandate that the child should have reasonable and frequent contact with both parents in a joint-custody arrangement and with the noncustodial parent in sole-custody situations. Each judge is apparently guided by his or her own standards. At the 1983 annual meetings of the American Academy of Marital Attorneys, a family judge stated that "regardless of the circumstances" he insisted that the children spend two weekends per month with the noncustodial parent. A well-known judge is noted for his predilection to insist that the noncustodial parent take up residence within walking distance of the custodial parent's residence and

---

[6] *Hutchins v. Hutchins,* 220 So.2d 438 (Fla. App. 1969).
[7] *Collins v. Newton,* 362 So.2d 174 (Fla. App. 1978).

that the children spend alternate nights in the divorced parents' separate homes. Most judges favor visitation plans which concentrate on vacations and holidays rather than on the needs of a specific child. Together with issues of monetary support, visitation conflicts are likely to be the most frequent reasons for petitions to modify custodial decisions.

OTHER FAMILY AND CHILD ISSUES

Child Abuse

All states have a variety of regulations and procedures designed to protect children's physical and emotional health. A community agency, operating under state laws, is usually vested with responsibility for identifying instances of child abuse and bringing these to the attention of the courts. The most frequent sources of such complaints are the reports of neighbors or the resource personnel at the child's school. When a complaint is made, the child is frequently taken from the home and placed in a protective-custody situation until the issue is settled at court.

The following represents the type of petition filed in such cases.

In the Circuit Court of the Thirteenth Judicial Circuit of
the State of Florida, in and for Hillsborough County
JUVENILE AND DOMESTIC RELATIONS DIVISION

CASE NO. X-137-B

In the Interest of: Jane Doe   83-6274A

—————————————————————— , Child ——————————————————

PETITION

To the Judge of the Juvenile and Domestic Relations Division: Your petitioner, Mary Smith, District Intake Counselor , respectfully represents under the Court that Jane Doe

---

residing at 123 Elm Street, Tampa, Florida of the age of 14 years, (is) (XXX) a dependent child within the intent and meaning of Chapter 39 of the Florida Statutes, in that, the petitioner is informed and believes, that: Jane Doe is an abused child in that her parents permitted the child to live in an environment which would likely cause physical, mental, or emotional injury to the child or cause the child's physical, mental, or emotional health to be in danger of being significantly impaired. To Wit: On March 6, 1983, James Doe threatened to strike Jane with an awl, and a belt. Further, Mr. Doe hit Jane about the body. Jane states that on numerous occasions she has been threatened with physical harm by her father and she is very fearful of him. Mrs. Doe admitted putting bruises on the child's arm when the child did not clean the bathroom as told.

Jane Doe is an emotionally neglected child in that her parents, although financially able, deprived the child of, or allowed the child to be deprived of, the necessary medical treatment or permitted the child to live in an environment when such deprivation or environment causes the child's mental and emotional health to be significantly impaired or to be in danger of being significantly impaired. To Wit: Mr. Doe admitted to emotionally neglecting and threatening the child with a belt. Mr. Doe has stated he feels his child does have serious emotional problems which he has not sought counseling for in the past.

The names of the parents or legal custodians of the child ___Jane___ are: __James and Mary Doe__
residence and address is ___123 Elm Street, Tampa, Florida___ whose relation to said child ___Jane___ to that of ___parents___ . Wherefore your petitioner requests that the Court take jurisdiction of the child ___Jane___ and if the facts alleged are true, adjudicate the child ___Jane___ to be __a dependent__ child _____ .

Date: ___3.29.83___

___Mary Smith___
Petitioner

State of Florida
Hillsborough County } SS.

_____Mary Smith_____ , the petitioner who subscribed ___her___ name to the foregoing petition in my presence, being duly sworn, deposes and says that the allegations contained in said petition are, to the best of information and belief, true, that this petition is filed in good faith.

___J. D. Brown___

Most communities have arrangements for the investigation of such charges by caseworkers. Psychological evaluation of the child and the parents is frequently conducted by mental health professionals on the staff of local institutions or by independent professionals who are retained as experts. The parents have the right to retain their own mental health professionals to evaluate the parties in the alleged abusive situation. Judges rely quite heavily on the reports of social workers, psychologists, and psychiatrists in these matters.

Juvenile Misbehavior

Juvenile offenders tend to be treated with special concern and leniency by the courts. Judges tend to be much more sanguine about rehabilitating youthful offenders than adult felons.

In matters of delinquency, the juvenile, usually under 17 years of age, has traditionally been "taken over" by the court, which acts as *parens patriae*, or responsible custodian. In 1967, the Supreme Court held that juveniles have a wide range of rights.[8] In these criminal cases, judges are very responsive to social service investigations and psychological reports when deciding the disposition of the case.

The larger group of judicial proceedings involving juveniles is called "status offenses" (truancy, running away, lack of parental control, promiscuity, drinking, and so on). Judges have very wide discretion in the disposition of such cases (Glaser, 1979). Reports from social workers, caseworkers, and mental health experts are well received by most judges. For first offenders, probation or warnings and remedial recommendations are usual.

Adoption

Although very elaborate procedures have been developed by most adoption agencies, and state laws can be quite specific, the advice of professional mental health workers is rarely sought before an adoptive decision is made. Adoption procedures vary greatly: The rather casual, physician-arranged adoptions stand in contrast to the often rigid agency requirements focusing on socioeconomic status, age, community stability, and so on. Rarely are psychologists called upon for an expert opinion in these matters. Occasionally, when prospective parents are "questionable," a psychological evaluation may be requested to attest to their aptitude and stability in respect to parenting.

Marital Reconciliation and Mediation

Although a divorce is easier to obtain than ever before, as noted in the introduction to this chapter, some judges are reluctant to grant dissolution of a marriage until the couple has sought professional help in an effort to save the marriage. In such instances where the reconciliation fails or where the couple wishes to challenge the reconciliation mandate, the psychologist may be called upon to evaluate the partners and render an opinion as to the feasibility of reconciliation.

Although this is less likely to occur now than in the past, most states have passed or are considering legislation mandating that mediation to

---

[8] *In Re. Gault*, 387 U.S. 1, 87 S.Ct. 1428, 18 L.Ed.2d 527 (1967).

settle adversary issues be recommended before formal court litigation in a marriage dissolution takes place. The concept of mediation is well-intentioned. Mediation consists of several (usually half a dozen) sessions with the disputing marital partners and an attorney as well as a mental health professional, who may be a psychologist, a social worker, or a family specialist. The goals or benefits of this nonjudicial procedure include:

1. A less stressful environment to help ease the bitterness of the marital breakup
2. A less expensive modality than the adversary system
3. Time savings for the court and the marital partners
4. Assistance in working through custody issues with fewer damaging side effects than in traditional adversary resolutions
5. Opportunity to benefit from therapeutic intervention due to non-threatening procedures and professional expertise

Many lawyers and judges have serious questions about mediation as a realistic solution to divorce conflicts. Some lawyers feel that divorce mediation may be the unlawful or unethical practice of law. Laws concerning property are more complex today than ever before, and a matrimonial lawyer in a mediation situation may not be able to protect the rights of both parties. A single attorney in a mediation situation may become hopelessly involved in a conflict of interest in dealing with both spouses. Some states mandate that an attorney may not form any kind of partnership with a nonlawyer in matters related to the practice of law.[9] Although many matrimonial attorneys have given their time to early settlement programs, such programs differ from mediation in that no fee is charged.

It has been suggested that mediation represents a philosophical attack on the adversary system in marital dissolution. It is suggested that if two attorneys are involved, there is less of a chance that some significant aspect of the law will be missed to the detriment of one or both spouses. In mediation, one lawyer is more likely to miss such points. In favor of the adversary system, it is argued that without competent counsel the passive partner in a divorce may agree to things not in his or her best interests. In mediation, the mediators may not fully inform each participant of their rights for fear of encouraging hostility or negativism in the mediation setting. Thus many attorneys fear that mediation can result in uninformed and ill-advised settlements.

Although most matrimonial lawyers applaud the concept of mediation to enhance a positive relationship between the divorcing spouses, there is concern that such efforts may be made at the expense of a spouse's long-term legal rights. Additionally, since only about 5% of all matrimonial matters are tried as contested cases, some lawyers question the value of

[9] Disciplinary Rule 2-103, New Jersey Bar.

adding a procedure that may, in the end, increase rather than decrease court time (Executive Committee, 1983).

Some attorneys believe mediation can work in spite of the concerns noted above (Gourvitz, 1983). The Association of the Bar of the City of New York has set forth some safeguards in these matters:

1. The lawyer must clearly and fully advise the parties of the limitations on his or her role and, specifically, of the fact that the lawyer represents neither party and that, accordingly, they should not look to the lawyer to protect their individual interests or to keep confidences of one party from the other.

2. The lawyer must fully and clearly explain the risks of proceeding without separate legal counsel and thereafter proceed only with the consent of the parties and only if the lawyer is satisfied that the parties understand the risks and understand the significance of the fact that the lawyer represents neither party.

3. A lawyer may participate with mental health professionals in those aspects of mediation which do not require the exercise of professional legal judgement and involve the same kind of mediation activities permissible to lay mediators.

4. Lawyers may provide impartial legal advice and assist in reducing the parties' agreement to writing only where the lawyer fully explains all pertinent considerations and alternatives and the consequences to each party of choosing the resolution agreed upon.

5. The lawyer may give legal advice only to both parties in the presence of the other.

6. The lawyer must advise the parties of the advantages of seeking independent legal counsel before executing any agreement drafted by the lawyer.

7. The lawyer may not represent either of the parties in any subsequent legal proceedings relating to the divorce.[10]

Thus the law is well on its way to setting guidelines and limits in mediation style. As yet, no substantial research is available to suggest whether mediation is useful, and if so, under what conditions.

Property Agreement Challenges

On rare occasions, a contested divorce action may involve property settlement issues where one of the spouses agreed to a business matter, such as transfer of property, stock ownership, corporate voting rights, and so forth, during the course of the marriage. At the time of the dissolution, the spouse who previously gave up property or rights may indicate that he or she did so under unusual emotional strain and was not able to act in his or her own best interests.

---

[10] N.Y.C. B.A. Comm. on Professional & Judicial Ethics No. 80-23 (Feb. 27, 1981).

An example of this might be the case in which a wife was an officer in her husband's corporation, holding a significant block of stock in the corporation. During a stormy period in the latter phases of the marriage, the wife discovered that the husband had become emotionally involved with a woman executive in one of their subsidiary corporations. During the course of their various arguments, the husband proposed that the wife sign over all her stock rights to him, so that this issue would not interfere with their efforts to reconcile. The wife, a severely dependent person, fearing the loss of the husband, complied. Four years later the husband filed for divorce. In evaluating the assets of the marriage prior to the final agreement, the wife's attorney discovered the circumstances of the stock transfer and filed a claim for the wife's original share of the corporation. The husband's position was that the wife willingly exchanged the stock for other considerations and was not entitled to the value of the original stock. The wife had seen two different psychologists during the stressful period of the marriage. Both were deposed by the wife's attorney to determine whether she indeed was unable to make business decisions in her own best interests at the time of the stock transfer. One had conducted an evaluation, and the other was the wife's therapist. Both were able to testify that their records showed that the wife was an inordinately dependent person, morbidly fearful of losing her husband, and willing to do almost anything to placate him and keep the marriage intact.

As psychology continues to expand its research base, both in new areas and in replication studies, the range of opportunity for psychologists to serve as experts in family law is likely to broaden.

THE PSYCHOLOGIST'S ROLES

There are, at this writing, no standards for the delivery of psychological services to families in legal conflict or to courts seeking help from expert witnesses in dealing with difficult and complex custodial decisions. Standards already developed by the American Psychological Association for the delivery of professional services (APA, 1977), the code of ethics of psychologists (APA, 1981), and the principles for the use and interpretation of psychological tests (Chapter 5) apply to the work of psychologists in domestic relations or family court issues.

Traditionally, psychologists have been called upon for evaluation and expert testimony in a variety of matters in family court:

1. Psychological status and needs of a child and the best interests of a child
2. Fitness of the mother as sole parent
3. Fitness of the father as sole parent

4. Parents' potential as joint custodians
5. Significance of grandparents in the child's life
6. Change of custody petitions
7. Current scientific thought on issues of child development and family dynamics
8. Visitation plans
9. The child's potential for dangerousness to self and others
10. Potential of parents as abusers
11. Issues of mental status at time of property agreement

No research area in psychology is growing more rapidly than child development and family interaction. As new research is forthcoming, supporting some concepts and casting question on others, the psychologist who serves as an expert witness in these areas cannot afford to testify on the basis of what he or she learned in graduate school or "several years ago." The fields of family interaction and structure as well as child growth and development are dynamic, benefiting from a continuing infusion of data from research programs and demonstration projects. The work of the psychologist as an expert witness is subject to public scrutiny in the courts and should reflect excellent training, professional competence, awareness of current research, and adherence to the highest ethical and professional standards. Examples of the work of psychologists as expert witnesses in family law will be presented in some detail.

The Psychological Status of the Child and the Child's Best Interests

In the effort to administer custody decisions, the courts often seek professional advice, guidance, and even justification, and when the courts are addressing the best interests of the child, an evaluation of the child's psychological status is often helpful. Ideally, such an evaluation would include:

1. *The Facts of the Case.* The psychologist should be provided with as objective a set of facts in the matter as possible. This may prove difficult when the expert is retained by the attorney for one parent or the other in an adversary matter. Sometimes, the psychologist must accept the attorney's presentation of the facts, which should be obtained in writing since attorneys are usually more objective when committing the facts of a case to a document. When the expert serves as amicus curiae in custodial issues, the judge usually presents both the facts of the case and the questions to be addressed by the expert.

2. *Background Factors.* Ideally, the psychologist will take a history from both parties in the disputed issue. This is not always possible, and if

history is taken from one parent only, the psychologist must view the parent's judgmental responses cautiously. If both parents are interviewed, discrepancies in the history should be noted and, as far as possible, omitted from the psychologist's assessment process. Interviews with the child are important. Those who do not use psychological tests may depend heavily on interviews (Gardner, 1982).

3. *School Adjustment.*   An interview with the child's teachers is often helpful in assessing the child's adjustment to the most significant segment of time in his or her life. Children spend 30–40 hours per week in school, and their response to this setting is an important consideration in the evaluation of the child's adjustment.

4. *Psychological Status.*   Decisions concerning custodial placement, visitation, treatment, or remedial education should be made with an objective view of the child's current status, special abilities, needs, and problems. Such an examination should generally include:

    a. A thorough evaluation of intellectual status and potential

    b. An evaluation of neuropsychological factors

    c. An assessment of academic achievement

    d. A personality evaluation and measures of personal adjustment

Specific tests and procedures will depend on the age and background of the child.

5. *Report of Findings.*   A report of the findings of the psychological evaluation must be made available to the retaining attorney. In addition to the objective findings, the psychologist should summarize the results and state, as specifically as possible, the child's current developmental status, the child's anticipated needs, and specific remedial or therapeutic recommendations. The expert should remember that the decision as to custody will be made by the court. The psychologist must avoid making that decision in the report of the evaluation of the child.

In reporting a child's current psychological status, the psychologist must be aware of current research concerning the effects of divorce on children so that findings of psychological dysfunction are not misattributed to inappropriate causalities. Much is known about the child's reaction to family conflict (Beal, 1979; Glick, 1979; Hetherington, 1979; Hetherington, Cox, & Cox, 1979; Luepnitz, 1978; Rutter, 1971; Wallerstein & Kelly, 1975). The psychologist who acts as an expert witness in custodial matters should be aware of the contrasts between children of fractured families and children of intact families.

These suggested procedures are ideal but not always practical or possible. The extent and completeness of a psychological evaluation may be influenced by the constraints placed on participants by the attorneys in the case or by the judge. Where these constraints seriously interfere with the conduct of an adequate evaluation, the psychologist must make this known, in writing if necessary. Should the constraints continue, the psychologist may have to withdraw from the case.

The following psychological report and testimony involve a petition for change of custody. Initial contact was made by the attorney representing the father. The divorce took place when the male child was 16 months of age. Both the mother and the father had remarried. The father had maintained regular contact with his son via visitation arrangements set by the court. As the boy began to mature, the father became concerned about the youngster's emotional development and sexual identification. A petition for change of custody was filed, and the psychological examination was conducted to determine whether such a change was likely to be in the child's best interests.

Originally, both the mother and father were to be interviewed as part of the assessment. The attorneys for the mother decided that the mother should not be interviewed, so the entire history was given by the father. School records were retrieved and provided by the father. The following report resulted from the evaluation of the youngster.

PSYCHOLOGICAL REPORT

June 13, 1978

NAME: Doe, Jack

DATE OF EXAMINATION: 5/19, 6/2, 6/5, 6/14/78

ADDRESS: 123 Elm Street,
Palatka, Florida 31702

TELEPHONE: 000-0000

BIRTHDATE: 3/10/70   AGE: 7-9

OCCUPATION: Student

EDUCATION: 2.9

Referral

This youngster is referred via R. M. Roe, esquire. Mr. Roe is attorney for Albert M. Doe, the father, who is concerned about his son's emotional adjustment. The boy has been living with his mother. The mother remarried in 1975. Mr. Doe feels that from that point on communication between himself and his child deteriorated rapidly.

The purpose of the assessment is to answer a number of questions:

1. Is there cause for concern as to how this youngster is developing psychologically?
2. What kind of custodial arrangements are likely to be best for the boy at this stage in his life?

3. Is he in a setting likely to be conducive to masculine identification and optimum opportunity to develop his potential?
4. Are there any specific recommendations that would be made in view of psychological findings?

Background Factors

The information is provided by Mr. Doe. He states that he and his ex-wife were married in 1964 while the father was in college. He feels that he married because it was the "normal thing to do." He found that their personalities did not match. They have been divorced for six and one-half years at the time of this assessment. Mr. Doe states that he is regretful that his son has had to pay a price for the divorce.

The mother, Mrs. Jane Smith, received her divorce in 1972 after seven years of marriage to her husband. Jack was 16 months of age at that time. The mother is said to be 34 years of age. She has a bachelor's degree in education. She is described as a heavy smoker and overweight.

The stepfather is Mr. Bill Smith, about 37 years of age. He is a computer salesman.

The real father, Albert M. Doe, is a 38-year-old accountant. He received his education at Yale and at Case. He is in good health. He remarried two years ago. The stepmother, Harriet, is a 29-year-old HRS Child Support Enforcement professional. She has a bachelor's degree from Georgia State University.

The custody arrangements at the present time are that Mr. Doe picks up the youngster every two weeks. Mr. Doe also has five weeks in the summer. Mr. Doe complains that his ex-wife refers to him as "Al" and doesn't encourage the boy to call him "Father" or "Dad." The mother has been describing the stepfather as "Jack's Father." Mr. Doe insists that he has never spoken to his son negatively about the boy's mother. He feels however that his ex-wife speaks disparagingly of him.

Jack sees the paternal grandparents on Sunday afternoons. He also sees the maternal grandmother. As far as Mr. Doe knows, they all get along well.

He weighed eight pounds at birth. Early growth and development are described as occurring essentially within normal limits. He has attended with a general practitioner in Tampa, according to the father. The father plans a thorough dental evaluation in the near future.

He still maintains some childhood habits. He cannot complete his own bathroom behavior and tells the father he needs wiping.

The father states that the boy hit a wall at age seven and one-half and was "unconscious" according to the youngster's reports. He sleeps fitfully and reports nightmares.

The boy had preschool at Mulberry, and the first grade at Palatka Heights. As far as the father knows, the boy is doing average work. Father visited the school three months ago. The boy seems to seek attention and is slightly disruptive.

At the father's home he has his own room. The father tries to encourage him to get outdoors. The father is concerned that he may be watching too much TV at the mother's home. The father has occasionally spanked him. The father has taken him camping. Jack enjoys boating, fishing, and swimming. He likes to look for fossils.

The father gives him a dollar every two weeks as an allowance. The father tries to associate this with instructions to mind the mother and to do what is expected. Bedtime is between eight and eight thirty.

On occasion Mr. Doe and his ex-wife have had some altercations about Jack's visitation and how holidays might be spent.

Currently Jack suffers from constipation. He seems to be fitful in sleep. There has been a little bit of stuttering for the past year and one-half. He reports nightmares and will call out to his father two or three times a night. He is still fearful of the dark, and at home he is said to sleep with a night-light. He is somewhat dependent, slightly shy, and tends to be moody at times.

Mr. Doe forwards a report from Jackson Epp, M.D., who reports in a brief letter to Woodworth Pell, esquire that Jack was evaluated on January 27, 1978, using a psychiatric interview, a Bender-Gestalt, and a Draw-a-Person Test. He states that there is no evidence of organicity or psychosis. He states that Jack appears to be adjusting well in his present situation. This cannot be considered an adequate psychological evaluation.

Examination Procedures

Wechsler Intelligence Scale for Children–Revised, Peabody Picture Vocabulary Test, Torque Test (repeated), Indiana Reitan Neuropsychological Short Form, Metropolitan Achievement Tests, Thematic Apperception Test, Draw-a-Person Test, Child Sentence Completion Test, House-Tree Test, History, Observation, and Interview.

Response to Evaluation

Jack is a round-faced youngster with brown hair and brown eyes. He appears to be close and affectionate with his father. He looks somewhat like his father. His speech is clear with a slight scratchiness. Hearing is within normal limits. Motor behavior is controlled. He fidgets slightly, appropriate to age. He socializes in a quiet, polite manner. He enjoys playing and interacting. Cooperation is good. His confidence seems fairly good.

He has had camping experience, but he says he is not too sure he is going to enjoy it again.

Results of Examination

A. *Intellectual Factors*

Results of the WISC-R are as follows:

Factor	Deviation IQ	Percentile
Verbal scale	123	93rd
Performance scale	132	98th
Full scale	131	98th

The above results suggest that this youngster falls in the Superior to Very Superior range of intellectual capacity. There is a slight lowering in arithmetic reasoning and attention span, but all other factors fall in the Superior ranges. The lowering is probably an artifact of age and development.

Results of the Peabody Picture Vocabulary Test place Jack at the 96th percentile, confirming the results of the WISC-R. The youngster has a mental age of approximately 11 years at the present time.

B. *Neuropsychological Factors*

The Torque Test indicates that Jack is solidly right-handed and left-brained with no evidence of mixed cerebral dominance. The Indiana Reitan Short Form indicates that central nervous system development is appropriate for age. No signs of anomalies.

C. *Achievement Factors*

Objective results of the Metropolitan Achievement Tests are as follows:

Factor	Grade Equivalent	Percentile (End of 2nd Grade)
Word Knowledge	3.7	86th
Word Analysis	2.6	44th
Reading Comprehension	2.9	64th
Spelling	2.7	42nd
Math Computation	4.2	94th
Math Concepts	3.4	68th
Math Problem Solving	3.7	86th

The above results indicate that this youngster is ahead of his grade placement except for Word Analysis and Spelling. He should do quite well in the third grade and probably ought to have a stimulating intellectual environment in his school.

D. *Personality Factors*

(1) *Interpersonal Activity.*   This is a youngster who for his age is quite cautious about expecting success. He seems fearful of thinking about good things coming to him. He enjoys physical activity most of all. His basic values and character are good.

(2) *Early Identifications.*   Primary identification is with the father. The unconscious picture of the father is that of a fairly aggressive person who is powerful. He sees the father unconsciously as an individual who tries to separate emotion from intellect. The father is seen as a person who feels pleasant with his child. Father has a poor tolerance for hostility and sees calmness and control as a primary value. Father can be quite stubborn. He controls his emotions and does not like to be too spontaneous.

The mother is the love object. She is seen unconsciously as a person who has high aspiration. She is often unable to face her own limitations, denying that they exist. She denies stress. She can be quite impetuous. She can blow up in a volatile manner. When frustrated, she becomes extrapunitive, blaming those around her. He sees her unconsciously as having a poor tolerance for frustration. She can be quite nourishing to her children. She insists that they be dependent upon her. She has a compulsion to know everything that's going on and prefers the children have no secrets. She is a relatively traditional, available mother.

(3) *Anxiety Structure.*   Jack is going through a very important emotional stage in his life. He is fearful of many things. One of the most frightening things to him is the expectancy of maturity. He fears he cannot do the large number of things he sees coming up in the future. He has a great many masculine-aggressive impulses but fears that these are unacceptable. He thinks that expressing anger is intolerable to older people.

He is unsure about the nature of the real world and tends to substitute television values. These are quite aggressive and frightening to him.

He is quite frightened of taking risks. He would like to take the initiative, but he fears this. He is developing fairly normal negative attitudes toward his mother as he prepared to move into the latency period where he will relate more to males than to females. He fears being engulfed by the mother and yet feels vulnerable about the future without her. Thus he has a dependence–independence conflict with her.

(4) *Defense Structure and Outlets.*   His intellectual defenses include a tendency to be very dependent and compliant. When he is frightened, he seeks all kinds of intellectual reasons to avoid trying new things. He gets a great deal of relief through fantasy, although this is somewhat frightening to him.

When his anxiety is not settled by intellectual defenses, and avoiding what is uncomfortable, he begins to regress to earlier levels of behavior. He gets some relief from his science-fiction fantasy. He is beginning to develop phobias in order to punish himself for his guilt feelings about his own anger. Swimming seems to give him a great deal of relief.

Summary and Recommendations

Psychological evaluation of Jack Doe indicates that he is a youngster of Very Superior intellectual capacity who seems to be growing intellectually and physiologically according to expectancy. His academic achievement indicates that he is ready for the third grade with no expectancy of difficulty. It is possible that the public school does not challenge him enough. The personality structure is that of a youngster with a mental age several years beyond his chronological age who is beginning to look to the future and wonder about his own capacity to meet expectancy. He suffers the anxiety and the dominance–submission conflicts of most youngsters who are victims of a split family. There is some evidence that his anxieties are being magnified by the amount of television that he watches. The personality structure is that of a youngster who is holding in and has been quite successful in this for some time. One can expect more rebelliousness in order to relieve the natural tension that comes with this stage of growth. The following recommendations seem appropriate:

1. He needs some additional stimulation to that which can be provided by the ordinary school setting. Special projects, visits to museums, traveling whenever possible to see educational types of presentations would be helpful. There is a gifted-child program at the University of South Florida, which operates on Saturdays, that would be helpful for him. He is eligible.

2. He ought to have summer camp and a chance to split off from the tense family situation.

3. He should be given as much encouragement as possible to experiment with new things, and both parents would do well to make an effort to give the boy less "no" and more "try."

4. He should have sex education from his father and appropriate materials will be provided.

5. Between now and his 11th year, he would profit considerably from fairly intense joint activity with his father. This should include building things, such as a tree house, going to the Go-Karts on weekends, learning fundamentals of physical activity, such as running, jumping, swimming, and so forth.

6. He should share common experiences with the father in learning traditional masculine values.

7. I believe for the next couple of years this boy should not watch any weekday television. Weekend television can be fairly unrestricted, but the presence of an adult to help him interpret complex situations, particularly aggression, would be helpful.

8. Both parents would do well to prepare to tolerate negativism and aggression. This is a natural part of a child growing up and learning

about his own power in the world. He should not be forced to be a
"compliant" child any more.

It is difficult to specify an exact custodial arrangement. No fractured marriage is good for children. They are going to be in conflict regardless of the
custodial arrangement. At this particular time in Jack's life, the more time
he spends with his father, probably the better, but this of course should
not be to the exclusion of regular interactions with the mother.

When the report was given to the father in a follow-up interview, it was
suggested that most judges consider a change of custody only when the
child's physical or psychological well-being is threatened. In spite of this,
and the fact that the father was clearly aware that his petition had little
chance of succeeding, he chose to go forward with the petition since he felt
strongly that his son's best interests would be served by a change of
custody.

Custody hearings are generally much more informal than the litigation
that takes place in a courtroom. The judge will often hear petitions in a
small conference-type room adjoining his or her office. Although legal
protocol and language characterize the proceedings, the degree of exactness in procedural matters reflects the degree of divisiveness between the
litigating parties. Where the issues are hard-fought, procedures tend to be
similar to those found in open court. Where the custodial issues are fairly
clear-cut and the adversary parties are on reasonably good terms, the judge
is likely to encourage an easier style of information exchange. Figure 8.1
shows a typical "judge's chambers" where custody issues are often heard.

The psychologist is asked to appear during the evidentiary portion of

FIGURE 8.1. A typical judge's suite, with C as the usual setting for custody hearings. A:
Office of the judge's secretary; B: judge's chambers; C: judge's hearing room; D: hearing room
reception area; and E: witness or lawyer's conference rooms.

the proceedings and is led through qualification and direct examination by the attorney for the petitioner. Following direct examination, the attorney for the defendant-parent is given the opportunity to cross-examine the witness. Often the psychologist's report is offered in evidence by the petitioner's attorney.

After attorneys for both the petitioning parent and the defendant-parent complete their examination of the expert witness, the judge usually has a period of questioning where he or she will attempt to clarify issues that will play a significant role in his or her custodial decision. Following the testimony by the psychologist in the case of Jack Doe, the judge chose to examine the expert as follows:

The Judge:	Mr. Doe touched on one matter that I am interested in. You had this young man tested for a period of some nine hours, and you had some contact with his father at a different time. I assume your interview with him was outside the presence of Mr. Doe, the father, wasn't it?
Dr. Blau:	My interview with the child? Oh, yes.
The Judge:	It was private?
Dr. Blau:	Those nine hours are spent only with the child. No parent is involved.
The Judge:	At any time did Jack, either voluntarily or spontaneously or in response to your questions, express his feeling about the stepfather or the stepmother?
Dr. Blau:	No, sir, he did not.
The Judge:	In neither case?
Dr. Blau:	No, sir. It is my experience that children of fractured families will bend over backward to give a neutral or positive recommendation to all parties concerned. They do not want to be the cause of any difficulty—none whatsoever. As I say, I make the assumption that all four natural and surrogate parents are first-rate. I saw no evidence to the contrary.
The Judge:	What opinion, if any, do you have, doctor, with respect to the workability of divided custody in the case of a child of this age, under these conditions?
Dr. Blau:	My only opinion is that the more complex a custody arrangement, the more complex the child's adjustment to it. It would depend entirely on the amount of stress placed on the parents because the child is going to be a reflection of the degree of personal comfort and self-satisfaction of the parents. Happy parents do tend to make happy children. Miserable parents seem to share it with the children, whether they wish to or not.
The Judge:	Does either counsel have any further questions?

PROPERTY OF
RIVERWOOD COMMUNITY MENTAL HEALTH

One can see that the judge is clarifying in his own mind that the child has nothing terrible to say about the new stepparents in Jack's two families. Also, the judge is seeking the expert's opinion as to whether sole custody is "workable" (read: "anything but disastrous for the child"). The report suggests that the best interest of Jack, at this stage of his development, would be served by his living with his father. The presiding judge's reluctance to modify a custody arrangement except under the most stringent circumstances involving the child's physical and psychological well-being is reflected in the order denying a change of custody:

ORDER DENYING CHANGE OF CUSTODY, EXTENDING VISITATION, AND INCREASING SUPPORT PAYMENTS

Both parents of the 8½-year-old child, Jack Doe, were before the court with counsel for consideration of the mother's request for an increase in support and the father's petition for change of custody. Extensive testimony was taken with particular emphasis on an evaluation of the child conducted in June 1978 by Dr. Theodore H. Blau, eminent clinical psychologist.

After considering all the testimony and evidence, including results of the child's tests and measurements and his psychological profile, skillfully presented by Dr. Blau, the results of which are not being disputed by either party, the court summarizes his finding of fact as follows:

1. Jack Doe was placed with the mother by stipulation during the divorce proceeding approximately seven years ago and has had visitation with his father every two weeks commencing Friday night and extending until Sunday.

2. Both parents have remarried, and each concedes the other to be a fit parent.

3. The evidence shows the child to be extremely bright, with a high potential for learning and achievement. It also reveals that he needs greater intellectual stimulation than he receives in public schools with large classes and that he is not performing in school to the level of his capacity. He appears to enjoy a satisfactory relationship with both his stepfather and his stepmother and is the only child in either household. While evidently reflecting some degree of emotional trauma and anxiety as an aftermath of his parents' divorce, the child is revealed as a reasonably well adjusted, normal, and bright youngster with capabilities of a child several years older. Psychologically, he is found to need the warmth and protectiveness of his mother but also is believed to need the firmer, better-disciplined guidance of his father—a paternal "bonding" process which Dr. Blau describes as essential for a male child's proper development.

4. The evidence shows that the father's financial resources have improved since the dissolution of marriage between the parties. The child's present needs are in excess of the father's current contributions thus making it incumbent upon the stepfather to make up the deficit.

5. There is no showing that the child will be placed in any immediate jeopardy, emotionally or physically, if custody is not changed. It is clear however that he should be allowed to spend more time in the company of his father without maternal interference.

Applying the principles of *Hutchins v. Hutchins* (2d DCA) 220 So.2d 438 and *Collins v. Newton* (2d DCA) 362 So.2d 174 (1978) to the above facts, the court is of the opinion that a change of custody is not warranted at the present time. It is thereupon

ADJUDGED, ORDERED, AND DECREED as follows:

1. The petition for change of custody filed by Albert Doe is denied.

2. Visitation of Jack Doe with his father will be extended so as to allow his father to have the child visit with him each weekend, commencing Friday evening and ending at 2:00 P.M. on Sundays, until further order of the court, subject to the right of the parents to vary the aforesaid precise hours of visitation by mutual consent.

DONE AND ORDERED at Palatka, Florida, this 15th day of November 1979.

L. A. Coleman
Circuit Judge

Examining Parents

The issues involved in parental fitness can be very complex. Age, health, intelligence, financial stability, community involvement, and morality are but a few of the factors a judge may evaluate in deciding the fitness of a parent. If it can be clearly documented that the parent poses a potential physical, intellectual, or emotional danger to the child, the psychological expert's task is fairly easy.

The following illustrates an examination of a mother thought to be unfit to have custody of her own child. Because of the mother's Hispanic background, the court wisely mandated that the examination be conducted by a psychologist of the same cultural background as the defendant-parent. The examination was conducted in Spanish, and the following report was submitted to the court by Maria Molinar, Ph.D.

PSYCHOLOGICAL EVALUATION

NAME: Anselma Niza   DATE SEEN: 4-6-83

C.A.:   32   REFERRED BY: HRS & Fam. Prot. Team

BIRTHDATE: 4-25-51

EDUCATION: attended thru 9th

Reason for Referral

Ms. Niza is the mother of six children. The two oldest children reside with her mother. The four younger children, aged, according to her, between 8 and 14 years, are in foster care. She is seeking the return of these four children into her care. A psychological evaluation was requested, focused on her ability to care for her four children. She was seen for two and a half hours; the evaluation was conducted in Spanish.

Background Factors

A detailed history is available elsewhere; thus only some salient factors will be repeated. Ms. Niza, who at times has insisted her last name was spelled *Nisa*, is a Mexican-American born in Texas. She recalls traveling with her family but says she did attend school in Texas. She stopped attending at the age of 14.

She believes the father of her two oldest children is dead. The father of the two youngest children is now out of the picture. For the last nine months she has been living with a man by the name of Roberto Marón. This man is apparently applying for disability payments and is said to have some visual problems. She is also getting some type of assistance. They have a house that has three beds. She understands that, should the children be returned, she must clothe them and see that they attend school regularly. She states she cannot have any more children, wishes to have her children back, and feels that she will be able to provide adequate care.

Evaluation Measures

Wechsler Adult Intelligence Scale (EIWA–Spanish version); Indiana Reitan Neuropsychological Screening Test; informal reading evaluation in Spanish and English; Draw-a-Person Test; Thematic Apperception Test; Rorschach Psychodiagnostic Test; and clinical interview.

Observation and Test Results

Ms. Niza is a dark-complexioned woman, overweight, who looks her stated age. She was cooperative and not distractable. The evaluation was conducted primarily in Spanish, but at times she seemed to understand English better than Spanish. There were some communication difficulties, partly on the basis of vocabulary but partly because Ms. Niza substitutes some sounds, omits others, and transposes yet others. At times she had difficulty understanding instructions, and even once she understood them, she had difficulty remembering instructions. That is, they had to be repeated for each item within a subtest rather than just being given at the beginning and for one or two items. When she did not know the answer to a question, she was quite likely to give some kind of answer as if by doing so she would not be pressured to respond further. This tendency may also be in part cultural; that is, it would not be polite not to answer. If one does not know the answer, one attempts to give some kind of answer. Affect was not inappropriate as much as flat. She was very passive, not physically restless. She said she was not on any medication related to any emotional problems. Hearing and vision were grossly normal. She is left handed.

Ms. Niza was not well oriented. She had much difficulty, could not give the year different things had occurred, had even difficulty in giving how many years she had lived, for example, with the father of the last two children she had. She has lived, she states, at the present address for eight or nine months but cannot give the address. When asked if she had been told the wrong date for the evaluation (since she had gone strawberry picking the morning she was to be picked up), she pointed out that a neighbor had told her that the appointment was the next day.

The Spanish version of the Wechsler Adult Intelligence Scale (EIWA) was administered. The present psychologist had seen Ms. Niza in the fall of 1977 when, at that time, question had been raised as to the advisability of returning her four younger children to her care. Thus it had been five and a half years since the prior evaluation, and there was negligible practice effect. She had had another evaluation using much of the material from the Performance scale in 1979, but using United States norms rather than Hispanic norms against which to evaluate her functioning. Enough time has elapsed to ignore the practice effect. On the EIWA she earned a Verbal scale IQ of 63, which falls within the mildly mentally retarded range; a Performance scale IQ of 88, which falls within the dull normal range, and a Full scale IQ of 74, which falls within the borderline deficient range. These results are practically identical to those reported in 1977.

The norms used against which to evaluate the performance of an individual on a test are of utmost importance. The Spanish version of the Wechsler has unfortunately not been revised since 1968 and was normed on a Puerto Rican population. If one takes the three subtests from the EIWA, which are identical or practically so to the same subtests on the Wechsler Adult Intelligence Scale–Revised, which is normed on a carefully chosen sample from the United States (testing done 1976–1980), then it becomes clear that in comparison to the general population in the United States she is functioning at a mildly retarded level, estimated IQ of 65.

These test results are significantly higher than those reported on the Wechsler Adult Intelligence Scale in 1977 and 1979 (48, 43) when her functioning level was evaluated in comparison to a United States population. It has been found that the EIWA tends to overestimate the functioning level of adults when compared to expectancy in the United States.

However, even taking into account the many difficulties there are in evaluating a person from a deprived environment and, in addition, a bilingual person, Ms. Niza did not give evidence during the interview of functioning anywhere near the level one would predict on the basis of overall mild mental retardation. She cannot write except to print her name and does not do this either consistently or correctly. Secondly, while she can name some letters of the alphabet, she cannot read in Spanish at all and can only read a very few words at a first-grade level in English. Her number concepts are extremely limited, below expectancy for a beginning first-grader. One would predict that the typical individual who is functioning at a mildly retarded level would acquire the basic reading and number skills of at least third grade.

She was asked to complete the Indiana Reitan Neuropsychological Screening Test. Her functioning on this suggests the presence of moderate intracranial pathology. She does not report any seizures, loss of consciousness, dizziness. This is most likely to be a chronic situation. The likelihood of some organic factors being present and helping to account for some of her difficulties was suggested a few years ago.

Ms. Niza's difficulty in coping with, in earlier years, the school situation and, at present, in coping with adult responsibilities is not primarily due to her lack of intellectual ability. Her underlying emotional disturbance became quite evident in her responses to the personality tests. These represented for her unstructured and stressful situations. Her thinking became quite confused, her logic autistic. Her reality contact was obviously disrupted. Certainly she views the world as a dangerous place but the outstanding characteristic of her responses is not depression, as reported earlier, but rather serious distortion of thought processes, very poor reality contact. Ms. Niza is not at this time overtly psychotic but is suffering from a Schizophrenic Disorder, Residual Type, 295.6. This is in line with the diagnosis made in November 1977.

Summary and Recommendations

Ms. Niza's functioning on formal tests is within the mildly mentally retarded range. However, this is not the primary reason for her difficulty to function independently and care for her children. Rather the primary factor interfering with her ability to function is a chronic schizophrenic reaction. Her emotional problems, not her intellectual limitations, interfere with her ability to cope adequately with her environment. She is able to remain outside an institutional setting as long as she can live within a relatively simple and supportive environment wherein other adults provide an informal network of care. Despite the fact that she expresses love for her children, she is unable to provide minimally adequate care for herself, much less for four children.

During the judicial hearing, after the expert witness presented her report in the direct examination, the court examined her as follows:

The Court:	Thank you, Doctor Molinar. Did you conduct your examination entirely in Spanish?
Dr. Molinar:	Yes, your Honor, for the most part.
The Court:	Do you feel that Mrs. Niza understood what you required of her and was able to do her best on your interviews and examinations?
Dr. Molinar:	Yes, your Honor.
The Court:	Thank you for your excellent report, Doctor.
Dr. Molinar:	Thank you, your Honor.

Following the close of the hearings, and after due deliberation, the judge ordered the children to be placed in a foster home and the mother in a community halfway house, with ancillary treatment opportunities.

The psychological expert must be exceedingly cautious about making absolute pronouncements or adhering to a rigid value system in issues of parental competency. Except where issues are as clear-cut as noted above, evaluations and decisions must be conservative, cautious, and made with a thorough awareness of wisdom and constraints based on current research in parenting roles and behaviors.

Most litigation concerned with parental fitness is much more complex than the previous example. In the absence of clear-cut, measurable psychological deficiencies associated with an inability to perform usual parental duties, mental health professionals should be extremely cautious in agreeing to serve as experts unless there is a very specific question concerning the parent. Most custodial battles have more to do with the intense feeling between former spouses than with the best interests of the child. At this writing, there is no body of research that suggests a psychological profile of the "fit" or "unfit" parent. Such decisions are moral determinations to be made by the court. The best that can be done by a behavioral scientist is to present a psychological assessment to the court. Judges differ considerably in their psychological sophistication, intelligence, and philosophical views of the family. The way in which a general psychological evaluation of a parent will be used by the court in determining fitness is likely to be a reflection of the judge's values, with the psychological report interpreted, misinterpreted, accepted, or rejected accordingly.

Some judges request psychological evaluation of parents preliminary to a custodial decision as part of a broad process of attempting to serve the child's best interests while protecting the parents' rights. The judge does not ask for an evaluation of fitness but a general evaluation to help know better the parties who will be affected by the judicial decisions. Such reports may be helpful, depending on the way the judge uses them.

Most requests for evaluation of parents relate to specific accusations of unfitness, and in a sense, the psychologist is being asked to examine the parent and tell the judge whether the parent has a propensity for child neglect or child abuse. Except in the extreme cases noted previously, such determinations are of very questionable validity. In adversary hearings, mental health experts are usually brought in by the attorneys for both sides and the court is treated to a "battle of the experts."

In spite of the lack of research data to support pronouncements by experts about parental fitness, this continues to be an area of considerable activity for psychiatrists, social workers, marriage and family counselors, and psychologists who work in family courts. Courts in larger jurisdictions often have access to agencies that specialize in evaluating the fitness of parents disputing the custody of a child or the accusation of abusive actions by parents toward their children. Evaluations, often quite cursory, are done regularly and submitted to the court couched in language similar to laboratory reports, implying a validity and reliability of the findings not warranted by the evaluative procedures. Using personal observation and interviews of family members as the bases for pronouncing on the fitness of parents, some mental health experts see themselves as "impartial observers" (Gardner, 1982). Such gratuitous self-evaluations perpetuate the participation of experts in court matters beyond their genuine scope or skill.

If the psychologist believes that an evaluation of a parent will aid the court in the complexities of the Solomonic decision, the expert should scrupulously avoid predicting positive or negative behavior on the part of the evaluated parent. There is no research to substantiate the accuracy of such moral decision making, and to do so would be to make unethical use of psychological procedures, laying the expert open to charges of unprofessional behavior. All references in reports to the court should be made in terms of substantive findings, based on reliable and valid techniques. The moral evaluation and prediction must remain with the court.

In the past, mental health experts have testified in these matters, giving wide-ranging opinions about the character and potential of parents. Judges and attorneys are becoming much more aware of the limits of the reliability and validity of human behavior data in the areas of personality and character. Experts in the mental health professions can expect vigorous challenges to opinion not substantiated by data and/or generally accepted in the expert's special field. An example follows.

In a recent custodial matter, the father of the children was accused by the wife of being an amoral, hard-drinking person whose values were questionable. The ex-wife was requesting the end of visitation privileges for the father. A psychologist examined both parents and wrote reports, favorable for the mother and unfavorable for the father. He recommended that the father's visitation privileges be revoked since the psychological evaluation showed the father to have "a confirmed character disorder with psychopathic tendencies." The psychological examination consisted of a Wechsler Adult Intelligence Scale–Revised, an MMPI, a Rorschach examination, and an interview (not an unusual battery for such cases). On the basis of a history of enjoying skydiving and scuba diving, a 4–9 profile on the MMPI, the Performance scale exceeding the Verbal scale on the WAIS-R, and two unstructured color responses on the Rorschach, the psychologist opined that the father was an unfit parent for his two children, ages eight and six. During the custodial hearing, in the judge's chambers, the following cross-examination of the psychologist, Dr. Elfred Gordon, was conducted by Mr. Robert Harper, attorney for the father:

Mr. Harper: I found your testimony very interesting, doctor.

Dr. Gordon: Thank you, counselor.

Mr. Harper: As I understand it, because the father has what you call a "4–9" profile, you have decided he is unstable—is that correct?

Dr. Gordon: That is correct. Those who have the 4–9 profile tend to be aggressive, with little conscience, and likely to engage in asocial and antisocial acts.

Mr. Harper: I see—and so you believe that because the father's MMPI profile is a 4–9, he ought not to see his children.

Dr. Gordon: Yes—such people usually live on the fringe of society and are much more likely to get into trouble than the average citizen.

Mr. Harper: Are we to understand then that all men with 4–9 MMPI profiles ought not to be fathers?

Dr. Gordon: Well, I'm not sure I'd put it that way—

Mr. Harper: Are men with 4–9 MMPI profiles *ever* good fathers?

Dr. Gordon: Well—I don't know if *all* wouldn't be good.

Mr. Harper: So it is *possible* that a man with a 4–9 profile could be a good father?

Dr. Gordon: I suppose it's *possible*.

Mr. Harper: Are you familiar with MMPI 4–9 research in general?

Dr. Gordon: Yes, in general.

Mr. Harper: Would you be so kind as to tell the court the MMPI coding of successful police officers in the Los Angeles Police Department selection studies?

Dr. Gordon: Well, they had 4–9 profiles but . . .

Mr. Harper: Are you aware that replication studies of the Atlanta Police Department resulted in similar findings?

Dr. Gordon: Well yes, but . . .

Mr. Harper: Are you aware that these two police departments are considered among the finest in the country?

Dr. Gordon: Well, no . . . but . . .

Mr. Harper: Doctor, would you have us believe that none of the thousands of successful, effective, policemen in Los Angeles, California, and Atlanta, Georgia, are unfit to be fathers?

Dr. Gordon: Well, I couldn't say that.

Mr. Harper: And by the same token I submit that you couldn't and *shouldn't* say that about the father who you have condemned based on his performance on your MMPI!

Certainly Dr. Gordon was entitled to discuss the *probable* behavioral responses of a man with an MMPI 4–9 profile. His error occurred in moving from description to prediction in his report and making a prediction about a person's future moral behavior and fitness as a father without substantiating it by any significant research at this point in time. Few courts will give credence to personalistic, unsubstantiated, or unspecific statements by experts directed at depriving a parent of the right of access to his or her children.

Summing up, psychologists who intend to give testimony about the fitness of parents are well advised to conduct a careful, standard evaluation; report results in a cautious, supportable style; and avoid addressing issues of fitness until such time as substantial evaluative research appears that would support such predictions.

Evaluating Child-Rearing Settings

Psychologists are not infrequently asked to give opinions as to the quality of home settings and developmental environment provided by custodial or noncustodial parents. Being an expert in this area requires extensive education, training, and experience possessed by few psychologists. It is an error for a pyschologist to believe his or her specific psychological training and experience are sufficient for the evaluation of environmental assets and liabilities. Social workers, public health nurses, caseworkers, and other professionals who understand the complexities of environmental safety, opportunity, stimulation, and support should conduct such evaluations. The most competent expert knows his or her limitations and does not exceed these regardless of pressures to do so by bar or bench.

Evaluating Marital Partners

Aside from child custody and parental fitness issues, psychological experts are sometimes called upon to testify as to the state of mind or the psychological adjustment of one partner or the other at some time during the marriage or in respect to the dissolution procedures. Most frequently, the focus of the controversy is financial. In some way, the mental state of one of the partners is considered to be of crucial importance in an equitable division of jointly held assets. The psychologist is advised to consider the following questions before entering into an agreement to be an expert in this or other areas where the psychological factors are tangential to the adversary issue:

1. Are the questions to be answered by the expert within the usual and ordinary framework of the science and profession of psychology and the psychologist's training, knowledge, and experience?
2. Would other highly skilled and respected colleagues use similar evaluation procedures and come to similar conclusions?
3. Can the expert present his or her findings in a conservative manner with appropriate disclaimers and alternate possibilities?
4. Is the expert prepared to define the limits of his or her expert opinion and resist any manipulation by attorneys or judges to extend testimony or opinion beyond reasonable limits?

These are the acid tests of whether a psychologist can serve as an expert in an ethical and professional manner.

Examples of psychological evaluations of marital partners seem warranted. In the first, a psychologist was consulted by the attorney representing a man seeking extensive alimony payments from his wealthy wife in conjunction with the dissolution of the marriage. The husband claimed that his wife's excessive demands and domination ruined his artistic potential, causing him such distress that he could not produce salable art during their marriage. The attorney sought a psychological evaluation to assess the degree to which the husband's artistic productivity was negated by the wife's behavior and influence. The psychologist properly refused to accept the role as expert in this case. The questions asked of the psychologist clearly failed at least two of the four acid tests of an acceptable adversary issue with which an expert can become associated.

In another marital dissolution conflict, initially discussed in the section "Property Agreement Challenges," the attorney representing the wife approached a psychologist with a request to serve as an expert in determining the wife's mental condition and state of mind at a time years previous to the dissolution proceedings. At issue was a block of stock in the husband's company signed over to him by the wife some eight years previously. The wife contended that the husband manipulated her dependency on him to force her to sign the stock over. The husband contended that the wife "willingly and knowingly" made the transfer and was entitled to no part of that stock in the dissolution agreement.

The wife had consulted with the psychologist just previous to the stock transfer in question. He had conducted an extensive psychological evaluation of the wife at that time in response to her request for help. She was confused, deeply depressed, and almost nonfunctional. The psychological evaluation, consisting of several hours of history and interviews, complete intellectual, neuropsychological, interest, marital, and personality assessment, revealed her to be a woman of superior intellectual endowment, of emotionally impoverished family background, deeply and pathologically dependent on her brutally manipulative husband, who was similar in character to her own father. During the assessment, the issue of signing over the stock arose. The psychologist advised the woman to consult an attorney and to begin psychotherapy. The wife was able to start therapy with a skillful female therapist but was too fearful to oppose her husband's domination by seeking legal counsel. She shortly thereafter stopped therapy and signed over her stock when her husband threatened to leave her if she did not do both. The husband made his demands known not only to his wife but to the psychologist and the wife's therapist.

The attorney representing the wife requested a copy of the psychologist's original report and a letter stating his opinion as to whether the wife's decision to sign over her stock was made under any degree of mental duress. The psychologist forwarded the following response:

> Pursuant to your letter of November 7, I contacted your client, Ms. Gladys Rumfree, and received her permission to send a copy of my psychological report dated April 7, 1976, and this letter responding to your questions. Ms. Rumfree has reviewed both the report and this letter before granting her permission to release them. I saw Ms. Rumfree on six occasions previous to my writing the enclosed report. Our initial consultation was arranged by her husband with the referral comment "she needs straightening out."
>
> Ms. Rumfree herself expressed the wish to understand herself better and gain some degree of independence. Psychological evaluation indicated that though she was of superior intellectual endowment and possessed many skills and talents, she was pathologically dependent and unable to resist the demands and manipulations of her family. The enclosed report provides details of procedures and findings regarding this.
>
> During the course of the assessment Ms. Rumfree reported that she was deeply distressed by her husband's suddenly demanding that she sign over to him her stock rights in a closely held family company. She didn't want to do this, but the husband threatened to leave her if she didn't comply.

Ms. Rumfree was advised to consult an attorney regarding the legal aspects of her situation and was referred to an experienced female psychotherapist, Dr. Mary Isch, to deal with the emotional pressures she faced.

Although Ms. Rumfree finished her psychological evaluation, received the results, and began her psychotherapeutic program, she was unable to consult an attorney for fear it would offend her husband. She stopped her therapy very shortly after she began for the same reason. Several telephone calls received from Mr. Rumfree (noted in my report) conveyed his feelings to me that this psychological work was "putting bad ideas" in his wife's head.

It is my opinion that, at the time I examined Ms. Rumfree, she was a deeply distressed, dependent person, unable to act in her own best interests in any issue opposed by her husband. Although not incompetent to manage ordinary affairs of life, she was exceedingly vulnerable to threats and manipulations at that time.

After contacting Dr. Isch, Mr. Jones, the attorney representing Ms. Rumfree, arranged for depositions from both psychologists who had seen Ms. Rumfree. After qualification and preliminary questions, the following direct examination of Dr. Isch was conducted by Mr. Jones.

Mr. Jones:	As I understand it, Dr. Isch, Ms. Rumfree stopped seeing you after 10 sessions of psychotherapy.
Dr. Isch:	That is correct.
Mr. Jones:	Had she finished or did you dismiss her?
Dr. Isch:	No. She had just begun her therapy.
Mr. Jones:	Why did she stop?
Dr. Isch:	She told me that her husband had demanded she sign over her stock to him and discontinue the therapy.
Mr. Jones:	Did Ms. Rumfree want to do this?
Dr. Isch:	No, she did not. She was deeply disturbed during our last session, indicating that she would prefer to continue in psychotherapy.
Mr. Jones:	Why did she not continue?
Dr. Isch:	She said that her husband threatened to leave her, and she was so fearful of being without him that she was going to sign her stock over to him and stop her psychotherapy to comply with his wishes.
Mr. Jones:	Did you believe that Mr. Rumfree made such demands on her?
Dr. Isch:	Yes, I did. During the time she was in psychotherapy, I received several telephone calls and a visit from her husband. At first he demanded to know what we discussed in his wife's sessions. When I told him I couldn't discuss that, he told me that this was "nonsense" and he knew more about what was

good for his wife than anyone. He told me that he would have her stop the therapy and put her total faith in him.

Mr. Jones: Did you report his comments to your patient?

Dr. Isch: Of course.

Mr. Jones: Thank you very much, Doctor.

Psychotherapists are generally reluctant to serve as expert witnesses since their work is conducted with due concern for confidentiality. Once a patient uses his or her psychological status as a basis for litigation, however, he or she is no longer entitled to claim privileged communication. This poses a variety of ethical and professional issues for psychotherapists, and these will be addressed in detail in Chapter 12.

Guiding the Court

The psychological expert will find that in family or domestic courts the degree to which judges are knowledgeable or sophisticated in matters of child development, marital relationships, and parenting varies considerably. Few judges are formally trained to discharge their awesome responsibilities with an awareness of what psychological research suggests in these specialized areas. Some judges develop personalistic and even bizarre ideas of what constitutes good parenting or the best interests of the child. Many judges are aware of the imbalance between their power to influence a family and their knowledge of family structure and dynamics. Well-founded information is usually welcomed by such judges.

Psychologists are uniquely qualified by education and training to be helpful in complex family decisions. As part of the expert witness's role, the provision of current psychological theory and research can be extremely helpful.

If the court is dealing with decisions that should include information from the behavioral sciences, the psychological expert should provide such information, which may be requested by the court or by attorneys for either party in an adversary action. Certain guidelines are desirable in providing such recommendations or evaluations to the court, including the following:

1.   The topic or subject must be within the expert's area of training, education, and experience.

2.   Opinions proffered by the expert should be supported by appropriate research references.

3.   The report should be conservatively written and in keeping with usual standards of objectivity.

4.   Advocacy should be avoided.

Several examples of learned treatises that have been presented to courts by psychologists follow.

Visitation Plans.   In virtually all marital dissolutions that involve minor children the judge will lay down a set of visitation rules to ensure reasonable contact between the children and the noncustodial parent. The issue of visitation, together with custody and financial sharing, constitutes essentially all the conflict one finds surrounding dissolution of marriage. Whereas change of custody is rarely granted, judges are more willing to modify visitation plans in order to ensure equality between parents and reasonable contact between the child and the noncustodial parent.

The first report presents a psychological visitation plan concerning the problem of a father living in a state quite distant from the residence of the mother-custodian and the child. One of the mother's concerns is that visits with the father should not be traumatic for the child. The mother is also of the opinion that the child should not have caretakers other than the mother. The following report was submitted to the court, after first being reviewed by attorneys for both the mother and the father.

A RECOMMENDED VISITATION PLAN

in re

Jones v. Smith

Referral

Jonothan Doe, esquire, requested consultation in this matter on July 15, 1981. Mr. Doe represents Mr. Smith, natural father of William Smith, age 22 months, for whom the mother, Jane Jones, seeks sole custody. Mr. Doe states that his client, Mr. Smith, seeks reasonable visitation privileges with his son. Mr. Smith and Mr. Jones state they would like to have a visitation plan devised which would allow Mr. Smith to have frequent and continuing contact with his son while fully supporting the welfare and best interests of the child.

The parents are divorced. Ms. Jones liver in Florida, while Mr. Smith's primary domicile is in Ohio. The child William is currently 22 months of age.

The purpose of this proposal is to recommend a visitation plan that would be fair and equitable to the parents while supporting the best interests of the child and ensuring maximum opportunities for optimum growth and development.

Psychological Factors

Classically and scientifically, the first year of life has been considered the critical bonding phase of growth and development. There is considerable controversy as to whether attachment responses of infants represent emotional bonding (Waters, 1980). At the end of the first and beginning of the second year of life, flexibility, rather than dependency, is the hallmark of the typical infant–adult relationship. Distress and disorganization based on separation from the primary caretaker are of developmental significance before one year of age. Simplistic concepts of mother bonding and separation anxiety are not borne out by infant studies (Ainsworth, 1973). During the past decade it has become clearer that the *quality* of the child–parent bond, as opposed to the *strength* of the attachment bond, is of greater significance to development. Discrete behavior indices or reports of attachment are not reliable. As bonding and attachment increase beyond the 12-month level, such behavior becomes incompatible with exploratory behavior. Thus early separation from the mother may be deleterious, while later separation can be developmentally helpful (Joffe & Vaughn, 1982). Fathers tend to spend more and varied interactional time with firstborn male children (Clarke-Stewart, 1978). No developmental time period beyond the very early months has been found to have unique and irreversible importance (Sroufe, 1979).

During the past decade, considerable research on language acquisition suggests that the early interaction between the mother and the child is crucial to language development. This begins early in infancy. This special communicative interaction is called "motherese." The important stages for this interaction appear to be between a few days after birth and about two years of age (Molfese, Molfese, & Carrell, 1981).

Ages two to three represent exploratory opportunities, which include socialization, communication, problem solving, skill development, and social training. If infant day care is a significant part of the child's development between 3 and 29 months of age, there are no significant developmental differences between children who were at a well-run, nurturant, responsible group-care center and a matched group raised at home. Only in concept formation did the children raised at home appear to be superior to those in a day-care center. These findings only apply to responsibly and conscientiously implemented day-care centers defined as follows:

A conscientious and nurturant caretaker in a group setting is keenly aware of the psychological diversity among the children in the setting as well as the differences in the values between each parent and herself. As a result, she is unlikely to hold rigid standards of behavior for each child regarding talkativeness, cooperativeness, cleanliness, aggression, quality of play, or the age when particular developmental milestones should appear. She is likely to be more relaxed about these standards than the parents because she is less profoundly identified with the children in her care. It is neither a source of deep pleasure if one of her children is slightly precocious in learning to drink from a cup nor a source of anxiety if a motorically retarded child spills his milk every day. This tolerant attitude toward diversity in growth patterns leads the caretaker to give each child considerable license to behave in accord with his temperamental disposition and relative level of maturity. As a result, with the exception of extremely destructive or regressed children, the caretaker does not impose constraints on the children when they seem occupied and happy. As a result the average child does not generate serious uncertainties about the caretaker's actions when he is exploring his environment.

For purposes of the research reported above, the typical mother is "identified and emotionally involved with her young child. She has a set of discrete standards for his behavior, and she vigilantly watches for deviations from those standards."

Thus, *assuming certain characteristics,* day care probably does not interfere with children's development (Kagen, Kearsley, & Zelazo, 1977).

Joint, cooperative parenting that involves issues of interstate custody often requires extensive mediation and when joint-custodial parents are separated by great distances, frequent consultation is difficult and misunderstandings can be magnified (Bodenheimer, 1981).

Legal Considerations and Expectancies

Conciliation efforts are being required by many courts (Orlando, 1978). Rights of fathers have received increasing attention, including the rights of unmarried fathers (Bedwell, 1979).[11] More and more the focus has been directed to the best interests of the child when the courts must decide on custody and visitation (Goldstein, Freud, & Solnit, 1973). In almost 90% of cases, custody has been awarded to the mother without contest by the father (Weitzman & Dixon, 1979). The classical *tender years* doctrine for custodial award to the mother has come into question in the past decade. About 40 states, including Florida, have rejected this doctrine. The Uniform Marriage and Divorce Act (National Conference of Commissioners, 1971) recommends:

The court shall determine custody in accordance with the best interests of the child. The court shall consider all relevant factors including: (1) the wishes of the child's parent or parents as to his custody; (2) the wishes of the child as to his custodian; (3) the interaction and interrelationship of the child with his parents, his siblings, and any other person who may significantly affect the child's best interests; (4) the child's adjustment to his home, school, and community; and (5) the mental and physical health of all individuals involved. The court shall not consider conduct of a proposed custodian that does not affect his relationship to the child.

[11] *Rothstein v. Lutheran Social Services,* 59 Wis.2d 1, 207 N.W.2d 826 (1973).

Judges continue to depend on subjective judgment as to the child's best interests (Ruback, 1982). More recently, the advice of mental health professionals has received favorable reception by the Bench (Litwack, Gerber, & Fenster, 1980; Woody, 1977). The recent trend toward joint custody seeks to preserve and protect the child's relationship with both parents, ensure easy access to both parents, and allow opportunities for both parents to be supportive of each other's parenting efforts (Weiss, 1979).

On July 1, 1982, Florida Statutes required shared responsibility by parents at the discretion of the court and establish family mediation or conciliation services to assist parties in resolving controversy.[12] The statute proposes as public policy that:

1. Each minor child be assured frequent and continuing contact with both parents.
2. Parents share the rights and responsibilities of child-rearing where the Court so decides.
3. Both parents retain full parental rights and responsibilities.
4. Parents confer on major decisions affecting the welfare of the child.

Final decisions in all these matters reside with the court.

Visitation Plan

For Ages 24 Months through 60 Months

The following visitation proposal is made in respect to the following considerations and assumptions:

1. No visitation plan can replace a warm, accepting dual-parent environment.
2. The most propitious developmental opportunities and expectancies for a child between 24 months and 60 months of age are clarified and understood.
3. Both parents are willing and able to participate in shared responsibility, mutual support in the child's interest, and mediation when irresolvable conflicts arise.
4. Both parents are willing to preserve the child's attachments to the opposite parent.
5. Both parents are willing that the child have frequent and continuing contact with both natural parents.
6. The proposal meets with expectancies and requirements of Florida Statutes.

[12] Fla. Stat. §§61.13, 61.21 (1982).

The plan is divided into four age-developmental stage-related segments. These segments correspond to important developmental milestones and are designed to help the parents achieve all the considerations noted above. Both parents must be willing to view these proposals as somewhat flexible in respect to realistic stresses that may occur in their own environments.

1. *24–30 Months of Age.* During this stage of development William is likely to extend his language development, curiosity, and exploration. Almost constant motor activity can be expected. Although still very dependent on a familiar environment, the child will welcome all sights, sounds, and pleasant sensations. The child's capacity to interact with more than two or three adults continues to grow. Recommended visitation frequency and style for the father would include one or two visits a month, of one week each. Although the visitation plan which is herein recommended requires a great deal of inconvenience for the father, the gradual development of familiarity is deemed very important for the child. Each visit might follow a sequence of familiarity as follows:

   a. *1st Day.* Father arrives and spends one hour at child-care center with William.
   b. *2nd Day.* Father will pick up William at mother's home and spend one hour at child-care center.
   c. *3rd Day.* Father will pick up William at home, spend two hours at child care with him and return child to mother's home at the end of the day.
   d. *4th and 5th Days.* Father will pick up the child from mother's home, spend the entire day with William, and return William to the mother's home.
   e. *6th and 7th Days.* Father will pick up William, keep him overnight, and return him to mother's home at end of seventh day, saying "good-bye" until the next visit.

2. *31–36 Months of Age.* During this phase fairly complete transfer from motherese to communicative speech should be taking place. Early identification can begin here, and the father as a unique, safe parent becomes known. "Daddy" becomes a pleasant and meaningful concept. Games and play with father become more motoric and complex. Six to twelve visits during this phase would again be desirable, depending on father's availability. The sequence of events during visits that is recommended for the father is:

   a. *1st Day.* Father should spend two hours at the child-care center with William.
   b. *2nd Day.* Father should pick William up at home, take him to the child-care center, and spend two hours there. The rest of the day

should be spent with father, and then William should be returned to the mother's home.

c. *3rd Day.* Father should pick up William at home and spend all day with him. Father should return William to the mother's home after supper.

d. *4th–7th Days.* Father should pick up William at home, keep him three nights and days, and return William to the mother's home the final evening before supper.

3. *37–48 Months of Age.* Language should be well developed during this phase. William should be now be capable of short telephone conversations. He should have pictures of his father and himself framed in his room. He should receive occasional letters from his father that should be read to him and kept in his room. By now William should be sleeping in a single bed of his own, have a toy chest in which he keeps all toys, and be fully toilet trained. Communication, exploration, development of new motor skills, game playing, and limit testing will be part of his daily life. He should now know "Daddy" by picture, by voice on the telephone, and by sight. Visitation during this phase can be once every two months for a two-week period at the father's residence. The sequence should include:

a. Anticipatory explanation of forthcoming trip by both parents.

b. *1st Day.* William should meet father in the morning and spend the day with him. He should return to the mother's home that night.

c. *2nd Day.* William should be picked up by father in the morning and they should fly to the father's home.

d. *3rd–13th Day.* William will reside with father at the father's home. Father should ensure that William feels secure and comfortable. To this end the father should:

(1) Arrange William's room to be as much like his room at home in color, content, furniture, and decor as possible.

(2) Follow the same times for meals, bed, naps, and bathing as at home.

(3) Introduce new family members singly or in pairs quite gradually.

(4) Arrange daily telephone contact between William and his mother.

(5) Avoid sudden, unexpected, or intense stimuli experiences (Disney World, amusement parks, large parties, and so forth).

(6) Arrange play-school–like activities with other children Monday through Friday.

e. *13th Day.* Father and William should fly back to Florida, and William should be taken to the mother's home by father.

f. *14th Day*. Father should pick William up at home in the morning, take him to day care or play school, and say "goodbye," ending the visit with promises of telephone calls and the next visit. William should have a Polaroid snapshot of himself and his father taken during the visit.

4. *49–60 Months of Age*.   During this stage of development William will probably be in nursery school or prekindergarten. He will probably follow a regular routine during the school year. He should be able to spend summers and vacation time with his father, who by this time will be well known and a part of William's affective attachments and identifications. William should now be ready for many varied and stimulating experiences. The summer period might be split, one month with father, two weeks at midsummer with mother, then a month with father.

Beyond the fifth year, psychological assessment would be a helpful adjunct in making visitation recommendations, as testing could address in detail William's current intellectual, social, and emotional development and needs (Goldstein et al., 1973; Litwack et al., 1980; Soufe, 1979; Woody, 1977). Such an evaluation could be a milestone assessment to help the parents understand how William is developing, how well they are doing as parents, and what opportunities lie ahead for continuing to share the responsibility for William's growth and development.

Auditing

No visitation plan can be followed with exactness. Variations and modifications should be made with a view toward abiding by the positive spirit of shared responsibility. If conflicts between parents become irresolvable or intense, a moderating influence in the child's best interests should be invoked in the form of a professional mediator. Such a person should be selected and agreed to by both parents before issues arise, so that conflicts may be early considered and resolved.

References

Ainsworth, M. (1973). The development of infant–mother attachment. In B. Caldwell & H. Riccioti (Eds.), *Review of child development research* (Vol. 3). Chicago: University of Chicago Press.

Bedwell, M. A. (1979). The rights of fathers of non-marital children to custody, visitation, and to consent to adoption. *University of California, Davis Law Review*, (1981). *12*, 412–451.

Bodenheimer, B. M. (1981). Interstate custody: Initial jurisdiction and continuing jurisdiction under the UCCJA. *Family Law Quarterly, 13*, 203–227.

Brodsky, J. G., & Alford, J. G. (1977). Sharpening Solomon's sword: Current considerations in child custody cases. *Dickinson Law Review, 81*, 683–731.

Clarke-Stewart, A. (1978). And daddy makes three: The father's impact on mother and young child. *Child Development, 49,* 466–478.

Goldstein, J., Freud, A., & Solnit, A. J. (1973). *Beyond the best interests of the child.* New York: Free Press.

Joffe, L. S., & Vaughn, B. E. (1982). Infant–mother attachment: Theory, assessment, and implications for development. In B. B. Wolman et al. (Eds.), *Handbook of developmental psychology.* Englewood Cliffs, NJ: Prentice-Hall.

Kagan, J., Kearsley, R. B., & Zelazo, P. R. (1977). The effects of infant day care on psychological development. *Evaluation Quarterly, 1*(1), 109–142.

Litwack, J. R., Gerber, G. L., & Fenster, C. A. (1980). The proper role of psychology in child custody disputes. *Journal of Family Law, 18,* 269–300.

Molfese, D. L., Molfese, V. J., & Carrell, P. L. (1981). Early language development. In B. B. Wolman et al. (Eds.), *Handbook of developmental psychology.* Englewood Cliffs, NJ: Prentice-Hall.

National Conference of Commissioners on Uniform State Laws. (1971). Uniform marriage and divorce act. *Family Law Quarterly, 5,* 205–251.

Orlando, F. A. Conciliation programs. *Florida Bar Journal, 52,* 218–221.

Ruback, R. B. (1982) Issues in family law. In J. C. Hansen & L. L'Abate (Eds.), *Values, ethics, legalities and the family therapist.* London: Aspen Systems.

Sroufe, L. A. (1979a). The coherence of individual development: Early care, attachment and subsequent developmental issues. *American Psychologist, 34,* 834–841.

Waters, E. (1980). Traits, relationships and behavioral systems: The attachment construct. In K. Immelman et al. (Eds.), *Development of behavior.* New York: Cambridge University Press.

Weiss, R. S. (1979). Issues in the adjudication of custody when parents separate. In G. Levinger & O. C. Moles (Eds.), *Divorce and separation.* New York: Basic Books.

Weitzman, L. J., & Dixon, R. B. (1979). Child custody awards: Legal standards and empirical patterns for child custody, support, and visitation after divorce. *University of California, Davis Law Review, 12,* 473–521.

Woody, R. H. (1977). Psychologists in child custody. In B. D. Sales (Ed.), *Psychology in the legal process.* New York: Spectrum.

Sometimes the expert witness is called upon to express an opinion on a fairly unusual or bizarre visitation situation. In the following example, a father of record was found not to be the child's biological father. The biological mother divorced the father of record and then married the "biological" father. This couple sought exclusive custody of the child. The former father of record sought visitation rights. The attorney representing the biological parents requested an evaluative study of the likely psychological effects of forced visitation.

The following report was prepared for submission to the court after an evaluation of the facts in this convoluted case and a review of what appeared to be pertinent research associated with the question at issue: Should a child be forced to participate in a visitation plan involving a nonbiological parent with psychological attachments to the child?

EVALUATION STUDY
FORCED VISITATION AND THE BEST INTERESTS OF THE
CHILD

Introduction

This evaluative study was undertaken at the request of Richard Roe, esquire. The purpose of the study is to explore the potential psychological effects of a variety of visitation decisions on the best interests of Mary White, a minor female child of approximately five years of age.

Background Factors

Mr. Roe is attorney for Mr. and Mrs. B. Brown who filed suit seeking a determination that Mr. Brown is the biological father of Mary White. The suit further seeks a termination of Mr. White's rights of parenthood to Mary and that he be enjoined from contacting or visiting Mary. Mr. Roe has alleged the following:

1. Jane White, now known as Jane Brown, married Tom White on 1/18/75.
2. Jane White gave birth to a daughter, Mary, on 3/2/77 while married to Mr. White.
3. Jane Brown and Bob Brown claim that Mr. Brown is the biological father of Mary.
4. Mr. White claims he is the biological father of Mary.
5. In August 1978, Mr. Brown separated from his wife at that time, Susan Brown, and in January or February of 1980, their marriage was dissolved by final judgment.
6. Jane White separated from Tom White, and she together with the daughter Mary commenced living with Mr. Bob Brown.
7. On 10/3/80, Jane and Tom White signed a marital settlement agreement granting custody of Mary to Jane. Mr. White was to pay $400 per month for child support and have visitation rights. On 1/20/81, the marriage was dissolved by final judgment.
8. On 7/18/81, Jane White married Mr. Bob Brown.
9. In January or February of 1982, Jane Brown told Mr. White for the first time that he was not the biological father of Mary, but Mr. Brown was.
10. Jane White (now known as Jane Brown) was with Mr. Brown on a frequent basis from May 1977 until they commenced living together in 1980.

11.   After Mary's birth, the child was with her mother during the majority of the times her mother met Mr. Brown.

12.   Since the divorce, Mr. White has had visitation with Mary.

13.   An examination attested to by Dr. J. Jorgens, dated 5/26/82, states that the probability is 99.85% that Mr. Brown is the biological father of Mary.

14.   Since the filing of the suit for termination of Mr. White's rights of parenthood, no further child support has been accepted by the mother.

Questions to be Answered

In response to Mr. Roe's consultation request, a search of the pertinent behavioral science literature was made in pursuit of data to clarify the following questions:

1.   What are the general conclusions in the psychological literature about the best interests of a child, under six years of age, who is the product of a fractured marriage.

2.   What is the likely psychological effect on a child, under six years of age, of forced visitations to a former psychological father outside of the home in respect to a biological and psychological father in the primary custodial and caretaking residence.

The Best Interests of the Child

Divorce is a legal device designed to be a social remedy for terminating an unsatisfactory marital union. The emotional and developmental problems of children of broken unions represent one of the potentially most unhappy sequelae of divorce. Family disruption through divorce triggers regression, fretfulness, cognitive bewilderment, heightened aggression, and neediness in the preschool child just following the family split. The symptoms are usually temporary if continuity of physical and emotional care and love is restored and maintained by the parent and/or a competent substitute caretaker. The child's view of dependability and predictability is usually threatened, and his or her sense of order regarding the world is disrupted. In children with no prior history of psychological problems, about one-half show some psychological development problems one year following the marital fracture.

Where there is a diminution in the quality of the mother–child relationship following divorce, a deterioration in the psychological condition of the child is more likely to occur (Wallerstein & Kelly, 1975). Most researchers agree that the parents' personal and emotional response to the divorce and the quality of the child's relationship with parents immediately after divorce have a substantial effect on the child's coping and adjustment. Conflict between immature, poorly adjusted parents tends to nullify any positive effect of frequent contact with both parents. The positive influence of frequent visitations with a noncustodial father, especially with male children, is found if there is no father in the custodial home and the divorced parents are friendly and supportive (Hetherington, 1979).

Some broken families are able to retain many bonds, including new parents and the former spouses of the caretaking parent. Friendly relationships are maintained in about 30% of couples who have joint custody and about 20% of couples where the mother has custody. In a recent study of the child-sharing behavior of divorced couples, one year and two years following the divorce, it was found that some couples are sufficiently friendly and cooperative so as to decrease the negative effects of custody-visitation conflicts in the children of the divorce (Collins, 1982). Success or failure in multiple caretaking seems to be based on the quality of the relationship between estranged former marital partners. If feelings are warm and positive among the adults involved, there is a higher likelihood that the child will be less negatively affected by multiple parenting (Santrock & Warshak, 1979).

If parents or caretakers are in conflict, the interaction between them is likely to be transferred to the children of divorce through the mechanism of *child-focus*. The family members tend to deal with their interactional stress by focusing their anxiety, often unwittingly, on the child (Beal, 1979).

To date, what constitutes a child's best interests remains a controversial legal and clinical question. The simplest position in this matter has been taken by Goldstein, Freud, and Solnit (1973, 1979) who, in their book *Beyond the Best Interests of the Child,* suggest that the key to positive child development is day-to-day interactions with the *psychological parents* (those living in the child's present home). They urge that the custodial parent decide all conditions under which the child should be raised. They proposed that a noncustodial parent should have no legally enforceable right to visits which the custodial parent feels are not in the best interests of the child. It is suggested that the shifting and disruption in a child's life that occurs in visitation situations is likely to be deleterious to principles of healthy psychological development.

For any kind of custodial sharing to be effective, it is necessary that the adults involved be emotionally committed to mutual support, flexible sharing, and agreement on the implicit rules and share relatively unambivalent acceptance of the arrangement. Frequent moving back and forth is usually unsettling. Some children are of a nature as to need one home base rather than two. As children mature, they tend to exert pressure on a multihome visitation system. Some shared custody and visitation systems work out well for children, but it is more likely to be the exception than the rule (Abarbanel, 1979).

Parents often, with the best of overt intentions, try to make visitation work. In spite of such good intentions, where a genuine hostility or resentment exists between the parents, it will emerge in such ways as "forget-ting" the time the child is to be ready or to be returned, unconsciously disrupting a visit or a return, creating conflict through incautious remarks, being too rigidly conscientious regarding visitation times, and in other human, natural but disruptive behavior (Gardner, 1982).

In visitation arrangements, the *schedule* has been found to be a primary source of conflict between parents and, as a result, for the child. During discussions of scheduling, conflicts regarding time, consistency, money, causes of the divorce, and personal character often arise (Keshet & Rosenthal, 1978).

The absence of the father in a child's life has been studied extensively. Only about 10% of children live in single-parent homes with their fathers. The difficulties associated with an absent father are strongest for young male children. Father-surrogates work well to give children a balanced parental modeling framework. Females are less affected developmentally by the absence of a father (Biller, 1981); however, the complete absence of a father figure in a female's developmental years can disrupt discipline, social attitudes, and personality (Biller & Weiss, 1970). Some research suggests that "it takes a mature man, one who has found an unneurotic solution to his own oedipal conflict and has achieved a satisfying marriage relationship, to be able to offer his daughter desexualized affection at the crucial stages of her development" (Leonard, 1966).

General Conclusions about Conditions Following Divorce That Are Positive for the Child's Psychological Growth and Development

1. The mother or father is not overburdened by being a solo parent.
2. The child is fixed and stable in a consistent household with caring, warm, available, and stable mother and father figures.
3. The child is sheltered from exposure to conflict which may exist between the partners of the dissolved family.
4. Milestones and opportunities at expected ages and stages of the child's development are not disrupted by custodial or visitation mandates.
5. There is an absolute minimum of the compensatory mechanism of child-focus by former spouses in conflict with each other.
6. Female children develop best when living under the influence of a father who has achieved a satisfactory marital relationship, without neurotic oedipal problems (too great a need to be attached to a mother or daughter).

The Probable Psychological Effect of Forced Visitations

Given both the available research and questions still unanswered as to how children cope with conflict, the following is more likely to occur than not if interpersonal conflict and tension remain between the parents in a visitation situation unacceptable to one or more of the involved parental figures:

1. Child-focus conflicts
2. Impossible loyalty choices for the child
3. Disruption of the parenting by the psychological and biological father
4. Disruption of the routine and schedule of the child's home and peer environment
5. Increased awareness of the original spousal conflict for the child
6. Consequent symptoms of social, academic, and personal maladjustment

References

Abarbanel, A. (1979). Shared parenting after separation and divorce. *American Journal of Orthopsychiatry, 49*, 320–329.

Beal, E. W. (1979). Children of divorce: A family system perspective. *Journal of Social Issues, 35*, 140–154.

Biller, H. B. (1981). Father absence, divorce, and personality development. In M. E. Lamb (Ed.), *The role of father in child development*. New York: Wiley (1970).

Biller, H. B., & Weiss, S. D. (1970). The father–daughter relationship and the personality development of the female. *Journal of Genetic Psychology, 116*, 79–93.

Collins, G. (1982, December 20). Some broken families retain many bonds. *New York Times*.

Gardner, R. (1982). *Family evaluation in child custody litigation*. Cress Kill, NJ: Creative Therapeutics.

Goldstein, J., Freud, A., & Solnit, A. J. (1973). *Beyond the best interests of the child*. New York: The Free Press.

Hetherington, E. M. (1979). Divorce: A child's perspective. *American Psychologist, 34*, 851–858.

Keshet, H. F., & Rosenthal, K. M. (1978, January). Fathering after marital separation. *Social Work*, pp. 11–18.

Leonard, M. R. (1966). Fathers and daughters. *International Journal of Psychoanalysis, 47*, 325–333.

Santrock, J. W., & Warshak, R. A. (1979). Father custody and social development in boys and girls. *Journal of Social Issues, 35*, 112–125.

Wallerstein, J. S., & Kelly, J. B. (1975). The effects of parental divorce: Experiences of a preschool child. *Journal of the American Academy of Child Psychiatry, 14*, 600–616.

Tender Years Doctrine.   Although most states have fairly recent statutes casting some question on the traditional concept that the child of young and tender years belongs with the mother, judges are reluctant in many instances to give up this shibboleth. In the following example, attorneys for a father, seeking custody of his sons, requested a learned treatise on the current psychological thought regarding the parenting needs of younger children and the quality of fathers as custodial parents.

THE TENDER YEARS DOCTRINE: CURRENT PERSPECTIVES

Traditionally the court has awarded custody of most children of dissolved marriages to the mother under the shibboleth that "the child of young and tender years belongs with the mother." Judicial interpretation of "young and tender years" has varied considerably.

With the advent of greater sophistication in matters of child development among jurists, the focus has shifted to the "best interests of the child" and beyond (Goldstein, Freud, & Solnit, 1973, 1979). More fathers began to be named custodial parents (Molinoff, 1977), and more recently, joint custody, or shared responsibility, has become the decision of choice with growing frequency. The recent Florida statute mandates:

> It is the public policy of this state to assure each minor child frequent and continuing contact with both parents after the parents have separated or dissolved their marriage and to encourage parents to share the rights and responsibilities of child-rearing. Upon considering all relevant factors, the father of the child shall be given the same consideration as the mother in determining custody *regardless of the age of the child*" [italics added].[13]

This idealistic approach is unlikely to be effective or helpful to the child in all cases, and the statutes frequently provide for mediation of disputes before sole custody is granted. Significant numbers of divorced parents are unable to work equitably and effectively in the child's best interests, once again burdening the court with the Solomonic decision.

In most divorces (85%) custody is awarded to the mother without contest by the father (Weitzman & Dixon, 1979). Until the middle of the nineteenth century, it was believed that fathers were better able to care for children (Weiss, 1979). From the 1850s until the 1950s custody was routinely awarded to the mother unless she was judged unfit. Once the children passed the "tender years," it was assumed that the father would be given custody of the boys, while the mother would retain custody of the girls, although the courts have always been reluctant to separate siblings (Krause, 1977). More recent research suggests that fathers are quite capable of being competent custodial parents (Orthner & Lewis, 1979). Since the early 1970s, the tender years doctrine has been rejected by legislative act or court decision in 38 states (Freed & Foster, 1981).

Children's needs during the growing years have been extensively studied, and an understanding of developmental needs and how they may be met is readily available to all parents. Experts agree that divorce is harmful to all children. They also agree that it is desirable for the children to stay with one of the parents and to be helped, sometimes by a professional, to maintain a good relationship with the absent parent through regular and

[13] Fla. Stat. §61.13 (1982).

sensible visiting plans (Granger, 1978). Between ages three and six, children require sensible, knowledgeable, and consistent parental supervision, particularly as the child develops toward school entrance, beginning with nursery school (Hymes, 1976).

The nature of the infant–mother relationship has been extensively studied over the years. Research does not support the concept of a tie between the infant and the mother as a specific parent. The so-called mother–infant bond has been found to exist with any close figure in the infant's development, including soft, warm inanimate objects. Although human infants are predisposed toward becoming attached to some person, if given the opportunity, it is *not* predetermined to whom they will become attached. These attachments become increasingly complex through the twenty-fourth month of life and develop into a *secure base* from which the child can learn and grow through exploration. An attachment figure is important but need not be a "mother" per se.

The child is considered to have developed secure relationships with an attachment figure when he or she greets the parent positively, actively attempts to reestablish proximity or interaction after separation, and does not display strongly negative behaviors during reunion episodes in a strange situation. Sustained early separations (birth to 12 months) from attachment figures may inhibit or prevent attachment.

Children who are securely attached by 18 months of age tend at four to five years of age to be described as highly resilient (resourceful in initiating activities, curious, exploring, self-reliant, and confident). Children who have not formed attachments by 18 months are described by teachers at four to five years as restricted (inhibited, disengaged under stress, anxious when the environment is unpredictable). The basic attachments, good or bad, tend to occur with the primary caregiver from birth through the eighteenth month of life (Joffe & Vaugn, 1982).

Specific studies of father–infant interaction indicate that the mother as primary caretaker is a stereotype of society and not specifically necessary and reinforcing for the infant. Fathers are potential equals where the role of primary caretaker is concerned. Over a wide age range throughout infancy, fathers, when placed in one-on-one relationships with their babies, interact as well as mothers, as demonstrated by a variety of studies. Fathers may operate somewhat differently with infants than do mothers (more playful, more physical than verbal, and more task oriented) but are equally competent as primary caretakers. Boys show a clear preference for fathers over mothers by the end of the second year of life (Hodapp & Mueller, 1982).

In a recent review, Warshak (1982) summarizes current research regarding the positive values of fathers as custodial parents. There seems to be some consistent evidence that male children, in particular, are less adjusted when the mother is the custodial parent and more adjusted when custody resides with the father.

Where mother–child attachment is concerned, Bowlby (1969) states: "Although the growth of attachment behavior during the first year of life is reasonably well-chronicled, the course it takes during subsequent years is not." The ideal early developmental interaction involves the mother–child–father triad. After the first year of life the father's role becomes increasingly important (Clarke-Stewart, 1978).

Current research in respect to the child of young and tender years doctrine suggests:

1. Joint-parental custody is the most desirable situation when both parents are stable, competent, available, and cooperative.

2. Whatever exclusive mother–child bonding may exist is probably most significant during the first year of life.

3. During the twelfth to thirtieth months, mother–child–father influences are most important.

4. After 30 months there is no research to suggest that children develop better in a single-parent custodial situation with the mother than with the father.

5. If a single-parent custodial situation is necessary, male children, in particular, seem to show better long-term adjustment when such custody resides with the father.

References

Bowlby, J. (1969). *Attachment and loss*. New York: Basic Books.

Clarke-Stewart, K. A. (1978). And Daddy makes three. *Child Development, 49*, 466–478.

Freed, D. J., & Foster, H. H., Jr. (1981). Divorce in the fifty states: An overview. *Family Law Quarterly, 14*, 229–284.

Goldstein, J., Freud, A., & Solnit, A. J. (1973). *Beyond the best interests of the child*. New York: Free Press.

Goldstein, J., Freud, A., & Solnit, A. J. (1979). *Before the best interests of the child*. New York: Free Press.

Granger, R. H. (1978). *Your child from one to six* (HEW Publication No. OHDS 78-30026). Washington DC: U.S. Government Printing Office.

Hodapp, R. M., & Mueller, E. (1982). Early social development. In B. Wolman (Ed.), *Handbook of developmental psychology*. Englewood Cliffs, NJ: Prentice-Hall.

Hymes, J. L. (1976). *Three to six: Your child starts school*. New York: Public Affairs Pamphlet No. 163.

Joffe, L. W., & Vaughn, B. E. (1982). Infant–mother attachment: Theory, assessment, and implications for development. In B. Wolman (Ed.), *Handbook of developmental psychology*. Englewood Cliffs, NJ: Prentice-Hall.

Krause, H. D. (1977). *Family law in a nutshell*. St. Paul, MN: West Publishers.

Molinoff, D. (1977, May 22). Life with father. *New York Times Magazine*.

Orthner, D. K., & Lewis, K. (1979). Evidence of single-father competence in child rearing. *Family Law Quarterly, 13*, 27–47.

Warshak, R. A. (1983) Custody disposition and children's psychosocial development. Unpublished manuscript.

Weiss, R. S. (1979). Issues in the adjudication of custody when parents separate. In G. Levinger & O. C. Moles (Eds.), *Divorce and Separation.* New York: Basic Books.

Weitzman, L. J., & Dixon, R. B. (1979). Child custody awards. *University of California, Davis Law Review, 12,* 473–521.

The Court's Response to Psychological Experts

Most family court judges welcome the opinions and testimony of mental health professionals in family issues (Litwack, Gerber, & Fenster, 1980). Although some judges deem themselves competent authorities in family matters, most are sensible enough to recognize their limitations in technical aspects of child growth and development, personality, and family systems. Judges tend to be most positively inclined toward experts who attempt to be objective (Kazen, 1977). Some jurisdictions employ staff psychologists to conduct child custody investigations and provide information to the judge. These psychologists serve as *amicus curiae,* and their reports are available to the lawyers of both parties in the adversary issue (Gozansky, 1976).

Although judges frequently laud the contributions of experts in family matters, what they say may not represent what they do. Carol Lowery (1981) studied 70% of the 85 available state circuit court judges and 32 commissioners in the state of Kentucky in respect to the factors they considered important in deciding custody in a divorce. Using an 11-point rating scale for each of 20 items, the judges and commissioners ranked the importance of each variable in deciding custody issues. The items, in rank order of importance, are presented in Table 8.1.

One must assume that judges vary considerably, among themselves and in response to various case situations. The above suggests that although professional advice is almost always welcomed, it may, in the final analysis, have modest impact on the judge's final decision.

Judges appointed or elected to serve judicial roles in family matters now enter their jobs with broader backgrounds in psychology as a result of the increasing likelihood that attorneys today will be exposed to psychology as part of their undergraduate courses. It is probable that psychologists will be called upon by family judges to serve more frequently and in a greater variety of roles than in the past. As curriculum builders in law schools become more aware of and more responsive to the emerging partnership of psychology and the law, an increase in both quantity and quality of psychological involvement in family legal issues can be expected.

Because, in effect, courts have understood little of the complexities of child growth and development and family dynamics, experts from a wide range of the behavioral sciences have been deemed acceptable as expert witnesses. With the growing sophistication of attorneys and judges in fam-

TABLE 8.1.   RANK ORDER OF FACTORS CONSIDERED BY JUDGES IN AWARDING CUSTODY

Rank	Item
1	Mental stability of each parent
2	Each parent's sense of responsibility to the child
3	Biological relationship to the child (when one parent is a stepparent)
4	Each parent's moral character
5	Each parent's ability to provide stable community involvement
6	Each parent's affection for the child
7	Keeping the child with siblings
8	Each parent's ability to provide access to schools
9	Keeping a young child with the mother
10	Physical health of each parent
11	The wishes of the parents
12	Professional advice
13	Biological relationship to the child (when one parent is an adoptive parent)
14	Each parent's financial sufficiency
15	The child's wishes
16	Length of time each parent has had custody
17	Each parent's ability to provide contact with the child's other relatives
18	Each parent's ability to provide access to other children of about the same age
19	Each parent's ability or intention to provide a two-parent home
20	Placing a child with the parent of the same sex

Source: Lowery (1981).

ily practice, experts will no longer be able to testify in vague generalities, personalistic notions, or outdated concepts. Such "experts" are likely to be discouraged by the learned treatise attacks of knowledgeable attorneys or the rejection of their opinions by judges who know that a body of research exists and who expect responses concordant with the concept of "expert witness."

9

The Expert Witness and Personal Injury Litigation

A personal injury lawsuit takes place when an individual feels that he or she has suffered an injury or a loss and seeks advice or assistance from an attorney in an attempt to obtain remedy. Personal injury litigation may be simple or complex. There are many grounds for legal recovery that may support a claim for personal injuries. The most common categories include the following:

1. *Negligence (Simple or Gross).* This usually involves a duty owed to the plaintiff by the defendant. That duty has been breached by the defendant's act or omission, creating an unreasonable risk of harm (in some cases, such as health-care delivery, a deviation from a reasonable standard of care). As a result of the defendant's breach of responsibility, an injury or damage is claimed. If the negligence case is against a professional, the legal standard of care is usually determined by reference to the activities of similar professional practitioners. The legal definition of a casual relationship between a defendant's breach of responsibility and a plaintiff's damages varies considerably from state to state. In such matters there are often "derivative actions," which are secondary injuries to a person related to the plaintiff, such as a spouse filing an action for loss of consortium (ordinary benefits expected in a marital relationship) or parents filing an action for medical expenses for an injured child.

2. *Willful or Wanton Misconduct.* A person's attorney may file for damages (usually punitive) if there has been a willful or wanton misconduct on the part of an individual who was to deliver services or provide in some way for the plaintiff.

3. *Nuisance.* An individual or a group may seek damages from a defendant who has created a public nuisance or a private nuisance. This covers a wide range of behaviors of commission or omission.

4. *Breach of Warranty.* In this type of personal injury action, the plaintiff may seek an attorney to file suit against the defendant who has ex-

pressly avoided fulfilling a warranty or a guarantee. This can include such things as merchantability of goods, usefulness of materials or objects, or habitability of buildings or dwellings.

5. *Strict Liability.*   This refers generally to product liability or ultrahazardous or abnormal activities. In product liability, action may be instituted against those who own or manufacture a product because of direct damage, which has been done, or because of a failure of some type of warranty. Ultrahazardous or unusual activities involving water, fire, electricity, gas, pesticides, nuclear waste, or nuclear explosions can result in claims that the defendant did not do the right thing in regard to products or activities. Strict liability also applies to unacceptable behavior of animals, to accidents or misconduct at sea, and to responsibilities of individuals or organizations as defined by statute.

6. *Defamation.*   Seeking personal injury recovery because of libel or slander is a complex issue, generally requiring that the plaintiff prove that the defendant had an avowed intention to defame the plaintiff.

7. *Fraud, Deceit, and Misrepresentation.*   Personal injury that results from these actions is usually associated with a claim of intentional efforts on the part of the defendant to deceive or defraud the plaintiff. Negligent misrepresentation is also included in this category. Even if an individual who perpetrates a fraud, a deceit, or a misrepresentation is found innocent, a personal injury suit may be filed against him or her.

8. *Intentional Acts.*   Personal injury that results from assault and battery, false arrest and imprisonment, malicious prosecution, abusive process, alienation of affection, criminal conversation, invasion of privacy, intentional or reckless infliction of mental suffering, trespass, outrage, or bad faith is considered an intentional act for which recovery is possible by personal injury litigation.

9. *Breach of Contract.*   Wherever a contract exists that is not fulfilled in the eyes of one party, such party may seek remedy by filing a personal injury lawsuit.

10. *The Effect of a Statute, Regulation, or Ordinance.*   Personal injury lawsuits may be filed against a variety of individuals or agencies where the defendant's duty has not been carried out and has resulted in some kind of injury to the plaintiff. Such personal injury lawsuits can involve wrongful death statutes, survival statutes, the Workmen's Compensation Act, Death on the High Seas Act, the Federal Employees' Compensation Act, the Federal Employees' Liability Act, and a wide range of other statutes involving safety and consumer protection.

Some attorneys and indeed some statutes categorize personal injury actions according to the basic facts of the situation. The most common patterns of fact in personal injury litigation include:

1. Personal injury resulting from the activity of vehicles or transportation situations
2. Injuries occurring on premises
3. Contractor and construction cases
4. Personal injury occurring from the function or malfunction of manufactured products
5. Malpractice
6. Aviation accidents
7. Admiralty actions
8. Sports and athletic suits
9. Toxic torts involving exposure to and injury by a variety of pollutants, chemicals, or radiation sources
10. Personal injury suits involving government bodies as the defendant.
11. Personal injury cases involving family responsibilities and actions
12. Special personal injury actions, including prenatal injuries, preconception cases involving harmful or mutigenic substances, actions for wrongful life, bereavement, and wrongful discharge of employees

The above suggests that personal injury litigation is one of the broadest areas of civil law. The procedures are long and complex (Norton, 1981).

Personal injury litigation falls under the *law of torts* (French for "wrong"). The purpose of the tort is to arrange corrective justice, to ensure that there are principles whereby a plaintiff can achieve a fair compensation from a liable defendant. Under these statutes, injured parties are entitled to compensation under a wide variety of conditions. In essence, all of the above can be summarized in three main theories of tort law. In the first, a plaintiff is entitled to recovery for harms *intentionally inflicted* by a defendant upon a plaintiff. In the second instance, an opportunity is provided for recovery for harms that are *inflicted negligently* through the lack of reasonable or ordinary care. The third general area entitles a plaintiff to recover under the concept of *strict liability,* by which the harm may be inflicted on the plaintiff *without intention or negligence* on the part of the defendant. There are, of course, an enormous variety of variations in the above (Gregory, Kalven, & Epstein, 1977).

THE ROLE OF THE PSYCHOLOGICAL EXPERT IN TORT LITIGATIONS

Psychologists and other experts may be called upon to provide expert opinion in a number of evidentiary aspects of personal injury litigation.

The expert may be used to provide technical or professional opinions in almost any aspect of the litigation where the triers of fact require special aid in deciding on the cause, outcome, or consequences of alleged injuries or losses. Experts may be called upon to provide information and opinion as to:

1. *The Existence of an Injury.* The plaintiff's attorney must convince the triers of fact that a loss has been suffered. The loss may relate to decreased intellectual capacity in a brain-injured accident victim or the bereavement of the survivors of a tragic and wrongful death. A corporation may claim a loss of business as a result of trademark infringement. Experts are called as witnesses to define, in terms understandable to the average juror, the nature and extent of the loss that is alleged by the plaintiff to have occurred.

2. *The Cause of an Injury.* In addition to rendering opinions as to whether the plaintiff has suffered an injury, and the extent of that injury, experts are usually asked for an opinion as to the probable source or causal factors leading to the plaintiff's injuries or loss. Before a jury can assign liability, a causal connection between the plaintiff's loss and the defendant's accountability must be demonstrated.

3. *Permanence, Replacement, or Remediation.* To aid the triers of fact in making decisions about just and fair remedies, experts are asked to render opinions as to the degree of which an injured person will recover, the plaintiff's future capacity to function, and estimates as to his or her rehabilitation potential and requirements. An expert may be asked to estimate the gap between an individual's likely or eventual quality of life in work, family relationships, health, or recreation as a result of the injuries suffered in comparison with an estimated quality of life had the injury not occurred.

When a person is injured in an automobile accident or is hurt in any of the many kinds of accidents that injure millions of persons each year, personal injury litigation frequently follows the event. Whether it involves a child profoundly brain damaged after being hit by an automobile or a person suffering a very limited orthopedic strain as a result of being bumped by a cart in a hotel, personal injury litigation may result. A psychologist may be called by the plaintiff's attorney to evaluate the psychological deficits and consequences of the injury, and the psychologist's testimony would be part of the attorney's efforts to convince the jury that the plaintiff has suffered and deserved compensation. A psychologist may be retained by the defense attorney to provide expert testimony to demonstrate to the jury that the psychological effects of the injury are minimal. Personal injury litigation is sometimes referred to as "the battle of the experts," since the effects and future outcomes of personal injury can be evaluated and perceived in different ways by different experts. In almost every community there are experts in various health professions who are known as "plaintiff's experts" or "defense experts." This may mean that the expert has specialized in some aspect of his or her profession that lends itself uniquely to the goals or tasks pursued by the attorney for the plaintiff or the attorney for the defense. More frequently, such a label suggests that the expert has a bias for one side or the other and is willing to expand subjective opinions to meet the competitive adversary requirements of the attorney who retains the expert. Such a stance is to be scrupulously avoided by psychologists who function as experts in the courts.

A considerable variety of situations occur in tort litigation where psychological experts have been called on to testify. A number of usual and unusual litigations will be presented to illustrate such situations, as well as the procedures that psychologists should follow in order to perform competently as expert witnesses.

Accidental Injury

This is the tort litigation in which a psychologist is most likely to be called as an expert witness. When the attorney (representing a person injured in an automobile accident, a malfunctioning elevator, a fall over an object, or any of thousands of tort litigation situations) calls a psychologist, it may be assumed that the attorney has reason to believe that the psychological expert can be a helpful witness. The attorney for the plaintiff anticipates testimony supporting claims of loss or deficit, while the attorney for the defendant seeks expert testimony to raise questions about such claims. The psychologist must remain as neutral as possible in the case, for no matter how encouraging, suggestive, flattering, or manipulative the lawyer, it is the expert's job to render an honest, complete, conservative opinion well within the ethical and contextual framework of his or her science and profession.

Intake Interview.   During the initial interview with the retaining attorney (usually by telephone), the psychologist should consider the following before agreeing to accept the case:

1. *The Facts of the Case.*   Attorneys are usually willing to give the expert a concise summary of the facts of the case and the attorney's position as plaintiff or defense counsel. The expert must know what happened, when it happened, and the apparent results.

2. *Anticipated Court Date.*   It takes a month or more to prepare adequately to be an expert in an accident case. Pressure from attorneys to examine an injured patient and be prepared to testify "next week" should be politely but firmly rejected. If the attorney has a court date that conflicts with the expert's availability, this should be clear at the outset.

3. *Hypothetical Questions.*   During the initial interview the psychologist should find out the probable hypothetical questions that will be asked by

the attorney. This ensures that the attorney's expectancies are within the technical, scientific, or professional expertise of the psychologist. It is important that the psychologist make clear the boundaries or limits of psychology in respect to the facts of the case and the anticipated hypotheticals.

4. *The Condition and Availability of the Plaintiff.*   During the initial conference the psychologist should find out whether any limitations or constraints exist that might prevent a thorough evaluation. In some cases the judge may have limited the number of hours that the plaintiff is available for evaluation. If the constraints are so stringent as to prevent a thorough and competent professional evaluation, the consultation should be refused.

5. *Retrieval of Records.*   Since the expert will be asked questions concerning the plaintiff's current level of psychological functioning in comparison with the level that existed before the accident, every possible source of objective data concerning psychological status previous to the accident should be obtained. As an officer of the court the attorney is able to obtain such records more efficiently than the expert, and his or her willingness to do so should be ensured at the outset. School records, with a specific request for test scores and counselor reports, should be sought. Work, military, and treatment records are all potentially important since they may provide objective evidence of premorbid levels of function. The psychologist should also ask the attorney to forward all hospital and posthospital treatment records. It is most important to have the attorney find out whether other psychologists have examined the plaintiff and, if so, the dates of such examinations. This will ensure that tests are administered with sufficient time lapse to avoid test–retest effects.

6. *Fee Arrangements.*   During the initial interview the expert should ensure that the retaining attorney understands and agrees to financial arrangements and responsibilities required by the psychologist. It is suggested that the expert cover the following during the initial interview:

   a. *Fee Structure.*   The expert should inform the retaining attorney of the hourly rate charged by the expert for all direct work in the case accomplished by the psychologist. This should ordinarily be the psychologist's usual hourly fee for professional services.

   b. *Approximate Cost.*   Since the attorney is frequently accountable to his or her clients for consultative fees, the psychologist should be able to tell the attorney the approximate costs for the anticipated professional work.

7. *The Psychologist's Product.*   During the initial interview the psychologist should inform the retaining attorney about procedures that are likely to be conducted, the scope of preliminary work, and the type of evaluative procedures tentatively planned. The psychologist should indicate what areas of exploration will be pursued and the kind of report that can be expected. It is always appropriate to indicate at this early stage that other

evaluative directions may seem appropriate as information is collected. The psychologist should tell the attorney that should additional assessment or exploration be necessary, the psychologist will discuss this with the attorney before proceeding. The psychologist should inform the attorney that an interim or formative report will be made by phone as soon as the psychologist has enough information to form an opinion.

8. *Scheduling.*   Scheduling should be done through the attorney's office in order that some responsibility for the client's keeping appointments can be shared by the attorney. Missed or forgotten appointments can seriously interfere with an orderly and timely collection of the data necessary for decision making by the psychologist. Coordinating appointments through the attorney's office can be important when the plaintiff must be examined by a variety of experts.

The Assessment Process.   The number of assessment tests and procedures available to psychologists for use in personal injury issues is considerable (Buros, 1933–1978). New tests and assessment instruments are continually being developed and marketed. The choice of tests or procedures to be used is a matter of professional judgment, based on well-defined principles. The psychologist must always keep in mind that the assessment procedures selected in any case must be appropriate for the hypothetical questions in the case at hand, appropriate for the individual who is being evaluated, and recognized and accepted within the profession. (See Chapter 5.)

The psychologist should conduct the assessment under the best-standardized conditions possible. Plaintiffs may be quite uncomfortable about being interviewed and tested, so the psychologist must make every effort to ensure that the testing atmosphere is comfortable and conducive to the plaintiff's asserting his or her best efforts.

Before beginning the assessment, it is important that the psychologist identify himself or herself, indicate the name of the attorney retaining the expert, and specify that a report of the assessment will be forwarded to that attorney. If the psychologist is retained by the attorney adversary to the examinee's case, the examinee should be reassured that the report will be given to the examinee's attorney.

Before scheduling and conducting an assessment, the psychologist should be familiar with all background materials and records about the examinee so that pertinent facts associated with the issues and questions in the case can be taken into consideration in selecting and administering the assessment procedures. It is important to keep in mind that the plaintiff may be examined by several psychologists, thus raising the issue of test–retest effects.

Reporting Findings.   Once the psychologist has reviewed all records relating to the facts of the case, has conducted the evaluation, has checked all scoring and profiling, and is satisfied that the assessment is complete, the report should be constructed in first draft and the psychologist should list findings, conclusions, and opinions (responses to the hypothetical questions). Before writing the formal report, the psychologist should telephone the retaining attorney and report briefly as to what was done, what was found, and the expert's opinions. At this point the attorney may pose additional questions for the psychologist to answer on the basis of the findings. If the results add nothing to the case, the attorney may terminate the consultation at this point and ask the psychologist to submit a final bill. In most cases the attorney requests that the psychologist submit the final report.

There is no one style of psychological report, and throughout this book there are examples of different styles. As long as the report is complete, is within the ethics and standards required of the profession, and is understandable, there is considerable leeway permissible in style. Very careful copy reading is important since the written report is the document from which the psychologist will render expert testimony at deposition or at court.

The following psychological report was submitted in an accident case.

PSYCHOLOGICAL REPORT

October 8, 1981

NAME: Mullen, Ruth   DATE OF EXAMINATION: 10/7, 10/8/81

ADDRESS: P.O. Box 721, Oxford, Florida   TELEPHONE: 000-0000

BIRTHDATE: 9/22/61   AGE: 19–11   OCCUPATION: None

EDUCATION: 10th

Referral

James East, Esquire, made a telephone request on the 8th of September for psychological consultation concerning the case of *Mullen v. Bently Corp. et al.* He states that the plaintiff, Ms. Mullen, was attending a promotional festival in Hilton County when a polesitter giving an exhibition landed on her. The result of this interaction was a head injury which was first treated at Lundeen General Hospital and then at the Murtry Regional Medical Center. There she was found to be bilaterally decerebrated. Jack Lott, M.D., performed a left posterior parietal craniotomy, with evacuation of left epidural hematoma.

Ms. Mullen did fairly well according to history. She was subsequently examined twice by Bill Surt, Ph.D., and once by Pearl Flack, Ed.D. Mr. East requests a review of the background records, and psychological evaluation of Ms. Mullen.

Background Factors

This young woman was born on September 22, 1961. The information following was given by her mother, Jane Potts, on 10/8/81. Ms. Potts says that she is 41 years old and is not working at the present time. She was a fruit packer. Before that she did factory work. She received an eleventh grade education at Grove, Michigan. She quit in the eleventh grade. She is in good health. She is currently beginning to work selling Amway products.

She was married to Arthur Mullen, who is the father of Ruth. They divorced on May 8, 1974. At that time Ruth was twelve, according to the mother. The real father does not work. He used to be a semi-truck driver. He quit school in the eleventh grade. She and her brother saw the father last in 1978.

Since June of 1979 Mrs. Potts has remarried, and Ruth lives with her and with the stepfather. There is a brother, Jack, age 21, who is with the U.S. Navy and who "puts bombs on airplanes."

In giving the history it is noted that Mrs. Potts has a remarkably similar speech distortion to her daughter, Ruth. She speaks in a very nasal, twangy manner. The mother is unable to remember dates and facts and must refer to a series of sheets of paper which she keeps in her purse concerning all important dates. During the interview it became obvious that the mother has a very poor memory.

She gives the history that Ruth weighed four pounds and four ounces at birth. Ruth was born a month early, and they "didn't expect her to live." Ruth spent a month in the incubator. The mother states that Ruth was born with weak eye muscles. She received her first eye operation in June of 1966 and another one in July of 1967. The mother states that for all practical purposes Ruth is blind in her left eye. "There is not enough that it would be noticed for her to see." Ruth wears glasses for her weak right eye. Ruth was also born with a hip problem. She had to wear a brace on her shoes and between one year and one and a half years of age had to sleep with a brace.

She has been under the care of Dr. Storr of Williston. She had her first menstrual cycle at age 17. The mother claims that Ruth has been irregular since the accident. Early medical problems are denied.

Ruth started kindergarten at the Olney Elementary School at the age of six. Mrs. Potts says this was because of her birthday. She then went from the first through the third grade in the Olney Elementary School, and then the family moved to Waycross, Georgia, during the third grade, and then four months later they moved to Williston, Florida. Ruth failed this grade, and the mother says that this was because of the move. During the history the mother indicates that Ruth was nine years of age at that time, but it may be that she was really ten since the mother was very confused about ages and miscalculated several times.

The third grade was repeated in Williston, where she completed the fourth, fifth, and sixth grades. Mrs. Potts insists that Ruth's work was "average" and that she was "an average student." (The school records do not support this.)

Ruth, according to her mother, entered the seventh grade in the Maple Junior High School and did average work through the eighth grade. In the ninth grade she entered the South Maple High School and did "pretty good." In the tenth grade she didn't do well, but Mrs. Potts said that this was because "she got mixed up with a bunch of kids and let her grades drop but still she passed." When asked how old she was when Ruth finished the tenth grade, at first Mrs. Potts said "seventeen" but by looking at ages, it turns out that Ruth was 18 at that time. Mrs. Potts said, "I don't really remember her failing another year."

Mrs. Potts says that Ruth makes friends very easily. Ruth has her own room at home but will not sleep there, preferring to take cushions from the couch and put them by her mother's bed and sleep there. The mother doesn't seem to mind this, and although they have made efforts to get Ruth to sleep in her own room, these have been unsuccessful. The mother states that Ruth is now going to a psychiatrist and has been for the last four weeks. The psychiatrist says that "we should not try to force her—he will get her back into her own bed." The psychiatrist is Thomas Berd, M.D. He has been giving her some medication "for her nerves." This consists of two yellow capsules two hours before bed.

The mother says that Ruth never joined the Girl Scouts, and the only activity that she can remember was in the fifth grade when Ruth twirled the baton. Ruth has always liked dolls and has collected quite a few. She had a boyfriend before the accident, but he was getting too serious so she dropped him because she wasn't ready to settle down. Ruth gets no allowance, but the mother and the stepfather give her money when they think she needs it.

She helps her mother around the house all of the time. She is a fanatic about cleaning, according to the mother, and keeps their house very well. Ruth collects aluminum. Since July when the mother began working with Amway, Ruth has been helping her. The mother states that Ruth does most of the selling. She says that Ruth has a good style and people like her. The mother says, "I don't let her drive that much alone, but she does most of the selling. She writes up the orders on her own. She has been doing better since she got started at this. It wasn't very good for her to be laying around at home."

Ruth is very insecure. If the mother and stepfather forget to tell her at least once a day that they love her, she comes to them and says, "You don't love me anymore," until they very pointedly tell her that they love her.

The mother gives the facts of the accident. She was present. She states that she, Ruth, the brother, and a neighbor friend were standing by a building in the shade. A loudspeaker announced that there would be a polesitting exhibition and anyone who wished to see it should go to the field. Ruth ran toward the field. The mother then noticed that the son was screaming, "I think it's Ruth." The mother says that the polesitter swooped down and tried to "catch" Ruth. Instead he hit her and dragged her. He was holding onto her and then apparently dropped her. When he did, her head hit on the blacktop of the road. This is the mother's version of the accident.

When asked what changes have occurred, she indicates that since the accident Ruth has cried more, has difficulty talking as well as she did before, has nightmares, wakes up screaming, gets tired more easily, and has dizzy spells. These come sometimes once a day and sometimes not for a week. Her balance is not as good as it was, and she tends to stagger. The mother feels that Ruth gets upset easily. The mother feels the memory is real bad. The mother feels that Ruth wants to say something but doesn't know the words to use. Ruth is very sensitive and feels that the parents criticize her too much. The difficulty in sleeping alone since the accident has been noted previously.

Medical Records

The accident took place on May 19, 1980. After Ruth was hit by the polesitter and dragged, she was given some first aid. She was then brought to the Lundeen General Hospital. She was apparently comatose at that time. Blood was coming from her left ear. She was immediately transferred to the Murtry Regional Medical Center, where she was found to be bilaterally decerebrated. Examination by Dr. Jack Lott (neurosurgeon), including an emergency CT scan, suggested left posterior parietal epidural hematoma and a small left temporal epidural hematoma. The patient was taken to the operating room, and Dr. Lott performed a left posterior parietal craniotomy and evacuation of left epidural hematoma. The preoperative diagnosis of left acute epidural hematoma was confirmed.

The patient did fairly well and was followed by Dr. Lott. Subsequently she received two psychological examinations from Bill Surt, Ph.D. (assisted by Karl Coller in the first evaluation and Edward Moody, Ph.D.). Dr. Surt found neuropsychological dysfunctions but in particular noted a strong negative emotional response that he attributes to the accident. Ms. Mullen was also seen by Pearl R. Flack, Ed.D., a counselor.

Dr. Lott's records consist of admission notes beginning on 6/19/80. There is a description of the operative procedure (left posterior parietal craniotomy with evacuation of left epidural hematoma). It was stated that the patient tolerated the operation well and returned to consciousness. She was discharged on 7/6/80 and was placed on Dilantin in order to prevent the occurrence of seizures.

A postoperative follow-up on 7/27/80 notes that this patient had "roving eyes since birth." The doctor increased the Dilantin to 400 mg per day.

A postoperative note of 8/21/80 indicates that the neurologic examination was "very good." The doctor notes, "The patient has not sustained permanent physical injury." He further states that it is too early to find out about her mental condition.

In a postoperative note dated 1/18/81, Dr. Lott says that the neurologic examination is entirely normal but that this patient has suffered mental impairment. He recommends additional psychometrics to follow Dr. Surt's evaluation in the fall of 1980. He notes that the family is having financial problems and that this is affecting the patient.

In a postoperative follow-up note of 6/17/81, he notes that the patient suffers headaches which are probably from tension. The neurological evaluation is again normal. The doctor states that the "economical situation" is a significant factor in the situation.

Dr. Lott notes that this patient is extremely thin and notes her weight to be 80 pounds. This is unusual and one would wonder whether there is the possibility of anorexia.

The first psychological examination reported by Dr. Surt is apparently a standard psychological evaluation. Dr. Surt indicates that the patient was 19 at the time of the examination, with 11 years of education. There are no indications that this is true, since we have records showing that she finished the tenth grade. He notes that the girl is right-handed. She was referred by an attorney by the name of Yurtey. The examination occurred four months after the accident, and it could be expected to show the maximum deficit since it was so close to the time of the accident.

Ms. Mullen was tested for six hours in a one-day session. This may have been pretty tiring to her. The examination consisted of some standard administrations and partial administration of the Halstead-Reitan Neuropsychological Battery.

The Wechsler scores were as follows:

> Verbal scale—95
> Performance scale—83
> Full scale—89

The above scores included Comprehension with a weighted score of 12 and Similarities with a weighted score of 11.

Dr. Surt found poor memory, better performance on tactile tasks with the left hand than the right, better tapping with the right hand than the left (30 in 10 seconds as opposed to 27 in 10 seconds). He found her to be at the twentieth percentile on the Controlled Word Association Test, although no normative reference is given.

The Wide Range Achievement Test indicated the following:

Factor	Grade Equivalent	Percentile (No Norms Given)
Reading	6.6	18th
Spelling	6.7	19th
Arithmetic	5.3	12th

The personality was referenced to the MMPI, which showed "a troubled and anxious individual." No notation is made of the effects that poor reading may have on the MMPI. The report refers to changes that are reported by either the patient or the parents.

Dr. Surt apparently examined Ms. Mullen in August of 1981. A letter to Dr. Lott indicated that an examination took place on the 14th of July, 1981, at the offices of Dr. Edward Moody in Garville.

Dr. Surt expressed a great deal of alarm about Ms. Mullen's emotional condition and suggested immediate intervention. No details of his examination were enclosed. Although this letter came approximately six weeks after the examination, Dr. Surt apologized for the press of time preventing him from giving a more detailed report. He did indicate that a more detailed report would follow. Dr. Flack apparently did some kind of rehabilitation evaluation. The tests administered were simply the Bender, the Wide Range Achievement Test, and the WAIS-R.

Results of the WAIS-R were as follows:

Factor	Deviation IQ
Verbal scale	84
Performance scale	84
Full scale	82

His report indicates that the patient received a weighted score of four in Information and Picture Completion, a score of six in Vocabulary, Arithmetic, and Object Assembly, a score of nine in Digit Span and Digit Symbol, and a score of eleven in Picture Arrangement.

The results of the WRAT were as follows:

Factor	Grade Equivalent
Word Recognition	6.8
Spelling	6.9
Arithmetic	6.6

School Records

It is unclear what school district produced these records. Some of the records are clear, and some of them are quite unclear. They cover the years 1969 to 1977 for six grades of school. Absences of as long as 30 or 36 days were noted in many of the school grades. In some cases they were attributed to illness, and in some cases there were question marks for the cause. She was given a conditional promotion from grade two to three and a social promotion from grade three to four. She was absent 16 days in the seventh grade. She was absent 34 days in the eighth grade. For junior high school she received C's and D's in all subjects except a B in home economics and a B in vocational courses.

Her Metropolitan Achievement Test total achievement scores were as follows:

Year	Grade Equivalent
1970	1.9
1971	2.3
1972	2.9
1973	3.5
1974	4.3

She took grade nine between 1978 and 1979, and she received three F's (basic science, general math, and civics). She received four D's (English, general math, world geography, health) and two C's (physical education, drivers' education). She received one B (physical education) in the second term.

In grade ten, which was taken between 1979 and 1980, she received two D's (general science and fundamentals of business), three C's (agriculture, general math, physical education), three B's (basic English, agricultural occupations, and general science). This is the last record noted. Apparently she had completed the tenth grade when she was $18\frac{1}{2}$ years of age.

Metropolitan Achievement scores for the intermediate and junior high school years were as follows:

Age	Grade	Date	Tot Reading	Tot Language	Tot Arith	Tot Battery
13-6	5	4/75	4.7	5.5	5.4	5.2
14-5	6	3/76	5.0	5.7	5.2	5.1
15-5	7	3/77	6.1	5.7	6.9	6.4
16-6	8	4/78	5.1	4.7	6.6	5.5
17-5	9	3/79	7.0	5.7	—	—

The above results indicate that this young woman has had a very difficult time in school. She has never achieved above the elementary school level. She was 17½ years of age when she finished the ninth grade. There are no indications of where she failed in school. She apparently began school in 1969, but she may have been seven and a half years of age at that time if the birthdate of 10/61 indeed represents her birthdate. Even so, there is evidence that she must have failed at some grade level.

The particular school system she attended gave some intelligence tests called the SFTAA. These results were as follows:

Chronological Age	Language IQ	Nonlanguage IQ	Total IQ
13-6	78	88	82
15-5	85	85	84
16-6	74	80	75

In a letter received on October 26, 1981, Bill Surt, Ph.D., enclosed a copy of his second examination and report, which he dated October 3, 1981. He essentially administered the same examinations that were given in October of 1980. He reports a WAIS VIQ of 89, a PIQ of 97, and a Full Scale of 92.

In his summary he states that some recovery has occurred for selective higher mentative functions but that other cognitive abilities, especially those associated with the left hemisphere, have not improved. He again emphasizes that the patient's reaction to these losses has intensified emotional problems. Timely therapeutic intervention at this critical juncture in her life is strongly recommended.

It is instructive to look at a basic measure of the patient's functional skills-intelligence. The following table presents the highest level of intellectual function as measured by the Short-Form Test of Academic Aptitude in comparison with three measures of intelligence given during three psychological examinations since the accident:

SFTAA and Wechsler Results

Factor	School Records SFTAA 3/77	Surt #1 10/24/80 WAIS	Flack 1/20/81 WAIS-R	Surt #2 7/14/81 WAIS
Verbal scale IQ	85	95	84	89
Performance scale IQ	85	83	84	97
Full scale IQ	84	89	82	92

The above measures suggest on objective evaluation that at the time of the last intellectual assessment, Ruth Mullen's Verbal Scale Intelligence, Performance Scale Intelligence, and Full Scale Intelligence exceeded the best intellectual performance that she demonstrated between the ages of 13 and 16 while in school. Thus, her postaccident results are not reflective of lower intellectual functioning since the accident.

Examinations Given during Current Evaluation

Peabody Picture Vocabulary Test, Form M; Flanagan Aptitude Classification Tests (Inspection, Coding, Memory, Precision, Mechanics, Assembly, Scales, Coordination, Judgment and Comprehension, Arithmetic, Patterns, Components, Tables, Expression); Gates-MacGinitie Reading Test— Form 1; Metropolitan Achievement Test—Advanced 1, Form JS, Reading and Mathematics; Wechsler Memory Scale, Form I; Luria-Nebraska Neuropsychological Battery; Draw-a-Person series; Sentence Completion Test; House-Tree Test; Millon Clinical Multiaxial Inventory (items read to patient); History Taking, Interview, and Follow-up Interview. (THB—$2\frac{1}{3}$ hours, SD—$11\frac{1}{2}$ hours).

Response to Evaluation

Ms. Mullen is a young woman with brown hair and brown eyes who is quite small and thin. Her mother also has a very tiny body image. She wears glasses. Her voice is clear and light. She speaks in a somewhat nasal manner. Hearing is within normal limits. She is slow and deliberate in writing and drawing. She forms fancy letters. She is polite, friendly, shows good manners, and is very "sweet." She cooperates well and seems to have good confidence. She works quite slowly, and this results in some lower scores, since she does not attempt a number of the items. The air conditioning was not functioning properly and it was quite warm in the test room. This made everyone somewhat uncomfortable during the testing session on October 7.

Ruth herself was interviewed; she and her mother both were told the purpose of the examination and by whom Doctor Blau was retained. Ruth talked very positively about her family. She states that her mother remarried when she was about 15, and that Ruth likes her stepfather. For recreation she likes most to go to the game room uptown. She likes to help her mother out. She enjoys watching TV three or four hours a day. She has been selling Amway for months and goes all over with her mother.

Since the accident Ruth feels that she forgets more, but when she is reminded she will remember. She feels her math and English are worse, and she notices this since she is studying in a GED book to try to prepare for this examination. She feels that "things" in general bother her more.

Results of Examination

A. *Intellectual Factors*

The intellectual evaluation consisted of the examination of previous results, and since Doctor Surt conducted a WAIS examination in July, it was felt that a reexamination at this time would confuse the issue with practice effect. A review of the intellectual test results is presented on Page Eight of this report.

Ruth was given the Peabody Picture Vocabulary Test and she fell at the second percentile in this test. She had a relatively narrow range of response with a basal score at 99 and ceiling at 132. Her raw score was 118, which resulted in a mental age equivalent of 11 years and 10 months. This would suggest that she has the mental facility to do sixth to seventh grade work.

B. *Neuropsychological Factors*

On the Wechsler Memory Scale, the total scale resulted in a Memory Quotient of 90. This compares favorably with the various Intelligence Quotient results noted previously. Her performance would be considered Low Average.

On the Luria-Nebraska Neuropsychological Battery, Ms. Mullen exceeded the Critical Level in six of the fourteen scales (Rhythm, Receptive Speech, Writing, Reading, Arithmetic, and Intellectual Processes). This would place her in the brain-disordered range of performance.

Primary areas of difficulty are apparently in the left parieto-occipital area and the right temporal areas.

Specific neuropsychological skill deficits demonstrated on this test include the reading of simple material, motor writing skill, logical grammatical relations, concept recognition, relational concepts, arithmetic calculations, complex verbal arithmetic, and simple phonetic reading. She has some mild difficulty with kinesthesis-based movement.

These results show that Ms. Mullen is a person of somewhat deficient neuropsychological function. Her difficulties are likely to show up in any academic area or in any situation which requires applied intelligence. She will show some modest discrepancies in rhythmic motor movements, she will misunderstand directions in some cases, she will show difficulty in writing and reading as well as in arithmetic. In general her intellectual processes show limitations.

The pathognomonic scale is moderate, indicating that at the present time there is no highly active disease process affecting the neuropsychological system.

C. Achievement Factor

The Metropolitan Achievement Tests—Advanced Form 1 indicate that general reading is at the 3.5 grade level when given a speed test, while mathematics falls at the 6.3 grade level.

The reading was further investigated using the Gates-MacGinitie, and the following results were obtained:

Factor	Grade Equivalent
Reading Speed	3.5
Reading Accuracy	3.3
Vocabulary	5.8
Comprehension	3.9

Viable independent reading starts at the 3.5 grade level. These results show that Ms. Mullen is penalized by time and does rather poorly under any kind of time pressure for reading. Her vocabulary is at about the fifth grade level, and her comprehension at about the fourth grade level. This is somewhat lower than previous testings have indicated, but the Gates-MacGinitie and the Metropolitan are somewhat more demanding tests.

D. Aptitudes

Results of the Flanagan Aptitude Classification Tests were as follows:

Factor	Percentile (Compared with High School Graduates about to Enter Trade School)
Inspection	2nd
Coding	8th
Memory	8th
Precision	8th
Assembly	17th
Scales	17th
Coordination	17th
Judgment and Comprehension	8th
Arithmetic	8th
Patterns	2nd
Components	2nd
Mechanics	50th
Expression	2nd

The above results indicate that Ms. Mullen has poor skills to prepare her for any kind of trade training.

Doing an Aptitude Classification Analysis, her highest prediction for trade training would be in the area of agriculture and farming. Here she falls at approximately the seventeenth percentile in predicting success from such training.

E. *Personality Factors*

The projective techniques performed by Ms. Mullen are at a preteen to early teen level. She tends to see the world in fairly simplistic ways. Her values and her interests are that of a 12- to 13-year-old teenager. She would appear to be extremely dependent, particularly upon the mother.

Problems are approached quite simplistically. She has a fairly active fantasy life. She shows a great deal of anxiety about new situations and independence. She enjoys being sociable and thrives on approval and praise.

The results of the Millon Clinical Multiaxial Inventory show this young woman to be a fairly dependent and submissive person who suffers a moderate amount of anxiety. There are indications that she has "ups and downs." She fears abandonment, and this leads her to seek nurturance by acting in an overly compliant and obliging way. She can act gregarious and pleasant. She often dramatizes her own behavior. She has a naive attitude about interpersonal problems, and her thinking is unreflective and some-what scattered. When faced with tension, she will make an effort to maintain an air of pleasantness and deny that things are bothering her. To maintain dependence she will tend to admire and accommodate to and be responsive to the needs of other people. She prefers to play an inferior role to accomplish this, and she often looks for situations to feel useful, sympathetic, strong, and competent. She actively solicits praise. Harmony with others is very important to her even at the expense of deeper values or beliefs. She is quite unassertive. She has little sense of her own identity because she spends most of her time trying to please others and gain their approval. She values herself in terms of the persons to whom she is attached. She feels most comfortable when she feels that the bonds with others are unshakable. She seems quite sensitive to hostility from others and does everything she can to minimize the danger of their disapproval. When faced with responsibility, she feels helpless. She becomes depressed when she is afraid of the loss of dependency. She will display guilt, illness, anxiety, and depression to deflect criticism and to transform threats of disapproval into support.

Clinically she may show distressing phobias, indecisiveness about tiny matters, acute physical discomfort, insomnia, muscular tightness, headaches, tremors, and cold sweating. She can feel pessimistic about the future.

She would probably be seen as a *Generalized Anxiety Disorder* (300.02) with a possible secondary diagnosis of *Dysthymic Disorder* (300.40).

She has probably long had a dependent personality disorder.

The major personality features herein described reflect long-term or chronic traits that are likely to resist resolution. Therapeutically, Ms. Mullen will welcome the opportunity to form rapid therapeutic identification. This will create the impression of rapid progress. It will be extremely difficult for the therapist to terminate the relationship. Developing independence will be very difficult.

Summary and Recommendations

Psychological evaluation of Ms. Ruth Mullen, her background, her history, and previous professional reports indicates that she is a young woman of limited intellectual endowment and current function. She falls at the Borderline level, although this seems to vary to some extent. She demonstrates neuropsychological deficit in a variety of areas. She has limited academic achievement as well as limited academic potential. She shows poor aptitude for trade training. She has had some modest success in domestic activities and in service-sales. She suffers moderate emotional distress and a fairly severe dependency state.

Possible Causes or Contributing Factors to the Current Conditions

1. There are indications that Ms. Mullen had difficulties at birth that could well have led to neuropsychological dysfunction.
2. Her academic progress has been at best borderline, and could well reflect the difficulties noted in Item 1 or perhaps Item 3.
3. Ms. Mullen may have some inherent genetic limitations. Neither of her parents demonstrated very extensive educational or intellectual attainments. Her speech patterns, which are characteristic of mild articulation disorder, are very similar to her mother's.
4. Ms. Mullen sustained a brain injury at age 18 which required neurosurgery. Some of her current condition might be attributable to this.
5. There is no way that her current condition can be solely attributed to her recent accident. The consistency of intellectual performance over a period of years, as well as the obvious difficulty in matters involving reading, arithmetic functions, and other academic ventures, suggests that there has always been some neuropsychological deficit. To attribute her current condition to the recent accident would require a very marked difference in her state and status before and after the examination. Such a difference is only suggested in terms of her emotional response and some limited neuropsychological dysfunctions. There is evidence that the personality is such that many of the symptoms would emerge to demonstrate and enhance the very strong dependency needs that were found.

Recommendations

1. I believe that Ms. Mullen would profit from supportive psychological and psychiatric care.
2. Anything that can be done to prepare Ms. Mullen through training for a service-sales occupation at a rather basic level with strong support and supervision would probably be helpful. She might consider domestic service, since she has demonstrated interest and skill in this area.
3. She would probably profit from simple, straightforward social skills training.

This report clearly indicates the importance of retrieving early records where estimates of psychological deficit must be made following an accident. In this instance, both Drs. Surt and Flock assumed Ms. Mullen had at least average intellectual capacity before the accident. Close examination of school records indicated that the assumptions made by Drs. Surt and Flock were inaccurate, rendering their findings questionable.

Bereavement and Wrongful Death

The survivors or the estate of an individual who dies as a result of the negligent or wrongful activities of a person or corporation may seek remedy as the injured party or plaintiffs in civil litigation. In addition to the usual approaches of determining the monetary value of what the deceased may have earned in his or her lifetime, the statutes make provision for recovery or compensation for pain, suffering, bereavement, and loss of *consortium* (the benefits of the deceased person's company) experienced by surviving members of the deceased's family. Psychologists may be called upon to testify as to the intellectual, academic, or achievement potential of the deceased. This testimony would be based primarily on an examination of school and other records. In issues of bereavement, evaluation of the significant survivors is also part of the assessment by the psychologist in order that an opinion may be rendered as to bereavement effects.

Bereavement effects can be measured by applying well-known, standardized psychological assessment procedures. Shneidman (1978) had reported that the effects of a tragic death can be extensive, even devastating, on survivors; others report similar findings (Fulconer, 1942; Glick, Weiss, & Parks, 1974).

Intake Interview.   During the initial interview with the attorney seeking expert consultation, the psychologist should ask for the facts of the case and other basic information, very much as indicated in the accidental-injury type of case presented at the beginning of this chapter. The intake sheet (Chapter 4) would be completed in the usual way.

Of special importance in a bereavement case is a complete list of all family members who are likely to have suffered, or will suffer in the future, as a result of the tragic death. At this point, the psychologist should indicate to the attorney the number of evaluations that are likely to be necessary to identify the extent of bereavement among the various surviving family members. Since this can mean a very extensive set of evaluations and considerable expense, practical issues of time, availability of family, and likely cost should be discussed during the initial conference. It is important to recommend at this time that all significant family members receive complete physical examinations since the survivors of a tragic death seem much more at risk for development of a serious medical condition than they might be without the stress of the tragic loss (Rahe, 1972; Holmes & Masuda, 1973; Petrich & Holmes, 1977).

The Assessment Process. After all records and other background information have been evaluated, the psychologist should plan a complete assessment of each significant family member likely to be affected by the tragic loss. The assessment will ordinarily be a basic psychological evaluation, consisting of history, interview, assessment of intellect, neuropsychological screening, and personality assessment. The procedures should all be conducted within the guidelines for assessment detailed in Chapters 4 and 5.

Reporting Findings. Preliminary results and opinions should be reported to the attorney by telephone as was suggested previously. At this point, the results may suggest additional assessment (neurological or medical evaluation, vocational assessment for a surviving spouse, and so on). After all evaluations are complete, the report is written and forwarded to the retaining attorney. The following bereavement report illustrates some of the procedures described in this section.

BEREAVEMENT EVALUATION

January 3, 1979

NAME: Murtrey (Mr. George, Mrs. Rae, Ms. Alice)

DATE OF EXAMINATION: 1/3/79

ADDRESS: 2314 Oak St., Ocala, Florida   TELEPHONE: 000-0000

BIRTHDATE: H— 4/10/38 AGE: 40-10 EDUCATION: 12 OCCUPATION: Electrician
W—11/12/38   39-2   12+   Housewife
D—12/17/61   17   11   Student

Referral

John B. Grandly, Esquire, of this city, refers the Murtrey Family. On the 14th of July, 1978, a pickup truck in which Colleen Murtrey and Alice Murtrey, daughters of Mr. and Mrs. Murtrey, were riding was struck by a train. Colleen, 15, was killed at that time, while Alice was injured as was the driver of the vehicle, the maternal grandmother, Mrs. Harcourt. The purpose of this evaluation is to determine whether there is any psychological evidence of residual bereavement as a result of the tragic death.

Evaluation Procedures

Family Interviews, Interviews with each member of the family separately, Minnesota Multiphasic Personality Inventory, Thematic Apperception Test, Draw-a-Person Series, Sentence Completion, Wechsler Adult Intelligence Scale Sub-Tests, Wechsler Memory Scale, Observation, Family History.

Initial Family Contact

An entire day was set aside for the bereavement evaluation. Mr. and Mrs. Murtrey and Alice Murtrey were brought to our clinic at 8:00 A.M., January 3, 1979, by James Cowley, Esquire, and introduced. The initial hour was spent in determining how comfortable the family would be and trying to make them as comfortable as possible for the evaluation. The time of the accident was discussed briefly and the conditions under which the two girls were visiting their grandparents at that time. The week previous to the tragic incident was reviewed with the family. Discussion of the family patterns, eating habits, religious preference, leisure time activities, and general style of life was developed during this initial interview. All members of the family were found to be cooperative. The remainder of the day was spent in alternately examining individual members of the family and conducting subsequent individual interviews. A final family interview was completed, and this constituted the evaluation. Each member of the family was given approximately seven hours of psychological evaluation.

Interviews

Mr. George Murtrey

This is the first tragic death experience for Mr. Murtrey. He himself was born and raised in Krelltown, and his parents are both living and well. He was one of six children. He works as an electrician, and the family income he brings in is about $16,000 a year. They are buying their own home. He has no hobbies but enjoys family things. He reads the newspapers and watches TV. Most of his leisure activity is focused on camping and fishing. Since Colleen's death they have not done any camping.

He is under the care of Doctor Chalmers. His last physical examination was in August, and he is in good health. No illness since the tragic death.

He smoked until two years ago, and he drinks beer. He sleeps well. He had early dreams about Colleen, but they stopped after about six months. After the accident he thought of her every day, but recently his thoughts are on Colleen only two or three times a week. The family talks occasionally about her.

The effect on him of this tragic death, in his opinion, includes the idea of death itself, missing Colleen as part of the family, and feeling that the closeness has been disrupted. He is not sure how his life has really changed as a result of Colleen's death, but feels it's something that could happen to anyone. He feels that his wife is the person most affected by the tragic death.

MRS. RAE MURTREY

Mrs. Murtrey was born in Krelltown, Tenn. Both of her parents are still living. She has had no tragic death previously. She feels her mother, who was driving the truck that was hit by the train, was severely affected by the death. Her mother is seeing a psychiatrist in Tampa.

Mrs. Murtrey has been studying genealogy, enjoys music, and at one time liked camping. The family can't seem to do it since Colleen died. She doesn't want to repeat those activities where they were all together.

The family are regular churchgoers and they attend the Baptist Church in Krelltown. All go on Sunday, and the women go on Wednesday night. Mrs. Murtrey has always worked with children, but after Colleen's death she had to stop working with younger children, because she simply couldn't go camping. It reminded her of her time with Colleen.

Sometimes she gets close to accepting Colleen's death but feels that other times that she can't. Since Colleen's death she has had an odd eating pattern where she will avoid eating and then go on eating binges. She has gained 80 pounds since Colleen died. She has found that she is unable to cook supper after Colleen's death, since Colleen used to "bounce in" to the home at 4:30 very hungry and mother would cook something for her. The family used to have a definite pattern of eating, with supper at the kitchen table. No one eats at the kitchen table now because it reminds the mother of Colleen. They tried to change Colleen's bedroom two weeks after her death, but any furniture that the mother associates with Colleen is disturbing.

Mrs. Murtrey has found herself seriously withdrawn sexually from her husband since the death of Colleen. She will cry suddenly. She feels she has not been happy since Colleen died. She feels that a lower section of her heart has been ripped out and can identify this as the lower left quadrant of her heart. She says she is searching for someone who can tell her why she has this very specific response.

She is not aware of being depressed, although the doctor has told her she is. She feels she is fine until people bring up Colleen, and then she cries. She cries when she is in the house. Christmas has been particularly difficult, because they did not hang up a stocking for Colleen.

Since Colleen's death, Mrs. Murtrey has been under the care of Doctor Kane and Doctor Chalmers. They found she had thyroid problems. She was in the hospital last month. She had a biopsy for a mass in the breast, but it was benign. She is out of balance in her thyroid, and she is anemic. She has had urinary infections. Her cervix will be cauterized soon. The anemia and infections have all occurred since Colleen's death. She has never had this sort of trouble before.

She takes thyroid medication and vitamins. She has had only two dreams of her daughter, and she doesn't dream now. She believes there are meanings to her dreams.

Ms. Alice Murtrey

Born in Krelltown, Alice is in high school and says that she likes it quite a bit. She is a member of the French and Latin Club. She loves to play the piano and do crafts. She collects miniature figures. She states that she doesn't like to read. She likes physical activities, such as rollerskating, swimming, volleyball, fishing, tennis, paddle ball, etc. She has a boy-friend, but they don't really date.

She is under the care of Doctor Frank Lane. He is concerned about her weight, but she has always been thin. She has had occasional dreams about Colleen. She feels they were very close, and they always did things together. She is lonely without her sister. She has become "sort of quiet" since her sister's death.

She finds that she is bothered when going over a railroad track. She finds herself overly cautious and watchful. She finds she is very responsive when other people are depressed or hurt. She denies being upset emotion-ally about her sister's death at the present time. She states that it helped her rather than bothered her. She feels it brought her closer to God. It hurts her that her sister is not around, but she is willing to accept it as the way it is and feels that she cannot change things. She has been praying more since Colleen's death and attends church regularly. She denies that the death bothers her at the present time. She still thinks of Colleen once or twice a week, the things they did, and the good times they had together. She believes the mother is having the hardest time accepting Colleen's death.

Summary of Interviews

The Murtreys look very much like bereaved families. They all superficially accept Colleen's death and are trying to make adjustments. There are some permanent kinds of difficulties which are residual even though it has been almost 18 months since the death. They avoid their family activity—camping—because it reminds them of Colleen. From the clinical point of view, it seems that Mrs. Murtrey is suffering the most severe bereavement reaction and is able to show some of it. The next most severe reaction is being suffered by Alice, although this is almost entirely repressed and could become a dangerous situation in the future. Mr. Murtrey seems to be tolerating the tragic death the best of the three family members.

Results of Psychological Evaluation

Mr. George Murtrey

A. Response to Evaluation

Mr. Murtrey is a man of average height and weight with dark hair. He shows little emotional expression. He speaks in a clear, rapid voice. Hearing is within normal limits, and motor behavior is controlled. He jokes occasionally as he becomes comfortable. He seems to avoid spontaneity. He was cooperative throughout.

B. Personality Structure

(1) *Interpersonal Activity.* Mr. Murtrey is a person who focuses his life on his home and his children. His interests in child-rearing and home life are greater than the average male. He is seen by others as ambitious and persevering. He is known for having common sense. He is rather quiet and passive, although he attempts to be helpful when he can. His basic values are simple and rather rigid. He likes children. He can be quite stubborn. He is what would be called a fairly traditional person who is intolerant of unconventional beliefs.

(2) *Sources of Anxiety.* In general, Mr. Murtrey is most anxious about matters which require decisions. He is fearful of risks and prefers an orderly life. He has a great deal of difficulty exposing his feelings. He likes things to be "the way they usually are" and is uncomfortable with new things. He realizes that he is rather passive, and he worries about it sometimes. He has a hard time doing things just for himself.

In respect to the tragic death, he is very anxious about revealing bitterness. He tries to hide this. He feels that perhaps in some vague way he was not a good enough father, which may have in some way been associated with the occurrence of the tragic death. He doesn't necessarily feel at a deep level that he caused it, but perhaps it is a punishment for not having done all he could have for his family.

(3) *Outlets for Anxiety.*   Intellectual outlets in dealing with anxiety include the need to appear controlled, passivity, subtle criticalness, usually in a joking form, and suppression of a lot of feeling. He relieves a lot of anxiety by being dependent on his wife and children. His work occupies much of his tension and relieves stress. He achieves much satisfaction and balance through family ties. When anxious, he usually blames himself first. Strong emotional feelings are denied. He deals with the tragic death through a variety of these defenses as well as a tendency to externalize and see death as inevitable.

C. Mr. George Murtrey's Adjustment to the Tragic Death

(1) *External Adjustment.*   Mr. Murtrey accepts the death as having happened, denies emotional response, avoids interaction about it when possible, but passively goes along when it appears.

(2) *Internal Response.*   Mr. Murtrey uses the mechanisms of denial, in turning his bitterness inward, as well as "accepting the inevitable." He has some guilt feelings which vaguely connect him with his daughter's death, thinking he was in some way not "good enough."

(3) *Quality of the Bereavement Response.*   Mr. Murtrey would be ranked as one on a scale of zero to four for current response to the tragic death. He has not completely recovered, without residuals, but has recovered considerably with only a sporadic bereavement reaction. He is functional in the usual everyday responses of living.

(4) *Prediction.*   At the present time, Mr. Murtrey seems to be doing fairly well. His eventual adjustment is going to be highly dependent on the reactions of his wife and his surviving daughter in the future, since he is so thoroughly dependent on his family for his own adjustment.

Mrs. Rae Murtrey

A. Response to Evaluation

Mrs. Murtrey is a tall, obese, cheerful woman with gray/brown hair. Her speech is clear and hearing is within normal limits. Motor behavior is controlled. She socializes in an open but subtly angry and tense manner. Cooperation is good. She apparently has a very strong need to ventilate.

B. Personality Factors

(1) *Interpersonal Activity.*   Mrs. Murtrey suffers a chronic and intense anger that she is unable to express openly. In dealing with people she is sociable and has a strong need to be the center of attention and to be

appreciated. She has strong emotions and can be volatile. The family is important, and she expects it to represent her, particularly her children. Although she is seen as a conformist, her ideas are quite different from the average person. She tends to be watchful and dominant. She is controlling her impulses but having great difficulty with this. Her deep and bitter feelings tend to emerge in sudden spurts. She is desperately busy doing many different things.

(2) *Anxiety Structure.*   Mrs. Murtrey internally is full of anxiety and explosiveness. She is very fearful of being wrong, being rejected, or being guilty of anything. The daughter's death has instigated an enormous amount of anxiety about her own worth. Her defense against her loss is to be angry and enraged. She is terribly fearful of anger and rage and therefore represses it. She has great fear of losing control and being destructive. She had a very intense dependency interaction with her youngest child, and this loss has devastated her. Since she is terribly concerned with how she appears to others, she hides these deep anxieties.

(3) *Outlets.*   Intellectual defenses are beginning to deteriorate. She uses mechanisms of denial, holding in, suppression, and compulsive concern about tiny details to hold in anxiety. She leads a life of busy desperation trying to hold down her real feelings. She swallows her anger and her resentment. Her expressions of anger are passive, indirect, or humorous. She is a severely overcontrolled person. She may experience brief efforts of anger or explosiveness, but to date they are fairly mild. She is growing much pickier and much more suspicious than she has ever been in her life.

Her primary mechanism of dealing with her deep anxieties is repression. She is not even aware of how violently angry and resentful she is. She has turned much of her stress and anxiety into overeating, and she has an obesity syndrome where she has somatized her anxiety. Additional ways of dealing with anxiety include sexual maladjustment and a tendency to distort the world as it really is.

As her defenses fail, one can expect suicide potential to be activated, and one can expect acting-out through fugue episodes, dissociation, violence, or psychotic episodes. Although Mrs. Murtrey seems pretty well compensated on the surface, she is a deeply disturbed person.

C.   *Adjustment to the Tragic Death*

(1) *External.*   Externally Mrs. Murtrey is the family leader, energetic, concerned with church work and other projects. She is severely overcontrolled. She has occasional expressions of sudden lability.

(2) *Internal.*   Mrs. Murtrey is severely disturbed, with anxiety and resentment growing and opportunities for expression decreasing. Her rage is both suppressed and repressed. She is becoming more dangerously explosive. Her guilt is becoming intolerable. She has somatized much of this and has moved into an obesity syndrome. Her adjustment is extremely precari-

ous, and her external defenses are just barely controlling the internal explosiveness.

(3) *Quality of Adjustment.*   I would rate Mrs. Murtrey four on a scale of zero to four with zero being complete recovery from the effects of the tragic death with no dysfunction and four being where she would be considered debilitated, dysfunctional, continuing in the bereavement reaction, and in danger of more severe reactions.

(4) *Prediction.*   Unless Mrs. Murtrey is given immediate and extensive treatment, and a great deal of support, as well as opportunity to externalize the guilt and resentment, we can expect some explosive episode which might take the form of a dissociation or a fugue. Violence either internalized or externalized, possibly in connection with a psychotic episode, should be considered a real possibility.

Ms. Alice Murtrey

A. Response to Evaluation

Ms. Murtrey is a tall young woman of about 5 feet 6 inches in height. She weighs about 100 pounds. She has green eyes and brown/auburn hair. She chews gum intensely. She speaks in a clear manner and is quite loquacious. Hearing seems within normal limits, although occasionally she misunderstands directions. She is fidgety, socializes pleasantly, and is quite cooperative.

She talks about going to nursing school after high school. She hopes to marry and have children. Her primary interest is in helping others in the future.

B. Personality Factors

(1) *Interpersonal Activity.*   The external picture of Ms. Murtrey's personality is that of a youngster who tries to be too perfect and do the right things all the time. She tends to be idealistic, seems mature to others, and tends to be popular. People see her as honest, peaceable, and persevering. Her values are traditional and rather rigid. Most people see her as a serious person, conscientious, who always tries to put on a good face. She can be somewhat Pollyannaish.

(2) *Anxiety Structure.*   Ms. Murtrey has the usual anxieties about the future, her role as a woman, and expectations of her. Her greatest fear is that of committing herself to a particular course in the future. On the one hand she would like to be independent, seek a career, and "do good in the world." On the other hand she has a mutual dependency interaction with her mother which has been made enormously strong and intense by the loss of her sister. She feels her mother needs her and that she may be useful to the mother. By maintaining this close interaction with the

mother, her own dependency needs are met, and it is unnecessary for her to make a decision.

She is very frightened of expressing feelings. She is fearful of asking questions and clarifying her own anxieties. She has great trouble competing with other females. She feels the expression of any kind of anger is forbidden, and she is frightened of her own anger.

(3) *Outlets.* Some of her intellectual defenses include doing her best to appear well adjusted and helpful in every situation. She truly believes it is more important how you look than the way you feel. She focuses a great deal on religion to relieve tension. She is very close and dependent on the mother. She withdraws from pressure or risks. Some of her anxieties are expressed in hyperactivity. She tends to be drawn to dependent males because she feels useful. She denies her fear of anger, and externalizes, seeing almost everything as "God's will" or "That's the way it is." She tries to keep busy and work at many different things in order to relieve anxiety. Her prime focus is helping others.

Less intellectual defenses include a very rich fantasy life about which she feels somewhat guilty, a proneness to anniversary reactions of depression, an inwardly gloomy picture about the future, occasional subtle cries for help, and the avoidance of really close relationships. Both repression and denial are primary mechanisms of defense against anger.

She is likely to make a choice soon between marriage, which will give her a strong defense of dependency, and a career, which will allow a defense of "doing for others." She will probably give up the career idea in order to be close to the mother if the mother needs her. This suggests that one of her choices will be an early marriage in order to maintain dependency and closeness to the mother.

C. *Adjustment to the Tragic Death*

(1) *External.* The primary reaction to her sister's death by Alice is denial. She sees it as over and done with, and she has pushed it away.

(2) *Internal.* Her dependency on her mother has tightened, and her degree of adjustment is quite dependent upon the degree to which the mother needs her. She does feel guilty and anxious about her sister's death, but this is well hidden. If her mother adjusts well, her internal reaction will be seeking a career to help others.

(3) *Quality of Adjustment.* I would consider Ms. Murtrey to be adjusted at a level of two on a scale of zero to four, where two would represent recovery from extreme reaction to the death and functional performance at the present time. She experiences regular bereavement reactions on an internal basis, with a tendency for these to be periodic and based on anniversaries. I would consider her recovered but still experiencing stress.

(4) *Prediction.* The quality of the continued adjustment to her sister's death is going to be heavily dependent on the mother's adjustment. If the

mother resolves her enormous tension, it is likely that Alice will go on to balance her deeper anxieties by seeking a career and denying her anger by doing things for others. If the mother continues to be deeply distressed, it is likely that Alice will give up her career, seek an early marriage, and remain at home in order to be of help.

Summary and Recommendations

Bereavement evaluation of Mr. George Murtrey, Mrs. Rae Murtrey, and Ms. Alice Murtrey indicates that indeed the entire family has suffered from the tragic death of Colleen Murtrey which occurred almost a year and a half ago. The most severe reaction is taking place internally for Mrs. Rae Murtrey. Both Mr. George Murtrey and Ms. Alice Murtrey have accommodated to the death, and their bereavement is sporadic and does not interfere with their ability to be functional. They are, however, both intensely dependent on Mrs. Murtrey, and if her precarious adjustment fails, both of them will immediately be thrown into a very intense anxiety reaction and will become dysfunctional. The following recommendations seem appropriate:

1. The first order of business is immediate, intense support and crisis intervention for Mrs. Murtrey. Competent mental health professionals who are experienced with bereavement reaction should be contacted, and early appointments scheduled. It is likely that there will be a need for intensive work for a period of six months to a year.
2. Family sessions which will include Mrs. Murtrey, Mr. Murtrey, and Alice should be scheduled on a once-a-month basis for the next six months. The degree to which these are successful will be to some extent dependent on the success of Mrs. Murtrey in individual therapy.
3. Alice Murtrey should have some individual vocational/personal counseling sessions to help her work through the painful dependent/independent pressures that are going to be coming upon her in the next year.
4. All members of the family should have regular physical examinations every 6 months for the next 18 months. The research suggests that in 70 percent of families where there has been a tragic death, another member dies within an 18-month to 2-year period following the tragedy. Mrs. Murtrey seems the most probable candidate for this danger at the present time, and medical supervision is very urgent.

Prognosis is guarded. A lot depends on the success of the intervention with Mrs. Murtrey. I would consider that this family is suffering a moderate to severe bereavement reaction on the basis of the tragic death they have experienced in their family. The effects are likely to continue for several years. Final outcomes will be very dependent on the success of treatment and the avoidance of further tragedy, particularly in respect to Mrs. Murtrey.

References

Abraham, K. (1927). *Selected Papers of K. Abraham*. London: Hogarth Press.

Becker, H. (1933). The sorrow of bereavement. *Journal of Abnormal and Social Psychology, 27*, 391–410.

Britchnell, J. (1970). Early parent death and mental illness. *British Journal of Psychiatry, 116*, 307.

Doyle, N. (1972). *The dying person and the family* (Public Affairs Pamphlet No. 485). New York: Public Affairs Committee.

Eliot, T. B. (1932). The bereaved family. *Annals of the American Academy of Political and Social Sciences, 160*, 184–190.

Fulconer, D. M. (1942). *The adjustive behavior of some recently bereaved spouses*. Doctoral dissertation. Northwestern University.

Glick, I. O., Weiss, R. S., & Parkes, C. M. (1974). *The first year of bereavement*. New York: Wiley.

Grollman, E. A. (1967). *Explaining death to children*. Boston. Beacon Press.

Hagin, R. A., & Corwin, C. G. (1974). Bereaved children. *Journal of Clinical Psychology. 3*(2), 39–40.

Hilgard, J. R., et al. (1959). Strength of adult ego following childhood bereavement. *American Journal of Psychiatry, 30*, 788–798.

Lindemann, E. (1944). The symptomatology and management of acute grief. *American Journal of Psychiatry, 101*, 141–148.

Marris, Peter. (1958). *Widows and their families*. London: Routledge and Kegan Paul.

Maurer, A. (1966). Maturation of concepts of death. *British Journal of Medical Psychology, 39*, 35–41.

Ogg, E. (1976). *A death in the family* (Public Affairs Pamphlet No. 542). New York: Public Affairs Committee.

Shneidman, E. S. (Personal communication, 1974).

Shneidman, E. S. (1978). *Voices of death*. New York: Bantam Books.

The inclusion of appropriate references is sometimes helpful in a report which is out of the ordinary experience of the referring attorney. Many attorneys who practice tort litigation want to become more familiar with the available research associated with the case at hand and such references are usually appreciated.

Malpractice

When the services of a professional person in some way cause pain, loss, embarrassment, or other conditions considered to be a result of negligence, fraud, deceit, misrepresentation, or willful misconduct, the aggrieved party may institute litigation to recover damages. Sometimes psychologists are called upon to testify as experts in usual and acceptable standards of care or ethics in psychological procedures or services.

More frequently, the psychological expert is likely to be called to evaluate the psychological effects of an alleged malpractice. Specific examples would be cases where someone allegedly suffers brain damage as a result of improper or insufficient intubation procedures by an anesthesiologist during surgery or claimed loss of intellect as a result of seizures caused by improper medication. In such cases psychologists are generally asked to examine a plaintiff and indicate whether psychological deficits are found, to what degree they are found, and whether such findings can be ascribed to the alleged malpractice.

In recent years, litigants have begun to claim damages for "psychological distress" or "posttraumatic stress syndromes" based on alleged professional misconduct. The claim may be the result of situations where the plaintiff was forgotten, left untreated, subjected to an operation later found to be unnecessary, or other conditions representing malpractice.

Charges of sexual misconduct by a professional person are being filed more frequently than ever before by plaintiffs who claim injury and loss as a result of the professional's alleged improper attention. In such cases, "psychic trauma" or consequent psychological anguish and disturbance are commonly cited as the effects for which compensation is sought. Psychologists, together with other mental health professionals, are frequently sought as experts to define the presence and extent of the claimed deficits.

Intake Interview.   In ascertaining the purpose of the psychological consultation during the initial interview with the attorney, the psychologist should try to get the attorney to be as specific as possible as to the effects claimed by the plaintiff as a result of the alleged malpractice. Whether the attorney who contacts the psychologist represents the plaintiff (the party claiming injury) or the defendant (usually the accused professional's insurance company), the psychologist can expect a fairly strong, possibly biased account of what supposedly happened and the residual effects of that happening. Such statements as "He was psychologically devastated by the experience" or "We think she's faking" are not uncommon. The psychologist should do everything possible to clarify, in measurable terms, what kind of deficits are being claimed by the plaintiff.

Assessment.   The nature of the assessment in a malpractice case will depend on the nature of the alleged injury and the effects of the malpractice. The most frequent type of referral received by psychologists is for evaluation of a plaintiff who claims loss of function as a result of improper treatment or care. In such cases the assessment is similar to accident cases for which the attorney seeks an opinion as to the nature and extent of psychological deficit to be found in the plaintiff and the extent to which the deficit may be considered a result, direct or indirect, of the alleged malpractice. Assessment procedures, instruments, and focus are similar to those cases described previously.

In some malpractice cases the psychologist is asked to serve as an expert in "usual standards of care." The psychologist may be called upon to render an opinion as to proper assessment procedures, the accepted standards for psychotherapy practice, issues involving duty to warn, and so on. In such cases the assessment may require interviews with the accused professional, as well as examination of records and depositions. Before accepting such a consultation, the psychologist should be sure he or she possesses the experience and resources for information necessary to judge the behavior and performance of a coprofessional. A thorough familiarity with state licensing requirements, state and national codes of ethics, standards for delivery of professional services, and appropriate state and federal statutes, which may be involved in the issues at hand, is mandatory.

Reporting Findings. Guidelines for reporting that have been outlined in previous sections are applicable here. The psychologist should avoid making any value judgments concerning guilt, innocence, or liability in malpractice suits. Answering hypothetical questions as clearly, accurately, and succinctly as possible is the expert's job.

Where the psychologist functions as an expert in professional standards and ethics, the written report should be directed to the referring attorney (or, in some cases, a judge or an administrative master). The report should address the questions at issue, and copies of pertinent statutes, codes of ethics, and recommended professional standards should be appended to the report.

It is quite rare that a psychologist will be called to testify on standards of care in a malpractice suit. It is more likely that an assessment of the effects of the alleged malpractice will be the focus of the psychologist's assessment. The following report presents psychological findings in a medical malpractice suit in which the issue of a survivor's grief and bereavement was one aspect of the injuries claimed.

PSYCHOLOGICAL REPORT

September 9, 1978

NAME: Raul Perdida   DATE OF EXAMINATION: 8/21, 8/22/78

ADDRESS: 324 Mare St., Apt. 11,
Cedar Grove, FL 33178   TELEPHONE: 000-0000

BIRTHDATE: 3/11/49   AGE: 29-6   OCCUPATION: Broker

EDUCATION: 13

Referral

Mr. Perdida is referred by Edwin R. Won, Esq. A psychological evaluation for the purpose of determining the impact upon his life caused by the untimely death of his wife is requested.

At the time Mr. Perdida and his wife, Maria, were married for approximately one year, she entered the Cedars Hospital in March 1977 for what was projected to be a normal delivery of their first child. During the delivery, it was decided that a caesarian section was necessary. This procedure was accomplished the following day, at which time Mrs. Perdida suffered severe hypoxia. The infant which was born, a female, suffered from brain damage due to hypoxia in the mother. On the day of the caesarian section, Mrs. Perdida went into coma (this was the day of their first wedding anniversary). Seven days later, after repeated negative brain scans, the life support system on Mrs. Perdida was disconnected by the County Medical Examiner, and she was pronounced dead. Mr. Perdida continues to grieve regularly as a result of these events.

Mr. Perdida was examined on August 21 for approximately three and one-half hours and on August 22 for approximately six hours. At that time, he stated that he sees his daughter every day. She lives with his parents. It is a painful experience for him. He always remembers the plans that he and his wife had. It's his worst time. Whenever he sees other families with their children being happy he becomes deeply depressed. He is very bitter, wondering, "Why did this happen to me?" When he is home alone he has a lot of memories. Anything that his wife gave him, such as a present or a piece of clothing or some music, will ruin his day. He is very depressed. He is irritated. He is aggressive with people when it isn't their fault.

In the last few months it has eased somewhat in the sense that it doesn't happen daily, but when it does happen, it is just as strong. He cried a great deal at the beginning, but he is crying less now.

He married his wife on April 29, 1976. He had known her for five and one-half years. He met her after he was in the service. He was 26 at the time of the marriage. The daughter, 16 months of age, is named Maria Elana after her mother. Mr. Perdida fulfills his obligation as a father, but each day is extremely painful to him.

Background Factors

Born in Havana, Mr. Perdida came to the United States when he was 11 years of age. His mother, 54, living and well, is a housewife. His father, 59, living and well, works at a gas station. Mr. Perdida attended Latimer School, and then Cedar Senior High School where he graduated. He spent some time at Cedar Junior College. He entered the U.S. Army at the age of 20 and spent two years as a clerk/personnel specialist. He was discharged E-5. He spent four years in the Reserve.

Presently he works as a loan broker—specializing in commercial loans— at the Springs National Bank in Maitland.

Although he goes to movies and attends club meetings and eats out in restaurants, his social life is minimal. He prefers to read and listen to music. He tried to get out and do some boating as a result of some recommendations by a psychiatrist, but he stopped this.

He is trying to date and to see someone regularly, but he is not serious. He can't seem to form a relationship with anyone. He is continually comparing her to his dead wife. He is trying hard, but it has been difficult. He still has pictures of his wife in the house, and he will talk about her perhaps too much.

He saw a psychiatrist for about a year, Doctor Alvarez. It was helpful to a certain point, and he did everything he could. At that time Mr. Perdida claimed strong suicidal tendencies, and he feels Doctor Alvarez helped him.

The sleep pattern is typical of deep grief reaction. There were many problems the first nine to twelve months. He started taking some pills for sleep but felt this was bad for him, and he quit this. He usually goes to sleep sometime after 11:30 and wakes up about 7:30. Sometimes he wakes up in the middle of the night. He has many dreams about his wife and the life they would have had. He often dreams that she is not dead. He sometimes dreams that he found someone exactly like her. His dreams are repetitive.

The course of events in his life has given him a reality basis for an anniversary depression. In the March-April time sequence he has his own wedding anniversary, his father's birthday, his dead wife's birthday, his child's birthday, his wife's death, and the occurrence of a trauma where he got a knee injury which prevented him from playing professional football anymore (this was his original career choice).

Examination Procedures

Wechsler Adult Intelligence Scale, Ammons Full Range Picture Vocabulary Test, Wonderlic Personnel Test, Vocational Guidance Summary, Wechsler Memory Scale, Indiana-Reitan Neuropsychological Short Form, Depression Calendar, Hand Dynamometer Test, Rey 15 Symbols, Thematic Apperception Test, Qualify Of Life, Minnesota Multiphasic Personality Inventory, Draw-a-Person Test, Sentence Completion Test, Edwards Personal Preference Schedule, House-Tree Test, FIRO-B, History, Observation, and Interview.

Response to Evaluation

Mr. Perdida is a tall, well-built man with black hair. He dresses very well. He wears a mustache. He speaks in a soft voice, with Hispanic accent. His hearing is within normal limits. Motor behavior is controlled, and he is right-handed. He socializes in a polite, comfortable manner. He seems flat and depressed. He cooperates well. Confidence varies. He reports that he still often thinks in Spanish, making it difficult for him to take some tests where the directions are complex and in English.

Results of Examination

A. *Intellectual Factors*

In spite of language barriers, Mr. Perdida falls within the High Average range of intellectual capacity. In comparison with his own normative group of high school graduates he falls at the seventy-sixth percentile. His best intellectual trait is verbal comprehension. He has significant lowering in attention span and ability to concentrate. Memory is significantly lowered also. These factors are associated with stress.

B. *Neuropsychological Factors*

Mr. Perdida's performance is within normal limits and is shown to be contraindicative of any central nervous system difficulty. The Rey Tests of Memory—Malingering are performed within normal limits indicating no effort to "falsify bad."

C. *Personality Factors*

(1) *Interpersonal Activity.* At the first level of interpersonal activity, Raul Perdida showed a number of Need-Drives (above the seventy-fifth percentile for adult men) and Need-Avoidances (below the twenty-fifth percentile for the same group) as follows:

Need-Drives	Need-Avoidances
Exhibition	Orderliness
Intraception	Abasement
Heterosexuality	Change
Consistency	Endurance

The above pattern is characteristic of people who are strongly drawn to saying witty and clever things, talking about personal adventures, being the center of attention, having others notice and comment on appearance, and talking about personal achievements.

He prefers situations which require analyzing one's motives and feelings, observing others, trying to understand why people do what they do rather than simply what they do, putting oneself in another person's place, attempting to analyze the behavior of others, and predicting how they will act.

He favors being with members of the opposite sex, engaging in social activities with the opposite sex, being in love, participating in sexual activity, being regarded as physically attractive by the opposite sex, reading books about sex, and being sexually excited.

He prefers being consistent in the expression of needs.

People who show this pattern are most comfortable when they avoid having written work neat and organized, making plans before starting out, keeping things neat and orderly, making advanced plans, and keeping letters and files according to a system.

He dislikes feeling guilty when something goes wrong, accepting blame when things do not go right, feeling personal pain and misery beyond the point where it does any good, being drawn to punishment for wrongdoing, feeling better when punishment is given, preferring to give in rather than fight, tending to feel depressed by inability to handle situations, and feeling timid in the presence of superiors.

He is not comfortable doing new and different things, traveling, meeting people, breaking the daily routine, going to different places, participating in fads.

He does not like keeping at a job until it's finished, completing jobs undertaken, working at a task even though progress is slow, but excluding other extraneous demands until the job is finished, sticking to problems, and being interrupted while at work.

In diadic interactions, Mr. Perdida is a very energetic and dynamic person. He is drawn to those who have a very strong need to exchange their inner ideas with him and to tolerate his expressing his inner thoughts. In the area of Control, he is drawn to a strong person who can guide and direct him. In the area of Affection he has an enormous need to both give and to receive affection. It is a profile of overreaction and withheld feeling that is characteristic of bereavement profiles.

On the surface Mr. Perdida attempts to express himself as "doing okay." He has a Quality of Life Index of 390. This is quite unusual in depressed persons, but the matter clarifies as we look at his Minnesota Multiphasic Personality Profile and we find that he has suppressed the depression, in favor of an agitation and stress reaction. He literally "keeps busy" to avoid and deny the deep feelings of bereavement and depression.

At a deeper interpersonal level people see Mr. Perdida as a person who is loyal, is honest, has good manners, and is conscious of his status. He tends to be dependent and inwardly pessimistic. A cautious person, he is nevertheless desperate for friendship. He tends to be bitter about life and what it has dealt him.

(2) *Early Identification.*   No distortions are noted here. Primary identification is with the father, who is seen as a quiet, industrious person very dependent upon the wife. A person quite talented in practical matters. Admired. A sacrificing person who was not too much involved in raising children.

The mother is the love object. She is seen as a concerned, available person somewhat cautious and unsure of her own intellect. She is seen as having been a person who held in a lot of emotional feeling. Quite nourishing.

(3) *Anxiety Structure.*   The deepest source of anxiety is the combination of guilt regarding his wife's death and the fear of risking future interactions. He feels that he caused his wife's death. At a deep and unconscious level he feels it should have been he that died. He has unconscious rage toward his child, feeling that the child should not have survived but that his wife should have survived.

Alone now, he fears that there will be no mate figure who could guide and direct him. He fears making any kind of attachment, expecting that he might be deserted again. He is still severely traumatized by the death of his wife.

His anxiety is stirred by feelings of loneliness and the inability to make close relationships in one-to-one interactions. A deep and abiding bereavement reaction has been found in the anxiety structure.

(4) *Defense Structure.*   Intellectual defenses include a tendency to internalize his feeling, rigid attempts to control his life and show nothing of his real feelings, overcontrolled responses to his feelings of vengeance about his loss, and an intense attempt to "work" out his stress. All of this increases his stress. He tries to protect himself by expecting the worst in life, seeking for strong supervisors to depend on, and trying to "make the best" out of anything that comes along.

His deep resentment of the surviving child is going to come out very shortly. He is beginning to suffer an agitated depression where instead of seeming sad and withdrawn, he cannot tolerate his energies. He is beginning to somatize and is exceedingly prone to illness and accidents at the present time. The data on bereavement suggest that there is a strong chance that surviving members of a family in which there has been a tragic death may themselves die or become seriously ill within 18 to 24 months after the tragic death (Fulconer, 1942; Shneidman, 1978; Ogg, 1976).

He arranges to have nothing but superficial relationships with females in order to avoid the risk of involvement in further trauma in life.

Mr. Raul Perdida suffers a very severe grief reaction in response to his wife's death, and a consequent agitated depression.

Summary and Recommendations

Psychological evaluation of Mr. Raul Perdida indicates that he is a man of above-average intellectual capacity who has suffered a traumatic loss, and a consequent intense, acute, and chronic grief reaction. The following seem to be the direct results of the bereavement experience:

1.   Mr. Perdida now has the personality structure that is liable to set him up for anniversary depressions of increasing severity.

2. His grief follows a pattern of severe bereavement, and under the best circumstances, he still has one to three years of intense grieving.

3. There is evidence of lowered attention and memory as a result of the agitated depression.

4. There is a real and present danger that Mr. Perdida may suffer severe illness or even accidental death as a result of his grief reaction to tragic death.

5. He is beginning to somatize distress that has developed since the death of his wife, and this stress seems to be increasing. The rigid internalization is going to lead to further agitation.

6. Because he is fearful of making relationships that will disappoint him, his basic dependency needs are not being met, increasing the probability that the grief will continue.

7. His experience of grief is intensified by self-blaming and resentment, much of which is hidden.

Therapeutic Recommendations

I believe that Mr. Perdida is in clear danger of suffering any one of a number of aftereffects of a severe bereavement response, including his own illness or death. The following recommendations seem urgent:

1. He must have a very complete physical evaluation immediately. This should be followed by physical evaluations at six-month intervals for the next three years.

2. He must immediately have some professional help to deal with the growing depression. This would include:
   a. Concentration on his feelings of self-blame
   b. Evaluation of his inner feelings of blame toward his child
   c. His fearfulness of trusting new dependency relationships
   d. The agitation that comes from not having his dependency needs met
   e. The importance of settling the grief work before marrying again

Mr. Perdida puts on a "good front." From a mental health point of view he is in very dangerous straits. Immediate help is needed and will be required for some period of time.

References

Becker, H. (1933). The sorrow of bereavement. *Journal of Abnormal and Social Psychology, 27,* 391–410.

Doyle, N. (1972). *The dying person and the family* (Public Affairs Pamphlet No. 485). New York: Public Affairs Committee.

Eliot, T. B. (1932). The bereaved family. *Annals of the American Academy of Political and Social Sciences, 160*, 184–190.

Fulconer, D. M. (1942). *The adjustive behavior of some recently bereaved spouses.* Doctoral dissertation. Northwestern University.

Glick, I. O., Weiss, R. S., & Parkes, C. M. (1974). *The first year of bereavement.* New York: Wiley.

Lindemann, E. (1944). The symptomatology and management of acute grief. *American Journal of Psychiatry, 101*, 141–148.

Marris, Peter. (1958). *Widows and their families.* London: Routledge and Kegan Paul.

Ogg, E. (1976). *A death in the family* (Public Affairs Pamphlet No. 542). New York: Public Affairs Committee.

Shneidman, E. S. (1978). *Voices of death.* New York: Bantam Books.

After completing the assessment, Mr. Won, the referring attorney, was called and a preliminary report rendered. Mr. Won was incredulous about the suggestion that Mr. Perdida might suffer physical manifestations of his grief. He pointed out to the psychologist that Mr. Perdida had been a professional football player, was only 29 years of age, and looked to be a "perfect physical specimen." The psychologist reviewed the grief and bereavement research with the attorney and urged him to arrange a complete physical examination for his client.

A week later Mr. Won called and stated that the physician who examined Mr. Perdida found his blood pressure to be 185/120 and had begun treatment for hypertension. The psychological evaluation aided not only in a satisfactory legal settlement but in early identification of a potentially life-threatening illness.

Product Liability and Negligence

The psychologist is most likely to be called as an expert if a plaintiff claims a loss or disability of some kind that allegedly results from use of or exposure to the effects of a substance or piece of equipment causing loss, pain, or suffering. In this respect, most opinions sought from psychologists are concerned with psychological deficit. These cases differ little from those where a person is injured or affected by an accident or malpractice.

In other instances, a psychologist may be called upon to render an opinion based on current scientific thinking, which in some way relates to the issue at hand. The issue may involve a product or service.

Intake Interview.   During the first interview with the referring attorney, the psychologist, as in all other cases, should ascertain very clearly what questions, in measurable behavioral terms, are going to be addressed by the psychologist's opinion. The hypothetical "Was this plaintiff caused any psychological injury, distress, or deficit as a result of the accident caused by the explosion of the defective gasoline tank in his car?" is quite clear and lends itself to psychological procedures, conclusions, and opinion. The question "Did this child become unsocialized and dangerous to herself and others because of her exposure to unrestrained violence presented on evening television?" is a much more vague, diffuse, and perhaps impossibly difficult question for a psychologist to address competently at our current stage of scientific understanding. A clear understanding of expectancies during the initial interview with the attorney is especially desirable in product liability cases.

Assessment.   If the product liability case involves alleged psychological effects on a plaintiff, the assessment procedures are similar to those used with an accident victim. The selection of tests and procedures is based on the nature of the questions concerning psychological deficit.

Should the psychologist be retained to render an opinion as to the nature and effect of a product, the approach follows procedures more identified with evaluation science than with professional clinical practice. Evaluation is the assessment of merit. Standards and procedures have been developed to guide evaluation studies (Rossi, 1982). Such evaluation reports are usually rendered by psychologists with a strong scientific background and evaluation resources and skills. Serious, in-depth literature review is often the primary assessment tool of such evaluations.

Reporting Findings.   If the case consultation involves a traditional assessment of psychological deficit, the report procedures differ little from accident cases. If evaluation of scientific issues is concerned, the product of the psychologist's work is an evaluation report that attempts to answer the referral question.

The psychologist's report may be an evaluation study. An evaluative report may review the literature and render an opinion as to the quality of a product or a service. An example of this might be an experimental study of the sound characteristics of a particular siren and the range of human response to the warning device where this is a product liability issue.

The following report was conducted in response to a request by attorneys for the estate of a plaintiff who committed suicide while awaiting professional help at a crisis center.

EVALUATION REPORT

In Re: Prentiss v.
Armedia Health Centers

Referral

This case is referred by Jack C. Smith, Esquire, of Smith, Baine and Wilson of Armedia. Mr. Smith states that Mr. Prentiss, while on his way from

Atlanta to San Francisco, was removed from an airplane for inebriation. According to a police officer's report, Mr. Prentiss was brought from the airport to Central Intake, where he attempted to put a razor to his throat. Central Intake personnel transported Mr. Prentiss to Crisis Center at Armedia Hospital for psychiatric evaluation. There Mr. Prentiss was registered as a "volunteer patient." Apparently he spoke briefly with the psychiatric resident and was told to wait. At that point, Mr. Prentiss apparently left the building, went outside, and hung himself with his belt.

Mr. Smith would like an evaluation of all records, and an opinion based on current and customary practice as well as research as to the appropriate professional responsibilities in the above situation.

Materials Provided

1. *Armedia Hospital Emergency Department Treatment Record*

Dated 6/18/82, 10:30 P.M. Handwritten note. Signed by B. Carstair, M.D. States that Dr. Carstair asked the patient to sit in the lobby. About 10 minutes later, the staff were asked to find the patient and the staff looked around and did not find Mr. Prentiss in the immediate area. The staff went outside to look for the patient. The patient was found hanging from a tree outside in the parking lot, with a belt around his neck. Appropriate emergency medical procedures were instituted. Beneath Doctor Carstair's signature is the notation, "Reviewed by Doctor Farber, 6/20/82."

2. *Offense—Incident Report—Public Safety Department, Armedia County*

A police report signed by Officer M. Browne (Badge No. 4267). Listed as Case No. 2376-B, Attempted Suicide. This report dated 6/18/82 at 9:40 P.M. was in response to a call regarding a man who had hung himself with his own belt. The subject's name was listed as James Prentiss, with a birthdate of 11/15/35. The officer reported that he responsed to a 4-55 signal at the Crisis Center. The officer found a large crowd in the parking lot attempting to revive the subject Prentiss. Witness No. 1, Bill Kerr, an Armedia Hospital Security employee, stated that at approximately 9:45 an unknown female approached him at the Crisis Center stating that "a man is hanging in the tree out there." Kerr went to the man and found him kneeling. He felt for vital signs and finding none, he contacted PSD.

Witness No. 2, Mary Jones, employed at Crisis Intervention, stated that at approximately 9:45 P.M. an unknown patient came into the Crisis Center screaming, "There's a man hanging in the tree out there." Ms. Jones states that she and other staff members ran out of the Crisis Center and discovered subject Prentiss hanging from a branch of the tree with his knees on the ground and a belt around his neck. They observed Kerr standing over the subject. When they approached, Kerr said, "Don't touch him, I think he's dead, leave him for the police." Ms. Jones stated that she pushed Kerr aside and she and a nurse cut the belt from the subject's neck and gave CPR.

Witness Bill Font confirmed the above.

Witness Leroy Elvin confirmed the above, and states that he saw Jones and Font removing the belt from Prentiss's neck and he assisted them with CPR.

Sylvester Giff arrived after the belt was removed and gave mouth-to-mouth resuscitation.

Albert Goff, a medical student, arrived after CPR had begun, and he assisted in attempting to revive the subject.

Dr. Jane Brady arrived when Prentiss was on a stretcher under the tree. There was no blood pressure or pulse and Prentiss had dilated pupils. After some time, Brady was able to revive the victim, who was transported to the emergency room. Brady diagnosed considerable brain damage and possibly a broken neck. It was learned from Crisis's staff that the subject was brought from Armedia Airport to Central Intake because he appeared too drunk to continue his flight.

According to the Crisis staff, while at Central Intake the subject was found with a razor blade at his throat. Fearing for his safety, Intake personnel transported the subject to Crisis for a psychiatric evaluation. Crisis advised that the subject was clocked in as a voluntary patient but that he had not spoken with a psychiatrist.

3.   Deposition—Ben Carstair, M.D.

Taken November 29th, 1983. Dr. Carstair states that he is a psychiatrist at Armedia Hospital, Psychiatric Institute. He also has a private practice. Dr. Carstair states that in June of 1980 he was in his second year of residency. He states, "He was never my patient—the only thing I did, I started intake." He indicated that he saw Mr. Prentiss on June 18, 1982. He states that he was intoxicated with alcohol. He was brought from Central Intake to the Crisis emergency room, and the person who brought him said that the patient, while at the airport, tried to cut his neck with a pocket knife. He states that the people from Central Intake wanted to know what the patient had to say. He does not remember a lot of the details.

Dr. Carstair says that the person in charge was Dr. Albert Rez. Part of the transcript is blurred, and it is impossible to read page 8. Dr. Carstair states that there was a man from Central Intake with them when they spoke originally. He says that the patient denied the situation and said, "I don't know what I did." There is some discrepancy in his report as to whether the man said, "I don't know what I did," or "I don't know why I did." Dr. Carstair states that he explained to the patient that he would have to be treated for a night to be able to continue his trip. The patient said that he was living in Atlanta, was married, with his wife in Atlanta. He states that 10 minutes later the patient disappeared from the area. He sent for him, and he was found hanging from a tree with a belt around his neck. When asked what he did after he first spoke to Mr. Prentiss, he says that he returned to his other patient and told him to wait to be seen later on. When asked if Mr. Prentiss was under observation by anybody else, he stated that he was a voluntary patient, so there was no reason to have anyone looking at him. He denies recalling whether he instructed any other staff member to keep an eye on Mr. Prentiss. He states that even though he was a resident, there was not another doctor supervising him at that moment.

Dr. Carstair says that the case was discussed with the staff, with Dr. Farber supervising. This was a mortality mobility meeting.

Dr. Carstair contradicts himself about what he heard from Mr. Prentiss in terms of his inebriation.

4. Deposition—Mary L. Jones

November 19th, 1983. Taken by attorneys for the plaintiff in the presence of the attorney for the defendant. Ms. Jones states that she is employed at the Armedia Hospital and has been there for 18½ years. She functions as a unit secretary. Her job is to do hospital records.

She does not remember a lot of details. Mr. Prentiss came to the psychiatric room. She does not recall how. She states that in 1982 the whole area was "voluntary." If a person walks in, they have a triage area. A person up front greets the individual with the question, "Why do you want to see the doctor?" They would then ask the person to have a seat, and someone else would come to get information about background and financial status. She states that there was no security area at that time; it was open. Her recall is relatively poor. She states that Central Intake is an alcohol detoxification place. She states that they receive patients from Central Intake regularly. She states that the Central Intake people bring a form with them when they turn over a patient.

Suicide Research

The importance of suicide in America today is measured by the large numbers of citizens, young and old, who take their own lives every day.

1. Characteristics of Those Who Commit Suicide

Three-quarters of those who commit suicide had previously threatened or attempted to take their lives. All efforts or gestures toward suicide must be considered serious by those faced with such behavior. Suicidal behavior is most serious when it follows some sort of emotional crisis. The availability of professional psychiatric, psychological, and social work specialists for the treatment of a potentially suicidal person may mean the difference between life and death (Shneidman & Farberow, 1957).

Patients who have made suicidal attempts and are entered into treatment have the highest suicide rate of any patient group (Shneidman, 1976).

Those who actually commit suicide generally do so during an acute suicidal crisis. This period is usually a matter of hours or days at most, and the individual is either helped, cools off, or dies. Eight out of 10 who kill themselves have given definite warnings of their suicidal intentions. To intervene and prevent a suicide, hospitals and crisis centers must provide good rapport, contact the patient's family, give emotional support, and focus on the reduction of lethality during the period of the suicidal crisis (Shneidman, 1973).

B. Dealing with Potentially Suicidal Patients

It is a misjudgment professionally to classify a first act of self-injury as a purely manipulative gesture. This constitutes a warning and must not be ignored by mental health professionals. Any act of deliberately inflicted self-damage which looks like a suicide attempt, or serious efforts in this direction, ought to be regarded and treated as a serious venture (Worden, 1976).

Suicide risk is considerably increased when an individual is under the influence of alcohol. Professionals must be acutely tuned to inebriated patients who are overwhelmed by feelings of despair, fear, and uncertainty. As Kiev (1976) states:

> Many people, by virtue of their social class membership or life situation have ready-made explanations for their distress and as such, may not seek appropriate help and for this reason be considered at high risk. One such group is the patients who attempt suicide, are evaluated as non-serious and summarily discharged from emergency rooms.

Kiev goes on to state that the potentially suicidal patient may turn to excessive alcohol use to relieve despair. Professionals must recognize the emotional disturbance which underlies such behavior and be aware of the potential for suicidal behavior. Some individuals demonstrate their deep disturbance preceding suicidal behavior by being unable to adequately express ideas or by misunderstanding the ideas of others. In weighing the gravity of suicidal attempts, the professional should evaluate:

1. The dangerousness of the attempt
2. Efforts to prevent assistance
3. Precipitating stresses
4. The use of alcohol
5. The patient's tendency to be impulsive

Patients with the highest degree of impulsivity tend to be the most dangerous or lethal.

Good treatment consists of appropriate medication and a meaningful patient–therapist relationship. What counts most is warmth, sympathy, understanding, and orientation to reality. Crisis intervention is vital.

A patient who is obviously disturbed and shows defects in reasoning and deductive fallacies requires treatment which includes protecting the patient from his or her own impulses. Such a patient is the least predictable (Shneidman, 1960).

Many hospitals have specific, written, known security measures. An example from a California hospital follows:

SUICIDE PRECAUTIONS*

When a patient drops clues such as "life is no longer worth living, I caused the last war," alert yourself to observe patient further. Make your report to the nurse. If patient's doctor feels patient is contemplating suicide, he may write an order placing patient on Suicidal Status.

Your responsibility then would be:

1. To make the environment safe. Remove articles that could be harmful such as glass vase, ceramic ash tray, cords, etc. Replace with articles that are less harmful. Be alert to solutions kept in housekeeping cupboards; check equipment left out in treatment room; check bathroom and shower room. Use common sense. Remember, you could take everything away, and if a patient wanted to, he could still harm himself. Be alert to your window screens, that they are locked at all times.

2. To be alert to use of utensils in the dining room. Allow patient to use knife, fork, spoon, china plate, glass, etc., but observe his handling of them. If his actions indicate misuse, step forward and quietly put it back in place. Allow your patient to be as other patients. Don't leave suggestion that you expect him to harm himself. Most patients are ambivalent; they want to live and they want to die. Try to give them more reason to want to live.

3. To be alert to use of tools at activities, especially O.T. If patient is using sharp tools, sit next to him working on some object yourself. Do not become so preoccupied with your work that you forget the patient. If you notice his behavior indicates possible missuse, reach over and place the tool in its proper place. Talk with the patient and others at the table. When occupied with group, patient is less likely to think of attempting suicide. Check that tools are replaced before leaving the clinic.

4. When escorting outside, be alert to roadways and walkways. Do not allow your patient to be the first one standing on the curb. Keep him more in the middle of the group. If escorting alone, time your stride so you arrive at the curb after cars have passed. When walking on sidewalks that have walls on one side, keep patient to the opposite side. Sometimes the wall tempts the patient and he jumps over the wall, falling to the

---

* Reprinted with permission from D. K. Reynolds and N. L. Farberow, Suicide Inside and Out (Berkeley: University of California Press, 1976).

ground below. Seldom have our patients who attempted this actually killed themselves, but they have sustained injuries such as broken ankles, heels, shoulders, and arms.

5. Supervise the use of sharps on the ward. Example: Patient asks to use the scissors. Ask what he plans to do with them. If you feel he can handle the scissors, then let him have them, but follow and observe his use of them. Chat with him. If you feel he is too impulsive, then go with him and tactfully use the scissors yourself. Sharps would be scissors, nail file, toe nail clippers, can opener, bottle opener, needle. These articles are kept in the Nursing Office in a locked cabinet.

6. Observe what patient picks up when you are escorting him. Patients see many things you and I would miss. Feel free to ask him what he has and take those things that qualify as contraband. Example: Sometimes a patient stops and picks up something from the ground. You step up and say, "What did you find?" Patient shows you a rusty razor blade. "Oh, that would cut someone's foot, it's good you saw it. We'll put it in a can so it can be safely discarded." What you say and how you say it is very important. If you notice patients are finding syringes and needles on the grounds, report this immediately to your nurse.

7. To be alert to patient when he is in the bathroom. Some patients plan to drown themselves in the lavatory. This means they will have to plug the sink. Drowning is difficult, so many patients plan to hit their heads against the faucet, hoping to become unconscious and face fall in the water. If patient's behavior indicates this type of thought, unplug sink and suggest they clean the sink. You are not expected to enter the individual closed commode area when such is present, but you observe the patient's feet which are showing. Example: Metal door is usually cut off about $2\frac{1}{2}$ feet from the floor. As long as patient's toes are facing you, or his heels, he's probably using the commode for the intended purpose; but if the sole of his shoe is showing, then investigate for the possibility that he may be trying to drown himself in the commode.

8. To be alert to your patient at medication time to see if he's saving medication. Example: Station yourself ahead of the patient if he's in a medication line. As he leaves line, observe movements of his arms as he walks away from you. If elbow bends and arm comes up, there is a possibility he may be spitting the medication out to save. When you make your report to Nurse, state you *suspect* the patient is not taking his medication. Role playing is used to demonstrate the approaches for effective use of safety precautions. Class is asked to suggest others not mentioned so far.

9. Close observation. Be aware of your patient—where he is, what he is doing. Try to keep him involved in activities or in area where others are present. Involve patient in your ward duties when possible. If you have been assigned to a special patient on suicidal status, he is your responsibility. Follow through on your safety precautions.
You do not need to breathe down his neck or hold on to him, but you need to be aware of where he is and what he is doing. If you have to leave the area, ask someone else to assume your specialing. Verbal and written reports of your observations and patient clues are very important

to the doctor and the nurse. Display a genuine interest in your patient as a person.

Problem Solving: You have been assigned to *special* an actively suicidal patient on status. Describe three additional safety precautions you would use.

Remember—Suicide is most likely to occur when the depression begins to lift.

Conclusions

Suicidal behavior is a frequent, tragic event in American life. It ranks as a major health problem. The conditions under which suicide occur have been extensively studied and are well known. Professionals in the mental health field are generally trained in identifying and dealing with a variety of suicidal phenomena. Suicidal emergencies require immediate professional attention of a warm, supportive, personal nature; the institutionalization of suicide precautions that include close observation of the patient, contact, and enlistment of significant others; and maintenance of these treatments through the crisis period. Previous suicidal ventures, excessive use of alcohol, mental disturbance, and impulsivity are the most dangerous signs of an imminent lethal effort.

Given the information regarding James Prentiss and his treatment at Armedia Hospital on June 18, 1982, the following evaluative comments seem appropriate:

1. The Crisis Center was apparently established to deal with patients experiencing mental crises, including suicidal thoughts and behavior.

2. The staff should have been trained in identifying and treating suicidal crises.

3. Mr. Prentiss was delivered from another treatment setting specifically for psychiatric treatment.

4. The ranking staff member:
   a. Communicated with Mr. Prentiss.
   b. Was aware he was being transferred from another treatment facility.
   c. Was aware Mr. Prentiss was inebriated.
   d. Was aware Mr. Prentiss acted in a peculiar or unusual manner at the airport.
   e. Was informed that Mr. Prentiss had engaged in self-dangerous behavior before coming to the Crisis Center.
   f. Was not able to elicit a coherent or sensible story from Mr. Prentiss.

    g.   Told Mr. Prentiss to "wait."

    h.   Did not consult with a superior in spite of the above and in spite of the physician's status as a second year psychiatric resident.

Usual and customary professional procedure for the circumstances in which Mr. Prentiss came to the Crisis Center would include:

1. Immediate efforts to determine in detail the circumstances preceding Mr. Prentiss's being brought to the Crisis Center.
2. Assignment of a staff person to establish rapport with the patient and ensure that impulsive behavior not occur.
3. Evaluation of the patient's current emotional status and potential dangerousness.
4. Consultation with a senior staff person if there is any doubt as to appropriate procedures, medications, or staff involvement in the patient's best interests.

As soon as a staff member establishes rapport with the patient, efforts should be directed to:

1. Identifying the precipitating incident for the crisis.
2. The lethality of the patient's suicidal ideation.
3. The degree of emotional disturbance being suffered by the patient.
4. Significant other persons who might level support to see the patient through the crisis.
5. Engaging the patient in making stable, realistic plans to ease tension and resolve conflicts.
6. Reassuring the patient of the availability of help and support.
7. Where necessary, arranging for the involvement of other staff or facilities to ensure that the patient survives the crisis.
8. Keeping the patient under observation at all times.

There appears to be a considerable discrepancy between the usual and customary procedure to be followed in treating a suicidal crisis and the treatment received by Mr. Prentiss on June 18, 1982.

References

Kiev, A. (1976). Crisis intervention and suicide prevention. In E. S. Shneidman (Ed.), *Suicidology: Contemporary Development*. 1976. New York: Grune & Stratton.

Litman, R. E. (1957). Some aspects of the treatment of the potentially suicidal patient. In E. S. Shneidman and N. L. Farberow (Eds.), *Clues to Suicide*. New York: McGraw-Hill.

Reynolds, D. K. & Farberow, N. L. (1976). *Suicide Inside and Out*. Berkeley: University of California Press.

Shneidman, E. S. & Farberow, N. L. (Eds.) (1957). *Clues to Suicide*. New York: McGraw-Hill.

Shneidman, E. S. (1960). The logical environment of suicide. *California's Health. 17*, (22), 193–196.

Shneidman, E. S. (1973). Suicide. In *Encyclopaedia Brittanica* (14th Ed.), Vol. 21, pp. 383–385.

Shneidman, E. S. (Ed.) (1976). *Suicidology: Contemporary Developments*. New York: Grune & Stratton.

Worden, J. W. (1976). Lethality factors and the suicide attempt. In E. S. Shneidman (Ed.), *Suicidology: Contemporary Developments*. New York: Grune & Stratton.

In this instance, the psychologist was used as a rebuttle witness (discussed in Chapter 10). As can be seen from these few examples of the use of psychological testimony or opinion in personal injury litigation, this area of litigation probably offers the broadest opportunity for the use of psychological scientists and practitioners in the courtroom.

10

Your Day in Court

The chances that you will prepare for the role of expert witness and then step into the courtroom to give testimony are quite slim. Most civil and criminal trials are settled by negotiation or plea bargaining. For every 15 or 20 cases the expert witness prepares, he or she is likely to give testimony in only 1, which is disconcerting to some psychologists, who experience a sense of incompletion.

In reality, justice and the promotion of human welfare are probably better served when the expert's work results in a conclusion before a trial commences. Magnificent as the American system of jurisprudence is in comparison with other systems, overcrowded dockets continually jeopardize the essential constitutional right to a speedy trial. Anything that aids in the resolution of adversary issues represents a major social contribution. Expert testimony, available to both the plaintiff and defense attorneys in civil matters and the prosecution and defense in criminal matters, often provides information that contributes to pretrial settlements.

The findings of the expert become known to the attorney who retains the expert (or to the judge for whom the expert is *amicus curiae*) when the report of findings is submitted. At that point, the retaining attorney may decide that the results are not useful for his or her trial strategy, and the expert is thanked, paid, and not listed as a witness; under these circumstances, the work of the expert is privileged and may not be revealed to anyone without the explicit permission of the attorney who had retained the expert.

THE DEPOSITION

Once the retaining attorney places the expert on the witness list, the opposing counsel has the right to know the essential content of the expected testimony by the expert. During what is known as the *discovery phase* before the trial, attorneys for both sides have the right to subpoena (demand) all records related to the expert witness's role in the proceedings. Sometimes the opposing counsel is satisfied to receive a copy of the ex-

212

pert's report. More usually, the opposing counsel obtains a court order called *subpoena duces tecum*, which, in effect, sets a date and hour when the witness is to produce all records connected with his or her role in the case and be prepared to answer questions posed by the opposing counsel.

Usual procedure is for the attorney's secretary to call the psychologist's office and ask for an hour or so of time when the opposing counsel can come to the expert's office and conduct the *deposition*. This formal procedure more frequently takes two hours, and the expert should block out this time accordingly. The psychologist should provide a place where five or six people can sit and work comfortably, since the deposition is a courtlike procedure involving the attorney who retained the expert, opposing counsel, a court reporter (complete with stenotype machine and tape recorder), and frequently one or two neophyte lawyers brought along by each attorney. It is during the deposition process that young lawyers learn their tradecraft much as do interns and residents during rounds in a medical setting.

Ordinarily, the attorney who retains the expert witness will call and ask to see the expert a half-hour or so before the deposition. During this time the attorney prepares the expert for the expected questions and reviews the psychologist's file in order to remove any materials that constitute *work product*. This legal term refers to materials that may relate to the attorney's trial strategy or plan and are *not discoverable* (available to opposing counsel during the discovery process).

It is the wise or experienced expert who, after agreeing to a deposition time, contacts the retaining attorney's secretary or assistant to ensure that they are aware of the date and time the deposition will take place and to further ensure a predeposition conference, so that the attorney prepares his or her expert and is aware of the content and limits of the psychologist's material.

Some attorneys encourage their experts to prepare no report before the trial. The purpose of this legal maneuver is to reveal as little as possible to opposing counsel regarding the expert's findings and position. What might constitute clever case strategy for an attorney can be potentially unethical or professionally unacceptable behavior for a psychologist. Within the clear limits imposed by law, the psychologist as expert must conduct scientific and professional activities as expected by the ethics and standards of psychology; the expert witness must always do exactly that and not be an advocate in the case at hand.

The deposition is conducted in a relatively formal manner, depending on the jurisdiction in which it occurs and the style of the attorneys involved. It usually proceeds as follows:

1. Swearing in
2. Qualifications
3. Direct examination

4. Cross-examination
5. Re-direct examination
6. Re-cross-examination
7. Records access
8. Certification of the deposition

Because a deposition is a matter of legal record, the court reporter will ask the expert witness to stand and "swear (or affirm) to tell the truth, the whole truth, and nothing but the truth—so help you God?" This makes the proceedings official. At that point, the attorney who scheduled the deposition begins the proceedings with *qualifications.* This introduces the expert witness and proffers his or her credentials as a basis for the forthcoming testimony. Questions include name, office address, number of years in the community, definition of professional role, education, training, accomplishments, experience, honors, and special credentials. During the course of this the retaining attorney may proffer the witness's curriculum vita or resume in order to save time. The expert should anticipate this request and have a copy of his or her curriculum vita available. This becomes an *exhibit* as part of the deposition materials.

Unless the opposing counsel objects to the qualifications of the expert as sufficient for testimony, at some point, he or she will "stipulate to the doctor's credentials as an expert," meaning that the expert is acceptable. At this point the direct examination begins. It is here that the expert witness "tells the story." Some attorneys ask the expert to tell how he or she was retained, what was done, and what conclusions were reached in very broad questions, allowing the expert to testify according to his or her own style—usually following the expert's report format. Other attorneys conduct direct examination point by point either in respect to the expert's written report or according to an internal format unique to the attorney. (In court, where direct examination is conducted by the retaining attorney, it usually follows a plan agreed upon by the attorney and the expert. In the deposition, the format of direct examination is controlled by the opposing counsel.) When the direct examination becomes picky, tangential, or hostile, the retaining attorney will usually "object for the record" and suggest that his or her colleague be more reasonable, patient, to the point, and so on, or "give the witness a chance to explain in her own way."

Once the attorney who conducts the direct examination has finished questioning the expert, retaining counsel may conduct a cross-examination on anything brought out during direct examination. During depositions the cross-examination (usually conducted by the attorney who hired the expert) is ordinarily quite brief, designed to clarify any misunderstandings but not to increase opposing counsel's knowledge of the case.

Following cross-examination, the attorney who conducted the direct examination may choose to ask a few more questions, and if he or she does, the retaining counsel is entitled to conduct a re-cross-examination. Charts and illustrations are ordinarily not presented during depositions, since this would require that the psychologist provide copies to be marked as exhibits and retained by the court reporter.

When these procedures are completed, the attorney who scheduled the deposition will usually ask for copies of reports, interviews, notes, test forms, and profiles in the expert's case folder. The expert may provide these using his or her own staff and equipment or may provide the entire file to the court reporter, who will reproduce it and later return the file to the expert. Some experienced witnesses simply reproduce everything in the file and have it ready for the deposition.

When all attorneys present agree that the deposition is finished, one of them or the court reporter will ask, "Will the witness waive reading and signing?" This means that the deposition can be typed and forwarded to the attorneys without the witness reading the transcription and attesting to its accuracy by signing it. Most lawyers recommend "waiving" as a convenience to the court reporter and as a time saver for themselves. *The expert should never waive reading and signing of the transcript.* The materials are complex, and even the best court reporter makes mistakes, such as "percentage" for "percentile," "chemical psychologist" for "clinical psychologist," ".10 level of confidence" for ".01 level of confidence," and so on. The transcript is the official, sworn statement of the expert and can in most cases be introduced during the trial during cross-examination. Errors should be identified and corrected in the interests of the expert and the clients served by the expert's testimony.

Of even greater importance is the opportunity for the expert to reproduce a copy of the deposition for the case file. In major cases, the expert may appear in court months after the deposition was taken. If the expert does not have a copy to review of what he or she has told opposing counsel during the deposition, the psychologist may find that his or her responses to specific questions posed months ago are all but forgotten. An ad lib response without access to the original transcript may put the psychologist in the embarrassing and precarious position of giving an answer on the witness stand that appears to be different from an answer given during the deposition. This could result in opposing counsel's claiming that the expert witness's credibility is impeached by the expert's own confusion. *Do not waive reading and signing of depositions.* Correct the transcript when received from the court reporter, make a copy for the case file, and review the transcript the day before the trial.

THE TRIAL

Should the case not be settled or plea-bargained, the trial will commence. The date of trial is set in a procedure sometimes called *docket sound-*

ing, in which the judge, with the various attorneys, apportions a certain number of days per trial or a certain number of trials per week during the court's calendar. Such dates are approximate. The expert witness is likely to receive a letter from the retaining attorney stating:

> The *Smith v. Jones* case is set on the docket for the week of February 16th. Please note this on your calendar and contact this office if for any reason you cannot be available for testimony during that week. This office will be in touch with you just before the trial to schedule your testimony in this matter.

Experienced experts understand that court dockets are flexible and that some cases take longer than anticipated. Some are settled "on the courthouse steps," freeing court time for the next case or for the calendar to be moved up. The expert should specify preferred times to appear during the week of the trial but remain somewhat flexible in respect to the uncertainties of trial procedures.

The expert witness has a relatively small, albeit usually important, part in the trial proceedings. Civil and criminal trials proceed in slightly different ways. The court has discretion in changing the order of trial proceedings, but in general both criminal and civil trials follow a format that includes:

1. Filing of motions by attorneys
2. Voir dire (jury selection)
3. Instructions to jury (judge)
4. Opening statements
   a. Prosecutor or plaintiff's attorney
   b. Defendant's attorney
5. Presentation of evidence—direct
   a. Plaintiff or prosecutor's case
   b. Defendant's case
6. Presentation of evidence—rebuttal
   a. Plaintiff's attorney or prosecutor's rebuttal
   b. Defendant's rebuttal
7. Opening final argument
   a. Plaintiff's attorney or prosecutor
   b. Defendant's attorney
8. Closing arguments
   a. Plaintiff's attorney or prosecutor
   b. Defendant's attorney
9. Instructions to jury

10. Decision
    a. Settlement for civil cases
    b. Guilt or acquittal in criminal cases

The expert witness appears during the presentation of direct evidence, proffered by the attorney for the plaintiff, the prosecutor (the state), or the defendant. Occasionally, the expert witness may be called during rebuttal, and on very rare occasions, the expert witness may appear as amicus curiae, or "friend of the court," called by the judge. Amicus curiae is more usual in juvenile court procedures or in appellate reviews (appeals).

PRETRIAL PREPARATION

Scheduling and Conferences

The expert witness should request that the attorney schedule his or her as the first witness in the morning or afternoon court session. Whereas some expert witnesses prefer to "be on call" and leave their offices 15 to 20 minutes before they are required, testify, and return to their waiting patients, it is unusual for psychologists to qualify and testify so briefly as to allow this. It is wiser to block out an entire morning or afternoon and ask to be the first witness called when court reconvenes at 9:00 A.M. or 2:00 P.M. Most attorneys will try to arrange this if it doesn't interfere with the order of evidence they've planned.

The afternoon before the expert is scheduled to testify, a call to the attorney's assistant will ensure that the trial is continuing and that there is no change in the expected time of testimony. It is disconcerting to arrive at the courthouse and discover that the trial was settled or postponed the previous day. These matters are complex, and sometimes witnesses are not informed of plans which change.

It is of cardinal importance that the psychologist arrange a final conference with the retaining attorney before the court appearance. All the following should be clearly determined between the attorney and the expert witness before the witness is called to the stand:

1. Questions to be used in qualification
2. The sequence of questions and responses in the direct examination
3. Hypothetical questions the attorney is likely to pose to the witness following direct examination
4. The limits of the psychologist's findings
5. Probable approaches to be used by opposing counsel during cross-examination

6.   Something about the demographics and responses of the jury members

7.   The presiding judge's style and special expectancies

8.   Any special limitations the physical environment of the courtroom may pose for presentation of charts or other visual materials

Some attorneys assume that the psychologist will give brief, generalized opinions, followed by answers "within reasonable medical certainty" to hypothetical questions posed by the attorney. During pretrial conferences the psychologist should be sure that the retaining attorney understands that psychological testimony generally involves an extensive presentation concerning what psychology is as a science and profession, the nature of probability, the nature of science, the purposes of psychological examinations, the qualitative and quantitative output of such examinations, and the limitations of findings and conclusions. The attorney must be helped to understand that all hypothetical questions he or she asks during direct or redirect examination should be addressed "within reasonable psychological probability." It is clearly better to resolve all these matters before the psychologist takes the stand.

Some expert witnesses find that a checklist of pretrial tasks is helpful to ensure that all preparatory steps have been taken in getting ready for court day. Figure 4.8 in Chapter 4 (page 39) presents such a checklist.

Charts and Illustrations

Sometimes a particular aspect of psychological testimony is best presented via a chart, a table, or an illustration. The decision to use visual aids should be governed by the opportunities and limitations of the physical environment of the courtroom, as well as the judge's patience. Visual aids that lend little to the expert's verbal explanations are poorly received by most judges and are sometimes rejected or excluded. Charts that are complex, difficult to see, or overly bulky disrupt the flow of testimony and lessen the witness's effectiveness. Easels, chalkboards, and projection screens are usually provided for chart display. Psychologists are advised to be extremely cautious about treating the judge and jury as undergraduates who must tolerate the professor's tangential or indistinct chalkboard illustrations or scribbled formulae. Charts should be very clear at a distance of 25 feet, since both judge and jury must view the material at the same time. Videotape and slide presentations tend to disrupt the smooth flow of a witness's testimony. Using a small number of charts to illustrate key data or conclusions in the expert's report probably represents the most reasonable approach to this matter. Figure 10.1, a simple but powerful example of the kind of chart that serves as a useful adjunct to an expert witness's testimony, illustrates total scores on the Holmes Stress scale for the plain-

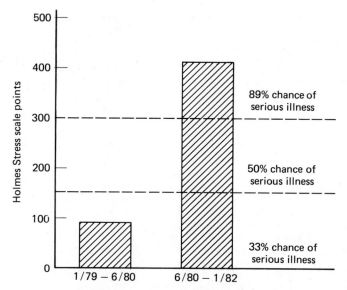

FIGURE 10.1.   A chart used during court to illustrate the stressful effects of a tragic death. A comparison of stress levels for Mr J. Doe for a period of 18 months previous to the tragic death of his wife and daughter and the 18 months following this event; also, the probable results of these stress levels on illness-vulnerability.

tiff who claimed that the stress level resulting from the tragic death of his wife and daughter in a railway accident contributed to the subsequent decline in his health.

Cue Book

Opposing counsel's job is to win for his or her client. Part of a winning trial strategy is to cast doubt on the credibility or standing of expert witnesses presented by an opponent. During cross-examination an opposing attorney may ask a wide range of tangential or esoteric questions in an effort to fluster the expert. Such questions as "What is the standard error of measurement?" or "Please tell the jury the standard deviation for Full scale Wechsler Adult Intelligence Scale–Revised for people between the ages of 55 and 64," or "What do psychologists mean by 'validity'?" are typical. Although retaining counsel may, on occasion, object to such questions as immaterial, irrelevant, or incompetent, in general, experts are expected to field such probes. Should the expert answer well, opposing counsel will be placed in the undesirable position of having demonstrated the quality and credibility of the opponent's expert.

The expert witness may wish to respond to all questions ad lib, but it is quite permissible to refer to materials and references. A *cue book* is a collection of materials that may be useful to support direct testimony or as reference in responding to questions during cross-examination. Taking a cue book to court ensures the availability of authoritative reference material should this be required. Figure 10.2 illustrates a table of contents of such a cue book. It will be noted in Figure 10.2 that some items in the cue book are quite basic, or general, while others are quite specific, directed to particular test instruments or issues in the case. Building a cue book in a large, three-

FIGURE 10.2.   A sample table of contents of a cue book.

ring, bound notebook will allow the expert to arrange it differently for each trial appearance.

Since the majority of cases are settled without a court appearance, preparation of charts, illustrations, and cue book materials should take place the day before the expert expects to testify.

Dress and Decor

Courtrooms are formal settings and they operate with a great deal of ritual. No matter what a witness may personally feel about the usefulness of such formality, experts who wish to be more effective in court will dress and conduct themselves accordingly. Dark suits and conservative, even muted, accessories are recommended. The expert witness is expected to be a serious, concerned, dedicated professional person whose grasp of information and ability to communicate stand out. Nothing in the expert's dress or demeanor should detract from the essential roles.

To transport case file, cue book, test materials, and other paraphernalia to court, the expert should consider obtaining a large briefcase or "sample case" specifically for court work. Since legal files tend to be quite bulky, such a case is a convenience as well as a part of the expert witness's self-presentation as a conservative person, serious and professional. The same is true of chart folders or chart cases, obtainable at either stationery supply houses or artists' supply stores. Black is the preferred color for these occasions, in keeping with the conservative theme.

Getting to Courtroom

The expert should know where the courtroom is located, how to get there, and what parking facilities exist, when necessary. Arriving late can have serious consequences for the retaining attorney's planned trial strategy and characterizes a thoughtless and unprofessional expert. Arriving somewhat early is advisable.

If the retaining attorney does not meet the expert at the courthouse, the expert should announce his or her presence to either the judge's secretary or to a bailiff in the corridor near the courtroom where the trial takes place. The judge's office is usually very close to the courtroom and is clearly identified. Bailiffs are men and women, usually in uniform, wearing a badge. They are available in the corridors and courtrooms whenever a trial is in progress. The witness should indicate who he or she is and ask that the retaining attorney be informed that the witness is present and ready. The judge's secretary or the bailiff may ask the witness to "wait" or may put the expert in a "witness room." There is a separate witness room for each side in the case. Under no circumstances should the expert converse in any way with persons associated with the opposing side in the case. This could result in the judge declaring a mistrial.

The witness must be especially careful not to enter the courtroom while the trial is in progress until called to give testimony. Judicial rules require that no witness in an adversary matter be exposed or have interaction with the presentation of trial evidence other than that to be given by the expert witness.[1] This procedure of keeping witnesses uncontaminated by the trial proceedings until their turn comes is called *invoking the rule.* Should an expert witness arrive early, sit in the courtroom during the trial, and then later be sworn in as a witness, the judge, on being informed of this, usually by opposing counsel or a bailiff, may declare a mistrial or even hold the expert in contempt of court, subjecting the witness to a fine (or even some time in the local jail if the judge is so inclined). In some jurisdictions, the judge does not invoke the rule on occasion, and the witnesses may sit in the courtroom and hear each other's testimony. A witness should always ask the retaining attorney if the judge "invokes the rule."

Sometimes it is necessary to wait in the witness room while some aspect of trial business takes place: Motions are filed, issues are discussed in the judge's chambers, the judge may declare a recess, or previous testimony may take longer than was anticipated. The well-advised expert will bring along some reading or busy work *not associated with the case at hand.* Going over reports or case materials while waiting to be called to the witness stand will only serve to make the expert more tense and probably less effective.

THE COURTROOM DRAMA

The expert witness may appear in a number of courtroom settings. Some of these settings may be moderately informal, such as the judge's chambers for custody hearings or a hearing room for disability determinations. Most settings and all procedures in which the expert witness will participate are quite formal. Figure 3.1 in Chapter 3 illustrates the state and federal court systems of the United States.

Experts are unlikely to be called to testify in municipal or lower district courts at the state levels or at magistrate courts in the federal system. Minor offenses and arraignments take place in these courts. Trials take place in the circuit courts at the state level and in federal district courts. Rarely are witnesses called during appeals at any level since most appellate courts review the records in issues being addressed.

Most courtrooms follow the same general architectural plan. A raised portion, called the *bench,* is the domain of the judge. Surrounded by flags and shields, the judge reigns supreme in this setting, sitting in a large swivel chair, surveying all and everything. To the judge's right (or sometimes left) is the jury box, also raised (but not as high as the judge's bench). As many as 15 to 30 chairs or seats will be found here, since potential jurors

[1] Rule of Sequestration. Fla. Rules of Crim. Procedure 3.131 B-3

are sometimes examined during the voir dire (jury selection phase of the trial). A table for the plaintiff or prosecution and one for the defendant, a table for the court reporter, a podium for the attorneys' presentations, chairs for the bailiffs, and a spectators section complete the usual courtroom environment. The expert witness sits in the witness-box, usually to the judge's right (in some courtrooms, if the jury box is to the judge's left, so is the witness-box). Figure 10.3 illustrates a typical courtroom setting.

When called from the witness room or corridor, the expert is generally ushered in by a bailiff. At this point the trial is in full swing. The jury has heard opening statements from both sides and a fair amount of evidence before the expert appears. Most expert witnesses are called toward the end of the evidence portion of the trial. The jury is ready to hear something that is not in their everyday experience and to learn and weigh the value of what the expert says in the matter at hand before facing the responsibility of rendering a fair verdict. The expert enters the courtroom after the judge has said to the attorney at the podium, "You may proceed, counselor." At this point the attorney who retains the expert usually says, 'I call Dr. _____."

Some bailiffs will explain what is expected of the witness, while others leave the witness to her or his own devices. When ushered into the courtroom (point *J* in Figure 10.3), the witness should stop and evaluate the setting. Nothing will happen until the witness is properly seated. First the witness should identify the location of the witness-box (*B* in Figure 10.3). Occasionally a courtroom will have *two* witness-boxes, one on each side of the judge's bench. The proper one for the witness is the witness-box being faced by the court reporter seated at *C* in Figure 10.3. The witness should walk directly to the corner of the witness-box and say *nothing* to anyone in the courtroom but nod to the judge as the bench is passed. Reaching the corner of the witness-box, *B*, the witness should turn, face the man or woman seated at *C* (the court clerk or reporter), and raise the right arm. Do not wait to be instructed. Do not hesitate. Nothing can be done until the witness is sworn. Following these procedures without hesitation announces to all present that this expert understands courtroom procedure and is, indeed, an expert.

At this point the court clerk will stand and raise his or her hand and say: "Do you swear (or affirm) to tell the truth, the whole truth, and nothing but the truth so help you God?"

There may be a slight modification of this in some jurisdictions, but this is the essential procedure. Occasionally, the court clerk will approach the witness with a Bible, asking that the left hand be placed on the Bible and the right hand raised. This is a rare procedure today.

After the witness says "I do" or "I shall," the court clerk usually says, "Take the stand" or "Be seated." The status and significance of witnesses is illustrated by the fact that the witness-box is raised one step—equal to the jury but lower than the judge.

FIGURE 10.3. A typical courtroom. *A*: judge's bench; *B*: witness-box; *C*: court reporter; *D*: defense table; *E*: prosecution or plaintiff table; *F*: jury box; *G*: bailiff's chairs; *H*: spectators, observers, and reporters; *I*: witness entrance; *J*: public entrance; *K*: jury entrance; *L*: judge's entrance; and *M*: attorneys' podium.

Once sworn, the witness should step up into the witness-box. There are usually a swivel armchair and a shelf on the front rail of the witness-box that can serve as a desk for the expert's materials. On being seated, the witness should turn to the judge, only two or three feet away, smile, and quietly say, "Good morning (or good afternoon), your Honor." This acknowledgment of the judge is good manners and helps to establish the witness's credibility with the bench. Briefcase and chart case should be opened but left on the floor of the witness-box, readily available when materials are to be retrieved.

THE EVIDENCIARY PROCESS

The expert has been called by one side or the other to be a part of the presentation of evidence to the judge and jury. The process may vary in content, but the structure is fairly rigid and quite predictable. It is a process of "taking turns" between two attorneys representing adversary positions in the matter at hand. Unless the witness serves as amicus curiae, he or she will be called during the evidenciary portion of the trial assigned to the attorney who retained the witness (see the section "The Trial"). Once the witness is called and sworn, the following process occurs for the purpose of entering the expert's statements and conclusions in the minds of the judge and jury and in the record of the trial.

The expert witness is usually called toward the end of the retaining attorney's presentation. The judge and jury have heard a variety of presentations from the attorneys and various witnesses. Most of the jurors and probably the judge have formed a framework for the evidence. They have been hearing other evidence and may even have reached some preliminary conclusion as to the decisions they will render in the case. The testimony of the expert may solidify or modify a series of conclusions, which are, to some degree, already formed. The expert will be identified to the jury as such by the attorney, with the approval of the judge. The jury will have been instructed by the judge that all decisions are theirs. They will be told that they are to weigh the opinions of experts as they weigh other evidence. They may accept, reject, or question expert opinion. The expert witness serves as a *source of influence* upon the *targets of influence* (see Figure 10.4). The retaining attorney has a right to expect that the expert will do everything possible to make the presentation thorough, defensible, scientifically reliable, and valid within reasonable psychological probability in a manner logical and understandable to the judge and jury.

The expert witness is not required and should not attempt to advocate for one side or the other, shade the data in favor of one adversary or the other, omit pertinent facts or expand inconsequential elements of a presentation. It is the expert's responsibility to resist and discourage such maneuvers. The expert should be neither surprised nor offended by any efforts by

FIGURE 10.4.   A model of social influence in the courtroom.

opposing attorneys to expand or aggrandize evidence in favor of their client—that is their job. The expert is an element of the adversary process but not an advocate. Anything the expert can do to avoid thinking in terms of "our side," "our case," "winning," or "beating them" will be helpful in maintaining perspective and appropriate behavior as an expert witness.

Qualification of the Witness

The witness is called by an attorney to provide information that, because of its uniqueness in relation to some science, profession, training, or experience, is unlikely to be common knowledge or in the experience of the average juror. The first step in the process is to demonstrate the expert's specialness or right to claim expert status. If opposing counsel and the judge accept the witness as qualified, the evidence may be presented. If opposing counsel objects to the expert's qualifications and the judge agrees with the objections or if the judge determines that the "expert" is not qualified, the judge will say, "You may step down," thus dismissing the proffered expert before testimony is given. The following is a representative sequence of questions and answers that may be used to qualify an expert in clinical psychology:

Mr. Jones
  (*Retaining attorney*): Please state your name.
Dr. Doe: John Doe.
Mr. Jones: Would you tell the Judge and jury your profession.
Dr. Doe: I am a clinical psychologist.
Mr. Jones: Where do you practice, Doctor?

Dr. Doe:	I am staff psychologist at the Kaufman Mental Health Center.
Mr. Jones:	Is that here in Okachobee?
Dr. Doe:	Yes, at 121 Main Street.
Mr. Jones:	How long have you been staff psychologist there?
Dr. Doe:	For the past 14 years.
Mr. Jones:	Please tell the Judge and jury what a clinical psychologist is in terms of education, training, and function.
Dr. Doe:	A clinical psychologist is a person who has received a bachelor's degree in psychology and has then gone on to recieve the doctorate in psychology, these degrees taking between 8 and 10 years to complete. During this time studies are taken in basic science, behavioral science, human development, learning, emotions, adjustment, normal and abnormal human behavior, and research in psychology. The individual learns techniques of diagnosis, therapy, and other helping interventions in supervised training and internship centers. Following the award of the doctor's degree, the psychologist must acquire a minimum of one year's postdoctoral supervised training in order to be eligible for licensing examination administered by the state. Licensed clinical psychologists diagnose and treat a wide range of mental disorders, emotional disturbances, family and marital problems, and difficulties associated with child development, adolescence, problems of aging, and so on. A clinical psychologist is an expert in the practice of the science of human behavior.
Mr. Jones:	Are you licensed in this state?
Dr. Doe:	Yes, sir.
Mr. Jones:	Are you an expert in neuropsychology?
Dr. Doe:	Yes, sir.
Mr. Jones:	In your work as a neuropsychologist, do you have occasion to examine patients and determine whether they have brain injury or brain disorder?
Dr. Doe:	Yes, sir.
Mr. Smith (*Opposing counsel*):	I object, Your Honor. There are no indications that this witness is a graduate of an accredited medical school.

This rarely occurs during qualification nowadays, but on occasion, where the lawyers are not familiar with the background of psychologists, this type of objection might be made. This can be handled in several ways. Mr. Jones, the retaining attorney, may ask, "May we approach the bench, your Honor?" for the purpose of discussing the psychologist's qualification and citing legal decisions or precedent qualifying psychologists in these matters. The counsel who retained the psychologist may debate the issue directly, before the jury, without asking to approach the bench.

Mr. Jones: Your Honor, I submit that psychologists have testified as experts in matters of brain injury, brain disorder, mental disease, and mental illness for many years. I submit that, according to the laws of the state, and federal procedure, Dr. Doe is fully qualified in this matter, and I would be happy to have him voir dired as to his specific qualifications.

The above statement refers to the attorney's response to opposing counsel's challenge, indicating that he is more than happy to show the jury how eminently qualified Dr. Doe is as an expert. At this point the judge may allow such questioning or may ask the bailiff to take the jury out so that the judge can conduct some questioning of the witness in order to determine that the witness is qualified to give testimony as an expert in the matters being considered.

As noted above, it is rare that psychologists of good qualification are challenged in any courts of the land. This is far different from the situation a decade ago. Ordinarily, the procedure is more likely as follows:

Mr. Smith: (*standing*) Your Honor, we wish to stipulate as to the qualifications of the witness.

This means that Mr. Smith does not want the jury to hear any more about the qualifications of Dr. Doe. At this point the retaining attorney may simply accept this. On the other hand, it may be of interest to him to have more of the qualifications presented to the jury. The judge is unlikely to allow the retaining attorney to "aggrandize" the witness. It is up to the retaining attorney to demonstrate the necessity of presenting the qualifications. This is sometimes done as follows:

Mr. Jones: Your Honor, I would like to continue with the qualification, since, in this case, the issue of addiction and the use of alcohol is of considerable significance. Dr. Doe has certain special qualifications that I believe are important as part of the qualification.

The Bench: You may proceed in your qualification, but I want you to be sure that you focus only on the pertinent background.

Mr. Jones:	Thank you, Your Honor. And now, Dr. Doe, have you had any special background or training in the treatment of alcohol or other drug-related conditions?
Dr. Doe:	Yes, sir, I have.
Mr. Jones:	Would you please tell the Judge and jury what special background you have in these areas?
Dr. Doe:	Following the receipt of my doctor's degree, I spent two years, first as a postdoctoral trainee and then as a staff psychologist, at the Alcoholic Rehabilitation Center at Camp Butner, North Carolina. During that time my duties were entirely involved with alcohol abuse, its diagnosis, its treatment, and rehabilitation. We also had a drug rehabilitation center attached to our unit, and I spent considerable time there both in training and in practice.
Mr. Jones:	Your Honor, I submit that Dr. Doe is qualified in this matter.
The Bench:	You may proceed, Mr. Jones.

The above statement by the judge means that Dr. Doe has been qualified to proceed with his testimony.

Direct Examination

The direct examination is conducted by the attorney who calls the expert witness. The purpose of the direct examination is to present as clearly and strongly as possible information supportive of the retaining attorney's case. Evidence presented by an expert witness is usually considered very seriously by the judge and jury. The attorney who retains the expert will usually conduct the direct examination in such a way that the findings and opinions of the expert are presented to the judge and jury in a smooth, logical, and understandable sequence of questions and answers. Some attorneys prepare their expert witnesses with one or more pretrial conferences, whereas other attorneys prefer their experts to testify "spontaneously" as to their findings. The psychologist who expects to be a credible and effective witness in the direct examination would be well advised to arrange a pretrial preparation of the direct examination. Agreement between the attorney and the expert as to the sequence of questions, length, style, and content of answers, use of charts or illustrations, and the form in which hypothetical questions are to be presented will help ensure a smooth, professional direct examination.

Because of the complexities and technicalities of psychological matters, much attention must be paid to the issue of carefully educating the judge and jury to these matters as the testimony unfolds. In some ways, the expert must perform as a teacher, explaining procedures and methods, before the results of an assessment or an opinion concerning an occurrence are presented to the judge and jury. The expert witness and the presenting attorney must strike a rather difficult balance in the direct examination, neither boring nor confusing the judge and jury with too much or too little information. Two or three experiences on the witness stand or even the reading of the court transcripts of direct examination of expert witnesses will probably be sufficient to convince most neophyte expert witnesses of the wisdom of the pretrial conference.

A traditional approach to making a clear and effective presentation requires a series of simple questions by the attorney and relatively short answers by the expert, gradually bringing out both the scientific bases of the testimony and the findings and opinions of the expert. This approach is extremely effective but puts great demands on the expert to be precise and concise at the same time. This particular communication skill, in a sense, defines the *expert* witness. No matter the credentials and technical knowledge possessed by the expert witness, the effectiveness with which the expert conveys information is the paramount issue in court.

All direct examinations have unique features, but a general format may be expected. The presenting attorney will first ask questions concerning how the expert became involved in the matter at hand. The expert will be asked what he or she did and the significance of the procedures. This will be followed by questions concerned with results and interpretations. The final questions will be *hypothetical questions* designed to summarize the expert's testimony, clearly but simply state the expert's opinions in the matter, and relate the testimony to the attorney's key premises and positions in the case.

The following illustrates how the direct examination begins in a case involving a 34-year-old woman who was the victim in an automobile accident which occurred two and one-half years before the trial. She was a passenger in a car that was struck head-on by a truck; was unconscious for 10 days following the initial trauma; and underwent surgery for the removal of a subdural hematoma in the left parieto-occipital areas of the brain shortly after admission to the hospital. Residual complaints include right-sided weakness, headaches, memory deficits, nervousness, clumsiness, double vision, and impulsive acts. Arithmetic skills are said by the patient to be lowered since the accident. The direct examination is by Mr. Albee, the retaining attorney, who represents the plaintiff, Mrs. Alberts; the psychologist-expert witness is Dr. White; and opposing counsel, representing the defendants (the driver of the truck and his insurance company) is Mr. McCracken.

Mr. Albee: When did you first become involved in this case, Doctor?

Dr. White: I received a call from you on September 18, 1982, requesting me to examine Mrs. Alberts.

Mr. Albee: What was the purpose of the examination, Doctor?

Dr. White: You asked that I conduct a psychological examination to determine whether Mrs. Alberts was at that time suffering brain
disorder, what the quality of her current psychological functions were, and whether any abnormal findings were related
to Mrs. Alberts' accident in June of 1980.

Mr. Albee: Were you provided with any background material or records?

Dr. White: Yes, sir.

Mr. Albee: Please tell the court and the jury what materials you reviewed
previous to your examinations of Mrs. Alberts.

Dr. White: I reviewed the emergency room records dated June 21, 1980,
from the Kaufman Memorial Hospital, the operating room
notes and summary report of Dr. Barclay, the neurosurgeon
who operated on Mrs. Alberts, various progress and treatment notes associated with her hospitalization, and the discharge summary written by Dr. Barclay. I have reviewed Dr.
Barclay's follow-up reports dated August 15 and November
12, 1980, as well as his notes dated February 6 and June 20,
1981. I've read Dr. Barclay's neurological evaluation, with enclosed CAT scan and EEG reports dated August 14, 1982. I've
reviewed the rehabilitation reports covering the period January 1981 to the present from the Coleman Rehabilitation Center. I've reviewed the psychological report and test materials
of Dr. Harkey, who examined Mrs. Alberts in August of 1981.
I believe that covers it.

Depending on the complexity of the case and the style of the attorney, the
interrogatory might continue into details as to the weight and meanings of
the background material. Sometimes this section of the direct examination
is for purposes of assuring the jury that the expert witness was thoroughly
familiar with the circumstances surrounding the plaintiff's injury.

Following the initial interrogatory, the lawyer will usually lead the expert witness into the presentation of information concerning the types and
purposes of the examinations and procedures conducted by the expert.

Mr. Albee: When did you examine Mrs. Alberts, Dr. White?

Dr. White: I saw Mrs. Alberts initially for a clinical history on October 6, 1982. Subsequently, Mrs. Alberts was examined
on October 12, 13, 16, and 18, 1982. She was seen for a
total of 14 hours of interviews and psychological examinations.

Mr. Albee: Did you conduct all the examinations yourself?

Dr. White: All the interviews and examinations were conducted by
me or under my direction and supervision by Mr. Bun-
ter, my psychological assistant.

Mr. Albee:	Approximately how many hours did you spend with Mrs. Alberts during this time?
Dr. White:	I spent a total of five and one-half hours examining Mrs. Alberts, and the remaining eight and one-half hours of the examination took place in my test room with Mr. Bunter administering various psychological tests under my direction.
Mr. Albee:	Is this usual and standard procedure for psychological examinations?
Dr. White:	Yes, it is.
Mr. Albee:	Please tell the court the types of examinations administered and the purpose or purposes of each.
Dr. White:	Mrs. Alberts was given a rather complete battery of psychological tests and procedures to determine her psychological status and condition. A clinical history was taken to establish the nature of Mrs. Alberts' background, development, family, education, and life experiences. The history also identified Mrs. Alberts' view of the difficulties she experienced since the accident.
Mr. Albee:	Would you please summarize the problems Mrs. Alberts associated with her accident.
Dr. White:	During the clinical history Mrs. Alberts stated that since the accident, she is "different." She stated that she has difficulty in remembering recent events, that she is much more nervous and irritable than ever before in her life, and much more impatient with her husband and her two children. She states that she is unable to lift things with her right hand and that her handwriting has become poor since the accident. She can no longer type effectively. Her arithmetic calculations are inaccurate since the accident. She suffers many more headaches than before the accident. She states that since the accident she suffers double vision frequently. She indicates that her social judgment, such as being critical, laughing too much or too loudly, and interrupting people without meaning to, has become a source of embarrassment since the accident.
Mr. Albee:	Do these symptoms mean anything to you, Doctor?
Mr. McCracken:	Objection, Your Honor. No premise has been laid to allow the doctor to speculate. The hypothetical is too vague.
The Judge:	Objection sustained.
Mr. Albee:	Let me back up a bit, Doctor. Were these responses a

	result of standard, generally acceptable interview procedures?
Dr. White:	Yes, sir.
Mr. Albee:	And did you evaluate Mrs. Alberts' statements according to known and generally accepted methods?
Dr. White:	Yes, sir.
Mr. Albee:	And in your field, Doctor, is there a standard interpretation or conclusion that psychologists would reach from such signs and symptoms?
Dr. White:	Yes.
Mr. Albee:	Would you tell the court your opinion as to the meaning of such symptoms reported by a person who had been in an automobile accident and suffered unconsciousness for 10 days following the accident?
Dr. White:	The experiences described by Mrs. Alberts are considered consistent with the sequelae, or aftereffects, of a severe closed-head injury.

The attorney has neatly brought out that the defendant's difficulties, associated with the accident, are characteristic of persons who have been brain injured. The objection raised by Mr. McCracken represents the proper response of a skilled attorney who has caught his opponent "rushing things" and seizes the opportunity to disrupt the smooth flow of the direct examination. Strategically, such disruptions serve the purpose of suggesting to the jury that the presenting attorney is less than perfect in his tradecraft. Mr. Albee takes this in stride and continues the direct examination, taking no issue with the objection, and hoping that the jury will view Mr. McCracken's objection as petty and unnecessary.

In the presentation of information about the use and interpretation of psychological tests, accuracy is of signal importance. Chapter 5 presents in detail the technical and ethical guidelines within which test data should be presented. During the direct examination the test data should be presented in a sequence that is logical and understandable in respect to the issues being considered by the jury.

Mr. Albee:	After the clinical interview, what procedures did you then follow, Doctor?
Dr. White:	I then began the formal psychological testing.
Mr. Albee:	What was your purpose in giving Mrs. Alberts psychological tests?
Dr. White:	The battery of tests given Mrs. Alberts consisted of standard psychological test instruments to help me determine if Mrs. Alberts suffered any psychological problems or deficiencies and, if so, what these might be.

Mr. Albee:	Would you tell the judge and the jury what type of tests were administered?
Dr. White:	Mrs. Alberts was given a series of tests of intellectual capacity, neuropsychological functioning, reading ability, skills, aptitudes, rehabilitation potential, and personality.
Mr. Albee:	Would this be considered a standard and proper test battery, in your profession, for a person in Mrs. Alberts' circumstances?
Dr. White:	Yes, it would.
Mr. Albee:	I would like, Doctor, for you to go through your examination and explain what you did, what you found, and what it meant. What tests were given first?
Dr. White:	Mrs. Alberts was first given the Wechsler Adult Intelligence Scale–Revised.
Mr. Albee:	What does this test measure?
Dr. White:	The Wechsler Adult Intelligence Scale is made up of 11 subtests measuring a variety of skills, abilities, and response capacities that can be generally grouped together and called "intelligence."
Mr. Albee:	Is this what we used to call "IQ" tests?
Dr. White:	Yes, sir, although the IQ is a fairly out-of-date concept. We can be much more accurate in describing intelligence today than we could 40 years ago when the concept of "IQ tests" was current.
Mr. Albee:	Then, Doctor, just what do these 11 subtests of the Wechsler measure?
Dr. White:	The Wechsler scales are the most generally accepted and most used tests of intellectual ability in psychological practice today. Developed and revised over the past 50 years, they measure an individual's ability to acquire information, organize ideas, use memory, perform logical operations—both verbal and nonverbal—and solve problems that are both simple and complex, verbal and mechanical. In short, human intelligence is a variety of abilities to process information, communicate, solve problems, use materials appropriately to perform a wide range of tasks. High intelligence represents efficiency, speed, and skill in these abilities, while low intelligence represents lesser or deficient skill and ability.
Mr. Albee:	Are there scores which a person makes on these tests?
Dr. White:	Yes. Scores on the 11 Wechsler scales are summarized into Verbal Scores, representing the tests that measure the general information a person has collected, ability to comprehend verbal material, attention span, memory for numbers, prob-

lem solving, vocabulary, and reasoning. A Performance Score represents such skills as eye–hand coordination, picking out key ideas, ability to manipulate objects skillfully and to put together various kinds of puzzles with speed and accuracy.

Mr. Albee: How do you determine the quality or the goodness of a person's test performance?

Dr. White: If a person's scores on various tests result in an Intelligent Quotient of 100, the performance is considered "Average." Psychologists prefer to use the concept of "percentile" in order to be more accurate about what test scores mean. A percentile is a person-to-person ranking that tells exactly how well a person performed when compared to a group of people in a specific population—such as men, women, high school graduates, and so on. An IQ of 100 would be the 50th percentile. This would mean that a person getting total scores which place them at the 50th percentile on the Wechsler Adult Intelligence Scale–Revised is able to perform equal to or better than 50 out of 100 people of their own age range in the general population. It also means that about 50 percent of the people in that group or population are likely to perform better than the person who achieves an IQ of 100 and falls at the 50th percentile. A person whose scores result in an intelligence quotient of 120 on the Wechsler scales falls at the 90th percentile. Such performance is considered Superior and equals or exceeds the scores of 90 out of 100 who have taken these tests. A person whose test scores result in an intelligence quotient of 80 on the Wechsler scales falls at the 10th percentile. This performance is considered Borderline. Ninety percent of those in the same age category as the person with the IQ of 80 perform better on the tests.

Mr. Albee: You administered the Wechsler Adult Intelligence Scale–Revised to Mrs. Alberts?

Dr. White: Yes, I did.

Mr. Albee: Please tell the Judge and jury the scores on Mrs. Alberts' intelligence tests.

Dr. White: Mrs. Alberts had a Verbal IQ of 104, which placed her at the 56th percentile, a Performance IQ of 70, placing her at the second percentile for these tests, and her Full scale IQ was 83, or the 14th percentile.

Mr. Albee: In practical, everyday terms, Doctor, what does this mean?

Dr. White: These results suggest that at the time I evaluated Mrs. Alberts, she was able to perform intellectual tasks with a strong verbal component, that is, involving communication—hearing, analyzing, speaking, calculating—at an average level.

That would be as good as about one-half of the people her age in the general population. By the same token, about one-half of the people in her age bracket in the general population are able to do these tasks more efficiently or better than Mrs. Alberts.

In Performance, or nonverbal tasks that require picking out key ideas, using social intelligence, eye–hand coordination, the ability to put things together, and new learning, Mrs. Alberts does as well as only 2 out of 100 in her age bracket; 98 out of 100 are likely to do better than she.

In short, Mrs. Alberts is able to do an average job in using intelligence that involves basic communication, but in practical areas of life she is severely limited.

Mr. Albee: Is this pattern of response something that Mrs. Alberts has always had?

Dr. White: Not likely. Mrs. Alberts is a college graduate. She has worked successfully for seven years before her accident as a marine biologist. It is unlikely that a person with the measured skills I've described could either graduate from college or work successfully or safely in the usual work setting of a marine biologist. At the time of her accident she was assistant chief of her research section with the U.S. Coast and Geodetic Survey.

Mr. Albee: Then if I understand you correctly, Doctor, your test results suggest that Mrs. Alberts is now less capable than she was at one time, such as during the years she acquired her education and during her professional career.

Dr. White: That is correct.

The attorney for the plaintiff has neatly led his witness through a presentation designed to demonstrate clearly to the triers of fact (judge and jury) that Mrs. Alberts has been carefully examined and found to have intellectual deficits. The attorney has also led the expert to an opinion that says that the plaintiff has suffered this loss after demonstrating intellectual capacity of a fairly high quality through education and work performance.

The attorney conducting the direct examination would continue his questioning of Dr. White to bring before the judge and the jury all aspects of Dr. White's psychological examination and the opinions formulated by Dr. White about Mrs. Alberts' deficiencies, losses, problems, rehabilitation efforts, and potentials. The interaction will tend to be smooth and comfortable for all parties if a pretrial conference between the expert witness and the attorney covered all aspects of the attorney's expectations and the expert's conclusions. In the style illustrated above, the attorney conducting the *direct examination* will being out the essence of the expert's examinations and conclusions. Following the presentation of the intellectual evaluation, the expert might then be asked similar questions concerning the neuropsychological evaluation, the aptitude assessment, and the personality examination. The effectiveness of the direct examination in terms of conveying the expert's opinion to the judge and the jury will largely depend on the competence of the expert, the experience and style of the attorney, and the amount of preparation they have put into the case, both separately and together.

After the presenting attorney has led the expert through examinations conducted and conclusions reached, the expert is likely to be presented with the key questions of the direct examination: the hypothetical questions.

Hypothetical questions bring together the salient issues of the case. The response by the expert witness is to focus attention on what the attorney wishes the judge and the jury to believe. It is critically important that the attorney and the witness are quite clear as to what will be asked and how the expert plans to respond before the expert goes to court. The earlier in the case the expert knows what hypothetical questions are liable to be asked, the more clearly he or she can tell the lawyer what answers can be given. It is disruptive and unprofessional to discover at the eleventh hour that expert and attorney have different ideas as to what hypotheticals will be asked and what answers will be forthcoming.

The following represents the hypothetical questions that might be asked after the direct examination in the case previously illustrated:

Mr. Albee: Now that you have explained your examination and your results to the jury, Doctor, I should like to pose a question to you: Assume that Mrs. Alberts is a successful college graduate, and further assume that before her accident of July 6, 1981, Mrs. Alberts worked professionally and efficiently as a marine biologist. Given your examination of the hospital records made available to you, given the results of your extensive psychological and neuropsychological examinations, given your broad experience and skill as an expert, is it your opinion that Mrs. Alberts now suffers measurable and significant brain disorder?

Dr. White: Yes, sir. That is my opinion.

Mr. Albee: Now, Doctor: Assuming all the above and that Mrs. Alberts functioned well up until July 6, 1981, further assume that since the time of her accident on that date, there has been no further injury or illness affecting Mrs. Alberts' brain. Is it your opinion, within reasonable psychological probability, that the aforesaid accident is the cause of Mrs. Alberts' present psychological and neuropsychological deficits?

Dr. White: Yes. That is my opinion.

Mr. Albee: No further questions, Your Honor.

The attorney has focused the attention of the jury on two conclusions: There is significant deficit in brain function and the most probable cause is the accident of 1981 for which the attorney is seeking damages and remedy for his client.

The Recess

In keeping with the tradition of "taking turns" in the adversary process, it is time for opposing counsel to question the witness. Before this takes place, the presiding judge, aware that the witness has been under questioning for an hour or more, is likely to interupt the interrogatory by striking his or her gavel and saying, "We shall have a 10-minute recess." At this point the judge gets up—a signal for *all* to rise—and leaves the courtroom.

Because lawyers spend much of their time in the courtroom, they may not be aware that judicial procedures are foreign to their witnesses who may be in the courtroom for the first time. The expert witness, when thus left standing in the witness-box after the judge has left, should assess his or her own situation. If there is a need to use the restroom, get a drink of water, or simply walk around, the proper procedure is to find a bailiff in the courtroom and indicate one's needs. It is important that one doesn't simply go out and find the nearest restroom that may be available. This might put the witness in contact with opposing counsel, witnesses for the opposition, or witnesses who are yet to be called. This could violate the *sequestration* rules that are established against interaction between witnesses. The bailiff is the person to ensure that this does not happen.

In less formal courtroom settings, the judge may invite the witness to chambers to have a cup of coffee and to "chat." This is not likely to be a usual process, but the expert should be prepared for this, particularly if the judge has been favorably inclined toward the expert's testimony.

The expert should not be concerned if the attorney who retained the expert does not immediately come to the witness stand and congratulate the witness on a sterling performance. This is one small part of the attorney's presentation, and there are many matters which are likely to take the attorney's attention at this point. The witness should not be disturbed if it is noticed that the two opposing counsels, almost bitter in their interaction during court, seem quite friendly and sociable during recess. They may be momentary antagonists, but they are professional colleagues.

The expert witness would be well advised to make best utilization of the recess, after consulting with the bailiff, by walking around, getting a drink of water, and using the restroom facilities. Psychological testimony tends to be rather extensive, and it is very inconvenient to the process for an expert to ask for a recess in the middle of some part of the trial. It is best to follow the judge's lead and use those recesses that are made available.

Should the judge declare a lunch recess or an overnight recess at the end of a portion of the expert's testimony, the expert should immediately approach the attorney who retained the expert and ask for directions and instructions. In the event it is a lunch recess, the retaining attorney may take the witness to lunch in order to discuss the testimony that has occurred up to that time. In a situation where the expert is still not finished with testimony at the end of the day and the judge recesses court until the following morning, it is likely that the judge will admonish the witness not to discuss the testimony or the anticipated presentation with anyone. With careful planning, this type of split testimony is likely to be rare.

Cross-Examination

The cross-examination is conducted by the attorney opposing the attorney who called the expert witness. The purpose of the cross-examination is to cast some doubt or question on the quality of the witness as an expert, on the thoroughness of the material presented, or on the credibility of the opinion that has been rendered by the expert. During the direct examination the expert may notice that opposing counsel has been taking notes and, in some cases, looking up references in various books on the counsel's table. This is in preparation to conduct the cross-examination.

It is unlikely that the expert witness will find the cross-examination similar to what is shown on television or in motion pictures about courtroom scenes. Each attorney has a particular style, and very few of them emulate fictional characters. It is important that the attorney impress and influence the jury, and few attorneys believe that they can do this by imitating familiar media characters.

Most attorneys begin cross-examination in a very gentle and persuasive manner. They are likely to be quite polite and even complimentary about the expert's testimony. Nevertheless, their hope and expectation is to leave the jury with the impression that the expert witness's testimony is to be given very little weight and credibility.

The most effective kind of cross-examination involves a process by which the opposing attorney can arrange for the expert witness to *impeach* himself or herself. The process of impeachment requires that the attorney ask questions that result in the witness making contradictory statements. If the lawyer can bring the witness to face and admit that he or she has said two different things about the same issue, the attorney will have succeeded in impeaching the witness and can then suggest that the entire testimony of the expert be disregarded.

It cannot be overemphasized that very careful professional work by the expert and extensive preparation for the trial between the retaining attorney and the expert will limit the effectiveness of opposing counsel's maneuvers to cast significant doubt on the expert's opinion during cross-examination. Poor professional preparation and lack of sufficient communication between the expert and the retaining attorney are likely to open many doors for successful cross-examination.

If the psychologist has "followed all the rules," it is unlikely that opposing counsel will do much during the cross-examination to lessen the credibility of the witness in the eyes of the judge and jury. Opposing counsel must take her or his turn, however, and Dr. White of the previous direct examination will be subject to something like the following cross-examination by Mr. McCracken, opposing counsel:

Mr. McCracken:	That was very interesting, Miss White.
Mr. Albee:	Objection, your Honor. Counsel is baiting the witness.
Court:	You will address the witness properly, Counselor.
Mr. McCracken:	I'm sorry, your Honor—I apologize, *Dr.* White, but it is true that you are not a medical doctor, is that not so?
Dr. White:	That is correct.
Mr. McCracken:	You are, in fact, only a doctor of philosophy?
Mr. Albee:	Objection. Counsel's remarks are immaterial and provocative. Dr. White's credentials have been ascertained and stipulated.
Court:	Sustained. I shan't warn you again, Counselor. Confine your questions to the issue.
Mr. McCracken:	I'm sorry, Your Honor, if it pleases the court, I shall continue.
Court:	You may proceed.

Although not a rule of thumb, some attorneys prefer to begin the cross-examination with a smokescreen of pseudochallenge to lay some doubt before the jury as to the credentials of the witness, knowing full well that the witness has been qualified and the questions will be ruled out of order by the judge. Some judges tolerate this type of trial strategy, while others may warn opposing counsel sharply. The witness may *not* enter in with rebuttal, counterquestions, or explanations outside of the direct question. Any such attempt by the expert will be immediately quashed by the judge. If the witness is unfamiliar with these procedures, the following might occur:

Mr. McCracken:	That was very interesting, Miss White.
Dr. White:	I'm afraid you've forgotten that I'm a doctor and that—
The Court (*interrupting*):	The witness will confine her responses to direct questions only. Do you understand, Dr. White?

Dr. White:	But, Your Honor, I—
The Court (*interrupting*):	Although you are designated as an expert witness, you must respond as I've just told you. Do you understand that?
Dr. White:	Yes, Your Honor.

No matter how unfair the attorney conducting the cross-examination may be, the witness may not complain, correct, or advocate. Either the opposing counsel or the judge may interrupt to prevent abuse of the witness, but the witness may respond only to the questions asked.

The tone of cross-examination of a well-qualified witness is more likely to be as follows:

Mr. McCracken:	Dr. White—please explain to the jury what psychologists mean by "standard deviation."
Dr. White:	Standard deviation is a statistical term. It is a measure of dispersion. By that, we mean the degree to which a test score may vary by chance alone. It is one measure of the stability of a test score.
Mr. McCracken:	And what is the standard deviation of the Wechsler Adult Intelligence Scale–Revised?
Dr. White:	Fifteen IQ points on the Full scale intelligence score represents one standard deviation.
Mr. McCracken:	That means, does it not, that any single IQ score is not an absolute, sure, certain, valid, reliable representation of what the person's "real" IQ is?
Dr. White:	Well, in a sense, I . . . .
Mr. McCracken:	Please answer my question, Doctor—yes or no?
Dr. White:	Well, yes . . .
Mr. McCracken:	Then the IQ scores you gave for Mrs. Alberts are really not "true" or "accurate" or "stable" scores, are they?
Dr. White:	Well, I wouldn't really . . .
Mr. McCracken:	If the Court pleases, could the good doctor be directed to be more responsive?
The Court:	Doctor, please answer Counsel's questions directly.
Dr. White:	Yes.

Opposing counsel has cleverly led the expert into a cul-de-sac using a basic statistical question to cast doubt on the quality, stability, or significance of the expert's conclusions offered during the direct examination.

The expert is not totally helpless in these matters. When opposing counsel uses a clever focus to cast question on the expert's conclusions, the attorney who retained the witness may raise issues of fairness or procedure to protect the expert. Most attorneys are somewhat reluctant to do this since it takes the jurors' attention away from the expert's testimony. It is much better for the expert to be capable of dealing with these issues without help. One very effective technique, which should be used sparingly, is the *qualification*. This enables the witness to explain why the opposing counsel's innuendo or implication is only *partially* correct. The witness makes this request *after* answering one of the opposing counsel's "clever" questions. Thus, in the case being considered above, it might go as follows:

Mr. McCracken: When it comes right down to it, Doctor, all the tests you gave and the results you reported on Mrs. Alberts really amount to little more than guesses, or "probabilities," as you call them—is this not so?

Dr. White: Well, in a sense, yes . . . but—

Mr. McCracken: And when you tell us that Mrs. Alberts has a lower IQ than what she probably had before the accident, this is nothing more than a guess, or "probability," and *not* a fact—is this not so?

Dr. White: Yes (*quickly turning to face the Judge*). Your Honor, may I qualify?

It is critical for the expert to be prepared to move quickly. Should the witness hesitate, the opposing counsel will go right on to the next question, leaving the impression with the jury that Dr. White's testimony was of little import. By quickly and politely appealing to the court, the witness requests permission to present her view fairly.

The Court: Yes, Doctor, you may qualify.

Dr. White: As an expert, I can only give my best and most carefully developed opinions. These are based on tests and other data that indeed are estimates of behavior and must be viewed in light of their inherent stability as measuring instruments. When I said that the difference between Mrs. Alberts' Full scale intelligence after her accident in comparison with her Full scale IQ before the accident, the probabilities are 95 out of 100 chances that the figures I gave are the "true" figures. Thus my conclusions are based on probabilities, but the chances that these conclusions are based on incorrect figures are less than 5 in 100.

The witness has shown Mr. McCracken's intimations of gross guessing and inaccuracy to be unfounded. The witness has clarified the issue in a simple, dignified professional style. Mr. McCracken's trial strategy has probably failed.

Under *no* circumstances should the witness ask opposing counsel if he or she may qualify. If that happens, the following is likely to occur:

Mr. McCracken: And when you tell us that Mrs. Alberts has a lower IQ than she probably had before the accident, this is nothing more than a guess, or "probability," and not a fact—is this not so?

Dr. White: Yes, may I qualify?

Mr. McCracken: No, your answer seems perfectly clear to me, and I'm sure that it is to the jury.

At this point, Mr. McCracken will probably turn his back on the witness and walk away, offering no opportunity at all to qualify. It is in the best interests of his case to do everything possible to place in the minds of the jury a question as to the competency, accuracy, and quality of the opposing expert's testimony.

Most successful trial attorneys attend workshops and seminars, often given by highly qualified psychologists, on how to deal with the expert witness in psychology. However, the matter is not completely simple for opposing counsel. If the lawyer attempts a gambit of trial strategy and the expert responds in a competent manner, the jury clearly sees that the opposing counsel is "tilting at windmills" and begins to develop sympathy for the expert witness. This is certainly not desirable for the opposing counsel. Thus after failing to discredit the witness after one or two attempts, the intelligent attorney will cease his or her efforts, since, in effect, the questions may actually enhance the expert's presentation to the jury.

Some attorneys attempt to discredit the expert witness by asking statistical questions, to imply that the expert is not "really" an expert:

Mr. McCracken: In discussing these tests, Doctor, I assume that you have some knowledge of them and their construction?

Dr. White: Yes, sir, I believe so.

Mr. McCracken: Would you explain to the judge and to the jury the meaning of the term *validity*?

Dr. White: Validity refers to the extent to which an instrument, such as a test, measures what it is supposed to measure. There are four main types of validity. Would you like me to outline each?

Mr. McCracken: Well, Doctor, I . . .

Dr. White: There is content validity, predictive validity, construct validity, and concurrent validity. These are statistical terms that are used in the validation of tests that are—

Mr. McCracken: Thank you very much, Doctor, I'm sure that's very instructive, but I would like to move on now.

Mr. McCracken's hope that Dr. White would stumble around and be unable to answer the question has not been fulfilled. To the contrary, Dr. White was prepared and demonstrated to judge and jury that she is indeed an expert. This is contrary to Mr. McCracken's plans, and he wishes to leave the discussion as quickly as possible. If the retaining counsel is sufficiently attentive, he may further enhance the expert's credibility by objecting to the quasi harassment being perpetrated by opposing counsel:

Mr. Albee:	Your Honor, I object. My worthy opponent first asks Dr. White a question and then does not allow her to finish. I suggest that Mr. McCracken is merely baiting the witness in an effort to discredit her testimony. If it pleases the Court, the witness should be allowed to complete her answer.
The Court:	Mr. McCracken, you will please allow the witness to complete her answer.
Mr. McCracken:	Yes, Your Honor. You may proceed, Doctor.
Dr. White:	Thank you. As I was saying, there are four main types of validity, and each one is a method of ensuring that a test is an instrument that measures what it is supposed to measure and the degree to which it actually does this. I could go into a long technical description of these matters if this is your desire.
Mr. McCracken:	No, thank you, Doctor, that's quite enough.

No expert can have at his or her fingertips all figures, definitions, and descriptions. This is the primary purpose of the cue book. When opposing counsel asks a question about which the expert is not quite sure, it is perfectly permissible to ask permission to make reference to the cue book. Again, this request is addressed to the court and not to opposing counsel. Opposing counsel may make a fuss about the expert referring to the cue book, but this can be dealt with readily, as follows:

Mr. McCracken:	Please tell us, Doctor, if indeed you are an expert, the meaning of the term *standard error of measurement*.
Dr. White:	Certainly (*turning to the judge, who after all is only about two and one-half feet to her immediate left*), may I refer to some of my materials, Your Honor?
The Court:	Yes, Doctor.
Dr. White:	(*turning to the appropriate page in her cue book*) The standard error of measurement is one way in which the reliability of a test may be expressed. It provides an estimate of the range of variation in a set of repeated measurements of the same thing. I'll illustrate this: Re-

peated administration of a test instrument will yield a frequency distribution of scores. That means that the scores may differ to some extent on repetition. The mean of these scores represents what we call the *true score* and yields a standard deviation that indicates the extent of variation of the scores. This standard deviation is the deviation of the errors of measurement, and this is called the *standard error of measurement*. It gives us an estimate of how frequently errors of a given size may be expected to occur when the test is used. A low standard error of measurement is an indication of a test's reliability.

Mr. McCracken:	Thank you, Doctor, but what is that book you are reading from?
Dr. White:	This is a book of materials that I refer to when I wish to be very accurate about a definition or a statistical conversion.
Mr. McCracken:	That means you don't really know the definition, is that not right?
Dr. White:	That means I would like to answer your questions as accurately as I possibly can.

Mr. McCracken is fighting a losing battle. Dr. White has demonstrated a quiet, direct, unthreatened response to Mr. McCracken's machinations. It is quite unlikely that he will go as far as we have indicated in the above interrogatories. He would have to be a very poor attorney not to realize that Dr. White is responding extremely well, creating a very favorable impression before the jury, and having her testimony enhanced by this cross-examination. By the same token, opposing counsel has begun to look like a nitpicker and is creating a relatively negative impression about himself before the jury. It is more than likely that one or two appropriate answers by the witness will cause opposing counsel to be very, very careful about continuing to ask potentially difficult or embarrassing questions.

The expert witness must be prepared to give up materials brought to court if these are used in any way by the witness during direct or cross-examination. It is wise to bring copies that can be handed over should opposing counsel request that such materials be marked and entered as an exhibit. The attorney may ask for tests, test materials, books, reprints, charts, or illustrations. In most cases this request serves no immediate purpose. Opposing counsel may be ensuring that the material being referred to is available for later examination and reference during the trial. The attorney may be "making a record" in the event the material might be helpful should the case be appealed. The opposing attorney may only be attempting to annoy the expert.

Should the attorney request something the expert is not prepared to give up, the expert must depend on the good offices of the presiding judge to protect the witness's property.

Mr. McCracken:	You referred to a group of percentiles in relating to the jury Mrs. Alberts' so-called intellectual deficits, did you not, Doctor?
Dr. White:	Yes, I did.
Mr. McCracken:	Is that something you worked out yourself?
Dr. White:	No, they are the percentiles developed from the normative sample used in the standardization of the Wechsler Adult Intelligence Scale.
Mr. McCracken:	Where does one find such percentiles?
Dr. White:	In the manual for the WAIS-R, the Wechsler Adult Intelligence Scale–Revised, published by Harcourt, Brace and Jovanovich in 1981.
Mr. McCracken:	Is that the manual that you are referring to—that booklet with the black cover?
Dr. White:	Yes, sir.
Mr. McCracken:	May I see it please?
Dr. White:	The table to which I referred for the percentiles is in Appendix D. It is labeled *Table 22*.
Mr. McCracken:	All right. Yes—I see that. Your Honor, I should like to enter this booklet as plaintiff's exhibit—let's see—number 43.

Once the material is stamped and entered, the witness will probably never see it again. This is an excellent reason to have a xerox copy of any material to be cited or demonstrated available to be turned over to opposing counsel should such a request be made. If, indeed, the opposing counsel tries to take the expert's tools or equipment, rather than expendable copies, the witness should appeal to the judge. Following the attorney's request for permission to mark the material as an exhibit, the witness should turn to the judge and say:

Dr. White:	Your Honor, if it pleases the Court, that booklet is used daily in my practice and is my only copy. May I reproduce the page in question and forward it to the court reporter?
The Court:	I think that we will let the Doctor keep her materials. If the bailiff will take the material to my office and have my secretary make a copy of the pages designated by Dr. White, we will mark those as exhibit number 43. Is that satisfactory, Mr. McCracken?

Mr. McCracken:	Yes, Your Honor.
Dr. White:	Thank you, Your Honor.
The Court:	Please proceed, Counselor.

Few judges allow an attorney to interfere with the personal property or professional tools used by the expert witness.

In concluding the cross-examination of an expert witness who has responded efficiently and has maintained credibility with the jury, opposing counsel may use a series of questions designed to convince the jury that the opinions of the expert should be disregarded or, at best, considered lightly.

Mr. McCracken:	And so, to sum it all up, Doctor, you're a psychologist, not a doctor, who has been hired to give Mrs. Alberts some tests and give your opinion. This opinion is based on "probabilities," as you call them, and not on hard absolute facts. Is this so, Doctor?
Dr. White:	Yes, sir.
Mr. McCracken:	No further questions, Your Honor.

Even though these questions and innuendos have appeared before, and Dr. White has responded effectively, opposing counsel wishes to have the last word in the cross-examination. The expert should not rise to the negative tone of the cross-examination. This is part of the courtroom drama and the adversary system. If the expert is on shaky ground or is not much of an expert, opposing counsel has the right and the duty to bring this out during cross-examination and to negate the effect of the witness against his or her client's case. The jury understands this, having experienced a number of exchanges between opposing attorneys before the expert has testified. The effective expert witness should rely on his or her knowledge, communication skills, and emotional control. There are any number of gambits and strategies opposing attorneys may use to upset a witness. A sensible dignity on the part of the expert will usually be perceived by jury members in a positive way.

Occasionally an opposing counsel may focus on the expert's fee during cross-examination, insinuating that the witness is "bought" or is a "hired gun." The following is an overdone but plausible cross-examination made up of dialogue from court transcripts. Mr. Mandell, a particularly hostile opposing counsel, questions the expert witness, Dr. Lawrence, who is experienced, calm, and unflappable.

| Mr. Mandell: | Your testimony has been very interesting, Doctor, I imagine that you testify in courts quite frequently. |
| Dr. Lawrence: | I have testified before. |

Mr. Mandell:	Please tell the jury how much you were paid to testify here today.
Dr. Lawrence:	I was paid nothing to testify.
Mr. Mandell:	Nothing?
Dr. Lawrence:	No, sir. My testimony cannot be bought. I was paid at my usual professional rates for my time, spent in evaluating and giving my opinion here today.

Mr. Mandell has attempted a standard ploy used in cross-examination to cast some doubts upon the expert's motivation and objectivity as a witness. Another such ploy is as follows:

Mr. Mandell:	As an expert, your name is quite well known. Haven't I seen it in some professional journals?
Dr. Lawrence:	That is possible. I've published several . . .
Mr. Mandell:	Oh yes! Haven't I seen an advertisement in some law journals where you offer yourself to anyone as an expert?
Dr. Lawrence:	Certainly not! I've never . . .
Mr. Mandell:	It's not that important, Doctor. I'm sure the jury understands.

This represents a strategy of desperation and is rare. When it does happen, it usually suggests that the opposing counsel is unprepared and willing to risk his or her client's case on a very long and very cheap shot. Few jury members are likely to be impressed by such nonsense. It behooves the expert to realize that such behavior will tend to damage the reputation of opposing counsel and not that of the expert witness.

Each attorney develops his or her own approach to cross-examination. An expert should be prepared for a variety of strategies, ranging from smooth, efficient probing to gross, tangential hacking. An attorney's behavior during deposition is sometimes a fair prediction of the style of cross-examination that can be expected in the courtroom.

Some attorneys scour the expert's deposition to find an opportunity to discredit the expert by getting the expert to impeach himself or herself. If the attorney can arrange for a witness to give different answers to the same question, the witness is *impeached,* casting grave doubts on the competence and veracity of the expert testimony. This is the primary reason for not "waiving the reading and signing" of the deposition when it is originally taken. To insist on reading and signing means the witness can make a copy of the deposition and review his or her pretrial testimony before getting on the witness stand. The following, taken from the record of a trial in federal court, illustrates what may happen if the expert has not reviewed the deposition. In this case, the federal prosecutor, Mr. Horwitz has a copy of Dr. Blau's deposition taken six months previous to the trial. Dr. Blau "waived reading and signing" on the advice of the attorney who retained him. The deposition was taken at a place far distant from the witness's office, and in order to expedite the trial process, the retaining attorney requested the waiving, assuring Dr. Blau that a copy of his deposition would be made available before the trial. Six months passed, and somehow the attorney "forgot." The following occurred during cross-examination:

Mr. Horwitz: Now, Doctor, you've testified that you conducted all of your examinations of the defendant at the Green County Jail. Is that correct?

Dr. Blau: That is correct.

Mr. Horwitz: And all of your examinations were completed on April 22, the one day you spent with the defendant?

Dr. Blau: Yes, sir.

Mr. Horwitz: And you've based all of your conclusions on your observations, tests, and recall of that day.

Dr. Blau: To a large extent, yes.

Mr. Horwitz: How many hours did you spend that day testing the defendant?

Dr. Blau: According to my records, I spent just over five hours with the defendant.

Mr. Horwitz: What time did you start your examinations?

Dr. Blau: About 10 in the morning. I drove to Deland from Tampa that morning. I arrived about 9:30 A.M. By the time an examination room was available and the defendant brought to me, it was about 10 or 10:30.

Mr. Horwitz: Were testing conditions good?

Dr. Blau: I've never examined anyone in a jail where testing conditions were "good." They were adequate in my opinion.

Mr. Horwitz: What did you do about lunch?

Dr. Blau: I beg your pardon?

Mr. Horwitz: You began your examination at 10 or 10:30. You examined the defendant for a period of about five hours. You were in an institution, a jail. What did you do to ensure the defendant would not miss lunch?

Dr. Blau: Well, ordinarily, when testing in an institutional setting, we tell the guards to let the person being tested eat at the usual time or bring a tray, and testing can be delayed while the person eats in the testing room.

Mr. Horwitz: What did you do in this case?

Dr. Blau: I believe the defendant went to lunch at his usual time— about 11:30—and returned shortly thereafter to continue testing.

Mr. Horwitz: So you began testing at 10 A.M. or so, worked until about 11:30, allowed the defendant to go to lunch, resumed testing after lunch, and finished during the afternoon. Is that about right?

Dr. Blau: Yes, sir.

Mr. Horwitz: So I take it, in following good testing procedure, you worked with the defendant giving tests and so forth, and then broke for lunch, and then continued until you were finished. Is that about right?

Dr. Blau: Yes, that seems about right.

Mr. Horwitz: (*taking a blue-backed deposition from a pile of documents on the prosecution table*) Dr. Blau, I'm going to show you a deposition taken from you on the 14th of May, and I would like you to look at it.

Dr. Blau: Yes.

Mr. Horwitz: Is this the transcript of a deposition I took from you at that time?

Dr. Blau: It certainly looks like it.

Mr. Horwitz: I have marked page 37 of this deposition, and I would like you to begin reading from the deposition where the red arrow is pointing (*handing the deposition to Dr. Blau*).

Dr. Blau: *Mr. Horwitz:* You did the entire examination at the jail? *Dr. Blau:* Yes, I did. *Mr. Horwitz:* You started at about 10 in the morning? *Dr. Blau:* Yes, that's about right. *Mr. Horwitz:* What did you do about lunch? *Dr. Blau:* Because the testing time that was available was quite limited, the defendant agreed that he would be willing to work right straight through lunch. The guards said that they would feed him after he was finished. We took several "bathroom breaks," and the guards allowed us to have some cold drinks, but we skipped lunch and worked right straight through.

Mr. Horwitz: (*taking the deposition from Dr. Blau*) That certainly doesn't sound like what you just said a few moments ago, Doctor.

Dr. Blau: Well, that was taken a long time ago and I . . .

Mr. Horwitz: So what you told us a few minutes ago is diametrically opposed to what you had just read from the deposition. Now, either you were wrong a few moments ago or you were wrong on the deposition. Which was it?

Dr. Blau: My recollection . . .

Mr. Horwitz: Would you please answer the question directly, Dr. Blau?

Dr. Blau: I was in error in my testimony before reading the deposition. Now that I have read the deposition I realize that we did skip lunch in order to complete the testing.

Mr. Horwitz:	So you do make errors in your testimony. Is that not correct?
Dr. Blau:	Well, I suppose . . .
Mr. Horwitz:	Either you do or you don't—which is it?
Dr. Blau:	I certainly made an error in that case.
Mr. Horwitz:	I submit Dr. Blau that this error may represent a whole class of errors that you may have made in your testimony—no further questions.

To the casual observer the above dialogue may seem to be inconsequential, and in point of fact it might be so, in terms of the quality of the witness's testimony. To the jury, however, Dr. Blau's credibility, his sharpness, and his ability to handle detail are called into question. This was a very clever and very effective ploy by the prosecuting attorney. This underscores the importance of *never* waiving the signing and the reading of the deposition. The expert witness should have in his or her possession a copy of every deposition given in the case about which he or she is going to testify. There should be no surprises.

In another criminal case, it is obvious that the expert witness has learned his lesson. In this case, a deposition was taken approximately five months before the trial. The expert did not waive the reading and the signing and obtained a copy of the deposition. The following dialogue takes place between Mr. Golden, the prosecuting attorney, and Dr. Blau, the expert witness:

Mr. Golden:	Now, Doctor, you've testified in direct examination that the defendant is "psychotic." Is that correct?
Dr. Blau:	No, sir.
Mr. Golden:	He is not psychotic?
Dr. Blau:	I said that my examination indicated that the defendant has a very disturbed and fragmented personality and that he experiences episodes of psychotic thinking and behavior.
Mr. Golden:	Then are you saying that the defendant was or was not insane at the time of the homicide of which he is accused?
Dr. Blau:	Neither. Insanity is a legal concept, and the decision as to insanity lies with the judge and jury, not with me as a psychologist.
Mr. Golden:	Then you don't say he was insane at the time of the homicide.
Dr. Blau:	I've not been asked that.
Mr. Golden:	Was the defendant insane at the time of the homicide of which he is accused?
Dr. Blau:	I don't know.

Mr. Golden: (*opening a deposition folder*) Dr. Blau—I have here a certified copy of a deposition given by you and certified by you in this matter. Please read this to the Judge and jury, beginning at the place I've marked with a red X.

Dr. Blau: (*reading*) *Mr. Golden:* Would you say he was insane? *Dr. Blau:* No, sir, I would not.

Mr. Golden: (*taking transcript*) So when I took your deposition you said he wasn't insane and now you say you don't know—is that it?

Dr. Blau: No, sir, it is not so.

Mr. Golden: What do you mean "No, sir"—in the deposition you said you wouldn't say the defendant was insane, now you say, here in open court, sworn to tell the truth, that you "don't know."

Dr. Blau: If you will read the previous page in the deposition I believe you will find that you asked me if I were a member of a jury, and if I were convinced that the defendant understood that he was doing wrong at the time of the homicide, and if I were convinced he deliberately took the life of the victim, would I consider the defendant "insane." To that I answered, "No sir, I would not." The question was totally different, *not* addressed to me as an expert.

Mr. Golden: Let me go on now to the next point, Doctor.

The value of not waiving the reading and signing of depositions so as to be sure to have a copy of one's deposition is obvious. Hostile or abrasive cross-examinations happen more frequently in movies or television drama than in the courtroom. Most experienced attorneys know that harshness, anger without real purpose, and abuse of expert witnesses is distasteful to most jurors and will result in a lessening of the attorney's esteem by jurors who might ordinarily be positively inclined toward the attorney's presentation.

Experienced opposing attorneys prefer that an expert discredit himself or herself on cross-examinations. In a first-degree murder trial, Dr. Artfield has testified that the defendant was insane at the time he shot and killed his former supervisor. Mr. Carnella conducts the cross-examination as follows:

Mr. Carnella: I found your testimony most interesting, as I often do when I hear you on the stand.

Dr. Artfield: (*unruffled*) Thank you, Counselor!

Mr. Carnella: I particularly note the calm, easy, absolute assurance with which you give your opinion that the defendant was insane when he shot and killed his former supervisor who had fired the defendant for repeated incompetence.

Dr. Artfield: He was insane.

Mr. Carnella: You have no doubt, no question, no slight unsureness?

Dr. Artfield: Certainly not!

Mr. Carnella: No possibility that you could be mistaken? be guilty of a slight error of professional judgment?

Dr. Artfield: (*becoming heated*) I told you—certainly not!

Mr. Carnella: As a professional, Dr. Artfield, don't you think it's unusual for a well-qualified expert to claim absolutely no room for error? Doesn't the psychiatric profession have a label or a diagnosis for folks who think they are never wrong?

Dr. Artfield: Damn it! I said the man was insane! He was crazy as a bedbug! Is that not clear enough for you?!

The Court: (*banging gavel sharply*) The witness will control himself. Answer the questions directly, Doctor.

Mr. Carnella: No further questions, Your Honor.

Dr. Artfield has shown himself to be easily annoyed, overemotional, and unprofessional. The jury, when later polled, indicated that almost to a member, they had disregarded his testimony because of his poor emotional control. Mr. Carnella very cleverly arranged for this expert to spoil his own testimony.

The cross-examination is the part of the procedure where the incompetent or poorly prepared witness may receive deserved comeuppance for poor preparation. In the following personal injury case, Dr. Pintz has testified that the plaintiff, Mr. Reading, suffers a brain dysfunction as indicated by poor performance on various psychological tests. Further, Dr. Pintz, in his response to hypothetical questions in the direct examination, has indicated that the disability results from an automobile accident that occurred in August, 1981. At this time, Mr. Reading was riding as a passenger in a vehicle that was hit from behind. The cross-examination proceeds as follows, with opposing attorney, Mr. Richard Bear, cross-examining Dr. Pintz, Mr. Siegal's witness:

Mr. Bear: So, Doctor, it is your opinion that Mr. Reading's neuropsychological problems are a result of a rear-end collision between automobiles, with Mr. Reading being a passenger in the forward vehicle.

Dr. Pintz: Yes—that is my opinion.

Mr. Bear: Is it your opinion that the neuropsychological damage occurred in the accident of August 1981?

Dr. Pintz: That is my opinion.

Mr. Bear: If the accident had happened in January 1981 or in December 1981, would that significantly change what you found in your psychological studies?

Dr. Pintz: I'm not sure I understand.

Mr. Bear: I'm asking if your results would be substantially the same if the accident occurred, say, four years ago or two years ago, rather than specifically three years ago?

Dr. Pintz: No—that would not be the significant factor. Our findings show that there is deficit, and the history identifies the trauma of the rear-end collision as the source of the deficit.

Mr. Bear: If there had been two, or three, or four rear-end collisions in which Mr. Reading was a passenger in the forward car during the past four or five years, would your tests or procedures have the capacity to identify which accident caused the damage?

Dr. Pintz: No, we couldn't tell that.

Mr. Bear: To your knowledge, has Mr. Reading been involved in any rear-end collisions other than the one at issue, which occurred in August 1981?

Dr. Pintz: Not to my knowledge.

Mr. Bear: If there *had* been other such rear-end collisions, would that change your opinion that the damage definitely, unquestionably be the result of the collision which occurred in August 1981?

Dr. Pintz: Of course!

Mr. Bear: Did Mr. Reading tell you whether he had any previous accidents?

Dr. Pintz: No, he didn't.

Mr. Bear: I have here, a deposition, taken from Mr. Reading on October 15, 1982. I should like to enter this into evidence, Your Honor.

The Court: (*To the court reporter*) You may mark that defendant's exhibit number . . . 22. You may proceed, Mr. Bear.

Mr. Bear: Dr. Pintz. I should like for you to read the material in this deposition beginning with the point marked with a red X.

Dr. Pintz: (*Taking the deposition from opposing counsel*) Let's see—oh—okay. *Mr. Bear:* Now, Mr. Reading, have you ever had any accidents in any way similar to the accident of August 1981. *Mr. Reading:* Do you mean just like it? *Mr. Bear:* Any accidents at all? *Mr. Reading:* Well, not so serious. *Mr. Bear:* Have you had *any* accidents other than the August 1981 accident? *Mr. Reading:* Well, on Christmas Eve of 1980 I was riding home from a party. My wife was driving, and we were hit from behind while we were stopped for a red light. The other driver was charged. *Mr. Bear:* Were you hurt? *Mr. Reading:* Well—not much. I might have been knocked out for a minute or two. *Mr. Bear:* Did you see a doctor? *Mr. Reading:* Well, we were taken to the hospital, and they gave me some X rays. I got over it pretty quickly. I had some headaches for a while, but they weren't as bad as after the accident in 1981. *Mr. Bear:* But you *did* have a head injury following a rear-end collision in 1980—almost a year before the accident of 1981? *Mr. Reading:* I suppose you could say that.

Mr. Bear:	Thank you, Dr. Pintz (*taking the deposition from the witness and giving it to the court reporter*). Is this information a surprise to you, Doctor?
Dr. Pintz:	Well, it, well I . . .
Mr. Bear:	During your evaluation of Mr. Reading did he reveal this incident to you on his own?
Dr. Pintz:	No, I don't believe he did, I really don't . . .
Mr. Bear:	Did you *ask* Mr. Reading, as part of your history, whether he had experienced any accidents or traumas other than the accident of August 1981 that might account for your findings of neuropsychological deficit?
Dr. Pintz:	No . . . I assumed that I'd been provided with all the pertinent medical records so I . . .
Mr. Bear:	If you *had* asked Mr. Reading about head traumas *other* than the accident of August 1981, he *might* have told you about his head trauma in a similar accident, which, in fact, did occur in December 1980, might he not?
Mr. Siegel:	I object, your Honor. Counsel is leading the witness.
The Court:	Objection overruled. Dr. Pintz—please answer the question.
Dr. Pintz:	(*uncomfortable and compromised*) I suppose he might have told me about the previous accident if I had . . .
Mr. Bear:	So, Doctor, you might say that you wish you had asked this question and obtained this additional information.
Dr. Pintz:	Well, yes . . .
Mr. Bear:	Had you known that Mr. Reading had *two* quite similar auto accidents with head trauma, you might not be so sure that your findings of neuropsychological deficit are attributable *only* to the accident of August 1981. Is this not a reasonable conclusion?
Dr. Pintz:	Yes—I suppose.
Mr. Bear:	Please, sir, do not suppose. Would this new information cast doubt on the August 1981 accident as the only possible source of your neuropsychological findings?
Dr. Pintz:	(*resigned and chagrined*) Yes, it would.

The expert witness has good reason to be chagrined. Opposing counsel has used his discovery of an omission in Dr. Pintz's evaluation which casts serious doubt on the expert's opinion as to the cause of the plaintiff's deficit that is critical to the defendant's claim for damages. It has been neatly demonstrated to the jury that Dr. Pintz is fallible and that his opinions must be doubted.

The expert witness who conducts his or her professional work properly, prepares a careful report, participates in a proper pretrial conference, follows the rules, and maintains decor and emotional control is unlikely to be discredited or embarrassed during cross-examination.

Re—Direct Examination

In keeping with the process of "taking turns" during the trial, the attorney who retained the expert follows the cross-examination with an opportunity to emphasize the strengths of the expert witness and to repair any damage that may have been inflicted to the expert's testimony by the cross-examination. No new material can be brought out. The attorney conducting the cross-examination may only refer to matters brought forth in the direct examination or raised in the cross-examination. If opposing counsel has "muddied the waters" during cross-examination by suggesting the expert or the expert's opinion is fallible, the attorney retaining the witness will attempt to reestablish the witness' credibility.

During cross-examination by opposing counsel, the attorney who retains the expert usually takes careful note of any issue that might give members of the jury concern about the credibility of the expert witness. While not annoying or antagonizing the jury with too many details unrelated to the issue at hand, the lawyer will do what can reasonably be done to convince the members of the jury that none of the issues raised in cross-examination is of significance and can be dismissed in the interest of justice. Re–direct examination may focus on substantial or peripheral challenges to the testimony of the expert witness. The following re–direct examination might occur in response to the earlier cross-examination of Dr. White on a peripheral issue concerning opposing counsel's attack on Dr. White's credentials.

The Court: Do you wish to conduct re–direct examination, Mr. Albee?

Mr. Albee: Yes—with the court's permission—just a few more questions for the good doctor. Now, Dr. White, my esteemed colleague asked you a few minutes ago if you were a "medical doctor." You are, in fact, a psychologist, are you not?

Dr. White: That is correct.

Mr. Albee: And I understand that you are licensed to practice psychology in this state?

Dr. White: Yes, sir.

Mr. Albee: Am I correct that medical doctors are *not* licensed as psychologists?

Dr. White: That is right.

Mr. Albee: Of what help would a medical degree be for a psychologist, Dr. White?

Dr. White: None, in my opinion.

Mr. Albee: Am I to understand that you have taught at a medical school?

Dr. White: Yes, sir, I have. At the Medical School of the State University.

Mr. Albee: So—you have *taught* medical students, have you not?

Dr. White: Yes, I have.

The attorney who retained Dr. White is pointing out to the members of the jury that opposing counsel, Mr. McCracken, has tried to cloud the real issues. Mr. Albee hopes that his polite, low-key questioning of Dr. White will convince jury members that his opponent will do almost anything to keep the *real* facts from the jury. This point–counterpoint of courtroom drama is all part of the adversary process.

Some attorneys will conduct very little re–direct examination on the assumption that their cause will *not* be served by focusing on peripheral issues raised in the cross-examination. Re–direct examination based on that trial strategy might proceed as follows:

The Court: Do you wish to conduct re–direct examination, Mr. Albee?

Mr. Albee: With the Court's permission—just a question or two for Dr. White. Forgetting the side issues raised by Mr. McCracken, you *did* conduct a thorough and complete psychological evaluation of Mrs. Alberts, did you not?

Dr. White: I did.

Mr. Albee: And you have analyzed all the medical records, accident records, rehabilitation reports, and so on?

Dr. White: I have.

Mr. Albee: Given all of this lengthy, extensive, and thorough professional evaluation, it *is* your opinion, is it not, that Mrs. Alberts suffers a variety of psychological deficits about which you testified in detail?

Dr. White: That is true.

Mr. Albee: Would you say that she is not the woman she was before her accident and has suffered significant losses in intelligence, skill, coping ability, working skills, and quality of life?

Dr. White: I would say so.

Mr. Albee: No further questions, Your Honor.

Briefly, clearly, and sharply counsel has focused on the main reasons for the expert's presence. The expert is advising the triers of fact that the plaintiff, Mrs. Alberts, has been seriously affected by her accident. Later, the attorney will present other experts to support and justify the *remedy* he proposes to the jury, such as money for rehabilitation, pain, lost earnings, loss of consortium (emotional or sexual deprivation), or even punitive damages where gross negligence contributed to the plaintiff's condition. The expert witness forms one part of the attorney's effort to convince the jury and the judge of what happened, what results have occurred, and what remedy is appropriate.

Re-Cross-Examination

Opposing counsel has the last chance at the expert witness, but no new material or approaches may be raised during re-cross-examination. Focus must be on what was brought out in direct examination or what was explored in the cross-examination. It is opposing counsel's last opportunity to cast doubt on the quality of the expert witness's testimony or to dilute the impact of this testimony on the developing decision-making process of the jurors. The expert can expect to experience a variety of styles of re-cross-examination, since the focus and intensity of question, as in cross-examination, depends on the opposing attorney's trial strategy, personal style, and perception of the most vulnerable portions of the expert's presentation. If the expert has done his or her job thoroughly, little can be done to weaken the expert's opinion. If the expert has made mistakes or prepared poorly, a strong closing can be expected from opposing counsel on re-cross-examination. An example follows:

The Court:	Do you wish to re-cross-examine, Mr. Bear?
Mr. Bear:	Just a few questions for Dr. Pintz. Reviewing what we've said during the cross-examination, I believe you said that the fact that Mr. Reading "forgot" about an automobile accident, which occurred before the accident we are considering in this case, could modify your opinion regarding the cause of his psychological deficit, is that not so?
Dr. Pintz:	Well, yes, it could.
Mr. Bear:	So, Doctor, would it be fair to say that the opinions you gave concerning Mr. Reading's psychological deficits and their origins must be reexamined—by you and the jury—in light of the information you have received during this trial?
Dr. Pintz:	Yes—I suppose . . .
Mr. Bear:	Might I say that if you had a chance to rewrite your report, with this new information—that report would be *different*?

Dr. Pintz: Well—yes.

Mr. Bear: Thank you, Doctor—no further questions.

Opposing counsel, Mr. Bear, has underscored the fragmentation of Dr. Pintz's opinion which occurred during cross-examination. He has shown the jury that Dr. Pintz's original report and his conclusions are in error and that the expert's testimony must be given revised and more limited credibility.

Few attorneys will give up their "turn" at cross-examination even though the expert witness has been outstanding. A final effort to lessen the impact of such testimony might proceed as follows:

The Court: Will you proceed with the re-cross-examination, Counselor?

Mr. McCracken: Yes, your Honor. I'd like to ask Dr. White, as an expert witness retained by the plaintiff, whether she believes that psychology is an "exact" science?

Dr. White: I'm not sure what you mean by *exact*.

Mr. McCracken: Do you, and other psychologists, believe or claim that psychology as a science can make the statements and predictions with the accuracy and predictability of, say, chemistry and physics?

Dr. White: No, as yet . . .

Mr. McCracken: A simple no is quite clear. Am I correct that as a psychologist, you would agree that all the opinions you expressed here today are based on probabilities rather than absolute facts?

Dr. White: That is correct.

Mr. McCracken: No further questions, Your Honor.

Opposing counsel's purpose is to make every legitimate effort to dilute the impact of an opposing counsel's witness on the thinking of the triers of fact.

At this point, when re-cross-examination is completed, the expert witness is finished, except in rare circumstances. The judge may ask questions, offer the jury an opportunity to ask questions of the witness, or even ask the expert witness to come to the judge's chambers. Ordinarily, however, the procedure is as follows:

The Court: Well . . . alright. If there is nothing further, you may step down. Thank you for your testimony, Doctor.

Witness: Thank you, Your Honor.

The witness is now excused. All files and papers should be packed. Do not hurry. When ready, the expert should stand in the witness-box, turn and nod another "thank you" to the judge, step down, nod to the jury, and move toward the door through which the expert entered the courtroom.

The expert witness who expects to improve the quality of his or her testimony should stop briefly at the court reporter's desk, drop a business card there, and whisper, "Please make me a copy of my testimony and bill me for it." Given these instructions, the court reporter will transcribe the expert's testimony, usually within a week, and mail it to the expert. Charges range from $1.50 to $2 per page. Though expensive, it allows the expert to review the details of the testimony, identify discrepancies, inadequacies, and undesirable responses and to improve on skills as an expert witness. The testimony will ordinarily not otherwise be transcribed by the attorneys or the court unless the case is appealed.

Occasionally the judge will call the witness to chambers. The purpose is usually to tell the expert that the judge was pleased with the quality of the testimony. The judge may wish to ask the expert's opinion as to the defendant's rehabilitation potential in a criminal case. Judges have considerable leeway in the matter of questioning experts in chambers. Ordinarily, the expert will be told that the judge wishes to speak with the expert privately by a bailiff who will conduct the witness to the chambers. Here the judge is likely to be out of his or her robes, offer the witness coffee, and chat informally.

When finally dismissed by the judge, the expert should return to his or her office and make a note of the proceedings for the clinical file. Charges should be calculated, portal to portal, and a final invoice sent to the attorney who retained the witness. Unless specifically noted by the judge or one of the attorneys, "the rule" remains in force: The witness should not return to the courtroom as a spectator.

Rebuttal

On very rare occasions, one attorney or the other may call a "rebuttal" witness or witnesses. This would occur after all the regular witnesses have testified and before summation and final arguments. The purpose is usually to focus on an issue important in judging the quality of the evidence. Experts called during rebuttal may have little or no involvement with the plaintiff or the defendant in the case. The rebuttal witness is called to deal with a specific issue. The following presents the testimony of a rebuttal witness called by the defense in the sentencing phase of a criminal proceding.

Witnesses for the prosecution have testified that their examinations have shown that the defendant is dangerous and is likely to be homicidal in the future. The state has asked for the death penalty. Defense counsel has presented no witnesses for direct examination. Instead, his trial strategy is to call a rebuttal witness to discuss "dangerousness" as a scientific concept.

Mr. Spurrier:	If it pleases the Court, we should like to call a rebuttal witness.
The Court:	You may proceed.
Mr. Spurrier:	The defense calls Dr. Richard Jaeger. (*Witness is sworn and seated.*) Please state your name.
Dr. Jaeger:	Richard Jaeger.
Mr. Spurrier:	Where do you reside, Doctor?
Dr. Jaeger:	Greensboro, North Carolina.
Mr. Spurrier:	What is your profession, sir?
Dr. Jaeger:	I am Professor of Statistics and Evaluation Science at the University of North Carolina.
Mr. Spurrier:	Would you please explain to the Judge and the jury the nature of statistics and of evaluation science?
Dr. Jaeger:	Certainly (*whereupon the witness proceeds to succinctly explain his science and profession*).

The witness is qualified in the manner demonstrated earlier in this chapter. His credentials are stipulated to by opposing counsel, and the judge accepts the witness as an expert.

The Court:	You may proceed Mr. Spurrier.
Mr. Spurrier:	Thank you, your Honor. Dr. Jaeger, have you ever "examined" the defendant?
Dr. Jaeger:	I have not.
Mr. Spurrier:	Have you heard the testimony of the State's witnesses during this trial?
Dr. Jaeger:	I have.
Mr. Spurrier:	Are you familiar with the issue of "dangerousness" and its prediction?
Dr. Jaeger:	I am.
Mr. Spurrier:	Have you, yourself, conducted and published research on the prediction of such traits as dangerousness.
Dr. Jaeger:	I have.
Mr. Spurrier:	Doctor—would you please explain to the court the nature and quality of the research on dangerousness.
Dr. Jaeger:	Research on dangerousness is a part of behavioral science research on what we call *infrequent events*. This is as opposed to research on such things as *learning* where the

behavior is frequent, regular, and of such a nature that laboratory experiments can be designed to measure and understand the behavior. With human responses, such as dangerousness, the events occur quite infrequently so that scientific measurement and study is much more difficult.

Mr. Spurrier: Then it is harder to study dangerousness, for instance, than to study how a child learns to read?

Dr. Jaeger: Yes, sir.

Mr. Spurrier: Has dangerousness been studied very extensively?

Dr. Jaeger: Yes, it has.

Mr. Spurrier: Please tell the Court what the science of evaluation has contributed to this.

Dr. Jaeger: Evaluation studies of dangerousness indicate that it is not so much a trait of an individual but a phenomenon or occurrence that happens when certain conditions occur in almost any environment.

Mr. Spurrier: Please tell the Judge and jury about these "conditions."

Dr. Jaeger: Violence or dangerousness tends to occur when there are conflict and provocation, few alternative solutions to the conflict, physical proximity between opponents, the means and the opportunity to be violent, and, frequently, significant quantities of alcohol having been taken recently by one or both opponents.

Mr. Spurrier: Are you saying that almost anyone could be dangerous, given the circumstances and conditions you've described?

Dr. Jaeger: The research does so indicate.

Mr. Spurrier: You have heard that the defendant has been described by various experts in psychiatry and psychology, retained by the State, as "potentially dangerous." Have you any information on the reliability of such statements?

Dr. Jaeger: Yes, sir, I have.

Mr. Spurrier: Would you please tell the Court the source of this material.

Dr. Jaeger: Studies in dangerousness or violence have been based on a wide range of populations. Prisoners represent one of the largest populations that have been studied. In many judicial settings, predictions of dangerousness or violence have been made, and then the individuals in the study have been followed very carefully for years. In this way, the effectiveness of predictions of dangerousness can be checked or evaluated.

Mr. Spurrier: If a person is predicted to be dangerous, what is the likelihood that this prediction will actually come about?

Dr. Jaeger: Given the considerable number of studies, it is my opinion that a professional prediction of dangerousness based on psychiatric examination and/or psychological tests is likely to be correct no more than one-third of the time.

Mr. Spurrier: Do you mean to tell us that if an expert predicts that 100 criminals he has examined are likely to be dangerous in the future, that only 34 out of a 100 will turn out to be dangerous?

Dr. Jaeger: Yes, sir, that is true. The prediction of dangerousness tends to have about 66 percent "false-positive" rate. This means that the vast majority of people who are predicted to be potentially dangerous do not, according to a current research, actually turn out to get into additional trouble and appear again in the criminal justice system.

Mr. Spurrier: Then according to the information you provided us, Dr. Jaeger, when an expert makes a prediction of dangerousness, his chances are about twice as great of being wrong than of being right, is that not so?

Dr. Jaeger: That is approximately correct, sir.

Mr. Spurrier: Do you understand the concept of beyond a reasonable doubt?

Dr. Jaeger: I believe so.

Mr. Spurrier: In the law *beyond a reasonable doubt* means that the probability of a thing occurring is extremely high, probably well beyond 9 chances out of 10. Is that the way you understand it?

Dr. Jaeger: Yes, sir.

Mr. Spurrier: In your professional opinion, as an evaluation scientist, does the research on dangerousness justify a prediction of dangerousness on any individual beyond a reasonable doubt.

Dr. Jaeger: No, sir, not by a long shot.

The rebuttal witness has cast scientific doubt on fairly absolute statements made by the previous experts.

11

Emerging Applications and Issues

The opportunities for psychologists to serve as expert witnesses have increased significantly during the past three decades. New directions are emerging constantly. Although not long ago psychologists as experts in the court served roles similar to those of the psychiatric witness (Blau, 1959), today new opportunities appear regularly.

In order to show some of the diverse applications of psychology as a science and profession in American jurisprudence, some specific examples are presented in this chapter. Most of these applications are fairly new and, thus far, occur infrequently.

EYEWITNESS TESTIMONY

Although it still has a limited area of application, the concept of psychology's potential contribution to this important aspect of evidentiary testimony is quite old, having been proposed in Munsterberg's original treatise, *On the Witness Stand* (1908). In the half-century subsequent to Munsterberg's serious questions concerning the reliability of eyewitness identification, experimental psychologists have demonstrated that the testimony of witnesses based on what they believe they saw is not as consistent and accurate as the courts have traditionally assumed (Loftus, 1981).

The courts have not been unmindful of such findings. In 1967, the U.S. Supreme Court attempted to define some limits on eyewitness testimony of questionable reliability.[1] The safeguards provided a defendant with an attorney during pretrial eyewitness identification procedures.

Since judges and jurors must ultimately decide on the reliability of eyewitness testimony, most attention and concern has been focused on them. Tentative efforts to ensure that jurors are aware of some of the inaccuracies and discrepancies possible in eyewitness testimony are found in recom-

---

[1] *United States v. Wade*, 388 U.S. 218 (1967).

mendations for instructions by judges to jurors.[2] Such instructions caution jurors to consider the credibility of eyewitness testimony in respect to who renders such testimony and the conditions under which the event was witnessed. These concerns mainly deal with the dangers of solidifying vague eyewitness testimony by having witnesses identify a potential defendant in a police or investigative setting under conditions that imply or suggest guilt. This tends to encourage positive identification. Many factors can influence the fairness of a police identification lineup (Wells, Leippe, & Ostrom, 1979). The Supreme Court has ruled that eyewitness identification that may have been reinforced by exposure of the defendant's photograph to the eyewitness by police anxious to have a positive identification is inadmissible.[3]

More recently, efforts have been made to decrease jurors' unrealistic reliance on eyewitness testimony by using psychologists as experts in the courtroom. In such instances, efforts are made to qualify a psychologist as expert in the reliability and validity of eyewitness accounts. The psychologist gives direct testimony as to those factors that affect the reliability and validity of recall. A number of courts have ruled that the experimental findings regarding eyewitness identification are not a fit subject for expert testimony. Some courts have opined that the average juror has sufficient knowledge as to those factors that contribute to unreliable eyewitness identification.[4,5] An appellate decision ruled that the testimony of a psychologist regarding the reliability of eyewitness identification was not admissible since it might take from the jury their own determination as to what weight to give the evidence of the eyewitness.[6]

A more recent state appellate court opined:

> The State asserts that the facts affecting the reliability of an eyewitness identification are within the ordinary experience of jurors, that the conclusions to be drawn from the facts affecting the reliability of an eyewitness should be left to the jury, and that expert opinion should be excluded where the facts testified to are of a nature as not to require any special knowledge or experience to form a conclusion.[7]

This decision seems explicit, yet it states that "where the facts testified to are of a nature as not to require any special knowledge or experience." Some attorneys believe that further appellate review will eventually define areas of "special knowledge" where expert psychological testimony will be admitted at trial. To this end, attorneys may request that a psychologist prepare testimony that will be proffered or submitted as an "offer of proof"

[2] *United States v. Telfaire,* 469 F.2d 552 (D.C. Cir. 1972).
[3] *United States v. Crews,* 445 U.S. 463, 100 S.Ct. 1244. 63L.Ed;2d 537 (1980).
[4] *Dyas v. United States,* 376 A.2d 827 (D.C. 1977).
[5] *Nelson v. State,* 362 So.2d 1017 (Fla. 1978).
[6] *United States v. Amaral,* 488 F.2d 1148 (9th Cir 1973).
[7] *Johnson v. State* 393 So.2d 1069 (Fla. 1980), *Cert. denied* 454 U.S. 882 (1981).

to a trial judge, requesting that the psychologist be allowed to testify as to the reliability of eyewitness testimony. The following report illustrates such an offer of proof.

OFFER OF PROOF
Proffered Deposition

The Psychologist as Expert
in Witness Credibility

Prepared for Mr. Jones
of the Public Defender's Office
13th Judicial District
State of Florida

Qualification

A. Is the Field of Witness Credibility a Scientific Field within Psychology?

The hundredth anniversary of psychology was just celebrated in America. Perhaps 10 years before this founding in 1881, the first psychological laboratory was established by Wundt in Leipzig. All of the early experiments in psychology had to do with learning, memory, recollection, and accuracy of observation. The capability of human beings to observe and identify things in the environment has always been a major element of the study of psychology.

The question of how people see things, retain things, remember things, and make identifications of people and objects is a major subject of scientific study in psychology. The first studies of the testimony of witnesses in courts of law occurred in 1895 in Europe. Munsterberg's book in 1909 was the first to summarize research in this area. Since that time, the areas of psychology associated with accuracy of witnesses' reports, such as perception, memory, observation, recall, and so forth, have been elementary to the study of psychology.

The American Psychological Association publishes some 19 scientific journals. Studies of memory, perception, and learning can be found in almost all of these journals as a regular part of the scientific reporting system. Hundreds of thousands of experiments have been conducted to determine basic principles in these fields. It is certainly to be considered a field of scientific exploration and study.

B. Is It Likely That the Average Person Who Might Appear on a Voters' Registration List Would Understand the Basic Principles of Memory, Cognition, Learning, and Recall?

Many principles that have been developed in psychology are known to the general public, such as *reinforcement* (that which is rewarded will tend to be repeated). Other principles are not well known, such as the inability to identify and remember colors under low illumination. In the question of witness credibility, memory, and learning, there are many findings in the scientific field of psychology that are simply not known to laymen or, for that matter, to many psychologists who are not specialists in this field. One example might be whether witnesses who state what they remember with great certainty actually remember events better than those who express more doubt. Numerous experiments have been done in which subjects are asked to identify the degree of assuredness of their memory with a variety of true and false memories being tested.

The results consistently show that the intensity with which a witness reports the sureness of his or her recall has nothing to do with the accuracy of the recollection. In a study reported by Loftus in 1980, over 500 registered voters in the state of Washington were given a series of witness-report situations and asked what they knew about the accuracy of different kinds of observations under a variety of conditions. The results indicated widespread misunderstanding of the principles of memory. It is clear that the average venireman knows something about memory from his or her own experience but very little about the scientific data that has been developed over the past 100 years concerning the complex phenomena of remembering.

C. What Would Be the Qualifications of an Expert Witness Who Could Inform a Jury about Memory and Witness Credibility?

Certainly the Ph.D. in psychology is the basic and fundamental requirement for such expertness. The holder of the degree should have conducted at least a dissertation for the doctorate and perhaps even a thesis for the master's degree associated with the phenomena of learning and remembering. Those who have taught basic psychology with its emphasis on perception, cognition, and memory are in a better position to instruct the jury than a person who has done some research in this area or has simply read about it. It is helpful if the witness has conducted research in the area of memory, cognition, perception, learning, and recalling.

D. Would You Please State the Background Qualifications You Possess?

I received the bachelor of science, master of science, and Ph.D. in psychology. My courses of study included a great many which emphasized memory, perception, cognition, learning, and recall. My professors of experimental psychology included William Lepley, noted for the Lepley Hypothesis in Learning and Memory; Joseph DeCamp, experimental psychologist; W. Ray Carpenter, professor of social psychology; Joseph Grosslight, professor of experimental psychology (now head of the Department of Psychology at Florida State University); and others.

My master's thesis was a study of learning and memory as it was associated with physiological phenomena. I measured the pulse rate and blood volume of over 100 subjects while they were presented with "interesting" learning material and "noninteresting" learning material to attempt to identify those physiological factors that might be associated with material which is better-remembered. As one might expect by "common sense," interesting material tends to be remembered for a longer period of time than "noninteresting." It was found that this is associated with increases in systolic blood pressure. That study indicated, as have others, that memory is quite imperfect, and people will forget critical details and add details which are simply not there.

For my doctoral dissertation, I conducted studies as a research fellow for the Aero-Medical Research Unit of the United States Air Force studying the effects of high intensity noise on the intellectual performance and memory of Air Force personnel. That was the time when jet planes were initially being acquired for our Air Force, and discrepancies in learning behavior and in memory were being noted. My studies found that under conditions of noise, people remember about 9 percent better in terms of quantity than when people are learning and observing in quiet conditions. An analysis of what they remembered, however, indicated that all 9 percent of the increase in quantity was in the form of "errors." This suggested that under stress, memory may seem to be increased, but the increase is almost entirely inaccurate.

From 1964 until 1971 I was closely associated with the National Society for Programmed Instruction and conducted many studies of the effect of various kinds of perception and learning on immediate and long-range recall. I studied normal people, retarded children, college students, and many others. Based on our findings, we built an automated learning center in Tampa which utilized the most salient principles of high-performance learning. This learning center was eventually donated to U.S. International University, where it is used for training at the present time.

In 1974 I became a consultant to the Office of Education and then later to the National Institutes of Education. My prime role was to evaluate laboratories and centers that were doing work in developing material to increase the learning capacity and the effectiveness of instructional materials for children. At about that time I began to consult with the United States Army in a variety of settings, establishing research programs and conducting evaluations of training and learning procedures where memory, cognition, perception, and recall were intrinsic parts of all of the work that we did. All of these studies were published by the United States Army, and most of them are classified. In 1976 I published one released study, "Automated Educational Systems and Instructional Devices."

In 1979 I wrote a chapter for the book *Minimum Competency Testing,* an area of current great interest, which addressed learning and memory in public school children.

I have taught memory, cognition, and perception in a variety of settings. I taught for the Department of Behavioral Science at the University of South Florida (Introductory Psychology, Introduction to Human Behavior, Introduction to Behavior Modification), as well as for the Department of Psychology when that department was formulated at the university.

I have also taught at U.S. International University and have presented workshops in a variety of settings, including various Bar associations.

As a researcher, my skills have been sought by a number of journals where I have been asked to review and evaluate the quality of scientific psychological research. I have reviewed for such journals as the *American Psychologist,* the *Journal of Abnormal and Social Psychology,* the *Journal of Selected Documents in Psychology, Contemporary Psychology, Professional Psychology, Science,* and the *Journal of Perceptual and Motor Skills.* I have presented a number of papers and symposia at scientific meetings and to Bar meetings in the area of the use of psychology in the courtroom. My academic rank has been Full Professor, at the University of South Florida, the Medical School of the University of South Florida, and U.S. International University. I have been Visiting Professor at St. Louis University, the University of Maryland Medical School, the University of Oregon Medical School, California School of Professional Psychology, and the Illinois School of Professional Psychology. I am a member of the American Psychological Association, the primary scientific/professional organization of psychologists in the United States. At present there are 65,000 qualified psychologists who are members of this organization.

Witness Interrogatory

A. What in General Has Psychological Science Learned about the Memory Process and the Recollection of Events?

Human memory is part of the study of perception, cognition, and learning. The average person believes he or she knows a great deal about these things, but the gap between the average person's knowledge and the psychologist's understanding, based on scientific research, of human memory is quite extensive (Saks & Hastie, 1979). The superiority of the scientific approach to the study of memory lies in its systematic character. Stringent standards of proof are required before generalizations are accepted.

Psychologists are generally agreed that there are three stages of memory: *acquisition, retention,* and *retrieval.* In the first stage information is encoded, enters into the subject's memory system, and becomes part of the neural network. During the retention stage we have a period of time that passes between acquisition and utilization of the stored memory material. The third stage is the retrieval stage, or the utilization stage, in which stored information is recalled or activated.

In psychological studies of human memory, an attempt is made to account for the failure of people to retrieve or utilize information. There are many causes of retrieval failure, which can occur at any stage of the process. A person who sees an accident or witnesses a crime and is then asked to describe what he or she saw cannot call up an "instant replay." The preson must depend on memory, with all of its limitations. These limitations may be of minor import in ordinary daily activities. If the memory is unreliable and the truth is slightly altered, it is ordinarily not significant. When a person must act as a witness, however, inaccuracy can escalate in importance (Buckhout, 1974). Perception and memory are not "copying" processes but decision-making processes affected by all of a person's abilities, background, attitudes, motives, and beliefs. The environment in which things occur has an important influence on quality of memory. Retrieval of memory occurs when the individual evaluates fragments of recalled information and then reconstructs them.

B.   What Factors Have Been Found to Affect Memory during the Acquisition Stage?

Before an event can be recalled, it must be *perceived* in such a way that it can be stored in the brain (encoded in the memory). The event must be within a witness's perceptual range (loud enough, close enough, sufficiently well-lit—in other words, available to the senses). Certain elements of the acquisition stage have been carefully studied by psychologists. They include:

1. *Exposure Time.*   It is consistently true that the longer an individual has to look at something, the better he or she will remember it. By the same token, when things are observed in a "fleeting moment," they are less likely to be remembered accurately or at all (Buckhout, 1974; Loftus, 1979).

2. *Observation Conditions.*   This relates to the perceptual range of the observer. A fast-moving, threatening, or chaotic flow of events, such as a crime in progress, often conflicts with the perceptual capabilities of the human observer (Saks & Hastie, 1979).

3. *Violence of the Event.*   A person's observation about a violent incident during the acquisition stage will be less accurate than when observing an equivalent nonviolent situation (Clifford & Scott, 1978).

4. *Stress.*   During any kind of stress the heart rate will increase, adrenalin will flow, blood pressure will rise, and as a result of these physiological conditions, incidents will be more poorly remembered than when stress is mild. As stress increases, the accuracy of memory decreases (Buckhout, 1974; Loftus, 1980).

5. *Distorted Perceptions.*   People can acquire only a limited amount of information from their environment at one time. What they acquire consists of fragmented bits and pieces, and many of these will be distorted. When events are rapid, mistakes will be made and things

will be omitted upon recall simply because they were not acquired (Munsterberg, 1950; Gardner, 1933; Buckhout, 1974).

6. *Depth of Processing.*   Different stimuli in the environment are processed at various levels of depth during the acquisition stage, depending on the amount of time the person is exposed to it and the importance of the item to the person. The deeper the processing, the more accurate the later recall (Bower & Karlin, 1974).

7. *Social Expectation.*   As Whipple pointed out as long ago as 1909, "Observation is peculiarly influenced by expectation so that errors amounting to distinct illusions or hallucinations may arise from this source. . . . We tend to see and hear what we expect to see and hear." This is unfortunately illustrated each and every year when hundreds of hunters are killed and wounded by their friends who "expect" any moving object to be a deer, and it unfortunately turns out to be one of their fellow hunters. Expectancy errors are quite common and were clearly illustrated by Allport and Postman in 1945.

8. *Personal Needs, Biases, and Emotions.*   "Honest" mistakes occur when witnesses, in strong emotional states, express absolute recall about events that were fragmentedly acquired. They remember because they "want" or "need" to remember.

9. *Weapon-Focus Phenomena.*   Where a crime victim is faced with an assailant brandishing a weapon, the weapon captures a good deal of the victim's attention, frequently resulting in a reduced ability to recall other details from the environment. Thus fragmented peripheral impressions may be either forgotten or distorted (Loftus, 1980).

C.   *Can You Tell Us What Scientific Psychology Has Found Out about the Retention Stage of Memory?*

The retention stage is all that an individual has to work with when the time comes to retrieve information. There are a number of factors which determine the degree to which the retention will be complete and undistorted. Some of these are:

1. *The Motivational, or Emotional, State of the Witness.*   Retention is affected by the feelings of the witness at the time of the event. Alteration of the shape and content of the information occurs as a result of those factors (Marshall, 1969). Strong emotional states improve retention up to a point, but after that retention is interfered with (Hilgard, Atkinson, & Atkinson, 1975). This is called the Yerkes-Dodson Law.

2. *The Kinds of Questions that People Are Asked Will Influence Their Recall.*   Any hint by the kind of question or the form of the question that there was something in the situation (that really wasn't there)

can have the influence of creating a perception of memory (Loftus & Palmer, 1974). The kind of words that are used influence the richness and quality of the rememberer's response. In experiments where the same material is presented to groups of witnesses, one group was asked to recall without influence, and the other was asked specific questions. Where specific questions were asked, the influence on retention is strong and often biasing.

3. *Decay over Time.*   The longer the time delay between the original acquisition and the retrieval (retention time), the poorer the memory.

4. *Filling Gaps.*   Memory is a process of active construction. Descriptions and details become more complete over time and often include details that were not originally encoded during the acquisition stage. Thus, during the retention stage, the mind is active, "putting things together." A person will create and fill in concepts and add details to eliminate inconsistencies in memory (Bem, 1967).

5. *Postevent Information.*   Any new information that occurs after the original acquisition may be absorbed and distort the original memory. Discussion and exchange of ideas may increase agreement among witnesses. Nonexistent objects can be introduced into the memory when such objects are mentioned during discussions.

6. *Peripheral Activity.*   Where there has been a strong focus of attention, actions, people, or things which were in the periphery are either more poorly retained or more distorted than central details.

D.   What Has Psychological Science Found Out about the Retrieval Aspects of Memory?

As noted previously, memory is not an instant replay. When an individual retrieves a memory, he or she has a series of fragments that are "filled in." The degree of accuracy with which a person fills in varies considerably. The original event may be distorted. Some of the influential factors are as follows:

1. *Individual Differences.*   The accuracy of retrieval of events depends on personal and social factors. Marshall (1969) showed a 42-second film to a large group of subjects who had various degrees of education. Out of 115 possible memories, law students remembered on an average of 14, police trainees remembered 10.3, while low-income adults remembered 5.3. Subjects "remembered" things which didn't exist in the film.

2. *Age.*   Schaie and Gribbin (1975) found that free recall tends to deteriorate after age 40 and more so after 50 and even more after 60 years of age. Older people are poorer at dividing their attention (Loftus, 1980). As a result of this, poor retrieval can occur. Retrieval tends to

decline with age (Farrimond, 1968). People in their 60s recall about 60 percent of what people in their 30s recall.

3. *Introduction of False Items.*   When, in the recounting of an event, an individual unknowingly introduces a detail into his account which did not actually exist, his perception of the false item will be that of "absolute memory" and in the future will be included in his description of the event (Bartlett, 1957).

4. *Conformity.*   People tend to make reports from their fragmented memory conform with all kinds of expectations—personal as well as social. Two witnesses can and will agree on an *error* as well as on accurate observations. One will influence the other, particularly if the first opinion is strongly given. Buckhout and his students (1974) at the University of California presented an assault scene to 141 witnesses. Sworn statements taken from the witnesses shortly after viewing the scene showed details that were quite inaccurate in terms of the appearance, the dress, and the actions of the people in the assault scene. Witnesses reinforced each other's statements. It was estimated that only 25 percent of the details were correct.

5. *The Need to Reduce Uncertainty.*   There is a natural human tendency to avoid uncertainty. As a result, during the retrieval stage, witnesses will form opinions with great sureness and later find out that the facts are simply not so.

6. *Specific Questioning.*   Questions which are asked as a witness reports an incident can lead to more inaccuracy than if the witness is allowed to give a completely open narrative report.

7. *Relation of a Surety to Facts.*   The research shows clearly that the degree to which the subject is "sure" about details bears no relationship to whether the fact is accurate or not.

8. *Consistency of Errors.*   Ever since Whipple's original observations (1909), it has been found over and over again that even competent observers, making observations under favorable conditions, frequently make errors of observations. They will attest that the observations are correct but this does not guarantee accuracy. Repeating testimony will tend to fix the details.

In 1976, Lord Devlin undertook a review of the issue of eye-witness testimony for the courts of England. In his report to the House of Commons that year, he stated that "it is only in exceptional cases that identification evidence is by itself sufficiently reliable to exclude a reasonable doubt about guilt."

Bibliography

Allport, G., & Postman, L. (1945). *The basic psychology of rumor.* New York. NY Academy of Sciences, Series II.

Bartlett, F. C. (1957). *Remembering*. Cambridge: Cambridge University Press.

Bem, I. (1967, June). When seeing is believing. *Psychology Today*, p. 21.

Bem, D. (1966). Introducing belief in false confessions. *Journal of Personality and Social Psychology, 3*, 707.

Bower, G. H., & Karlin, M. B. (1974). Depth of processing pictures of faces and recognition memory. *Journal of Experimental Psychology, 103*, 751–757.

Buckhout, Robert. (1974). Eyewitness testimony. *Scientific American, 231*(6), 23–31.

Clifford, B. R., & Scott, J. (1978). Individual differences and situational factors in eye-witness testimony. *J. Applied Psychology, 63*, 352–359.

Farrimond, T. (1968). Retention and recall: Incidental learning of visual and auditory material. *Journal of Genetic Psychology, 113*, 155–165.

Gardner, D. S. (1933). The perception and memory of witnesses. *Cornell Law Quarterly, 18*, 391–409.

Hilgard, E. R., Atkinson, R. C., & Atkinson, R. L. (1975). *Introduction to psychology*. New York: Harcourt, Brace, Jovanovich.

Lindsay, R. C. L., Wells, G. L., & Rumpel, C. M. (1981). Can people detect eyewitness-identification accuracy within and across situations? *Journal of Applied Psychology*.

Loftus, E., & Palmer, J. P. (1974). Reconstruction of automobile destruction. *J. of Verbal Learning and Verbal Behavior, 13*, 585–589.

Loftus, E. (1979). *Eyewitness testimony*. Cambridge: Harvard U. Press.

Loftus, E. (1980). *Memory*. Reading, Massachusetts: Addison Wesley.

Marshall, J. (1969). *Law and Psychology in Conflict*. New York: Doubleday Anchor.

Saks, M. J., & Hastie, R. (1978). *Social Psychology in Court*. New York: Van Nostrand Reinhold.

Schaie, K. W., & Gribbon, K. (1975). Adult development and aging. *American Review of Psychology, 26*, 65–96.

Whipple, G. M. (1909). The observer as reporter: A survey of the psychology of testimony. *Psychological Bulletin, 6*, 153–170.

Woocher, F. D. (1977). Did your eyes deceive you? Expert psychological testimony on the unreliability of eyewitness identification. *Stanford Law Review, 29*, 969–1030.

Such documents may eventually result in a more thorough appellate review of the issue of allowing experts to testify concerning eyewitness testimony.

PSYCHOLOGICAL AUTOPSY

Can psychological procedures or methods provide reliable information concerning the premorbid psychological state of an individual after that person is deceased? Forensic pathologists commonly testify about conditions that existed prior to death, frequently in respect to the cause of death. In recent years psychologists have developed methods to construct a psychological portrait of the deceased, which has come to be known as the *psychological autopsy* (Shneidman, 1967). Originally a tool that was developed to determine whether a death was the result of natural causes or of suicide, a psychological picture of the deceased was constructed by an investigation team based on history; interviews with relatives, friends, and fellow workers; personal communication; and reported premorbid behaviors. Since then, the technique has been extended to the investigation of aircraft accidents (Jones, 1977) and the relation of a death by suicide to family dynamics (Rudestam, 1977). The psychological autopsy has been used to aid bereaved family members (Sanborn & Sanborn, 1976).

Although the techniques are relatively new, psychological and psychiatric autopsies have been admitted in court. Used in both civil and criminal cases, admissibility is determined by the judge in each case (Lichter, 1981).

The following example of a psychological autopsy was presented in a civil case. The plaintiff, Mrs. Horner, wife of Karl Horner, deceased, claimed that the conditions of her husband's new employment contributed to his untimely death and sought remedy in the form of both an immediate award and extended payments in lieu of the deceased husband's earning potential. Evidence was needed that the conditions of Mr. Horner's new work placed him in a more vulnerable status for a heart attack than his previous job. There also needed to be some objective evidence that the new job was more stressful than Mr. Horner's previous employment. The following report was the result of the psychological autopsy on Mr. Horner.

FORENSIC PSYCHOLOGY EVALUATION REPORT

December 15, 1980

In re: *Horner v. Brand and Sills Communications*

A. *Purpose of Evaluation*

A request for forensic psychological consultation was received from James West, Esquire, of West, Lowery and Ilt on 12/2/80. Mr. West requires expert consultation regarding effects of job activity on vulnerability to cardiac disease. Mr. West represents the estate of Karl B. Horner, the plaintiff in this issue.

B. *Sources of Information*

Deposition of Ron Sacker, Vice President, Brand and Sills Communications. Examination of work records and medical records. Interview with Mr. Horner's widow.

An interview with Mrs. Mary Horner, widow of Karl Horner, was held on December 12, 1980. The couple had been married for 20 years. There were five children. Mr. Horner had worked for A.T.&S. for nine and one-half years before moving to the job at Brand and Sills. He worked 40 hours per week while at A.T.&S. After three and one-half years in crafts, he moved to management. He took regular vacations, as required by A.T.&S. His social life revolved around his wife and children, although he and his wife also played cards and went out with friends. Mr. Horner swam regularly in the family pool. His family income was $23,000 per year.

When he moved to Brand and Sills his income increased to $40,000 per year. There were major changes in his living, working, and recreational activities. He worked long hours, evenings and weekends. He gave up bowling. He no longer swam regularly. His interaction with the family on a regular basis ceased. His eating and sleeping habits became erratic. He lost over 40 pounds between January 1, 1979, and the time of his heart attack on May 16, 1979. He received a speeding ticket while driving the company truck in Ohio. His life and life-style changed considerably and rapidly after January 1, 1979.

C. Summary of the Facts in This Case

Karl B. Horner, age 44, a high school graduate and father of five children, married 20 years, died on May 30, 1979. Between January 1, 1979, and the time of his death five months later he was employed by the Brand and Sills company. Previous to his move to Brand and Sills, Mr. Horner was employed for 10 years by A.T.&S. In that company he started in crafts and moved to management approximately three years after starting with A.T.&S.

Beginning on January 1, 1979, Mr. Horner worked for Brand and Sills under Mr. Ron J. Sacker, vice president of Data Basics, a subsidiary of Brand and Sills. In his deposition, Mr. Sacker describes their work as follows: "We supply manpower and overload-type manpower systems for just about every telephone company going." He further states his work is "strictly an overload-bodyshop-type operation." Mr. Horner was initially employed as a project manager (Engineering) for Brand and Sills. (The intent was not to leave him with Field Projects but to bring him into management.) During the five months he worked for Brand and Sills, Mr. Horner worked on projects in Arabia, Ohio, Georgia, Texas, Michigan, Oklahoma, Massachusetts, and New York.

He was "on the move" approximately three days per week and sometimes on weekends. He lived in hotels, a company apartment, and his employer's, Mr. Sacker's, house. He traveled extensively. He was working 60–80 hours per week. He worked many nights until midnight. His wife flew to various cities to meet him approximately three times. He visited home in Tampa rarely. He worked against stringent deadlines. When he died, Mr. Sacker hired three people to replace him. The project was minimally staffed for maximum work effort. It was the beginning phase of long-range plans, and Mr. Horner was required to put forth excessive effort to accomplish his missions.

The day of his first heart attack, on May 13, 1979 (Sunday), he was in New Orleans at Mr. Sacker's house. He arose early to catch a plane to Albany, N.Y., to work on a project. He had worked all day Saturday. The early departure on Sunday was for the purpose of stopping at Dayton, Ohio, to evaluate a project there while on his way to Albany, N.Y. All of this intensive activity, according to Mr. Sacker, was to "prove something to the corporate people in order to get this company off the ground." The volume of work from January 1 to May 13, 1979, increased steadily.

Mr. Horner entered the hospital on May 13, 1979. According to his wife he suffered a myocardial infarction. One day later he was said to have suffered complications in the form of pericardial inflammation. Three and one-half days following the initial attack he suffered a CVA, left hemisphere, with paralysis and aphasia. He died on May 30 of a second M.I.

D. Significant Factors

Occupational factors are very significant in development of stress disorders (Freese, 1976). Certain people are particularly prone to certain types of coronary disease when exposed to highly stressful, demanding vocational situations (Glass, Contrada, & Snow, 1980). Changes in residence, occupation, and sociocultural environment produce "social discontinuity" and increase coronary risk (Karassi, 1979). Feelings of work-overload (demands of job greater than can be handled given the available time, resources, and abilities) are associated with elevated coronary risk. Deadlines are a frequent source of overload (Gentry & Williams, 1975). In a study of 299 men in a wide variety of white-collar and blue-collar jobs, House (1972) found a composite measure of overload, and responsibility and role conflict was associated with greater risk for heart disease in the entire range of occupations studied.

Russek (1965, 1967) compared 100 young coronary patients with an equal number of controls. Prolonged emotional strain associated with job responsibilities preceded the heart attacks of 91 percent of the patients, while strain was evident in only 20 percent of the control group. Miles (1954) found that 50 percent of heart disease patients worked long hours with few vacations prior to their attacks, while only 12 percent of the control group did. The risk for coronary heart disease is 45/1000 in laborers and 90/1000 for professionals (Russek, 1975).

Rapid change in occupational environment predisposes men to heart disease. "Complexification," the rate at which things change or become increasingly complex in the occupational environment, is a form of overload. People whose work involves occupational and geographic mobility experience a greater incidence of heart disease, as do men whose occupational status is higher than their educational status (Gentry & Williams, 1975). Contact with a variety of occupational environments increases heart disease risk (Caplan, 1971). Emotional stress emanating from increased job responsibility is seen by some as more significant in the etiology of coronary disease than heredity, high-fat diet, obesity, body build, tobacco consumption, or exercise patterns (Russek, 1967). Some myocardial infarction victims may feel increased pressures to achieve goals which become threatened by a reduced life expectancy. Those who die of recurrent myocardial infarction have higher stress-prone scores. In comparison with other occupational levels managers and foremen are highest on stress scales of "job involvement" and "hard-driving" in terms of vulnerability for coronary incidents (Dembroski et al., 1978). Higher rates of coronary heart disease occur among persons experiencing various types of life change and mobility (NIH, 1979).

Where a job requires crossing time zones, body time zones become imbalanced and create stress. "Relax and recovery" time must be allotted to such individuals by top management (Boggiano, 1966).

Table A, abstracted from *Vital Statistics* (USHEW, 1963) indicates that risk for cardiac disease in general and coronary heart disease in particular is significantly higher in the manager/official occupational category than in the professional/technical category. At A.T.&.S. Mr. Horner was in the professional/technical occupational category (11 percent risk above base rate for coronary heart disease at his age). When he moved to Brand and Sills, his work placed him in the manager/official category (50 percent risk above base rate for coronary heart disease).

Table A.   Base Rate Data (Vital Statistics, Vol. 53, No. 3, 1963. Mortality by Occupation and Cause of Death. Guralnick, U.S. HEW)

Deaths from all causes—all occupations		327,271
Deaths from all causes—all occupations—ages 35–44		44,534
Deaths from *cardiac*—all occupations—ages 35–44		15,161
Deaths from *coronary*—all occupations—ages 35–44		8,044
Base rate for ages 35–44—all occupations—*cardiac*	40%	
Base rate for ages 35–44—all occupations—*coronary*	18%	

Percentage of Total Deaths—Ages 35–44 (1950)

Occupational Category

	Clerical	Professional/Technical	Managers/Officials
All *cardiac*	38%	35%	42%
Coronary	18%	20%	27%
	(At base rate)	(11% above base rate)	(50% above base rate)

E.   Psychological Analysis of Karl B. Horner's Response to Vocational Expectancies: 1978 and 1979

From information taken from the deposition of Mr. Ron Sacker and clinical interview with Mrs. Margaret Horner a picture is obtained of the environmental/vocational expectancies and conditions in Mr. Horner's life in 1978 and 1979. Mr. Horner is depicted as a conscientious, competent telephone-system project planner and expediter. He is further described as extremely reliable. Although hard-driving and time-urgent, he was not described as competitive and aggressive, suggesting that his personality only partially fits the Type A pattern.

The information available suggests that Mr. Horner's job with Brand and Sills Engineering produced or required the following:

1. Geographic mobility and frequent time-zone crossings without adaptation time
2. Changes in residence
3. A position superior to Mr. Horner's educational background

Table B. Holmes Stress Scale Items for Mr. Karl B. Horner
January 1, 1978–December 31, 1978, Compared with January 1, 1979–May 14, 1979.

Stress Scale Items and Their Values			
Jan. 1, 1978–Dec. 31, 1978	Value	January 1, 1979–May 14, 1979	Value
14. Gain of new family member	(39)	14. Same	(39)
30. Trouble with the boss	(23)	16. Change in Financial State	(38)
41. Vacation	(13)	18. Change to a different line of work	(36)
42. Christmas	(12)	22. Change in responsibilities at work	(29)
		25. Outstanding personal achievement (work)	(28)
		28. Change in living conditions	(25)
		29. Revision of personal habits	(24)
		30. Major change in working hours or conditions	(20)
		31. Change in residence	(20)
		34. Change in recreation	(19)
		36. Change in social activity	(18)
		38. Change in sleep habits	(16)
		39. Change in family gatherings	(15)
		40. Change in eating habits	(15)
		43. Minor violation of law	(11)
Total	87	Total	373

ILLUSTRATION A.   A comparison of stress levels for Mr. Karl Horner for Jan. 1–Dec. 31, 1978, while employed by AT&S and Jan. 1–May 14, 1979, while employed by Brand and Sills.

4.   A great increase in working hours per week
5.   Elimination of vacation time
6.   Highly stressful, demanding project requirements and time limits (overload)
7.   A change in sociocultural environment
8.   A considerable increase in responsibility
9.   Prolonged absences from home and family
10.   Rapid changes in the occupational environment
11.   Pressures to achieve goals far beyond his previous occupational setting
12.   Higher expectancies to be job-involved and hard-driving than his previous vocational environment
13.   A major change in recreation and social activity
14.   Many different social and cultural settings

The research is clear in associating all of the above factors with increased coronary disease vulnerability. In order to make an objective analysis of Mr. Horner's vulnerability to illness before and after coming to work with Brand and Sills, the information available was subjected to the Holmes SRE Stress Scale (Petrich & Holmes, 1977; Holmes & Rahe, 1967). This 43-item scale evaluates the stress impact of life changes on disease-proneness. Many of the items refer to the stress impact of vocational changes and expectancies. Table B shows a comparison of life-change events for 1978, the year before Mr. Horner began work for Brand and Sills, and 1979, the first four and one-half months of which he was in their employ before his death.

F.   Conclusions

Within reasonable psychological probability, the extraordinary stress conditions required by Mr. Horner's job with Brand and Sills and the relatively short period of time over which these changes were required raised his vulnerability and potential for severe illness to very significant levels, forming a stress basis for his coronary heart disease.

References

Boggiano, W. (1966, January). Time zone woes: Potential hazard to decision-making ability. *Business Travel*, pp. 10–11.

Caplan, R. (1971). *Organizational stress and individual strain: A social-psychological study of risk factors in coronary heart disease among administrators, engineers, and scientists.* Unpublished doctoral dissertation, University of Michigan.

Dembroski, T., Weiss, S., Shields, J., Haynes, S., & Feinlieb, M. (1970). *Coronary-prone behavior.* New York: Springer-Verlag.

Freese, A. S. (1976). *Understanding stress* (Public Affairs Pamphlet No. 538). New York: Public Affairs Committee.

Gentry, W. D., & Williams, R. B., & Williams, R. B. (1975). *Psychological aspects of myocardial infarction and coronary care.* St. Louis: C. V. Mosby, p. 29.

Glass, D. C., Contrada, R., & Snow, B. (1980). Type A behavior and coronary disease. *Weekly Psychology Update, 1,* pp. 1–6.

Holmes, T. H., & Rahe, R. H. (1967). Social readjustment scale. *Journal of Psychosomat. Res., 11,* 213–218.

House, J. S. (1972). *The relationship of intrinsic and extrinsic work motivations to occupational stress and coronary heart disease risk.* Unpublished doctoral dissertation. University of Michigan.

Karassi, A. (1979). *Acute myocardial infarction.* New York: McGraw-Hill, p. 74.

Miles, H. H. W. (1954). Psychosomatic study of 46 young men with coronary artery disease. *Psychosomatic Medicine, 16,* 455.

National Institutes of Health. (1979). Working group on heart disease epidemiology (NIH Publication No. 79-1667). p. 7.

Petrich, J., & Holmes, T. H. (1977). Life change and onset of illness. *Medical Clinics of North America, 61*(4), 825–838.

Russek, H. I. (1965). Stress, tobacco and coronary heart disease in North American professional groups. *J.A.M.A. 192,* 189.

Russek, H. I. (1967). Role of emotional stress in the etiology of clinical coronary heart disease. *Diseases of the Chest, 52*(1), 1–9.

Russek, H. I. (1975). *New horizons in cardiovascular practice.* Baltimore: University Park Press, p. 131.

USHEW. (1963). Mortality by occupation and cause of death: men 20–64. *Vital Statistics—* 1950, Special Reports. *53,* (3), 95–195.

Zyzanski, S. J. (1978). Coronary-prone behavior pattern and coronary heart disease. In T. M. Dembroski, S. M. Weiss, J. L. Shields, S. G. Haynes, & M. Feinleib (Eds.), *Coronary prone behavior.* New York: Springer-Verlag. pp. 29–39.

After reviewing the report, the judge in this case allowed the psychologist to testify. The three tables and the figure were admitted into evidence as plaintiff's exhibits.

GRAND JURY TESTIMONY

The Fifth Amendment to the U.S. Constitution provides: "No person shall be held to answer for a capital, or otherwise infamous crime, unless on a presentment or indictment of a Grand Jury." This is generally interpreted to mean that no person can be charged with a major crime unless he or she is indicted by a grand jury. In every jurisdiction there are usually one or more grand juries sitting at any one time. A grand jury is usually impaneled for several months, is constituted with powers similar to those of regular juries, and consists, usually, of 16 to 23 members, panelists, or venire chosen from current voters' registration lists. Aside from regularly scheduled grand juries, the court can summon additional or special grand juries "at such times as the public interest requires."

Grand jury hearings differ from open court in that only the witness, the grand jurors, the government attorneys, and a court stenographer may be present inside the grand jury room. There is no judge present in the grand jury room. Only the grand jurors may be present when deliberating or voting on an indictment. An indictment, or "true bill," can be returned only if 12 or more jurors vote for such an indictment in federal grand juries. In some state jurisdictions the grand jury consists of 12 members, and a vote of eight is necessary for an indictment. Deliberations in the grand jury room are secret and may not be discussed outside the grand jury room by the prosecutor or the jurors. Witnesses may afterward discuss whatever was asked of them and whatever their responses were, although some prosecuting attorneys may suggest or imply otherwise.[8] If the grand jury votes an indictment, it is returned to a judge in open court.

There are few statutory provisions governing the procedures by which witnesses are called and questioned. Rights and privileges are covered by common-law case law. Thus, without a judge presiding, few of the formalities and safeguards found in open court apply during grand jury testimony. The district attorney, state attorney, or federal attorney directs the activity, calls witnesses, and conducts both direct examination and cross-examination.

The grand jury can subpoena any witness without having to give a reason. Fourth Amendment constraints against stopping, searching, or seizure without probable cause do not apply to a subpoena requiring a person to appear and testify before the grand jury.[9] The grand jury does not have to reveal the nature of the investigation being conducted, and witnesses cannot challenge the relevance of questions.[10]

[8] *In Re Minkoff*, 349 F. Supp. 154 (D.R.I. 1972).
[9] *Fraser v. United States*, 452 F.2d 616, 620 (7th Cir. 1971).
[10] *Hale v. Henkel*, 201 U.S. 43, 65 (1906).

The witness appearing before a grand jury generally has no right to counsel during the grand jury hearings inside the grand jury hearing room. A witness can be excused to consult with counsel outside the grand jury room after any question is asked.

During a witness's appearance before the grand jury, jurors, as well as the prosecution attorney, may ask the witness questions. The witness may not, in turn, ask jurors questions.

It is most important for the psychologist who is called to testify before a grand jury to know the following:

1. There is no presiding judge.
2. The prosecuting attorney will generally guide or dominate the proceedings.
3. Any consultation with an attorney must be requested by the witness after a question is asked. The attorney must be outside the grand jury room. The witness is responsible for making notes about the question so that when the attorney is consulted outside the grand jury hearing room, the witness can be reasonably sure of the details of the question. Note taking by witnesses is allowed.
4. If a prosecuting attorney seems to be leading, distorting, or segmenting the witness's testimony, it is the witness's responsibility to redirect the jury's attention to the focus of his or her testimony.

As can be seen from the above, an understanding of how the grand jury process operates is necessary if a witness is to be comfortable and effective in this setting (Grand Jury Defense Office, 1982).

In the following example of expert testimony before a grand jury, the issue involved the use of deadly force by a police officer. When a police officer discharges his or her weapon in the line of duty, a departmental hearing is convened to determine whether the action was warranted and occurred within police department guidelines for the discharge of weapons and/or the use of deadly force. At the same time, particularly if someone has been injured or killed, the state attorney's office reviews the circumstances surrounding the use of deadly force. The state attorney's office may conclude that no charges are warranted, or the state attorney may file a charge, ranging from first-degree murder down to involuntary manslaughter if a death has occurred, or may refer the case to the grand jury. In the latter instance, the grand jury must hear evidence and then decide whether to issue an indictment, or a true bill, specifying the charges to be placed against the officer. If the grand jury finds insufficient evidence to issue a true bill, there is no indictment, and the officer is exculpated of any criminal blame (however, a civil suit can, and often is, filed by the survivors of the deceased).

In the following case, the psychologist, Dr. Smith, was retained by Richard Baker, attorney for Sgt. Charles White of the Narcotics Division, State Police. Sgt. White had discharged his weapon during a narcotics raid, killing one of the suspects. Although a departmental hearing cleared Sgt. White of wrongdoing, the state's attorney for that region considered placing the case before the grand jury to determine whether Sgt. White should be charged with some degree of homicide.

Mr. Baker requested psychological evaluation as part of his efforts to clarify the situation with the state attorney's office and settle questions that office might have concerning Sgt. White and thus negate the necessity of going to the grand jury. The following is the report prepared for Mr. Baker.

PSYCHOLOGICAL REPORT—DEADLY FORCE EVALUATION

NAME: WHITE, CHARLES   DATE OF EXAMINATION: 5/19/83

ADDRESS: Narcotics, State Police,   TELEPHONE: 000-0000
             Division 5, Nohoma, Illiana

BIRTHDATE: 3/15/42   AGE: 41-2   OCCUPATION: Police Officer
EDUCATION: Grade 12   (Sergeant)

Referral

Richard Baker, Esquire, refers this case. By telephone, he states that Sgt. White, a police officer, while on duty on February 5, 1983, in a drug raid in which 10,000 units of LSD and drugs were seized, shot and killed Jack Gardner. The facts of the case have been such that Prosecuting Attorney is considering Grand Jury review. Sgt. White is cloudy about his thinking following the time he killed Mr. Gardner with his service revolver.

Questions for evaluation include:

1.   Did Sgt. White have intent to kill at time of incident?
2.   Was Sgt. White's response self-protective, reasonable, and responsive to the situation?
3.   Is any psychological instability noted in Sgt. White which would suggest defective judgment?

At the time of the incident, the deceased had concentrations of opiates in his blood in the range associated with overdose and which could be toxic. He was known to be a mentally disturbed person. Mr. Baker wonders whether these circumstances could explain the deceased's disobedience of the police officers' orders which led to the homicide.

Procedures

Review of all pertinent records regarding the shooting during the narcotics arrest, pertinent events previous to and subsequent to this, laboratory reports, reports of witnesses, criminal records of defendants, and other material. History and interview with Sgt. White. Review of Sgt. White's records. Minnesota Multiphasic Personality Inventory, Holmes Stress Scale. Review of pertinent research relating to deadly force and its use by police officers. Review of dangerousness and violence research.

Essential Facts of the Case

On February 5, 1983, Sgt. White led a team of agents of the State Police to accomplish the arrest of a number of suspected drug dealers. During the course of the procedures, Sgt. White became concerned for the safety of his undercover men who were inside the house preparing to make the initial arrests. He led a team of officers through a locked, wrought-iron gate and through a door in order to assist the officers inside the house. Upon entering the front door of the house, the agent immediately preceding Sgt. White found one of the suspects disobeying a police officer's orders to stay against the wall. He pushed this suspect (Gardner) against the wall and instructed him to remain there. As Sgt. White came through the door, he noticed that this subject was not obeying the officer's commands, again. As he moved toward this suspect to ensure safety of himself and his men, the suspect suddenly turned to Sgt. White and moved himself quickly toward him. Sgt. White, in a position of readiness, was taken quite aback and assumed a proper defense posture. Before the move by the suspect, Sgt. White had his weapon at a 45 degree angle from his body, which was usual for such circumstances. As the suspect came at him, both surprising and threatening Sgt. White, Sgt. White attempted to move backward, in the limited space available, while at the same time, his partially raised weapon began to arc downward into a usable, protective position, as would be natural under such circumstances. At that point, Sgt. White discharged his weapon. The shot killed the suspect. Sgt. White reports a somewhat fragmented perception of events from that point until he made the telephone call requesting the proper personnel to deal with the death that had occurred during this police action.

Sgt. White's Perception of the Events

On interview, Sgt. White states that when he entered the door of the house he saw Officer Chavez put the suspect to the wall. He saw the suspect start off the wall. Suddenly, the suspect was "on top of me." Sgt. White says, "I was moving toward him with my gun at 'ready.' This would be about a 45 degree angle. He scared me. My heart was in my throat. I stopped and started to pull back, and pulled the trigger instinctively. I didn't 'see' this. Suddenly, there was something there. I didn't know what he was doing. After the shot he suddenly disappeared. I said to myself, 'Where did he go?' For an instant it surprised me. Then it dawned that I had shot my gun. I looked down and there he was. I thought to myself, 'We've got a shooting.' I remember going to the counter and starting to unload my gun. I realized they would need it for evidence. I called and advised the office of the shooting. I didn't even tell them who had been shot. I then called Lt. Fleming and told him."

Sgt. White remembers the officer who preceded him through the door shoving Mr. Gardner against the wall. He remembers feeling "I better get him under control" when he saw Gardner come off the wall. It was later noted that this man was wearing a hat. Sgt. White does not remember the hat. He states he never saw the suspect's hands. Suddenly, he had the feeling of this man's "presence" upon him. He does not remember any physical contact, but he does remember that he did not know what was "going on" (the defendant's intent in moving off the wall) and he reacted instinctively (automatically taking a defensive–protective action). When asked about his memory, Sgt. White stated that for at least 30 minutes after this he was in a "daze," in a state of shock. He remembers going out of the front door and seeing the people with the bolt cutters opening the wrought-iron door. He cannot remember saying anything from the time he shot the suspect until the time he used the phone. He says that some of his fellow officers said that he had said some things.

In discussing the events leading up to this, Sgt. White noted that one to two weeks previous to the event described above, in another case, he was in a similar situation where surveillance contact was lost. He had deep concerns for the safety of the officers who were involved in an arrest that was going on. He became extremely tense. Because of the communication problems, his two agents had to make the arrests by themselves. Although nothing serious happened, he was extremely upset by this, being fully aware of the grave dangers that occur during the very initial phases of narcotics arrests. He is acutely aware that this was the time that an officer is likely to be injured or killed by a perpetrator facing arrest. In the current incident, he states that the radio reports that he was monitoring upset him considerably. Hearing what he heard, he said to himself, "These guys are in trouble." His actions after that point were based on the concept that it was his responsibility to ensure that this police action would not result in injury or death to any of his agents.

Background Factors

Sgt. Charles White, 41-year-old police officer with $17\frac{1}{2}$ years of experience in the Illiana State Police, was born in California but raised in Oklahoma. His mother and father are both living and well. His parents divorced when he was very young, and his mother remarried in about 1945. He himself was raised by his grandmother on the mother's side as well as his father's mother and a great aunt. The great aunt was particularly important in his early life. He was raised in a very religious home with strong traditional standards. He has three brothers and a sister. He always considered his stepfather as his father, and they got along well. The stepfather died a year and a half to two years ago.

Graduating from high school in Oklahoma, Sgt. White worked at a number of jobs including the Safeway stores, the oil fields, as a carpenter, and as a worker in a baking company. He entered State Police training at the age of 23. After nine weeks of recruit training, he was assigned to Las Cruces station and remained a trooper until 1979. He served in a variety of locations. Twelve years of his service have been in the Narcotics Division, on and off in uniform. He entered Narcotics after six years on the force.

He had training in hand-to-hand combat and the use of firearms on the basis of one hour per day for nine weeks in his early training. Since that time he has had to qualify in the use of arms on a regular basis as is the policy of the Illiana State Police. He had special training as a first aid instructor, in search and seizure at the F.B.I. School, and in a three-week course leading to a Certificate of Competency from the U.S. Department of Justice, Bureau of Narcotics and Dangerous Drugs in the enforcement of narcotics and dangerous drugs. He has been to management school and a variety of State Police in-service training schools, including electronic intelligence.

Sgt. White is in good health. He has no physical condition of untoward nature at the present time. He has taken a total of ten days of sick leave while on the State Police Force. He uses tobacco, smoking about a pack a day. He rarely uses alcohol, confining himself to an occasional beer. He is in relatively good physical condition.

His work is very demanding, and he has relatively little time for himself. There is a good deal of pressure on him and his family. He enjoys being around the home. At one time he fished, but he does not have the time or the availability of facilities. He owns a motorcycle, and enjoys doing his own mechanical work. He and his wife like to ride the cycle, attend movies, go to town, and go to the Flea Market. He enjoys working in the yard.

His first marriage occurred when he was 18 years of age, and he stayed in this for 15 years. There are two sons and two daughters to this union. His second marriage occurred when he was 34 years of age. His wife at the present time had been formerly married. She has two children from the former marriage, whom he considers his own and whom he has raised as his own. They see him as their father.

He has discharged his weapon a total of six times in his $17\frac{1}{2}$ years in police work. There have been many incidents where he restrained himself from discharging his weapon in spite of the fact that the situation was dangerous.

Psychological Evaluation

The history of Sgt. White is not unusual in any way. Early family problems are frequently found in the histories of successful police officers and other persons who enter dangerous social service occupations. His focus on his strong early religious upbringing again is a factor often found in the family history of successful police officers.

Analysis of the Minnesota Multiphasic Personality Inventory indicates that Sgt. White falls completely within the normal personality range. No eccentricities, evidence of instability, poor judgment, inappropriate behavior, or other disturbance is noted.

A description of Sgt. White's personality would indicate that he has a tendency to overlook faults in himself, his family, and his circumstances, although this defensiveness would be considered quite mild. His cautious personality is standard for police personnel. Impulsive and grossly inappropriate expression of feelings would not be expected in this man. He can expect to be energetic, active, and, in general, an overworker. His highest scale on the MMPI is that scale generally found to be highest among successful police officers.

When faced with stress, Sgt. White is the kind of a person who will tend to internalize it rather than to express it. He may tend to suffer fatigue, aches and pains, and other somatic or depressed feelings rather than express his tension. He tends to be a controller of tension.

The personality is that of an individual who expresses strong conformist, traditional attitudes but who will tend to enter an occupation where he is required to deal with people who are marginal or dangerous. The personality pattern is that which we find in successful police officers and combat commanders. It is interesting to note that the personality research suggests that such individuals tend to have more dissociative phenomena than those persons who do not have this profile. This personality profile is that of individuals who tend to be aggressive and extra-punitive in their reaction to stress and frustration. There is no psychiatric diagnosis or disorder for such persons, and they are considered to be completely normal.

The Holmes Stress Scale was administered to Sgt. White. This scale evaluates the significant life changes that occur in an individual in order to determine the degree of stress under which he or she ordinarily operates. Stress is a measure of the changes in a person's life which intensify his or her pace of living and lead the person into situations where he or she is likely to experience more illness and more overreaction than the average individual. An analysis of Sgt. White's activities in life in the past 18 months results in a stress index that would be rated at 326 conservatively and 411 when including items that are somewhat equivocal. The research shows that individuals whose stress index falls below 120 suffer very little stress and are generally able to function in a wide range of situations without any type of overreaction or propensity to suffer illness as a result of the stress. Between 120 and 300, a 50–50 chance of overreaction or stress reaction can be expected. When a scale exceeds 300, the chances are 89 or more out of 100 that the person will have stress reactions. Certainly, Sgt. White can be considered to be under considerable stress at the present time, excluding the incident under consideration. This in itself is not unusual, since people in his type of dangerous work, which requires rapid, aggressive decisions, are generally found to suffer high levels of stress.

This accounts for the significant and unexpected occurrence of hypertension and other somatic diseases in police officers at relatively early ages. It also probably helps account for the high rate of suicide that occurs among police officers.

The psychological evaluation indicates that Sgt. White is a man of normal personality, ideally suited for his job as a police officer operating in stressful and dangerous situations, conscientious, and concerned about those serving under him. He is a man who is likely to act in what he considers to be the best interests of those he is responsible for. He, under pressure, has a higher propensity for mild, brief dissociative reactions than the average.

Deadly Force and Dangerousness Research

There is a large body of research concerning the use of deadly force on police officers and by police officers. An average of 102 police officers a year are killed by civilians, and approximately 275 legal interventions by police officers result in a civilian death.

In pursuit of their mandate to preserve life and keep the peace, police do kill or maim suspected lawbreakers. One of the most important indicators of whether such events will occur in a police force has been found to be the social or community propensity of the city's armed criminal suspects to act with assaultiveness and aggressiveness toward police. This differs from one town to another.

The research indicates that the better the police force in terms of training and selection, the higher will be the fatality rate from police-discharged weapons. For instance, the Los Angeles Police Department, considered the most carefully selected and best-trained police department in the United States, has a fatality rate of 37 percent for weapons discharged other than in training. The "hit" rate for officers' weapons discharged is 62 percent. By contrast, in Chicago, where selection and training procedures are considered to be extremely lax and where the police department has suffered a great deal of criticism, the "hit" rate has been 18 percent.

Police officers are aware of the dangers of their profession. Three law enforcement officers are murdered annually for every 10,000 officers in the United States. Since there are 21,000 police departments in the United States, there are certainly a great many dangerous events that police officers are aware may confront them in the line of duty.

The research shows that although police officers become much more cautious and concerned when they are aware that suspects may have a weapon, this is not particularly helpful in protecting themselves. In the research it was found that 71 percent of officer victims knew or had good reason to believe that the suspects were armed before any shooting started. This indicates that in spite of the fact that officers may be forewarned by their perception of the dangerousness of a situation, they remain at very high risk. The research shows that officers in tactical units are seven to nine times more likely than patrol officers to become involved either as shooters or as victims.

The largest study of the use of deadly force concludes, "The use of deadly force by the police is concentrated within an environment of community violence in general." Thus it is a community's culture of violence, or the neighborhood of the community in which the police officer is operating, that determines the likelihood of a police officer's shooting or being shot.

There is a general myth, mostly believed by civilians, that most police officers are shot by "unstable" individuals. The research indicates that this indeed is a myth. A police officer is in greatest danger from and most likely to be killed by a rational criminal who is attempting to flee the scene of the crime. The criminal's intention is secondary to his attempts to protect himself from capture. Thus the strongest signal to a police officer that he is in danger is a suspect indicating that he is about to make an effort to escape (Geller, 1982).

Dangerousness and violent people have been carefully studied during the past 25 years. The number-one fact emerging from all of this research is that dangerousness cannot be accurately predicted. Those people who are most dangerous are those who have a history of being dangerous, those who associate with individuals having a history of being dangerous, and those who live, work, or recreate in settings that have been known to be places where dangerous, violent behavior occurs. Violence is a basic human propensity. It is ordinarily used as a defensive measure, but in modern society we see many cases where violence and dangerousness are used for political purposes, personal gain, vengeance, and so forth.

Law enforcement officers must evaluate and gauge individuals in terms of their propensity to be violent and dangerous. Persons who become violent become activated by closeness of dangerous other persons. In social/psychological research, the concept of "buffer zone" has emerged. The probability of a violent act occurring increases geometrically with the decrease in distance between two potentially dangerous subjects. This is true for dangerous criminals, and it is true for law enforcement personnel in dangerous settings. In police training, this is referred to as the "critical defense zone." Dangerousness is defined as the capacity to use deadly force. This is part of the training and part of the requirements of all law enforcement officers on active duty. It is inconceivable that a law enforcement officer who would be hesitant to use deadly force in an appropriate situation could function or be trusted by the personnel working with him or her. If one cannot accept the concept that law enforcement personnel must have the capacity to be violent in appropriate situations, one must reject the entire concept of law enforcement.

The buffer zone is considered to be 24–48 inches. In dangerous situations, violence is likeliest to be activated as the distance between the stimulus individual and the response individual decreases. Given a police officer with a capacity to be violent in appropriate situations, this violence is likeliest to be activated when a dangerous stimulus moved physically closer to such a police officer, particularly as the distance decreases from 48 inches downward (Hays et al., 1981).

Summary and Conclusions

Psychological evaluation of the circumstances surrounding the incident noted above, the personality and the background history of Sgt. Charles White, and the research appropriate to the use of deadly force, dangerousness, and violence indicates the following:

1. Sgt. White shows no psychological pathology.
2. Sgt. White's personality is that which is expected and found among successful police officers.
3. Sgt. White works in a unit of law enforcement that is considered among the most dangerous.
4. In the narcotics trade, it is rare that weapons are not present where drugs are transferred or sold.
5. In the incident noted above, Sgt. White was in charge of the situation and responsible for his men.
6. In addition to the ordinary anticipation of danger to himself and to his men, Sgt. White had a recent experience where he was concerned for the safety of his men because of communication difficulty.
7. In the current situation, a similar miscommunication occurred, and he heard information over his radio that led him to believe that his men might be in difficulty.
8. Sgt. White's record, his history, and his previous performance indicate that his actions were concurrent with a law enforcement supervisor taking the responsibility of protecting the men of his unit on a dangerous assignment.
9. Psychologically, his state of mind at the time of the above occurrences was that of an individual under a great deal of stress, taking appropriate action under time-stressful circumstances with his men's lives at stake.
10. On entering the scene noted above, Sgt. White was aware that one of the suspects was disobeying the orders of one of Sgt. White's officers.
11. Sgt. White moved in, properly, to neutralize the suspect who again disobeyed police orders.
12. The suspect suddenly made sharp movements threatening Sgt.

White's defense zone, and Sgt. White reacted in a proper, instinctive, trained manner as any law enforcement officer would be likely to do under similar circumstances.

13. Sgt. White's reaction immediately following the incident, in which he does not remember details of what he may have said to other officers or in their presence, is well in keeping with a minor, not unexpected dissociative response. "A sudden temporary alteration in the normal integration functions of consciousness. A sudden inability to remember important personal information. A localized amnesia following a severe psychosocial stress. The termination of the amnesia tends to be abrupt and in less than an hour" (American Psychiatric Association, 1981).

Nothing in our psychological evaluation indicates that Sgt. White has ever had a propensity to unusual violence, malicious intent, or propensity to overstep his professional mandates. The evaluation suggests that an experienced officer dealing with a known dangerous situation had his buffer safety zone suddenly and intensely violated and reacted accordingly with a defense-of-life shooting.

References

American Psychiatric Association. (1981). *Diagnostic and statistical manual* (3rd ed.). Washington, DC: Author.

Geller, W. A. (1982). Deadly force: what we know. *Journal of Police Science and Administration,* 10(2).

Hays, J. R., Roberts, T. K., & Solway, K. S. (Eds.). (1981). *Violence and the violent individual.* New York: S. P. Medical and Scientific Books.

After consultation with Mr. Baker, Richard Bennett, state's attorney, decided he would place this issue before the grand jury "without recommendations." Dr. Smith was called to testify before the grand jury after it had reviewed all the evidence and heard testimony from police officers who were on the raid, from defendants, and from Sgt. White. Dr. Smith's testimony is reconstructed from his notes, taken during his grand jury appearance and completed immediately after he finished his testimony. (The proceedings of grand juries are sealed records.)

Mr. Bennett:	Would you please take a seat here, Doctor?
Dr. Smith:	Thank you.
Mr. Bennett:	Would you please state your name for the grand jury?
Dr. Smith:	Rupert Bob Smith.
Mr. Bennett:	And what is your occupation, Dr. Smith?

Dr. Smith:	I am a clinical and consulting psychologist.
Mr. Bennett:	Would you please tell the grand jury something about your background and training as a psychologist?
Dr. Smith:	I have received the bachelor of science, the master of science, and the doctor of philosophy in psychology. My specialty at Penn State was clinical psychology. Following my doctorate I spent two years in postdoctoral training with the United States Veterans Administration. My training has been in hospitals and clinics, involving children, adolescents, and adults. I have been trained in a complete range of human behavior from the normal to the abnormal. I specialize in assessment, evaluation, and treatment of human behavioral problems.
Mr. Bennett:	The issue before the grand jury concerns the use of deadly force. Have you any special background or training that would qualify you to testify in this matter?
Dr. Smith:	Aside from the fact that I was asked to make a psychological evaluation of mental status of the police officer in question, I have had a number of consultations involving the use of deadly force.
Mr. Bennett:	Would you describe these to the grand jury?
Dr. Smith:	For the past 12 years I have been consultant to the United States Army, and to the United States Department of State. In the course of these consultations, I have been called upon to evaluate training systems and the effectiveness of such systems where deadly force was a key issue. In many of these the deadly-force issue was related to combat situations. In other consultations deadly-force concerns involved the activity as well as expected constraints in special military forces. I have been associated with the training and evaluation of special personnel associated with antiterrorist activity and counterintelligence activity.
Mr. Bennett:	I believe that we can accept and stipulate to your qualifications as an expert . . .
Dr. Smith:	There are other . . .
Mr. Bennett:	I think we can go on. Did you have an opportunity to examine Sgt. Charles White?
Dr. Smith:	Yes, sir, I did.
Mr. Bennett:	How did this come about?
Dr. Smith:	I was retained by Mr. Richard Baker, attorney for Sgt. White, as well as the legal staff of the State Police. I was asked to conduct a psychological evaluation of Sgt. White

to understand his motivation at the time he killed a suspect during a buy/bust drug raid that occurred on February 5, 1983.

Mr. Bennett:	Did you examine Sgt. White?
Dr. Smith:	Yes, sir, I did.
Mr. Bennett:	Would you tell the grand jury about your findings?
Dr. Smith:	I'll go through my procedures and my report so that you can understand what I did and how I came to my findings.
Mr. Bennett:	That's not necessary, simply give us your conclusions.
Dr. Smith:	Some of them may pose some questions to the jury, without knowing the reasons why we conducted certain examinations and how we came to certain results.
Mr. Bennett:	We'll get to that if we have to. Please tell us what your conclusions were.
Dr. Smith:	Well, as a result of my evaluation of the circumstances surrounding the incident in which Sgt. White shot and killed a suspect, together with my taking of a history from Sgt. White and examining all of his State Police records, I compared Sgt. White, the circumstances, and the outcome with the research on deadly force that is available and with the research on dangerousness. My conclusions are as follows: Sgt. White shows no psychological difficulties or pathology. His personality is that which would be found among successful police officers. Sgt. White has worked in a unit of police enforcement that has a 7 to 10 times higher risk of danger than patrol work. He is in a situation where weapons are generally used by suspects. Sgt. White was in charge of the detail making the buy/bust. Sgt. White had a recent experience of miscommunication which almost resulted in disaster. A similar miscommunication occurred during the current buy/bust when Mr. Gardner was killed. Sgt. White's record, his history, and his previous performance indicate that he was doing exactly what a good supervisor should do on a dangerous assignment. Certainly Sgt. White was under a great deal of stress at the time. Sgt. White, during the drug buy/bust, was aware that one of the suspects was disobeying the orders of one of the police officers. Sgt. White moved in to control the suspect. He acted properly. The suspect made sudden sharp movements threatening Sgt. White's defense zone, or buffer zone. Sgt. White reacted in the proper, trained manner as would any person properly trained in dealing with

deadly force. Sgt. White's reaction immediately following the incident, where details were vague, was not unexpected and would be associated with a fairly common reaction called a "dissociative" response. This is defined as "a sudden temporary alteration in the normal integration functions of consciousness, a sudden inability to remember important personal information, a localized amnesia following a severe psychosocial stress. The termination of the amnesia tends to be abrupt and end in less than an hour." In short, nothing in our psychological evaluation indicates that Sgt. White has ever had a propensity to unusual violence, malicious intent, or a need to overstep his professional mandates. The evaluation suggests that an experienced police officer dealing with a known dangerous situation had his defense safety zone suddenly and intensely violated and reacted accordingly with a defense-of-life shooting.

Mr. Bennett:	Thank you, Doctor, and now I would like to show you this sketch of the crime scene (*demonstrating*). Do you recognize this?
Dr. Smith:	Yes, sir, I have seen this.
Mr. Bennett:	Would you step over here where we have chalked out the details of the room in which the shooting took place?
Dr. Smith:	Yes, sir (*getting up and moving with Mr. Bennett*).
Mr. Bennett:	Now I want you to stand in this place marked doorway while I stand against the wall with my hands on the wall. You are in the position that Sgt. White was in when he entered the crime scene. I'm standing in the position that Mr. Gardner was in. Does this fit the facts as you know them?
Dr. Smith:	Yes, sir, I believe so.
Mr. Bennett:	Now I will turn, as apparently Mr. Gardner did, into you (demonstrating). Now what would your reaction be?
Dr. Smith:	Are you asking me to put myself in Sgt. White's mind?
Mr. Bennett:	I'm just asking you to act as anyone might act in such circumstances.
Dr. Smith:	Considering that I have had defense-of-life training, and if I were in such circumstances, I would instinctively defend myself.
Mr. Bennett:	Do you think that will be absolutely necessary? Couldn't you use some sort of special karate?
Dr. Smith:	I think you are suggesting that in these split-second circumstances, a person might have a chance to review

	options and make a selection. I don't think that is what happens in such circumstances.
Mr. Bennett:	So you actually really don't know what Sgt. White was thinking at the time?
Dr. Smith:	No, sir, other than what I have already testified to. Sgt. White said that he acted instinctively, and I believe that that is a reliable report of what happened.
Mr. Bennett:	You may return to the witness stand.
Dr. Smith:	Thank you.
Mr. Bennett:	Now your experience has been entirely in the military, so this would be a different situation. Is that not true?
Dr. Smith:	You didn't let me finish my description of my background, so at this point I can tell you no. My experience included two and a half years of work with prison riot personnel and police personnel and issues of deadly force and when to use it. My work also includes antiterrorist training, where the decision to use deadly force is a key issue for evaluation.
Mr. Bennett:	But in this situation, we have a man discharging a deadly firearm in a home with civilian persons. This is quite different from your experience. Is it not?
Dr. Smith:	I believe you're suggesting that decisions regarding innocent civilians must be made by a police officer and that this is a special case.
Mr. Bennett:	Exactly.
Dr. Smith:	I would point out to you that a sky marshal, trained in antiterrorist activity, must make that decision, for instance, when an aircraft is skyjacked. Hundreds of innocent civilians are involved, and the sky marshal or the antiterrorist personnel involved must always calculate the risk to innocent bystanders. This is work in which we have evaluated the effectiveness of the training and the realities involved in the use of deadly force.
Mr. Bennett:	I believe I have no further questions. Perhaps some members of the grand jury would like to ask some questions of Dr. Smith.
Grand Juror A:	I believe I would like to ask Dr. Smith a question. Do you think that Sgt. White had any alternative other than to shoot the suspect?
Dr. Smith:	There are always alternatives. One of which might be to hold off and to receive a knife or gunshot wound if the defendant were armed. That is an extremely difficult de-

cision to make, and under the stressful circumstances, it was probably made with respect to Sgt. White's concern for the safety of his entire group.

Grand Juror A: Thank you, Doctor.

Grand Juror B: Doctor, I want to ask you a straightforward question— wasn't there a tragedy here?

Dr. Smith: Of course. Any death is a tragedy. Regardless of the circumstances, a human being perished. Approximately 270 people are killed each year as a result of the discharge of firearms by police officers. I certainly believe that this represents 270 tragedies. On the other hand approximately 120 police officers each year are killed by perpetrators attempting to escape the scene of a crime. This represents 120 additional tragedies. Violence is almost always a tragedy, and I think all of us work and hope for a lessening of violence as a way of resolving conflicts of all sorts.

Mr. Bennett: No one else seems to have any further questions, so we will excuse you now, Doctor. Thank you very much for coming to testify.

Dr. Smith: Thank you and thank you all.

As can be seen above, the usual courtroom procedures, governed by a judge, do not apply. The district attorney is in charge of the proceedings. In this case, he cut off the witness on a number of occasions before the witness could complete a statement. The district attorney can be very powerful in establishing the focus and direction of the expert's testimony.

The witness has certain rights and responsibilities under these circumstances. The witness can interrupt the district attorney. The witness can suggest that the district attorney is withholding or manipulating information. The witness can push onward even though the district attorney says that he is satisfied with the answer.

The greatest difficulty for the expert witness in grand jury appearances lies in the fact that there is no retaining attorney to carry the psychologist through a direct examination. Direct examination by the retaining attorney is the point at which the psychologist as an expert is helped to tell a coherent and concise story about his or her role in the proceedings. In effect, the psychological expert at a grand jury hearing must conduct his or her own direct examination. Although such appearances are relatively rare at the present time, as the value of psychological testimony becomes more apparent to lawyers and judges, psychologists can expect to be called more frequently to testify at grand jury hearings.

THE PSYCHOTHERAPIST AS EXPERT WITNESS

Psychotherapists are rarely called to testify as experts. Where a psychotherapist is subpoenaed, it is usually as a "treating doctor" or one who may have information as to some aspect of the case at hand. An attorney may call upon a psychotherapist during the discovery phase of any litigation, criminal or civil. The attorney seeks evidence that will support or enhance the position of the attorney's client.

The psychotherapist is rarely a willing expert. The essence of the psychotherapeutic relationship is considered by many as the seal of confidentiality on all matters discussed between psychotherapist and client. All communications are considered privileged. Few psychotherapists are familiar with the limits and constraints that exist for privileged communication (Chapter 12).

Some attorneys will approach a psychotherapist during the discovery phase of a trial, complete with a subpoena *duces tecum,* and insist on examining all the psychotherapist's records. The attorney may schedule a deposition during which the psychotherapist will be subjected to probing questions concerning the client's character, past, and personal revelations. Psychotherapists can be overwhelmed by such an authoritarian approach and reveal information about their client that the therapist is actually under no legal compulsion to reveal. In such cases, the psychotherapist may be guilty of breach of privilege and subject to various criminal, civil, or ethical charges.

Although the psychologist's code of ethics states principles of confidentiality in general terms, each state may have specific guidelines, constraints, and exceptions for the psychotherapist as expert witness. Furthermore, such legal guidelines and exceptions are continually subject to legislative modification, rendering the position of the psychotherapist quite difficult in deciding what can and cannot be revealed about a client. When faced with a subpoena *duces tecum* for the records of a client, the psychotherapist should do the following:

1. *Contact the Client.* The psychotherapist's first duty is to inform the client that a subpoena has been issued and that an attorney will be questioning the therapist. The psychotherapist should obtain the name of the client's lawyer. The psychotherapist should suggest that the client contact his or her attorney. The psychotherapist should request permission to call the attorney to discuss the subpoena and the anticipated deposition. The psychotherapist should ask what restrictions the client wishes to place on the psychotherapist for the deposition. Regardless of whether the client tells the therapist to "use your own judgment," "say nothing," or "tell about anything that isn't personal," the psychotherapist should ask the client to provide a written document that includes permissions or constraints expressed by the client.

2. *Contact the Client's Attorney.*   After the psychotherapist receives the client's permission to contact the client's attorney, the psychotherapist should make this call. The attorney should be informed of the contents of the subpoena *duces tecum* (the name of the attorney, the dates, the material requested) and should ask the client's attorney for advice and guidelines. The attorney should be asked to forward a copy of the most current statutes on privileged communication for psychotherapists.

3. *Review the Record.*   The psychotherapist should conduct a thorough review of the client's record in psychotherapy to determine whether there is information that could be deleterious to the client, should it be revealed during an adversary deposition. The psychotherapist should discuss this review with the client and the client's attorney, preferably in a joint session if the client agrees.

4. *Review Current Statutes.*   Before complying with the subpoena, giving up records, or testifying at a deposition or court hearing, the psychotherapist should review current statutes regarding privileged communication for psychotherapists. These are sometimes quite complex. If statutes are unclear, the psychotherapist should consult the client's attorney or the psychotherapist's own legal counsel for clarification. The psychotherapist must be prepared to refuse to answer questions that impinge on the client's rights to privileged communication. There are frequently exceptions to the rules of privileged communication, and this will be addressed in greater detail in Chapter 12.

Where a psychotherapist has seen more than one member of a family, especially in conjoint therapy, the issue can be extremely difficult. This most frequently occurs in cases of marital dissolution, child-custody litigation, and other family-involved adversary proceedings. In such cases, the psychotherapist may find that the privilege is owned by both parties in an adversary proceeding. One party may seek certain testimony to further his or her case, and the other party seeks to suppress such testimony. Both can claim privilege. Where one party waives privilege, the psychotherapist is usually *not* free to testify, since the privilege held by the opposing party still applies. The psychotherapist must understand this and refuse to testify unless ordered to do so directly by a sitting judge who holds jurisidiction in the matter at hand. Before doing so, the psychotherapist should clearly indicate to the judge which client has *not* granted the psychotherapist permission to reveal privileged material.

Should the therapist's notes reveal information of an embarrassing or private matter, unassociated with the legal issues at hand, there is a way for the psychotherapist to protect this information. Where such a situation exists, the psychotherapist should contact the client's attorney and request a hearing with the presiding judge for purposes of "sealing the record." These procedures may be termed "motion for a protective order" or "motion to certify questions." In such a procedure, which takes place in the judge's chambers, the psychotherapist will be asked to specify what portions of the record are, in the psychotherapist's opinion, of a privileged and confidential nature but not significantly related to the adversary issues of the case. If the judge, after hearing the psychotherapist's description of the information, agrees, he or she will order the record sealed for the material specified. After this procedure, the psychotherapist may refuse to testify about any of the matters under the seal of the court. The witness may request such a motion even during a deposition.

When a psychotherapist is called upon to testify as an expert witness in any issue, it is always helpful to consult with a colleague who has more experience in the forensic area for suggestions and guidance.

LEGISLATIVE TESTIMONY

When the U.S. Congress develops new legislation, the Senate or House Committee responsible for the bill as it will appear for vote in each respective house (the "final markup") frequently holds hearings on the proposed wording of the legislative act. During these hearings, those individuals and organizations with vested interests in supporting or opposing the legislation are invited to present testimony. Experts are scheduled to appear, usually in groups of two to five witnesses, to make a brief, oral presentation of their views and opinions. Longer, more detailed reports are accepted "for the record" before the witness testifies, to be published in the hearings' record after all testimony is complete. After making the oral presentation, the various senators or representatives on the committee that hears the testimony may cross-examine the witness. Figure 11.1 shows the typical congressional hearing chambers where such testimony takes place.

Those who are sponsoring the witness's appearance will usually ensure that several weeks before the hearing the witness submits a copy of the testimony to be given. This should be camera-ready, double-spaced manuscript copy. The sponsoring organization will usually submit as many as 50 copies of the anticipated testimony to the congressional staff, so that the expert's opinion can be reviewed by all interested parties on the subcommittee before the witness testifies.

On the day the witness is to testify, the sponsor has usually contacted congressional assistants on the subcommittee to determine the order of witnesses. Experts are usually assembled outside the hearing room just before the hearings begin (usually 9:30 A.M. or 2:00 P.M.). When the hearing-room doors are opened, the witnesses and their sponsors usually take seats at the front of the gallery. The witness is ordinarily introduced to other witnesses in the panel who will be called. When the chairperson of the subcommittee takes his or her seat at the center of the raised bench where the subcommittee sits and announces, "These hearings are now in session," the hearings have begun. The chair may make several announce-

FIGURE 11.1.   A congressional committee hearing room. *A:* chairperson of subcommittee holding hearings; *B:* members of subcommittee; *C:* subcommittee staff and assistants; *D:* committee legal stenographer; *E:* witness table; *F:* television and sound podiums; and *G:* spectator, witness, and lobbyist gallery.

ments, issue a statement, joke with the press, or comment about people in the gallery. Procedures and protocol range from very formal to very informal.

Although the language and interaction is very similar to that which an expert witness has heard in courtrooms and depositions, the interchange between and among members of congress may range from the serious to the humorous.

After the preliminaries, the chair will usually read the names of the witnesses scheduled for that session and invite them to take seats at the witness table. The expert will usually find paper cups and several pitchers of water, as well as a number of microphones, on the witness table. In most congressional hearings, a staff assistant will have placed a name card on the witness table for each expert. This helps the members of congress in identifying the witness to whom they later direct their questions.

The witnesses at the table are usually called to testify in a predetermined order, agreed upon before the hearings begin. Questions are usually not asked by the subcommittee members until all testimony has been presented, although this is not a hard and fast rule. The chair may interrupt a witness to suggest that the testimony be summarized, since the congressional staff have distributed copies of the expert's proposed testimony before the hearings. The witness should always courteously acknowledge the importance of the subcommittee members' time, promise to be as brief as possible, and then go on to give as much or as little of the planned presentation as the expert feels is necessary to convey the opinion properly.

After the experts have finished making their presentations, the subcommittee members are invited to question the presenters by the chair. The Chair may begin the cross-examination or may defer to subcommittee members. Each subcommittee member is usually allotted a specific amount of time to question the panel—usually about five minutes. Sometimes the subcommittee member may use this allotted time to make a statement as to his or her opinion about the matter at hand and will ask no questions of the witnesses.

The following is abstracted from the report of hearings conducted by a congressional subcommittee that was proposing to add cautionary labeling on all cigarette packages in addition to the longstanding Surgeon General's warning that appears on all cigarette packages and advertising. Among the labels proposed was one that would state, "Cigarette smoking is addictive." The following testimony was presented by a psychologist retained by a law firm representing the Tobacco Institute.

COMPREHENSIVE SMOKING PREVENTION EDUCATION ACT

HEARINGS

BEFORE THE

SUBCOMMITTEE ON

HEALTH AND THE ENVIRONMENT

OF THE

COMMITTEE ON ENERGY AND COMMERCE

HOUSE OF REPRESENTATIVES

NINETY-SEVENTH CONGRESS

SECOND SESSION

ON

H.R. 5653 and H.R. 4957

BILLS TO AMEND THE PUBLIC HEALTH SERVICE ACT AND THE FED-
ERAL CIGARETTE LABELING AND ADVERTISING ACT TO ESTABLISH
A NATIONAL PROGRAM UNDER AN OFFICE OF SMOKING AND
HEALTH TO INFORM THE PUBLIC OF THE DANGERS FROM SMOK-
ING, TO CHANGE THE LABEL REQUIREMENTS FOR CIGARETTES,
AND FOR OTHER PURPOSES

MARCH 5, 11, AND 12, 1982

Serial No. 97-106

Printed for the use of the
Committee on Energy and Commerce
U.S. Government Printing Office
Washington: 1982

Mr. Waxman. Dr. Blau.

Statement of Theodore H. Blau, Ph.D.

Dr. Blau.   Thank you, Mr. Chairman, for the opportunity of appearing
here today. I will be brief and submit details of the research background of
my statements to your staff.

My name is Theodore Blau. I hold a doctorate in psychology, received
from the Pennsylvania State University in 1951. I have been in independent practice of clinical psychology and consulting psychology in Tampa,
Fla., since 1953.

Formerly, I was professor of psychiatry at the Medical School of the
University of South Florida, and professor of psychology at that school and
others. I hold a diplomate in clinical psychology from the American Board
of Professional Psychology as well as the diploma from the American
Board of Forensic Psychology.

I am a member and past president of the American Psychological Association and am currently president of the American Psychological Foundation. I am also a member of the Evaluation Research Society and have
conducted evaluation studies for private corporations as well as evaluation
research for various branches of the U.S. military and other elements of the
Government. I am the author of 1 book, a number of chapters and approximately 50 articles.

For several years, I have been involved in an evaluation of the research
and current state of knowledge about the psychological aspects of cigarette
smoking. The evaluation includes a thorough review of historical factors,
current theories and research, quality of the research and publications
pertaining to dependence, addiction, laboratory and applied research and
cultural aspects of smoking behavior.

In addition to this literature review, I have also communicated with
active researchers working in the area. I am presently writing the section

entitled "Smoking Behavior" that will be published in the "Wiley Encyclo-pedia of Psychology."

It is my understanding that proposed bill H.R. 5653 would mandate a warning on cigarette packages stating that cigarette smoking is addictive. I will address myself today to that conclusion.

For almost 400 years the smoking habit has been an issue never lacking proponents as well as opponents. Some who smoke seem unable to give up the cigarette habit, at least during certain decades of their lives. Others can quit with apparent ease.

Few specific areas of applied psychological research have received greater attention than the cigarette smoking habit. Despite this intense scientific focus on the behavioral as well as physiological aspects of ciga-rette smoking, no general agreement among scientists exists in answer to the question of whether cigarettes or their contents are addictive.

The behavior and responses of cigarette smokers are quite different than those observed in individuals who are addicted to heroin and other sub-stances that are demonstrably addictive.

The scientific literature demonstrates the following:

There is apparently no difference in the severity of cessation responses between light smokers and heavy smokers. Research also has shown that these effects are felt more severely by those who reduced dosages but did not stop completely than by those who abstained totally.

A third aspect reported by various researchers is that smoking cessation effects are relatively mild and in some cases non-existent. They are of a nature which might be expected to follow the loss of psychological rewards from any loved object to which a person was long accustomed and which could be conceived of as forming an important part of the way the individ-ual sees themselves and their behavior.

It has been reported that many smokers are able to refrain from smoking for relatively long periods of time for practical, safety or religious reasons and to do so without apparent discomfort. Some examples are coal miners who may not smoke at the pitface, Orthodox Jews who give up smoking at sundown on Friday and cease smoking until sundown on Saturday, and so forth. Such behavior does not fit conventional views of addiction.

Whereas the effects of use and withdrawal are consistent and predicta-ble with known addictive substances despite a wide range of uses, descrip-tions of tobacco effects are extremely varied and inconsistent. In this re-gard, tobacco use is more like the use of caffeine rather than alcohol or opiates.

It has been reported by Costa, in 1980, that the continuance of smoking appears more related to a wide range of psychosocial motives such as pleasure, stimulation, sensory motor manipulation, and reduction of nega-tive effect than an addiction factor.

The U.S. Department of HEW reported in 1977 that 95 percent of those people who quit smoking do so on their own. This is not only a phenomena in sharp contrast to experience with demonstrably addictive substances but one which remains to be explored.

Clearly, many areas of smoking behavior are as yet unexplored including why some smoke very heavily and some do not. Carefully controlled animal studies must be done before a scientific description of the smoking habit can be expected. Promising work with Rhesus monkeys has been reported by Kiyoshi and Tanagita—in Japan and researchers at the Southwest Research Institute—Rogers—have reported conditioning laboratory baboons to smoke cigarettes. These developments suggest that we may be able to study cigarette smoking in a properly controlled laboratory setting.

Until such controlled animal experiments with reliable models of self-administration of tobacco can be devised and conducted as they have been with morphine, cocaine, and alcohol, the concept of tobacco addiction will probably remain a hypothetical construct only partly understood as suggested by Jarvik, 1977. And so, gentlemen, at this time the scientific data do not support the statement: Cigarette smoking is addictive.

I would very briefly like to tell you my clinical experience with smoking. During the past 30 years I have worked and continue to work with people who smoke cigarettes. In reviewing my experience with the thousands of people that I have seen professionally, many of whom were heavy smokers, I find some continued, some quit with stress, and some quit with little or no stress. These patients of mine in no way acted like the patients that I have seen who struggle to be released from the addictions of opiates or alcohol or amphetamines.

Cigarette smokers are very attached to their smoking behavior. They are often annoyed or distressed when they are not allowed to smoke. However, I have also noted people have equally strong attachments to tennis, jogging, candy, rock music, Coca-Cola, members of the opposite sex, and hamburgers; particularly in my adolescent patients.

With children, one sees very strong attachments to playmates, parents, certain articles of clothing, TV, blankets, and teddy bears. Removal from these activities, persons or objects can result in agitation, sleeplessness, irritation, depression, and other uncomfortable symptoms. They vary considerably in intensity and duration, as do the effects of abstinence from tobacco smoking.

I, myself, smoked cigarettes for 24 years. Two to three packages a day for the last 10 years of the habit. I stopped at the age of 35, 1 year before the first Surgeon General's report, and have not smoked since. I was somewhat uncomfortable for a short period of time, but was never highly uncomfortable. The craving never reached the level that I have experienced in medical weight loss programs or in alcoholic rehab clinics.

In short, although cigarette smoking is a common and pervasive habit, I can find no convincing basis in the scientific literature or in my own professional clinical experience to justify labeling it or treating it as an addiction.

Mr. Waxman.   Thank you very much, Dr. Blau.

Mr. Waxman.   So we can have people try cigarettes, and oftentimes we are finding young people trying cigarettes because of a lot of different factors, one of which is advertising. Dr. Blau says that cigarette smoking is not addictive; is that a correct statement?

Dr. Blau.   There is no scientific basis for a statement that cigarette smoking is addictive.

Mr. Waxman.   Do you think that the use of cigarettes, has some kind of relationship to people wanting to continue using them a little bit more than other kinds of products that might be used very often?

Dr. Blau.   I think that is a question of very serious concern. I made a visit to Dr. Evans' laboratory in Houston. He works specifically with the question of how do people start smoking, what keeps teenagers smoking.

I see a group every week made up of seven people between 7 and 13 years of age. During the past few years I have observed the genesis of the smoking habit. One thing impressive from the research, I might point out, is that there are some indications as to how these teenagers are drawn into the habit. The first element is the parental model, the second is the sibling model, the third, peer group pressure.

I am quite taken by the fact that many of my heaviest smokers, my teenagers that I work with, don't read. They are very poor readers. They are dropouts from school.

Mr. Waxman.   So there are different factors?

Dr. Blau.   Many factors.

Mr. Waxman.   Once they take up using the cigarette product, isn't there some attachment that keeps them smoking? More than just the original reasons to take it up?

Dr. Blau.   Yes, sir. I think there are probably a multitude of factors that have been reported in the literature. There are indications that the habit, after an initial aversive response becomes pleasurable; for some it relieves tension, it's a social grace in some people's mind. For a small group of so-called diddlers, it's important to have something to do with one's hands. It arouses some. It tranquilizes others.

The amount of research which is done has stirred many questions that must be explored and answered. I am fully confident in the future we will have a definitive answer as to how people learn to smoke, why they continue to smoke, and from that, clear-cut directions as to how to go about preventing the inception of a habit.

Mr. Waxman.   Do you believe the reason people continue to smoke after they start smoking has less to do with advertising and more to do with these other factors?

Dr. Blau.   I am afraid that I must plead innocent on knowledge of the advertising factors. I can only speak for the other factors. I think they are terribly strong, the psychosocial factors in my observation, and evaluation of the data.

Mr. Waxman.   Dr. Blau, you stated, apparently with some confidence, that there is no general agreement among scientists as to whether cigarettes are addictive. The Director of the National Institute on Drug Abuse and the Assistant Secretary of Health made it clear that in their opinion smoking was in fact addictive, and this was also the conclusion of the National Advisory Council on Drug Abuse and a special task force of independent researchers convened by NIDA's Division of Research.

That sounds like a consensus of opinion. Are you asking us to believe these distinguished physicians and researchers were wrong and you are right?

Dr. Blau. I appear before you as an evaluation scientist. Evaluation is the assessment of merit. It's sort of like asking the goats to guard the lettuce patch when you ask scientists to make long range general statements about their research. The very essence of science is caution. One of the outstanding researchers in tobacco, Dr. Stanley Schacter, a member of the distinguished board that you just mentioned said, and I quote from a Government publication, "Most of us who do research on smoking have at some time championed the hypothesis that cigarette smoking with nicotine as the active agent is an addiction."

"Sometimes, however, it's difficult to figure out why that conviction is so strong. The data supporting the proposition are not particularly good. In fact, looked at with a ruthless eye, they are rather flimsy. When scientists are asked to weigh the evidence with care in terms of the long range implications, they generally agree that we have a long way to go before we can give a scientific support to the statement, cigarette smoking is addictive."

Mr. Waxman. Thank you very much.

DANGEROUSNESS AND VIOLENCE

Psychological evaluations of dangerousness may constitute the largest single category of evaluation and opinion called for from psychologists by the criminal justice system. Mental health professionals are asked to determine the propensity for future violence of thousands of people each year who are under control of the courts and the criminal justice institutions in America. The reports of mental health professionals are used by the courts and the criminal justice system for a considerable variety of decisions (Shah, 1978). These include:

1. To hold without bail, grant bail, or release on personal recognizance
2. To move juveniles to adult courts to be tried for serious crimes
3. To grant a lesser sentence or probation after conviction of a criminal offense
4. To grant work-release status to offenders in prison

5. To parole or conditionally release offenders
6. To commit, mandate treatment, or release "sexually dangerous persons," "delinquents," and so on
7. To determine whether felons found incompetent to stand trial are also "dangerous"
8. To determine what felons are too "dangerous" for ordinary prison routine and require special incarceration
9. To determine whether drug addicts should be committed because of a propensity for violence
10. To commit mentally disturbed persons involuntarily because they constitute a danger to themselves or others
11. To decide whether to release involuntarily confined mental patients conditionally or unconditionally
12. To hospitalize defendants acquitted by reason of insanity
13. To transfer a mental patient to a high-security ward or special hospital for violent patients
14. To invoke special sentencing options for habitual or violent offenders
15. To recommend the death penalty for those convicted of capital crimes because of a likelihood of continued dangerousness

Although the final decision in all these matters is made by a judge or a responsible administrator, the information supporting such decisions often comes from the report or testimony of a mental health professional (Monahan, 1981; Robitscher, 1980).

Recent court decisions require mental health professionals to breach professional ethics and privileged communication to "predict" that a patient or client is about to act in a violent manner.[11] The professional then has a "duty to warn" endangered parties.

The mental health professional rarely appears at court to explain or defend the basis of a prediction of dangerousness or violence. On those rare occasions when the mental health professional does appear in open court to present findings, it is rare that the witness is appropriately cross-examined as to the reliability and validity of his or her opinion.

Too few mental health professionals include caveats, cautions, or concerns regarding the accuracy of their predictions of dangerousness. The courts and the administrators of the criminal justice system are in dire need of expert opinion to aid them in making decisions concerning potential dangerousness. This need has influenced the production of opinions viewed as reliable and valid but poorly supported by substantial research or professional agreement.

[11] *Tarasoff v. Regents of the Univ. of Cal.*, 13 Cal.3d 177, 529 P.2d. 553, 118 Cal.Rptr. 129 (1974).

Predictions of dangerousness and potential violent behavior are for the most part inaccurate. Predictions of dangerousness or violence that does not come about (false positives) are reported to range from 54 to 99% (Monahan, 1975). The courts are concerned with both a "public protectionist" philosophy, in which the public is protected from dangerous persons, and the "civil libertarian" view, in which individual rights are protected. Whereas false-positive predictions of dangerousness may protect the general public, this protection is achieved at great cost to the civil liberties of those restrained as a result of false-positive predictions (Steadman & Morrissey, 1981).

Although the general public has always linked mental disturbance to dangerousness and violence, there is little evidence that emotional disturbance is a primary component of a propensity to harm the self or others (Walters, 1981). The courts have begun to recognize that mental disturbance is not inevitably linked with dangerousness.[12]

In spite of all evidence to the contrary, courts and clinicians continue to interact in the matter of predicting dangerousness. In most instances, the clinicians view their task as one of using the best clinical judgment to arrive at a difficult decision (Schoenfeld & Lehmann, 1981). Monahan (1981) proposes a series of questions that the mental health professional should ask and attempt to answer when assessing potential for dangerousness. The following is an abstract of these questions:

1. Am I really being asked to predict future violence or dangerousness?
2. Am I competent as a professional to estimate future violence?
3. What events led to questioning the defendant's propensity for violence?
4. What are the defendant's demographic characteristics relevant to the issue of predicting dangerousness or violence?
5. What is the defendant's history of violent behavior?
6. What are the base rates for dangerous or violent behavior for individuals of similar background to the defendant?
7. What are the stress factors in the defendant's environment?
8. What psychological factors indicate that the defendant may be predisposed to cope with stress by behaving violently?
9. Are there indications that the defendant can cope with stress in a nonviolent manner?
10. If there has been violence in the past, how similar are the contexts in which the dangerous behavior occurred to the contexts in which the defendant will function in the future?

[12] *O'Connor v. Donaldson*, 420 U.S. 563 (1975).

11. Who might be the likely victims of the defendant's violent behavior in the future, and how available will such persons be to the defendant?

12. What means will the defendant have to be dangerous or violent in the future?

13. What ethical constraints exist to prevent the reporting of a prediction regarding future violence?

14. Regardless of the expectancies of the referral source, is this an appropriate case about which to offer a prediction?

Dix (1977) offers a series of pragmatic suggestions for mental health professionals who wish to conduct careful evaluations and submit realistic, ethical reports of their findings with respect to a prediction of dangerousness. Schoenfeld and Lehmann (1981) summarize these as follows:

1. As part of qualifying as an expert witness, a mental health professional should demonstrate reasonable acquaintance with the developing literature on prediction of behavior.

2. Testimony should be given only if it can be based upon all four of the following:
   (1) A complete and consistent diagnostic framework, with broad professional support;
   (2) An extensive personal clinical examination of the subject;
   (3) An exhaustive history, not limited to information obtained from the subject himself; and
   (4) The result of psychological tests.

3. A mental health professional should not express an opinion as to whether a subject will engage in certain behavior unless the professional has a complete understanding of the legal standard involved, including:
   (1) The acts that, if committed, would meet the standard;
   (2) The likelihood of those acts that the standard requires being committed;
   (3) The time frame of the question, i.e., how far in the future does the standard cover; and
   (4) The circumstances which are to be involved, i.e., does the standard ask about the likelihood of given acts if the subject is imprisoned, or if the subject is simply released to society without rehabilitative efforts.

4. No expert opinion should be expressed unless the subject has actually engaged in dangerous behavior, and an analysis of that behavior should be a major factor in the conclusion of the expert.

5. Any opinion should be expressed only in terms of comparative group probability.

6. The testimony should include a complete statement and explanation of the basis or grounds for any opinion expressed, including:

(1) Any statements made by the subject which are relied upon as accurate statements of fact;

(2) Clinical observations made during the expert's examination of the subject;

(3) Prior behavior of the subject, and the source of the information concerning that behavior; and

(4) Past mental history, such as prior hospitalization, diagnosis, and the like.

7. The opinion should include an objective statement of the empirical basis for the witnesses' classification of the subject and the predictive value of that classification.

Stringent as these criteria may be, they clearly help meet some of the most serious objections to the use by the criminal justice system of evaluations of dangerousness by mental health professionals.

Unfortunately, few psychological evaluations of dangerousness or potential violence are so carefully done as to meet all the criteria recommended above. The time, professional skill, and cost required for such proper assessments exceed the number of competent professionals and funds available in respect to the number of requests for evaluation of dangerousness generated by courts and criminal justice agencies.

The following two reports contrast a psychological evaluation performed in a busy forensic psychology unit in a state prison with a report of examination by a psychologist in independent practice in a community where the courts are known to value careful psychological evaluation and consultation.

The first report is characteristic of a professional setting where 8 to 10 examinations are conducted each week by the forensic psychologist in a western state prison.

PSYCHOLOGICAL EVALUATION

Forensic Unit
ABC State Hospital
January 16, 1980

Ronald, Reggie
MSH# 19,919

Referral

This 21-year-old male patient was referred by Dr. Will Jones, Director, Forensic Treatment Center, to assist in differential diagnosis and evaluation of dangerousness.

Tests Administered

Revised Beta Examination, Wechsler Adult Intelligence Scale, Sixteen Personality Factors Questionnaire, Minnesota Multiphasic Personality Inventory, and Thematic Apperception Test.

Behavioral Observations

Reggie appeared tense on the Revised Beta. His hands shook when he tried to draw the objects on subtest 5. He complained that subtest 4 was beyond his comprehension and refused to attempt it after spending five minutes on the practice section.

On the WAIS subtest "Comprehension," Reggie asked that the statements be repeated several times. "Arithmetic" subtest showed that Reggie uses his fingers to add and subtract. Reggie smoked excessively, especially when he responded that he didn't know a particular answer. On the "Digit Symbol" subtest, Reggie tapped his feet, wrung his hands several times, and appeared to be breathing hard. Reggie's hands shook very hard on the "Block Design" subtest.

Reggie's feet were rocking and tapping back and forth while answering the MMPI.

Test Results

The Revised Beta Examination indicated that Reggie was functioning in the "Below Average" range of the population equivalent of the Wechsler's "Dull Normal" (16.1 percent bottom range of the population). The Revised Beta Examination IQ was 83.

Wechsler Adult Intelligence Scale Full Scale IQ was 76—"Borderline" (6.7 percent bottom range of the population); Verbal Score IQ was 72; Performance Score IQ was 83.

The discrepancy between the Revised Beta and the WAIS indicates educationally that Reggie is not very fluent in the English language. His performance scores and the Revised Beta, which is a nonverbal instrument, seem to more clearly indicate the level of his intellectual functioning.

The personality tests revealed that Reggie was aggressive, suspicious, and likely to act impulsively.

The MMPI indicated that Reggie was suffering from a psychotic depression manifested in schizophrenic tendencies. The MMPI further indicated that Reggie is unsociable, unstable, and inadequate in his relationships with others. The MMPI indicated a high degree of impulsiveness and selfishness resulting in his inability to relate to others. Reggie seems dangerous inasmuch as he is prone to act out his anger against others.

The Thematic Apperception Protocols were short sketches about the present situation in each picture. Low affect appeared present inasmuch as

Reggie wasn't interested in developing a story line. No father figures in any of the Protocols.

Diagnostic Impression.   Schizophrenia, paranoid type (295.3).

The next report was done by a psychologist in a medium-sized California community where funds are provided by the courts for consultation by mental health professionals.

REPORT OF PSYCHOLOGICAL EXAMINATION

NAME: Wayne, Alan   BIRTHDATE: 5/12/62   EDUCATION: 12.7

Referral

Mr. Wayne is charged with rape and first degree murder. While "hanging out" with some of his friends at the beach, Mr. Wayne took a 15-year-old girl into his van, forced her to have intercourse with him, and then bludgeoned her to death with a tire iron. Mr. Wayne was being held at Juvenile Hall at the time of this evaluation. The judge will later decide whether Mr. Wayne will be dealt with as a juvenile or charged as an adult.

Background History

The family history is provided by the mother, Mrs. Blanche Wayne. The mother is 51 years old and employed in a school cafeteria. She completed the eleventh grade and has had some technical training in electronics. She describes her health as being "good until this happened." She states that now she has headaches, trouble with her nerves, trouble sleeping, and nightmares. She describes her personality as "a homebody." She used to drink for a period of about 10 years but denies drinking now. However, she does admit to being drunk at times. The mother describes Mr. Wayne's father, George, as being 60 years old and presently working for Alcoholics Anonymous. He had worked previously as a contractor. She thinks that he completed the tenth grade. She saw him last approximately seven years ago. Asked to describe his personality, her response was: "If you do, you're wrong; if you don't, you're wrong."

Mrs. Wayne indicates that she and the father were married in 1948 and separated in 1966. At that time Alan was four years old. She stated that the marriage started out "pretty good," and she describes Mr. Wayne as drinking "a little" at the beginning of the marriage but that the drinking became more and more frequent, to the point that the last few years of the marriage he was drinking all of the time. Several years before the marriage ended,

Mrs. Wayne stated that she got a job so that she could pay the bills for the family. She described Mr. Wayne as being mean and fighting with her when he was drunk. Asked to describe what she meant by fighting, she indicated that he yelled and used physical force. She indicated that she has several scars from injuries she sustained from his aggression and stated that "the law was called a lot." She indicated that he threatened her with both a gun and knives but actually only used as a weapon a baseball bat. She indicated a scar on her head as a result of having been hit by him with a baseball bat. She indicated that the children, including Alan, were around the house and observed Mr. Wayne's behavior. Asked what Alan would do when this physical fighting was occurring, she indicated that he would crawl back in a corner and cry. She indicated that Mr. Wayne was not as violent with the children as he was with her but would yell at them a lot. Asked if Mr. Wayne ever became physically violent with Alan, Mrs. Wayne replied that she really did not know because she was out working so much of the time when Alan was home alone or with the other children and the father.

Mrs. Wayne stated that her pregnancy with Alan was "bad." She indicated that she did not have the proper food and that she had no prenatal care at all. She indicated that her own mother died one month before Alan was born, so she was quite emotionally upset during this time shortly before his birth. She indicated that Mr. Wayne beat her up an unknown number of times while she was carrying Alan and, at least one time while she was carrying him, pushed her down the steps from one floor to the next. She indicated that Mr. Wayne served one year in jail for this abuse to her and her unborn infant.

Mrs. Wayne states that her son was full-term and that his birth was natural. She states that Alan was bottle-fed but that there was no money to buy milk for him a lot of the time. Asked what she would use for a substitute during this time, she stated sweetened water or weak tea. She indicated that he had no feeding problems as far as she could recall and described him as being weaned very early but was unable to remember exactly when. She stated that she began toilet training Alan at about nine months and that he was completely potty trained by the time he was one year old.

Asked what she remembered about Alan from the time he was born until he was one year old, she stated that he was "just terribly thin and absolutely white." She described him as being so white that at birth his blood was checked to see whether he was an albino. She described his second through fifth years as being a time when he was a good child, but if they had company he would try to show off. She indicated that "he had nothing to do with his dad." She stated that he was taken care of by his four older siblings during the time that she worked. Mrs. Wayne indicates that the family physician is Dr. Featherington but that Alan has not seen him for several years. She indicated that he has not had his tonsils or adenoids removed and has had no other surgeries. She stated that he had a broken finger about three years ago and a cracked foot about four years ago. She also indicated that Alan had the mumps when he was about eight or nine and that he had the chicken pox when he was about 14. The mother indicates that his immunizations are current and that he has had regular complaints about not seeing too well the last three or four years. The mother indicates that Alan began puberty at about 11 or 12 and seemed to develop quite fast. Asked who gave Alan his sexual education, the mother replied that she didn't know if anyone had. She thought maybe he had gotten some sexual education at school or from his older brothers but denied that he had ever asked her any questions about sexual matters. She stated that she had talked to him only once, when a film about venereal disease was shown at school, and she describes Alan as thinking that it was a film about railroads.

Mrs. Wayne indicates that there was one incident when Alan was about five or six years old when he was seen at a physician's office in Fontana (she could not recall the physician's name) when he became unconscious for five to ten minutes after being given a shot in the physician's office. She indicated that he was put on a respirator and cold towels were used. She also indicated that whenever he got the flu or other kinds of illnesses he always became sicker than her other children and would run high fevers in excess of 104 degrees. She could not recall any periods of dizziness not connected with illness but stated that he often got headaches, especially from the hot sun. She denied periods of poor sleep.

Mrs. Wayne indicated that Alan went to Head Start. She indicated that there were no problems while he attended kindergarten and first grade and described his grades as okay. The mother states that in the second and third grades Alan was absent a lot for what she described as "financial purposes." Asked what she meant by this, Mrs. Wayne stated that she did not have money to buy clothes for Alan that he could wear to school. She stated that this situation occurred quite frequently and that by the time he reached fourth grade, he was "a little behind in his group" and had to be placed in a special class. She indicated that this appeared to be when Alan began to really like school and indicated the reason that he liked school seemed to be that he helped with the school lunches in the cafeteria. He held this job through the sixth grade. She stated that in fourth, fifth, and sixth grades, Alan did "pretty good" in school with grades of C's and D's and presented no behavior problems.

The mother indicated that when Alan left the sixth grade, he did not go to school "for a year or so." The mother was unclear as to whether he was out of school two years or two terms, but she did indicate that Alan said he did not want to go to school, and so he just stayed home.

The mother stated that it was during this time period—when Alan was not going to school—that he took an overdose of phenobarbital. She estimates his age at about 12 or 13 at the time. She stated that she did not know how many he took but that he was treated at Riverside General Hospital and kept there for several days. She cannot remember whether counseling was recommended or not, but he received no counseling following this overdose and hospitalization, and the only interventive step that was taken was that Alan went to live with his older brother Jim for "a couple of months."

When Alan finally entered seventh grade, the mother indicates that he hated school and his grades were low. She stated that there were behavior problems and, asked what those were, indicated that "they didn't allow him to smoke." The mother also indicated that the eighth grade was "a bad year" for Alan. She indicated that when he entered high school, things began to get better for him in the ninth grade because he had football and wrestling. She stated, however, that "as soon as wrestling was over it got bad again." She stated that the tenth grade was essentially the same as the ninth, with things going along pretty well during football and wrestling season and deteriorating when wrestling was over. During the eleventh-grade year, Alan went to Oklahoma for approximately one month, and when he returned he entered continuation school.

At home, before Alan was arrested, he shared a room with his brother. The mother states that for the most part he kept it very neat and clean. She describes his recreational interests as fishing, weight lifting, having his friends over, and playing a lot of loud music. She indicates that she believes he got along well with his brothers and sisters but described Bill (the second-oldest child) as helping her discipline Alan when she had trouble doing this. Asked what brother Bill usually did to discipline, she stated that he usually talked to Alan. Asked if he ever hit him, the mother seemed unsure but thought he might have hit him a time or two. She denied ever spanking him even when he was very young.

Asked about Alan's dating behavior, the mother seemed to have essentially no information at all. She indicated that maybe he started to date in about the tenth grade and that there was one girl he would pick up and take to the football game and then take home afterward. She states that she could recall one time when Alan went to the wrestling match with this girl, but this was the extent of the information she had about Alan's dating behavior. She indicates that he receives no allowance nor has he ever been to summer camp. She described his bedtime as being about 9:30 P.M. during weeknights and between 11:00 and 11:30 P.M. during weekends. She indicated that his chores were to keep his own room clean, do the yard work, and sometimes share doing dishes and emptying the trash.

Mrs. Wayne describes her son's behavior as very moody with variable and unpredictable emotions, becoming irritable without cause and being impulsive. She was unsure as to whether he was stubborn but described him as quite independent. She was also unsure whether he was able to learn from experience but stated that he had difficulty in completing projects and following directions, believing that he could do neither very well.

Mrs. Wayne indicates that Alan sucked his thumb from the age of about one to three and that he has been a nail biter from infancy to the present time. She indicates that about the time the parents separated, Alan began to have verbal problems in sometimes saying words and phrases backward. She also indicates that at about this time he began to show temper-tantrum behavior whenever company would visit. She indicated this latter behavior continued until he was approximately eight and one-half years old. She describes Alan as always having excess energy, always being jealous, and always being a dependent child. She indicates that he began to lie at about the age of 12 and that at about the age of six he began to present a picture of lacking self-confidence and being overly sensitive. She describes mood swings as beginning when Alan was approximately 13 years old and continuing to the present time.

Asked to describe her son's biggest problems, she indicated the following three: (1) not going to school, (2) the friends he picked, and (3) his smoking of marijuana. The mother denied that Alan used any other drugs but then added "except benzedrine." Asked to describe how her son appeared when he smoked marijuana, she indicated "different ways." She stated that he seemed "happy, giggly, stupid—saying silly things." Asked how he behaved when she observed him to be drunk, she indicated that he seemed happy and would spend most of his time apologizing, coming up and putting his arm around her and kissing her. She indicated that she had seen him pass out from drinking approximately an hour after he had been observed by her as being drunk.

Near the end of the interview, when asked if there was anything else that was important to know about Alan, the mother indicated that when he was about 12 years old she caught him and one of his friends sniffing gasoline and they stated that they had done it several times. She also added that she feels she had a closer personal relationship with Alan than either Bill or Jim.

Interview with Alan Wayne

Mr. Wayne was seen at the Juvenile Hall. He stated his mother is Blanche, who lives in Escondido and works in a cafeteria for the school district. Mr. Wayne states that his parents separated when he was about eight years old and that the family never really talked about the parents' separation, and he remembers little about it. He states that his father is in San Francisco, and he remembers very little about his father, indicating that he does not keep in touch with the family.

Mr. Wayne is the sixth of eight children. He states that his oldest brother, Jim, is about 30 or 31 years old and works as a detective. He describes his brother Bill as being 28 or 29 years old, living in Pomona near his family and managing a gas station. He states that his sister Maria, age 26 or 27, lives in Baker and works at clean-up tasks with a construction company. He describes his sister Jane, age 24 or 25, as living in Pomona and working as a substitute teacher, though he states that she never went to college. He indicates that his brother Jack is 19 years old, a senior in high school, and lives at home with his mother. His younger sister, Vivien, is 15 and lives with his sister Maria. Finally, he indicates that his youngest brother is about 13 years old.

Asked how he got along with his mother, Mr. Wayne states that he and his mother always had an agreement. He indicated that she put very few limits on him as long as he let her know what he was doing. Even when he would exceed limits, for example, coming in after curfew, the mother was not particularly strict in enforcing consequences. He stated that the one stipulation which his mother seemed quite firm about was that she did not want him having girls in the house while he was alone, particularly if they went to his room and closed the door. He describes his mother as a nice person and caring for the children a lot. He also indicates that she worries a lot.

Evaluation Procedures

Culture Fair Intelligence Test, Peabody Picture Vocabulary Test, Wide Range Achievement Test, Brief-Reitan Short Form, Memory for Designs, Torque Test: A Measure of Cerebral Dominance, Sentence Completion, Sixteen Personality Factor Questionnaire—Form E, Clinical Analysis Questionnaire—Part II, Motivation Analysis Test, Chromatic and Achromatic House-Tree-Person, Draw-a-Person, Draw-a-Family, Self-Portrait, Thematic Apperception Test—Cards 1, 2, 3BM, 4, 6BM, 7BM, 8BM, 13MF, 18BM, 15, 14, 13G, and 13B, Observation, and Interview.

Response to Evaluation

Mr. Wayne was evaluated in Juvenile Hall for three and one-half hours on April 3, two and one-half hours on April 4, and one and three-quarter hours on April 6. Total evaluation time was seven and three-quarter hours. Mr. Wayne was cooperative and seemed adequately motivated to perform all tasks requested of him. He worked hard and was persistent even when he seemed to become a bit tired. He seemed honest in answering all questions even though, initially, he was somewhat guarded and cautious in his responses.

Results of Evaluation

A. Intellectual Factors

A nonlanguage measure of intelligence, the Culture Fair Intelligence Test, Scale 2, was administered to Mr. Wayne inasmuch as verbal intelligence measures frequently give inaccurate assessment to delinquent popula-tions. On this measure, Mr. Wayne obtained an intelligence score of 99, which can best be described as being in the Average range of intellectual capacity.

The Peabody Picture Vocabulary Test was given, and Mr. Wayne achieved a Mental Age of 12 years and 9 months. This would place him in the eleventh percentile, with a Calculated IQ of 80. This suggests that he has unusually poor ability to use or conceptually understand verbal material.

The discrepancy between nonverbal and verbal intellectual measures suggests that Mr. Wayne is within the Average range of intellectual poten-tial with nonverbal information but functions at the lowest end of the Low–Average range of intellectual functioning when language skills are re-quired.

B. Neuropsychological Factors

The Memory for Designs resulted in a raw score of 1, which, in terms of both raw score and difference score, places him within the Normal range. This score is contraindicative of brain disorder.

The Brief-Reitan was performed with slight distortions. The distortions were not significant and would not suggest brain dysfunction. Results of the Torque test indicate severe mixed cerebral dominance. This result has a possible genetic source inasmuch as Mr. Wayne is left-handed, as is his sister.

C. Achievement Factors

Results of the Wide Range Achievement Test were as follows:

Factor	Grade Equivalent	Percentile Rank
Reading	7.1	27th
Spelling	2.4	34th
Arithmetic	5.9	16th

The above results, compared with Mr. Wayne's present grade placement of 12, indicate that he is significantly below grade expectancy in all of his achievement scores. These scores reinforce the intelligence testing, and together indicate that academic and verbal tasks will be extremely difficult for Mr. Wayne.

D. Personality Factors

(1) *Interpersonal Activity.*   Mr. Wayne is likely to be somewhat tactless in dealing with people, though he will usually be perceived as honest and

candid. He will get along best in settings where occasionally saying the wrong thing is not a serious matter and where his frankness is appreciated. He is likely to have difficulty when diplomacy and tactfulness are important.

Mr. Wayne is likely to be more of a follower than a leader, but he is also likely to want things his own way. He is not comfortable around people, and when situations require that he relate with any degree of depth, he is likely to become emotionally detached, suspicious, threatened, and hostile.

He tries to base his decisions and judgments on rational consideration of facts, a "hard-nosed" approach to problems. The resulting insensitivity to both his own and others' feelings leads him to ignore human values in considering issues. Most sensitive people may find themselves uncomfortable relating with him.

(2) *Early Identification and Parental Influences.* Considerable anxiety and conflict exists for Mr. Wayne in this area. Superficially, as described in the interview section, Mr. Wayne indicates that his mother is essentially easy to get along with and that he has a good relationship with her. However, the unconscious picture of the mother is filled with fear, futility, and feelings of being overwhelmed. Superficially, Mr. Wayne perceives the mother as appearing strong and available to him, but he also sees her as really overwhelming and at the same time weak. At a deeper level, he perceives her as emotionally closed and unnurturing, empty and unavailable to him. The mother figure is seen as demanding, manipulative, and easily threatened. She is certainly the most significant figure in Mr. Wayne's life, but she is an individual who needs to know everything that is going on and likely has made the subject feel spied upon, invaded, and with little privacy. There is a great deal of depression surrounding the mother, and Mr. Wayne perceives that the mother is so weak and emotionally shaky that at any time she will collapse, and her collapse will come down and crush him. Testing shows strong overambitious striving to try to make emotional contact with the mother, but underneath there is futility and hopelessness that this striving will ever be effective. Test results indicate that Mr. Wayne is frightened of his mother and that she is a person who promises but does not keep her promises to him. Much of his relationship and contact with the mother figure is accomplished through excessive and strong fantasy.

Mr. Wayne perceives fathers as getting drunk and as sinners. He sees them as enjoying strength but also feels that while they make overtures of being available, they really are inept, weak, and unavailable. There is considerable disdain and anger for the father figure, but there is also a sense that the father views the son with hostility and depreciation. Mr. Wayne indicates a strong sense of striving for contact with a father figure but essentially feels that this striving brings no satisfaction, and he shows a sense of futility that real contact with a father figure will ever be successful. He does not know what to say to his father or father figures.

Mr. Wayne essentially is overwhelmed and crushed by the mother figure and abandoned by the father figure. Projective testing indicates that on the one hand he is afraid of losing his parental contact, while on the other hand he feels that this parental contact has already died or been lost to him.

(3) *Sources of Conflict and Anxiety Structure.*   There is considerable anxiety reflected in the test results of both a general and specific nature. Generalized anxiety is at a percentile level of 95 with specific areas including parental relationships, personal identity, hostility, comfort, security and fear, love and sex, and becoming psychotic.

The parental relationships with both mother and father are a deep source of anxiety for Mr. Wayne. He feels unfathered and yet disdainful toward the father, and he feels overwhelmed and at risk of being crushed by the mother.

Mr. Wayne shows a severe retardation in his emotional development. His whole sense of emotional and psychological identity ranges between that of a very young child of perhaps two or three to a preadolescent of 11 or 12. He feels helpless before the body drives which frequently overwhelm him, and he feels helpless and futile that his strong overinvested attempts at "being somebody" are ineffective. In spite of his superficial appearance of looking somewhat "together," his personal sense of self-worth is so low that 98 percent of adolescents his age feel more self-worth than he does.

Mr. Wayne strives for victory over those he perceives as opponents or enemies; violence and destructiveness are implied, although they may be repressed through legal and socially acceptable channels much of the time. Habitual, focused, aggressive behavior is less part of the pattern than is deeply felt hostility and a compulsion to compete and win. The hostility is likely to emerge unchanneled and uncontrolled under slight provocation and in moderately stressful situations.

Mr. Wayne enjoys personal comfort and ease, although habits of lesser self-indulgence are also present. Thus moderate self-denial can be expected in situations that demand and support such unselfishness, but a strong drive to avoid discomfort is likely to appear in less structured situations. In these kinds of situations, Mr. Wayne is likely to go to any length in an impulsive effort to reduce feelings of discomfort.

Mr. Wayne actively seeks security. He is deeply afraid, and while he fears realistic threats, such as illness, accident, and financial loss, there is also a strong underlying feeling of being easily threatened even to an irrational degree. This means that he is likely to perceive as frightening and even terrifying small things which many other people would not perceive as threats at all.

PROPERTY OF
RIVERWOOD COMMUNITY MENTAL HEALTH

Alan shows a strong response to sexual and romantic stimulation. Test indications are that he invests a substantial commitment of time and energy to this area, but there are also indications that he tries through sexual activity to obtain the love and emotional closeness which he wants even more than sexual involvement. There is severe frustration and anxiety noted in the area of emotional closeness, and Alan generally tries to meet this closeness through sexual behavior. Test results indicate that his attempts are not effective in making him feel more emotionally close, and extreme deprivation is noted in this area.

A final area of anxiety for Alan is a deep sense of unworthiness and self-hate. The depression shown in the test results is so strong as to suggest that he becomes confused to the point of psychosis. There is clear paranoid ideation with severe schizoid thought patterns and his tendency to distort reality is unconscious and generalized and not something which is available to Mr. Wayne's conscious awareness.

(4) *Behavior Controls and Defense Structure.* Alan's behavior controls are so low that more than 98 percent of adolescents are better able to control their impulses and conform their behavior within expected rules and regulations.

His defense structure is one which oscillates primarily between strong fantasy and acting-out behavior. Much of Alan's need satisfaction is obtained essentially through fantasy. He acts out his impulses at a level greater than 96 percent of other adolescents his age.

Much of the time he is not able, either through fantasy or acting-out behavior, to control the anxiety involved with his urges and impulses, and during these times he is likely to have breaks with reality contact to the point of becoming actually psychotic. Alan shows deep feelings of self-hatred and disgust, weariness and inability to cope with life, and obsessive ideas and impulses with generalized fears. The high level of anxiety appears to be a by-product of depression rather than a primary symptom; however, there are numerous specific areas which generate and contribute to both the depression and anxiety. Danger to the self is indicated, and there is some tendency toward suicide. While the tendency is not extreme and the actual likelihood of a suicidal attempt is small, it is not so small that it can be safely ignored. Suicide precautions should be taken. Distorted thinking and perception are rather clearly indicated, and some kind of antipsychotic medication may be helpful in controlling the symptoms. Elements of chronicity and long duration suggest a guarded prognosis with any kind of treatment.

Summary and Recommendations

In summary, Mr. Wayne can be described as a person who is probably within the Average range of intelligence when verbal and language skills are not required but functions with a significant handicap when verbal performance is required. He shows severe mixed cerebral dominance and probably suffers from some developmental lag because of this. His achievement scores are all significantly below grade expectancy and reinforce his difficulty with academic and verbal skill requirements. The personality is in the area of most serious concern. While Alan is likely to be considered frank and honest in some situations, he is also tactless with people. He is more of a follower than a leader, and he is not comfortable around people. He is insensitive to both his own and others' feelings and generally relates in a "hard-nosed," factual approach to interpersonal relationships as well as to problems. There is significant conflict regarding both parents. He sees the mother as overwhelming and crushing to him as well as empty and unnourishing. This is in spite of the fact that consciously he describes himself as having a close relationship with the mother figure. Alan perceives fathers, and men in general, as enjoying strength but really inept, weak, and with significant disdain. There is much anxiety both of a general and a specific nature. Areas producing anxiety and conflict include the parental relationship, primitive emotional development, very strong repressed hostility, a high unmet need for comfort, severe fear and insecurity, strong needs for love and emotional closeness which are attempted to be fullfilled through a strong sex drive but continue to go deprived, and deep feelings of unworthiness and self-hate. The degree of emotional disturbance is to such an extreme that depression becomes psychotic in degree, there is clear paranoid ideation with severe schizoid thought patterns, and there are high indications that reality is misperceived and distorted. The behavior controls are low to the point of often being nonexistent, and the high unmet needs and conflicts show a pattern of impulsivity so great that Alan is likely to behave in ways to fulfill these needs and impulses through almost any means.

Considering the results of the psychological evaluation, the following recommendations seem in order:

1. Whatever the outcome of Mr. Wayne's trial, he needs to be in a treatment program which will focus on and specifically address the following treatment needs:

    a. The underlying psychotic process must be addressed and attended to at all times, most likely including medication management that will counteract symptoms during active and acute episodes.

    b. The deep feelings of self-hatred and disgust which become extreme to the point of rendering Mr. Wayne a danger to himself.

    c. The antisocial feelings need to find expression through safe, legal channels which can provide a needed "safety valve," and these should be encouraged.

    d. Densensitization and other therapeutic techniques specifically for dealing with specific fears and obsessions.

  e. The conflicted parental relationships and the deep sense of having been unparented, at least in an emotional and psychological way.

  f. Effective ways of both defusing and channeling the strong repressed hostility.

  g. Appropriate means for meeting the needs for comfort that will neither repress the need nor give in to selfish disregard for other people's needs.

  h. Specific therapeutic work that will include attention to sexual education, sexual identity, and role characteristics and education and support in learning how to build reciprocally warm relationships with women.

2. Because Mr. Wayne is a moderate danger to himself, and therefore a suicide risk, attention should be paid to his behavior in this respect. When environmental stress factors are minimal, this danger may not exist at that particular time. However, when even minimal stress or threat exists, Mr. Wayne is likely to behave in self-destructive ways. This behavior may sometimes be extreme and overt, while other times it may be more indirect, such as taking drugs to the point of an "accidental" overdose.

3. Mr. Wayne needs opportunities to experience real situations that provide even moderate success in small endeavors. He superficially presents a self-confident picture, but beneath this exterior is a human being so devoid of self-worth that he feels himself to be of practically no value at all.

4. Encouragement and structured education and exploration in values clarification, particularly as it relates to moral and ethical issues, should be part of any planning program for Mr. Wayne from this point on. He needs both individual help and reinforcement for his attempts in this respect.

5. In whatever situations that he is in, he needs detailed plans and structures for carrying them out and specific feedback so that he perceives benefit to himself from that behavior and may more specifically learn the consequences of his actions and thus increase self-discipline and personal effectiveness.

Any treatment program for Mr. Wayne should include both individual and group psychotherapy specifically to deal with the treatment needs outlined in no. 1, as well as treatment conditions spelled out in recommendations 2 through 5. Any performance-oriented program produces a special counseling need for Mr. Wayne because he feels confused and unable to cope with reality and, in fact, distorts reality so significantly that at times he can be deemed psychotic. Extra explanation and counseling support with patience and yet firmness will be needed if a treatment program is effective.

Because of some elements of chronicity, prognosis for improvement with any treatment program is guarded. However, it is felt that unless a treatment program which incorporates *all* of these needs can be provided for Mr. Wayne, he is at serious risk of continuing to disregard the needs and feelings of both himself and other people because of his overwhelming impulsivity, poor behavior controls, and extreme psychopathology.

Although these reports illustrate a wide range of content, detail, and focus, neither included a disclaimer section clearly stating that opinions concerning future dangerousness and potential for violence are based on clinical judgment and that the research literature suggests that such predictions most frequently err in the direction of false positives.

On a more pragmatic note; both defendants described in the two reports were sentenced to long terms in prison. The defendant in the second report has had no reported incidents of violence during the past three years; the defendant in the first report has since murdered four people while in prison.

The applications and issues which involve psychologists with the legal system have by no means been fully cataloged in this chapter. As the relationship between psychology and the law becomes more extensive, new areas of application and further questions of appropriateness are very likely to emerge.

12

Ethics, Constraints, Concerns, and Standards

The burgeoning use of psychologists as experts in legal proceedings continues. Efforts to establish standards and guidelines are just starting. Differences of opinion are bound to arise and will be debated and resolved. Until generally accepted standards are promulgated by organizations familiar with and representative of the work of forensic psychologists, practitioners must make do with current ethical constraints, legal expectations, and professional standards.

ETHICS

There is no code of ethics that applies specifically to forensic psychologists. There may never be one, as such. The *Ethical Principles of Psychologists** (APA, 1981) may provide sufficient guidance so that further general ethical principles will be unnecessary. The first 8 of the 10 APA principles provide clear general constraints for the psychologist who serves as expert witness:

---

* Copyright 1981 by the American Psychological Association. Reprinted by permission.

Principle 1

RESPONSIBILITY

In providing services, psychologists maintain the highest standards of their profession. They accept responsibility for the consequences of their acts and make every effort to ensure that their services are used appropriately.

Principle 2

COMPETENCE

The maintenance of high standards of competence is a responsibility shared by all psychologists in the interest of the public and the profession as a whole. Psychologists recognize the boundaries of their competence and the limitations of their techniques. They only provide services and only use techniques for which they are qualified by training and experience. In those areas in which recognized standards do not yet exist, psychologists take whatever precautions are necessary to protect the welfare of their clients. They maintain knowledge of current scientific and professional information related to the services they render.

Principle 3

MORAL AND LEGAL STANDARDS

Psychologists' moral and ethical standards of behavior are a personal matter to the same degree as they are for any other citizen, except as these may compromise the fulfillment of their professional responsibilities or reduce the public trust in psychology and psychologists. Regarding their own behavior, psychologists are sensitive to prevailing community standards and to the possible impact that conformity to or deviation from these standards may have upon the quality of their performance as psychologists. Psychologists are also aware of the possible impact of their public behavior upon the ability of colleagues to perform their professional duties.

Principle 4

PUBLIC STATEMENTS

Public statements, announcements of services, advertising, and promotional activities of psychologists serve the purpose of helping the public make informed judgments and choices. Psychologists represent accurately and objectively their professional qualifications, affiliations, and functions, as well as those of the institutions or organizations with which they or the statements may be associated. In public statements providing psychological information or professional opinions or providing information about the availability of psychological products, publications, and services, psychologists base their statements on scientifically acceptable psychological findings and techniques with full recognition of the limits and uncertainties of such evidence.

Principle 5

CONFIDENTIALITY

Psychologists have a primary obligation to respect the confidentiality of information obtained from persons in the course of their work as psychologists. They reveal such information to others only with the consent of the person or the person's legal representative, except in those unusual circumstances in which not to do so would result in clear danger to the person or to others. Where appropriate, psychologists inform their clients of the legal limits of confidentiality.

Principle 6

WELFARE OF THE CONSUMER

Psychologists respect the integrity and protect the welfare of the people and groups with whom they work. When conflicts of interest arise between clients and psychologists' employing institutions, psychologists clarify the nature and direction of their loyalties and responsibilities and keep all parties informed of their commitments. Psychologists fully inform consumers as to the purpose and nature of an evaluative, treatment, educational, or training procedure, and they freely acknowledge that clients, students, or participants in research have freedom of choice with regard to participation.

Principle 7

PROFESSIONAL RELATIONSHIPS

Psychologists act with due regard for the needs, special competencies, and obligations of their colleagues in psychology and other professions. They respect the prerogatives and obligations of the institutions or organizations with which these other colleagues are associated.

Principle 8

ASSESSMENT TECHNIQUES

In the development, publication, and utilization of psychological assessment techniques, psychologists make every effort to promote the welfare and best interests of the client. They guard against the misuse of assessment results. They respect the client's right to know the results, the interpretations made, and the bases for their conclusions and recommendations. Psychologists make every effort to maintain the security of tests and other assessment techniques within limits of legal mandates. They strive to ensure the appropriate use of assessment techniques by others.

Principles 9 and 10, "Research With Human Participants" and "Care and Use of Animals," are unlikely to apply to the work of the psychologist as expert witness.

Although general in nature, no cogent argument has yet appeared to suggest that these principles would not apply when psychologists appear as experts in legal proceedings.

PRIVILEGED COMMUNICATION AND CONFIDENTIALITY

Many psychologists confuse the concept of "confidentiality" with that of "patient privilege." In certain respects, the ethical standard concerning confidentiality (the professional's obligation never to reveal information obtained in the professional relationship without specific permission from the client) is at odds with the legal concept of privileged communication (legal constraints on the psychologist not to reveal information about the client obtained in the course of professional contacts). The ethical constraint against revealing confidential information is almost absolute, allowing only the leeway of revealing a confidence in the duty to warn where dangerousness is predicted. Both the APA Code of Ethics and the law seem to agree that psychologists should be able to determine when a patient poses a serious danger of violence to others (Shah, 1977).

Privileged communication is granted by statute. Each state usually specifies in its professional codes the nature, extent, and limitations of privileged communication.

The following excerpts from the California Evidence Code (1009–1028) illustrate how privilege is granted and the 13 exceptions that specify the conditions under which a psychologist *cannot* refuse to testify in the State of California.

1009. General Provisions.

(a) Except as otherwise provided in this section, the right of any person to claim a privilege provided in Section 954 (lawyer–client privilege), 980 (privilege for confidential marital communications), 994 (physician–patient privilege), 1014 (psychotherapist–patient privilege), 1033 (privilege of penitent), or 1034 (privilege of clergyman) is waived with respect to a communication protected by such privilege if any holder of the privilege, without coercion, has disclosed a significant part of the communication or has consented to such disclosure made by anyone. Consent to disclosure is manifested by any statement or other conduct of the holder of the privilege indicating his consent to the disclosure, indicating his failure to claim the privilege in any proceedings in which he has the legal standing and opportunity to claim the privilege.

(b) Where two or more persons are joint holders of a privilege provided by Section 954 (lawyer–client privilege), 994 (physician–patient privilege), or 1014 (psychotherapist–patient privilege), a waiver of the right of a particular joint holder of the privilege to claim the privilege does not affect the right of another joint holder to claim the privilege. In the case of the privilege provided by Section 980 (privilege for confidential marital communications), a waiver of the right of one spouse to claim the privilege does not affect the right of the other spouse to claim the privilege.

(c) A disclosure that is itself privileged is not a waiver of any privilege.

(d) A disclosure in confidence of a communication that is protected by Section 954 (lawyer–client privilege), 994 (physician–patient privilege), or 1014 (psychotherapist–patient privilege), when such disclosure is reasonably necessary for the accomplishment of the purpose for which the lawyer, physician, or psychotherapist was consulted, is not a waiver of the privilege.

1010. "Psychotherapist."
As used in this article, "psychotherapist" means:

(a) A person authorized, or reasonably believed by the patient to be authorized, to practice medicine in any state or nation who devotes, or is reasonably believed by the patient to devote, a substantial portion of his time to the practice of psychiatry.

(b) A person licensed as a psychologist under Chapter 6.6 (commencing with Section 2900) of Division 2 of the Business and Professions Code.

(c) A person licensed as a clinical social worker under Article 4 (commencing with Section 9040) of Chapter 17 of Division 3 of the Business and Professions Code, when he is engaged in applied psychotherapy of a nonmedical nature.

(d) A person who is serving as a school psychologist and holds a credential authorizing such service issued by the state.

(e) A person licensed as a marriage, family and child counselor under Chapter 4 (commencing with Section 1780) of Part 3, Division 5 of the Business and Professions Code.

1011. "Patient."
As used in this article, "patient" means a person who consults a psychotherapist or submits to an examination by a psychotherapist for the purpose of securing a diagnosis or preventive, palliative, or curative treatment of his mental or emotional condition or who submits to an examination of his mental or emotional condition for the purpose of scientific research on mental or emotional problems.

1012. "Confidential communication between patient and psychotherapist."
As used in this article, "confidential communication between patient and psychotherapist" means information, including information obtained by an examination of the patient, transmitted between a patient and his psychotherapist in the course of that relationship and in confidence by a means which, so far as the patient is aware, discloses the information to no third persons other than those who are present to further the interest of the patient in the consultation, or those to whom disclosure is reasonably necessary for the transmission of the information or the accomplishment of the purpose for which the psychotherapist is consulted, and includes a diagnosis made and the advice given by the psychotherapist in the course of that relationship.

1013.   "Holder of the privilege."
As used in this article, "holder of the privilege" means:

(a)   The patient when he has no guardian or conservator.

(b)   The guardian or conservator of the patient when the patient has a guardian or conservator.

(c)   The personal representative of the patient if the patient is dead.

1014.   Psychotherapist–Patient Privilege; Application to Individuals and Entities.
Subject to Section 912 and except as otherwise provided in this article, the patient, whether or not a party, has a privilege to refuse to disclose, and to prevent another from disclosing, a confidential communication between patient and psychotherapist if the privilege is claimed by:

(a)   The holder of the privilege;

(b)   A person who is authorized to claim the privilege by the holder of the privilege; or

(c)   The person who was the psychotherapist at the time of the confidential communication, but such person may not claim the privilege if there is no holder of the privilege in existence or if he is otherwise instructed by a person authorized to permit disclosure.

1015.   When Psychotherapist Requires to Claim Privilege.
The psychotherapist who received or made a communication subject to the privilege under this article shall claim the privilege whenever he is present when the communication is sought to be disclosed and is authorized to claim the privilege under subdivision (c) of Section 1014.

1016.   Exception: Patient–Litigant Exception. There is no privilege under this article as to a communication relevant to an issue concerning the mental or emotional condition of the patient if such issue has been tendered by:

(a)   The patient;

(b)   Any party claiming through or under the patient;

(c)   Any party claiming as a beneficiary of the patient through a contract to which the patient is or was a party; or

(d)   The plaintiff in an action brought under Section 376 or 377 of the Code of Civil Procedure for damages for the injury or death of the patient.

1017.   Exception: Court-Appointed Psychotherapist. There is no privilege under this article if the psychotherapist is appointed by order of a court to examine the patient, but this exception does not apply where the psychotherapist is appointed by order of the court upon the request of the lawyer for the defendant in a criminal proceeding in order to provide the lawyer with information needed so that he may advise the defendant whether to enter or withdraw a plea based on insanity or to present a defense based on his mental or emotional condition.

1018.   Exception: Crime or Tort. There is no privilege under this article if the services of the psychotherapist were sought or obtained to enable or aid anyone to commit or plan to commit a crime or a tort or to escape detection or apprehension after the commission of a crime or a tort.

1019.   Exception: Parties Claiming Through Deceased Patient. There is no privilege under this article as to a communication relevant to an issue between parties all of whom claim through a deceased patient, regardless of whether the claims are by testate or intestate succession or by inter vivos transaction.

1020.   Exception: Breach of Duty Arising out of Psychotherapist–Patient Relationship. There is no privilege under this article as to a communication relevant to an issue of breach, by the psychotherapist or by the patient, of a duty arising out of the psychotherapist–patient relationship.

1021.   Exception: Intention of Deceased Patient Concerning Writing Affecting Property Interest. There is no privilege under this article as to a communication relevant to an issue concerning the intention of a patient, now deceased, with respect to a deed of conveyance, will, or other writing, executed by the patient, purporting to affect an interest in property.

1022.   Exception: Validity of Writing Affecting Property Interest. There is no privilege under this article as to a communication relevant to an issue concerning the validity of a deed of conveyance, will, or other writing, executed by a patient, now deceased, purporting to affect an interest in property.

1023.   Exception: Proceeding to Determine Sanity of Criminal Defendant. There is no privilege under this article in a proceeding under Chapter 6 (commencing with Section 1367) of Title 10 of Part 2 of the Penal Code initiated at the request of the defendant in a criminal action to determine his sanity.

1024.   Exception: Patient Dangerous to Himself or Others. There is no privilege under this article if the psychotherapist has reasonable cause to believe that the patient is in such mental or emotional condition as to be dangerous to himself or to the person or property of another and that disclosure of the communication is necessary to prevent the threatened danger.

1025.   Exception: Proceeding to Establish Competence. There is no privilege under this article in a proceeding brought by or on behalf of the patient to establish his competence.

1026.   Exception: Required Report. There is no privilege under this article as to information that the psychotherapist or the patient is required to report to a public employee or as to information required to be recorded in a public office, if such report or record is open to public inspection.

1027.   Exception: Child Under 16 Victim of Crime. There is no privilege under this article if all of the following circumstances exist:

(a)   The patient is a child under the age of 16.

(b)   The psychotherapist has reasonable cause to believe that the patient has been the victim of a crime and that disclosure of the communication is in the best interest of the child.

1028.   Exception: Unqualified Psychotherapist. Unless the psychotherapist is a person described in subdivision (a) or (b) of Section 1010, there is no privilege under this article in a criminal proceeding.

The psychologist who serves as an expert witness should be very familiar with the laws regarding privileged communication so as to be able to inform the client of both the privilege and the exceptions. In most circumstances where the client's psychological status is a part of the litigation, there is an exception to the usual privilege.

STANDARDS

Psychologists by and large are very concerned with issues of standards and competence (APA, 1977). American jurisprudence has developed certain standards for the expert witness. Rule 702 of the *Federal Rules of Evidence* (1975) states:

> If scientific, technical or other specialized knowledge will assist the trier of fact to understand the evidence or to determine a fact in issue, a witness qualified as an expert by knowledge, skill, experience, training, or education, may testify thereto in the form of an opinion or otherwise.

The principles regarding expert testimony were reiterated by the U.S. Court of Appeals for the Ninth Circuit in its Amaral decision.[1] The general principles regarding testimony by an expert witness can be summarized as follows:

1. **The Witness Must Be a Qualified Expert.**   During qualification, the judge hears a recitation of the proffered expert's education, training, and experience and decides whether the testimony of the witness is to be admitted.

2. **The Testimony Must Be about a Proper Subject Matter.**   To qualify, the testimony must present information beyond the knowledge and experience of the average jury panelist. Further, the testimony of the expert must not invade the jurors' province by evaluating evidence or witnesses.

3. **The Expert's Testimony Should Be in Accordance with a Generally Accepted Explanatory Theory.**   The expert's testimony is expected to meet the test put forth in *Frye v. United States* that the scientific community accepts and agrees about the reliability and validity of devices or machines that are used to come to conclusions or opinions presented by the expert witness.[2] This principle is seldom applied to the testimony of medical experts or psychologists.[3] This principle may be applied more stringently in the future.

---

[1] *United States v. Amaral*, 488 F.2d 1148 (9th Cir. 1973).

[2] *Frye v. United States*, 293 F. 1013 (D.C. Cir. 1923).

[3] *Coppolino v. State*, 223 So.2d 68 (Fla. App. 1968), *appeals dismissed*, 234 So.2d 120 (Fla. 1969), *cert. denied*, 399 U.S. 927 (1970).

4. **The Probative Value of the Testimony Must Outweigh Its Prejudicial Effect.**   Probative value refers to evidence that is important in determining culpability or liability. If the expert's testimony has no relationship to the issue of guilt or innocence or the issues of contention between two parties, it is generally not admissible. The judge must also ensure that the expert's testimony does not unduly or unrealistically prejudice the members of the jury or confuse the issue at hand.

There are those who have suggested that the *Frye* test is too stringent (Suggs, 1979), while others have proposed that psychologists should generally not be experts in the courtroom (Ziskin, 1981, 1981a). Bazelon (1974), Bonnie and Slobogin (1980), and Morse (1978) have proposed that the testimony of mental health professionals is of questionable value. Poythress (1982) has responded to these critiques by pointing out that psychologists are acting with reasonable restraint as credible experts. Poythress suggests that scientific or academic colleagues are sometimes unaware of the courtroom realities of testifying as expert witness.

McCloskey and Egeth (1983) have presented a thoughtful philosophical critique of the use of psychologists as expert witnesses in cases involving eyewitness testimony. They suggest such testimony may not only be unhelpful but could conceivably have detrimental effects on jurors' ability to evaluate eyewitness testimony. Loftus (1983) has responded to these arguments with pragmatic examples of the importance of psychological testimony in this area.

Given the amount of growing concern about what psychologists should and should not do in the courtroom, as well as the paucity of specific standards for such activity, it would seem that it is time to explore possible guidelines. The following are proposed:

A.   Quality of Work

1.   The psychologist should follow the principles and standards for scientific and professional conduct promulgated by the American Psychological Association.

2.   All procedures utilized by the psychologist in the process of research review, assessment, research, or evaluation preliminary to an appearance as an expert witness should be carefully documented and available for discovery procedures, direct examination, and cross-examination.

3.   Before testifying as an expert witness, the psychologist should submit a written report of findings and opinions to the attorney or the court that has retained the psychologist.

4.   The quality of work done, the practices and procedures used, and

the conclusions reached should follow the usual and customary standards of the profession.

5. The psychologist who gives evidence as an expert witness should be sure that the opinions rendered are consonant with the current research base in the behavioral sciences.

6. Opinions and conclusions rendered by the psychologist serving as an expert witness should be supported by a known and generally respected theoretical position.

B. Competence and Decorum

1. The psychologist who serves as an expert witness represents psychology when appearing in court and should conduct himself or herself with such professional skill and style as to bring credit to the science and profession of psychology.

2. The psychologist who represents himself or herself as an expert witness should be prepared to demonstrate education, training, and experience in the avowed area of expertise sufficient to meet the standards of psychology and the requirements of the court.

3. The psychologist as expert witness should be sufficiently familiar with local, state, and federal statutes regarding the role of the expert witness in order to serve that role without confusion or errors of ignorance.

4. The psychologist who serves as an expert witness should be sufficiently familiar with the case law associated with the matter at hand so that the evidence presented by the expert will be appropriate and probative.

5. The psychologist who serves as an expert witness should ensure that sufficient consultation takes place before deposition or trial so that the attorney who has retained the psychologist understands the extent as well as the limits of the expert's findings and opinions.

6. Where clients, patients, or defendants are involved in the matter at hand, the psychologist who is to act as an expert witness should understand, and clearly state to all parties involved, the nature and limitations of privileged communication in the case.

7. When in doubt about any practice or procedure, the psychologist preparing to serve as an expert witness should consult with an attorney and/or an experienced colleague for guidance, within the constraints of professional ethics and privileged communication.

8. When testifying as an expert witness, the psychologist should ensure that nothing in his or her report or testimony infringes on the responsibilities or privileges of the triers of fact by rendering opinions concerning the verdict in the litigation to which the expert testimony is directed.

C. Financial Arrangements

1. The psychologist should never accept a fee contingent upon the outcome of a case.

2. The fee structure and details of reimbursement should be established between the psychologist and the retaining attorney during the initial consultation. The understanding should be in writing between the two parties.

3. All outstanding fees should be paid before the psychologist testifies.

4. Misunderstandings or disagreements about fees should be resolved before proceeding in the case.

5. Psychologists who testify regularly as expert witnesses should devote some portion of their professional time to *pro bona publica* cases.

As psychologists gain more experience as expert witnesses in a variety of settings, it is expected that standards will be developed and promulgated. The guidelines above are tendered as suggestions, having no special quality or status.

In 1909, Wigmore wrote that the courts were not ready for psychology. In 1937, Wigmore revised his thinking and wrote that the courts are ready for psychology when psychology is ready for the courts. Psychology is ready.

Landmark Cases

Vincent E. JENKINS, Appellant,
v.
UNITED STATES of America,
Appellee.
No. 16306.
United States Court of Appeals
District of Columbia Circuit.
On Rehearing in Banc.
Reargued Feb. 9, 1962.
Decided by Judgment Entered
April 12, 1962.
Opinion Rendered June 7, 1962.

Defendant was convicted of housebreaking with intent to commit an assault, assault with intent to rape and assaut with a dangerous weapon. The defendant relied solely upon defense of insanity. From a judgment of the United States District Court for the District of Columbia, Edward M. Curren, J., the defendant appealed. The Court of Appeals, Bazelon, Circuit Judge, held, inter alia, that the court's sua

Reprinted with permission from 307 F.2d 637. Copyright © 1963 by West Publishing Co.

sponte exclusion of psychiatrist's testimony concerning his changed diagnosis of accused because psychiatrist did not conduct a personal re-examination constituted prejudicial error requiring reversal for new trial, and that the determination of a psychologist's competence to render an expert opinion based on his findings as to presence or absence of mental disease or defect must depend upon nature and extent of his knowledge, and it does not depend upon his claim to title "psychologist," and that determination, after hearing, which may be conducted in presence of jury unless special circumstances warrant its exclusion, must be left in each case to traditional discretion of trial court subject to appellate review.

Reversed and remanded for new trial.

Separate concurring opinion by Fahy, Circuit Judge, with whom Edgerton and Washington, Circuit Judges, concurred.

Separate concurring opinion by Burger, Circuit Judge.

Bastian, Circuit Judge, and Miller, Chief Judge, dissented with opinion.

1. Criminal Law ⟳ 741(4)

Testimony of psychiatrist, whose expert qualifications were unquestioned, that he could arrive at a valid diagnosis of accused's mental capacity on basis of earlier examination and later psychological test reports was improperly excluded since psychiatrist's ability to make revised diagnosis without conducting impersonal re-examination presented a question for jury in assessing weight of his testimony and not a question for court upon which it might rest exclusion of diagnosis as a matter of law.

2. Criminal Law ⟳ 486
   Evidence ⟳ 555

Opinion testimony based in part upon reports of others which are not in evidence but which the expert customarily relies upon in practice of his profession is admissible.

3. Criminal Law ⟳ 486

Where psychiatrist testified that he considered undifferentiated psychosis a possibility when he first examined accused, and improvement in accused's I.Q. scores was inconsistent with mental defect, and induced psychiatrist to abandon that diagnosis in favor of undifferentiated psychosis which was consistent with his earlier clinical observations and later test reports, opinion so formulated was admissible, and any infirmity arising out of psychiatrist's failure to re-examine accused would go to weight and not to admissibility of his opinion.

4. Criminal Law ⟳ 1170(1)

The court's sua sponte exclusion of psychiatrist's testimony concerning his changed diagnosis of accused because psychiatrist did not conduct a personal re-examination constituted prejudicial error requiring reversal for new trial.

5. Criminal Law ⟳ 1038(1)

Court of Appeals would consider alleged error in instruction to disregard testimony of defense psychologist notwithstanding accused failed to object to instruction where instruction presented question which was likely to arise upon a new trial.

6. Criminal Law ⟳ 479

Some psychologists are qualified to render expert testimony in the field of mental disorder.

7. Criminal Law ⟳ 469
   Evidence ⟳ 505

The test in determining admissibility of expert testimony is whether opinion offered will be likely to aid the trier in search for truth.

8. Criminal Law ⟳ 479
   Evidence ⟳ 474(4)

Generally, anyone who is shown to have special knowledge and skill in diagnosing and treating human ailments is qualified to testify as an expert, if his learning and treaining show that he is qualified to give an opinion on particular question at issue, and it is not essential that witness be a medical practitioner.

9. Criminal Law ⟳ 478(1)
   Evidence ⟳ 536

If experience or training enables a proffered expert witness to form an opinion which would aid the jury, in absence of some countervailing consideration, his testimony will be received.

10. Criminal Law ⟳ 481

The determination of a psychologist's competence to render an expert opinion based on his findings as to presence or absence of mental disease or defect must depend upon nature and extent of his knowledge, and it does not depend upon his claim to title "psychologist", and that determination, after hearing, which may be conducted in presence of jury unless special circumstances warrant its exclusion, must be left in each case to traditional discretion of trial court subject to appellate review.

11.   Criminal Law   ⊄ 481

The qualification of particular witness to testify as an expert is largely within domain of trial judge, and particular inquiries which may be appropriate in some cases may be inappropriate in others.

12.   Criminal Law   ⊄ 479

Although there are no statutory criteria for licensing psychologists in District of Columbia to assist trial courts, the American Psychological Association's list of approved graduate training programs provides some guidance, and when completion of such training is followed by actual experience in treatment and diagnosis of disease in association with psychiatrists or neurologists, the opinion of psychologists may properly be received in evidence.

13.   Criminal Law   ⊄ 479

If the post-doctoral experience required for certification has included substantial experience in a hospital or clinical setting in association with psychiatrists or neurologists, clinical psychologists who are diplomates of the American Board of Examiners in Professional Psychology should ordinarily qualify as expert witnesses.

14.   Criminal Law   ⊄ 479, 481

The lack of a medical degree, and lesser degree of responsibility for a patient care which mental hospitals usually assign to psychologists, are not automatic disqualifications of psychologists to testify as experts, but where relevant, these matters may be shown to affect the weight of their testimony, even though it be admitted in evidence, and critical factor in respect to admissibility is actual experience of witness and the probable probative value of his opinion, and trial judge should make a finding in respect to individual qualifications of each challenged expert.

15.   Criminal Law   ⊄ 481, 741(4)

Qualifications to experess an opinion on a given topic are to be decided by trial judge alone, and weight to be given any expert opinion admitted in evidence by judge is exclusively for jury, and they should be so instructed.

16.   Criminal Law   ⊄ 432

Determination of accused's eligibility to stand trial may be established by a finding of "restored competency" or a finiding that he never was incompetent, and hence assuming that a proceeding to set aside original adjudication of incompetency is required, substance of such proceeding was provided by hearing in which hospital psychiatrist testified that accused was not a mental defective and that there was no indication of organic brain injury or mental illness. D.C. Code 1951, § 24–301(b).

Mr. Gerald Golin, Washington, D.C. (appointed by the District Court) for appellant.

Mr. Anthony G. Amsterdam, Asst. U. S. Atty., with whom Messrs. David C. Acheson, U. S. Atty., Charles T. Duncan, Principal Asst. U. S. Atty., and Harry T. Alexander, Asst. U. S. Atty., at the time the brief was filed, were on the brief, for appellee. Messrs. Nathan J. Paulson and David J. McTague, Asst. U. S. Attys., also entered appearances for appellee.

Messrs. Arthur B. Hanson, Dean Farrington Cochran and Samuel J. L'Hommedieu, Jr., Washington, D. C., filed a brief on behalf of American Psychological Association, as *amicus curiae*, urging reversal.

Mr. Warren E. Magee, Washington, D. C., filed a brief on behalf of American Psychiatric Association, as *amicus curiae*, urging affirmance.

Before WILBUR K. MILLER, Chief Judge, EDGERTON, PRETTYMAN, BAZELON, FAHY, WASHINGTON, DANAHER, BASTIAN and BURGER, Circuit Judges, sitting *in banc*.

BAZELON, Circuit Judge.

Appellant relied solely upon the defense of insanity in a jury trial which culminated in his conviction for housebreaking with intent to commit an assault, assault with intent to rape, and assault with a dangerous weapon. He alleges that the District Court erred in (1) determining his competency to stand trial, (2) excluding diagnostic opinions of two defense psychiatrists on the ground that their opinions were without "proper basis," (3) instructing the jury to disregard the testimony on three defense psychologists that appellant had a mental disease or defect on the ground that "a psychologist is not competent to give a medical opinion as to a mental disease or defect," and (4) depriving him of a fair trial by conducting a lengthy and disparaging examination of some expert witnesses.

I. The Facts

The record discloses the following pertinent information. After indictment, appellant was committed to the District General Hospital for a mental examination on September 4, 1959, to determine his competency to stand trial and his condition at the time of the alleged offense.[1] Appellant was given a series of psychological tests on October 20 and 22, 1959, by staff psychologists under the supervision of the Chief Psychologist, Dr. Bernard I. Levy. Appellant scored 63, high moron, on the I.Q. section of the tests. He was also interviewed three or four times by Dr. Richard Schaengold, Assistant Chief Psychiatrist. Appellant's test performance and his "dullness and inability to relate correctly" led Dr. Schaengold to consider and reject the possibility of undifferentiated psychosis in favor of a diagnosis of mental defect: a basic, unchanging deficiency in brain function.[2] His findings were confirmed by Dr. Mary V. McIndoo, District General's Chief Psychiatrist, on the basis of interviews on November 23, 24 and 25, and a review of appellant's history and test results. By letter of November 25, 1959, signed by Dr. Schaengold and countersigned by Dr. McIndoo, the District Court was advised that appellant was "suffering from an organic brain defect resulting in mental deficiency and impaired judgment. He is, therefore, psychotic, incompetent, and incapable of participating in his own defense." Appellant was adjudicated incompetent to stand trial on the basis of this report and was committed to "Saint Elizabeths Hospital until he is mentally competent

---

[1] See generally Winn v. United States, 106 U.S.App.D.C. 133, 270 F.2d 326 (1959).

[2] Durham v. United States, 94 U.S. App.D.C. 228, 241, 214 F.2d 862, 875, 45 A.L.R.2d 1430 (1954).

to stand trial pursuant to Title 24, Section 301, District of Columbia Code, 1951 Edition, as amended August 9, 1955."

At St. Elizabeths, Dr. Lawrence Tirnauer, a staff psychologist, administered another battery of psychological tests on February 25 and March 2, 1960, in which appellant scored 74 on the I.Q. section. Dr. Tirnauer concluded that appellant was suffering from schizophrenia. Thereafter Dr. David J. Owens of St. Elizabeths interviewed appellant several times, "probably [for] fifteen or twenty minutes," and saw him at a staff conference on October 3, 1960. Dr. Owens found no evidence of mental disease or defect. He classified appellant as "a borderline intelligence." Dr. William G. Cushard, another psychiatrist at St. Elizabeths, who saw appellant at the staff conference, reviewed the test reports and agreed with Dr. Owens' findings. Dr. Margaret Ives, Chief Psychologist at St. Elizabeths, was also present at the staff conference. Subsequently, she reviewed Dr. Tirnauer's test results and appellant's past history and administered one part of a six-part Szondi profile test. She agreed with Dr. Tirnauer that appellant "had a mental illness by name of schizophrenia."

Ten days later, the Acting Superintendent of the Hospital notified the District Court that "it has been determined that he [appellant] is, at this time, mentally competent to stand trial and to consult with counsel and assist properly in his own defense. He is not suffering from mental disease * * *. Although he is not suffering from mental deficiency, he has only borderline intelligence." Upon appellant's objection to this report, the court conducted a hearing on November 4, 1960, wherein appellant was found competent and ordered to stand trial.

In preparation for their testimony at trial, Drs. McIndoo and Schaengold noted the later and different diagnosis and the apparent change in appellant's I.Q. reported by the St. Elizabeths psychologists. They requested Dr. Levy of their staff to re-test appellant in order to reconsider their diagnoses that he was mentally defective on June 10, 1959, the date of the alleged offenses. This time appellant scored 90 on the I.Q. test, an improvement inconsistent with mental defect. In reporting this result, Dr. Levy, who had previously been unable to make a diagnosis, concluded that upon review of all test data appellant "is psychotic and schizophrenic." Considering this report in the light of the hospital record and "reports" from St. Elizabeths, Drs. McIndoo and Schaengold revised their previous diagnoses without seeing appellant again. Dr. McIndoo concluded that appellant was schizophrenic, and Dr. Schaengold diagnosed his condition as undifferentiated psychosis.

II. Admissibility of the Psychiatrists' Opinions

The trial court, *sua sponte*, excluded the revised diagnoses of Drs. McIndoo and Schaengold and instructed the jury to disregard testimony of the three defense psychologists that appellant had a mental disease when he committed the crimes charged.

We discuss first the exclusion of Dr. Schaengold's testimony. After questioning him at great length about the basis of his revised opinion, the court rules: "All I will allow is that in his opinion on June 10, 1959 [the date of the alleged offenses], the defendant was mentally defective"; it excluded Dr. Schaengold's later diagnosis of mental illness because "there isn't any testimony here that is based on any proper evidence that he was suffering from a mental disease. I am not going to allow it on the basis of a report of a psychologist." The court gave no further explanation.

The Government suggests that the ruling rests on the familiar principle that an expert witness' knowledge of "basic facts" must be adequate to support his conclusion.[3] It urges that the later psychological reports could not provide Dr. Schaengold with such information, "absent a personal re-examination of appellant," since thirteen months had elapsed between his personal examination of appellant and his revised diagnosis. The proposition seems to be that a psychiatric witness may not rely on psychological test reports unless he has considered them in conjunction with a contemporaneous personal examination. We are aware of no authority for such a rigid and artifical stricture.[4]

[1] Dr. Schaengold, whose expert qualifications were unquestioned, testified that he could arrive at a valid diagnosis on the basis of an earlier examination and later test reports. The court must be deemed to have rejected this statement. We find no basis for such action. We think it clear that Dr. Schaengold's ability to make the revised diagnosis without conducting a personal re-examination presents a question for the consideration of the jury, under appropriate instructions, in assessing the weight of his testimony and not a question for the court upon which it may rest exclusion of the diagnosis as a matter of law.

[2, 3] It is at least as likely, however, that the court predicated its ruling on cases which bar an expert's opinion based upon facts not in evidence unless it is derived solely from his own observations.[5] But we agree with the leading commentators[6] that the better reasoned authorities admit opinion testimony based, in part, upon reports of others which are not in evidence but which the expert customarily relies upon in the practice of his profession.[7] The Wisconsin Supreme Court has forcefully stated the policy underlying the application of this rule to medical testimony:

"In order to say that a physician, who has actually used the result of * * * tests in a diagnosis * * * may not testify what that diagnosis was, the court must deliberately shut its eyes to a source of information which is

---

[3] Toho Bussan Kaisha, Ltd. v. American Pres. Lines, Ltd., 265 F.2d 418, 76 A.L.R. 2d 1344 (2d Cir. 1959); Haug v. Grimm, 251 F.2d 523 (8th Cir. 1958). The Government cites United States v. Alker, 260 F.2d 135, 155 (3d Cir. 1958), cert. denied, 359 U.S. 906, 79 S.Ct. 579, 3 L.Ed. 2d 571 (1959), where the proposition appears as dictum.

The Government's reliance upon Blunt v. United States, 100 U.S.App.D.C. 266, 275, 244 F.2d 355, 364 (1957); and Carter v. United States, 102 U.S.App.D.C. 227, 236, 252 F.2d 608, 617 (1957), is misplaced since our discussion of the absence of detailed testimony concerning the underlying basis for the psychiatrists' opinions related to the weight of the testimony and not its admissibility.

[4] Cf. Williams v. United States, 104 U.S.App.D.C. 277, 278, 261, F.2d 743, 744 (1958), where we held that a new trial would be required if appellant could establish his allegations concerning newly discovered evidence of changed psychiatric opinion "without additional examination of appellant."

[5] E.g., People v. Black, 367 Ill. 209, 10 N.E.2d 801 (1937) (alternative holding); Equitable Life Assur. Soc'y v. Kazee, 257 Ky. 803, 79 S.W.2d 208 (1935) (dictum). See generally McCormick, Evidence § 15 (1955).

[6] McCormick, Evidence § 15 (1955). See 3 Wigmore, Evidence § 688 (3d ed. 1940).

[7] Taylor v. Monougahela Ry., 155 F. Supp. 601, 604 (W.D.Pa.1957), aff'd per curiam, 256 F.2d 751 (3d Cir. 1958); Sundquist v. Madison Ry., 197 Wis. 83, 221 N.W. 392 (1928); Schooler v. State, 175 S.W.2d 664 (Tex.Civ.App.1943).

relied on by mankind generally in matters that involve the health and may involve the life of their families and of themselves—a source of information that is essential that the court should possess in order that it may do justice between these parties litigant.

"This court * * * will not close the doors of the courts to the light which is given by a diagnosis which all the rest of the world accepts and acts upon, even if the diagnosis is in part based upon facts which are not established by the sworn testimony in the case to be true" [Sundquist v. Madison Ry., 197 Wis. 83, 221 N.W. 392, 393 (1928).

The record in this case confirms the well-known practice of psychiatrists of relying upon psychologists' reports in aid of diagnosis.[8] And it shows that Dr. Schaengold's changed diagnosis did not rest solely on the later test reports which were not in evidence when he testified,[9] but also upon his own earlier examination.[10] This diagnosis was "the type of clinical opinion he is accus-

tomed to form and to rely upon in the practice of his profession. * * * Though [his] conclusions were not mathematically demonstrable certainites, neither were they mere conjectures, suspicions or hunches." Blunt v. United States, 100 U.S.App.D.C. 266, 275, 244 F.2d 355, 364 (1957).

[4] It follows from the foregoing that the court's *sua sponte* exclusion of Dr. Schaengold's testimony concerning his changed diagnosis was error.[11] Since the exclusion was clearly prejudicial, the conviction must be reversed for a new trial.[12]

Appellant also objects to the similar exclusion of Dr. McIndoo's revised diagnosis. She testified that the later tests induced her to change her opinion. But when the court, in very extensive questioning, made clear its view barring reliance upon psychological test reports, she stated that she "did not have a medical opinion about the new diagnosis." At one point she said, "I'm strictly confused now." Later the following occurred:

THE COURT: Would you express an opinion as to a person's mental conditon on the basis of a report given to you by a psychologist?

THE WITNESS: I do, Your Honor, very fequently.

THE COURT: Without even seeing the patient?

---

[8] Hidden v. Mutual Life Ins. Co., 217 F.2d 818, 821 (4th Cir. 1954); Scheflen, The Psychologist as a Witness, 32 Pa.Bar Ass'n Q. 329, 333 (1961). See McDonald, Psychiatry and the Criminal 162 (1958).

[9] Such reliance would amount to offering an opinion of another in violation of the hearsay rule. Cf. McCormick, Evidence § 15 (1955).

[10] Dr. Schaengold testified that he considered undifferentiated psychosis a possibility when he first examined appellant. The improvement in appellant's I.Q. scores was inconsistent with mental defect, and induced Dr. Schaengold to abandon that diagnosis in favor of undifferentiated psychosis which was consistent both with his earlier clinical observations and the later test reports. An opinion so formulated is admissible. Cf. Williams v. United States, supra note 4. Any infirmity arising out of Dr. Schaengold's failure to re-examine appellant would go to the weight and not to the admissibility of his opinion. Cf. Brill v. Mushinsky, 90 U.S. App.D.C. 132, 194 F.2d 158 (1952).

[11] See Hidden v. Mutual Life Ins. Co., supra note 8; Watts v. State, 223 Md. 268, 164 A.2d 334 (1960) (alternative ground).

[12] In holding Dr. Schaengold's testimony admissible, we do not intimate approval of his failure to re-xamine appellant. Compare Winn v. United States, 106 U.S.App.D.C. 133, 270 F.2d 326 (1959); Carter v. United States, 102 U.S.App.D.C. 227, 236, 252 F.2d 608, 617 (1957); Blunt v. United States, 100 U.S.App.D.C. 266, 275, 244 F.2d 355, 364 (1957).

THE WITNESS: In most cases I do see the patient. This person I had seen. He was showing certain signs and symptoms. I made a wrong diagnosis. The suggested diagnosis from a psychologist explains my wrong diagnosis.

Since the new trial required by the exclusion of Dr. Schaengold's testimony will afford an opportunity for clarification of Dr. McIndoo's testimony in light of our earlier discussion, we think it unwise to engage in the speculation required to resolve the meaning of her testimony at the trial under review. Hence we refrain from deciding whether the court erred in excluding her opinion.

III. Admissibility of the Psychologists' Opinions

[5]   The next assignment of error we discuss concerns the court's instruction to the jury to disregard testimony of three defense psychologists that appellant had a mental disease when he committed the crimes charged. Although appellant failed to object to this instruction, we consider it because it presents a question which is likely to arise upon a new trial.[13]

The first psychologist, Dr. Tirnauer, administered a battery of tests to appellant, studied his case history, and concluded he had been suffering from schizophrenia when he committed the crimes. In his opinion, the disease and the crimes were "related." The second psychologist, Dr. Margaret Ives, had reviewed Dr. Tirnauer's test results, had seen appellant at a staff conference, and had administered part of a Szondi profile test. She stated that appellant was suffering from schizophrenia and that

[13] Villaroman v. United States, 87 U.S. App.D.C. 240, 184 F.2d 261, 21 A.L.R. 2d 1074 (1950).

his crimes were the product of the disease. The third psychologist, Dr. Levy, interpreted test results obtained by members of the District General staff in October 1959, and administered two additional tests shortly before trial. He testified that defendant had been suffering from schizophrenia on June 10, 1959, but could give no opinion concerning the relationship between the illness and the crimes. At the conclusion of the trial the court instructed the jury:

"A psychologist is not competent to give a medical opinion as to a mental disease or defect. Therefore, you will not consider any evidence to the effect that the defendant was suffering from a mental disease or a mental defect on June 10, 1959, according to the testimony given by the psychologists."

[6]   The trial court apparently excluded these opinions because psychologists lack medical training. We agree with the weight of authority, however, that some psychologists are qualified to render expert testimony in the field of mental disorder.[14]

We begin by placing this problem in the context of the considerations governing the reception of expert testimony.

"An observer is qualifed to testify because he has firsthand knowledge which the jury does not have of the situation or transaction at issue. The expert has something different to contribute. This is a power to draw inferences from the facts which a jury would

[14] See Hidden v. Mutual Life Ins. Co., supra note 8; Watson v. State, 161 Tex. Cr.R. 5, 273 S.W.2d 879 (1954), rev'd on other grounds on rehearing. People v. Hawthorne, 293 Mich. 15, 291 N.W. 205 (1940) (dictum); State v. Padilla, 66 N.M. 289, 347 P.2d 312, 78 A.L.R.2d 908 (1959) (dictum). See generally, Scheflen, supra note 8; Louisell, The Psychologist in Today's Legal World, 39 Minn.L.Rev. 235 (1955).

not be competent to draw. To warrant the use of expert testimony, then, two elements are required. First, the subject of the inference must be so distinctively related to some science, profession, business or occupation as to be beyond the ken of the average layman, and second, the witness must have such skill, knowledge or experience in that field or calling as to make it appear that his opinion or inference will probably aid the trier in his search for truth. The knowledge may in some fields be derived from reading alone, in some from practice alone, or as is more commonly the case, from both. [McCormick, Evidence § 13 (1954), citing authorities.]"

[7–9] The test, then, is whether the opinion offered will be likely to aid the trier in the search for truth. In light of that purpose, it is hardly surprising that courts do not exclude all but the very best kind of witness. See 2 Wigmore, Evidence § 569 (3 ed. 1940). Accord: Fightmaster v. Mode, 31 Ohio App. 273, 167 N.E. 407 (1928). Thus a general practitioner may testify concerning matters within a medical speciality if his education or experience, or both, involves demonstrable knowledge of the subject. Sher v. DeHaven, 91 U.S.App.D.C. 257, 199 F.2d 777, 36 A.L.R.2d 937 (1952), cert. denied, 345 U.S. 936, 73 S.Ct. 797, 97 L.Ed. 1363 (1953); 2 Wigmore, op. cit. supra. Nor need a skilled witness on a medical subject be duly licensed to practice medicine. Ibid. The general rule is that "anyone who is shown to have special knowledge and skill in diagnosing and treating human ailments is qualified to testify as an expert, if his learning and training show that he is qualified to give an opinion on the particular question at issue." "It is not essential that the witness be a medical practitioner." 32 C.J.S. Evidence § 537 (1942). Thus, non-medical witnesses who have had experience in electrical work may testify to the effects of electrical shock upon the human body.

Vessels v. Kansas City Light & Power Co., 219 S.W. 80 (Mo.Sup.Ct.1920); Blakeney v. Alabama Power Co., 222 Ala. 394, 133 So. 16 (1931). Optometrists, whose training includes instruction in the symptoms of certain eye diseases, may testify to the presence of cataract discovered in the course of fitting glasses, Jackson v. Waller, 126 Conn. 294, 10 A.2d 763 (1940), and to the effect of a scar upon vision. Black Starr Coal Corp. V. Reeder, 278 Ky. 532, 128 S.W.2d 905 (1939). A toxicologist has been permitted to testify to the effect of oxalic acid, a poison, upon the human eye. Reynolds v. Davis, 55 R.I. 20-6, 179 A. 613 (1935). The kinds of witnesses whose opinions courts have received, *even though they lacked medical training and would not be permitted by law to treat the conditions they described,* are legion. The principle to be distilled from the cases is plain: if experience or training enables a proffered expert witness to form an opinion which would aid the jury, in the absence of some countervailing consideration, his testimony will be received.

Suggesting the diagnostic category into which an accused's condition fits, and relating it to his past behavior require skill far in excess of that possessed by laymen. Lest the jury be misled into relying on opinions which are not based upon relevant learning and experience, we must examine the reality behind the title "psychologist." Many psychologists may not qualify to testify concerning mental disease or defect. Their training and experience may not provide an adequate basis for their testimony. Some psychologists, for example, teach and engage in theoretical research in fields unrelated to the diagnosis and treatment of mental disease. Others are employed in personnel administration, still others advise industry on problems of employee morale. See Western Personnel Institute, Opportunities for Psychologists, Psychiatrists, Psychiatric Social Workers 8–10 (1958); Daniel and Louttit, Professional Problems in Psychology 250–52, 297 (1953). Such experience does not ordinarily provide the skill essential to offer expert testimony concerning mental disorders. Cf. Albee, Mental Health Manpower Trends 116 (1959). Some psychologists, moreover, have had no post-graduate instruction. Id. at 121–22.

On the other hand, the Ph.D. in Clinical Psychology involves some—and often much—training and experience in the diagnosis and treatment of mental disorders. Typically, candidates are trained, *inter alia*, in general psychology, theory of personality and psychodynamics, psychopathology, diagnostic methods, therapeutic techniques, selected aspects of physiology and anatomy, and clinical methods. A one-year internship in a mental hospital is required for this degree.[15] After graduation, many clinical psychologists administer and interpret diagnostic tests which elicit the patient's intellectual level, defenses, personality structure, attitudes, feelings, thought and perceptual processes. See 1 Rapaport, Diagnostic Testing 7–9 (1945). In many institutions and clinics their reports, which regularly include opinions concerning the presence or absence of mental disease or defect,[16] are important aids to psychiatrists who customarily have the final responsibility for diagnosis. Some psychologists, moreover, regularly administer psychotherapy and related non-organic therapies in the treatment of certain types of mental disorders.[17]

[10–12] The determination of a psychologist's competence to render an expert opinion based on his findings as to the presence or absence of mental disease or defect must depend upon the nature and extent of his knowledge. It does not depend upon his claim to the title "psychologist." And that determination, after hearing,[18] must be left in each case to the traditional discretion of the trial court subject to appellate review.[19] Although there are no statutory criteria for licensing psychologists in the District of Columbia to assist trial courts,[20] the American Psychological Association's list of approved graduate training programs provides some guidance. When completion of such training is followed by actual experience in the treatment and diagnosis of disease in association with psychiatrists or neurologists, the opinion of the psychologist may properly be received in evidence.

188–205 (1957). See also Joint Commission on Mental Illness and Mental Health, Action for Mental Health 244–50 (1961).

[18] The court may conduct this hearing in the presence of the jury unless special circumstances warrant its exclusion.

[19] Cf. Pollard v. Hawfield, 83 U.S. App.D.C. 174, 170 F.2d 170 (1948), cert. denied, 336 U.S. 909, 69 S.Ct. 514, 93 L.Ed. 1073 (1949). Compare State v. Padilla, 66 N.M. 289, 347 P.2d 312, 78 A.L.R.2d 908 (1959). See also McDonald, supra note 8.

The qualification of a particular witness to testify as an expert is largely within the domain of the trial judge. Particular inquiries which may be appropriate in some cases may be inappropriate in others. The majority of this court think the matter should be left to the sound judicial discretion of the trial judge, with no more specific guidance than is contained in this opinion.

[20] Such statutes are in force in several states. See, e.g., Conn. Gen. Stat. Ann. §§20–188 to 20–191 (1960); Md.Ann.Code Art. 43 §§ 618–620, 629–636 (1957); Mich.Stat.Ann. §§ 14.677(3)–14.677(11) (Supp.1959), Pub. Acts 1959, No. 257.

---

[15] See Report of the Committee on Training in Clinical Psychology of the American Psychological Association, in 2 Am. Psychol. 539, 543–58 (1947). The Association certifies only those programs meeting the standards laid down in this report.

[16] Scheflen, supra note 8.

[17] See Clark, America's Psychologists

[13] Some graduate clinical psychologists, moreover, are certified by the American Board of Examiners in Professional Psychology.[21] Certification, which indicates exceptional professional competence, is awarded upon completion of written and oral examinations in, *inter alia*, diagnosis and treatment.[22] Applicants must have four years, acceptable professional experience and must present credentials, including a sample of their work and letters of recommendation, showing sufficient professional achievement to warrant further examination.[23] The purpose of Board certification is to identify and evaluate psychologists at an advanced professional level. If the postdoctoral experience required for certification has included substantial experience in a hospital or clinical setting in association with psychiatrists or neurologists, clinical psychologists who are diplomates of the American Board of Examiners in Professional Psychology should ordinarily qualify as expert witnesses.

[14, 15] We need not decide whether the three psychologists who testified for the defense at the trial under review were qualified to offer expert opinions since they may not be called to testify at the retrial.[24] We hold only that

the lack of a medical degree, and the lesser degree of responsibility for patient care which mental hospitals usually assign to psychologists, are not automatic disqualifications. Where relevant, these matters may be shown to affect the weight of their testimony, even though it be admitted in evidence. The critical factor in respect to admissibility is the actual experience of the witness and the probable value of his opinion. The trial judge should make a finding in respect to the individual qualifications of each challenged expert. Qualifications to express an opinion on a given topic are to be decided by the judge alone.[25] The weight to be given any expert opinion admitted in evidence by the judge is exclusively for the jury.[26] They should be so instructed.

IV.   Competency to Stand Trial

[16]   Another ground urged for reversal is that the November 4 order adjudicating appellant competent to stand trial was not authorized by D.C.Code § 24–301(b). That section provides, in substance, that when an accused person *"is restored* to mental competency" and when the hospital superintendent so certifies, the court may enter an adjudication of competence "unless the accused or the Government objects, in which event, the court, after hearing

---

[21] Kelley, Sanford & Clark, The Meaning of the ABEPP Diploma, 16 Am.Psychol. 132–34 (1961). Prior to 1949, the Board waived the Ph.D. or examination requirements, or both, if a candidate was judged qualified on the basis of training, professional experience and his colleagues' endorsements. Id. at 132.

[22] Id. at 134, 138.

[23] Id. at 134.

[24] The trial judge might have concluded that one or more of the three defense psychologists were competent to testify as experts. All are clinical psychologists; all hold doctoral degrees from institutions approved by the American Psychological Association; all are associated with psychiatrists and neu-

rologists in a hospital setting in the diagnosis and treatment of mental illness. Two were chief psychologists at the hospitals where they were employed, and the third had diagnosed more than a hundred patients during his three years at St. Elizabeths.

[25] Sher v. De Haven, 91 U.S.App.D.C. 257, 199 F.2d 777, 36 A.L.R.2d 937 (1952), cert. denied, 345 U.S. 936, 73 S.Ct. 797, 97 L.Ed. 1363 (1953).

[26] O'Donnell v. Geneva Metal Wheel Co., 183 F.2d 733 (6th Cir. 1950), cert. denied, 341 U.S. 903, 71 S.Ct. 612, 95 L.Ed. 1342 (1951).

without a jury, shall make a judicial determination of the competency of the accused to stand trial." Emphasis supplied. Here, the Superintendent did not certify that appellant's competency had been "restored" but rather that appellant "is, at this time, mentally incompetent." Upon appellant's objection, the court conducted a hearing in which Dr. David J. Owens, a hospital psychiatrist, testified that appellant was not a mental defective, and that there was no indication of organic brain injury or mental illness. His testimony clearly implied that appellant had been competent when committed. Appellant presented no evidence, and the court adjudicated him "mentally competent to stand trial."

Appellant contends that the statute applies only to cases of "restored competency" and cannot be invoked, as here, to set aside an original adjudication of incompetency. He argues that an adjudication of "restored competency" was precluded by the evidence at the hearing which showed only that appellant's condition was unchanged.

Clearly the determination of appellant's eligibility to stand trial may be established by a finding of "restored competency" or a finding that he never was incompetent. Assuming, *arguendo*, as appellant implies, that a proceeding to set aside the original adjudication of incompetency is required, we think the substance of such proceeding was provided by the hearing conducted below. Appellant does not claim that he was surprised or otherwise prejudiced by the Government's evidence that he never was incompetent.

Appellant's remaining contention concerns the conduct of the trial court in questioning certain expert witnesses. Since this issue may not arise upon the new trial, we do not consider it.

The judgment of conviction is reversed and the case is remanded to the

District Court for further proceedings in accordance with this opinion.[27]

Reversed and remanded for a new trial.*

FAHY, Circuit Judge (concurring).

Having joined in the opinion issued October 26, 1961, reversing and remanding for a new trial, I join now in similar action taken by the court after rehearing en banc. I concur generally in the opinion, adding the qualifications to be stated.

While, strictly speaking, it is not necessary, as the present opinion states, to decide whether the three psychologists who testified for the defense at the trial were qualified to offer expert opinions, since they may not be called to testify at the retrial, it would be altogether appropriate to pass upon their qualifications on the record before us; for the record is here for our review of the rulings of the District Court in excluding their testimony. Upon the reasoning of both the original and the present opinions, considered with the facts, I would hold that these witnesses were qualified. A ruling to that effect now would be useful to the District Court.

The main feature of the present opinion, however, is its holding that psychologists may qualify as experts on the question of mental disease or defect under the standards set forth in the opinion. I am in entire agreement with this, which was the gist of the opinion of the division prior to the rehearing en banc.

I an authorized to say that Judges EDGERTON and WASHINGTON join in the views above expressed.

---

[27] See note 19 supra.

* The retirement of Senior Circuit Judge Prettyman became effective April 16, 1962. Prior thereto he concurred in the foregoing opinion and joined in the judgment entered April 12, 1962.

BURGER, Circuit Judge (concurring).

I concur in the remand because the court's basic holding that a psychologist is not barred as a matter of law from giving expert testimony about mental diseases makes it essential that we have a comprehensive record before us on the education and training of psychologists in general and clinical psychologists in particular. This is emphasized by recalling that appellant's entire case in this court, including his oral argument, was based on matter *outside* the record in the form of recitals of what various writers thought on the subject of whether, and to what extent, psychologists should be permitted to testify relating to mental *disease.* Similarly the majority opinion relies largely on "the literature." The literature cited and relied on by the appellant, and indeed by the majority opinion originally, was and is now a series of references selected to support one or the other point of view. They were not developed in the record by an adversary process or subjected to adversary examination. The reason we now remand is to have a record made in an orderly way and in that process authoritative texts, or parts thereof, may well be offered and received, subject, of course, to the established rules of evidence.

At the outset certain factors should be kept in mind. The issue is not now and never was whether a psychologist's testimony is admissible in litigation where "sanity" is in issue. Such testimony has long been admissible in the form of psychological tests and the analysis and explanation of such tests by a psychologist. No one doubts that such matter is admissible. The real issue in dispute is whether the clinical psychologists in this case, by which we mean persons having degrees of Doctor of Philosophy in Psychology, and also additional training as clinical psychologists, are competent in a scientific sense and hence legally qualified.

(1) to make a diagnosis of the existence and character of a mental disease, and
(2) whether there is a causal relationship between a disease and an unlawful act.

The issue can be stated also in terms of whether *medical* opinions and *medical* diagnoses can be made by and be the subject of expert testimony by a Doctor of Philosophy in Psychology with added clinical experience. For convenience I will hereafter refer to such a psychologist as a Clinical Psychologist.

While the issue is new to this court it is not new to medicine and psychiatry. In 1954 a Resolution was adopted by the American Medical Association, the Council of the American Psychiatric Association and the Executive Council of the American Psychoanalytical Association to the effect that psychologists and other related professional groups were autonomous and independent in matters where *medical* questions were *not* involved, but that where *diagnosis* and *treatment* of mental illness was involved the participation of psychologists "must be co-ordinated under medical responsibility."[1] This Resolution, while not

---

[1] The Resolution in full is as follows:
"For centuries the Western world has placed on the medical profession responsibility for the diagnosis and treatment of illness. Medical practice acts have been designed to protect the public from unqualified practitioners and to define the special responsibilities assumed by those who practice the healing art, for much harm may be done by unqualified persons, however good their intentions may be. To do justice to the patient requires the capacity to make a diagnosis and to prescribe appropriate treatment. Diagnosis often requires the ability to compare and

contrast various diseases and disorders that have similar symptoms but different causes. Diagnosis is a continuing process, for the character of the illness changes with its treatment or with the passage of time, and that treatment which is appropriate may change accordingly.

"Recognized medical training today involves, as a minimum, graduation from an approval [*sic*] medical school and internship in a hospital. Most physicians today receive additional medical training, and specialization requires [*sic*] still further training.

"Psychiatry is the medical specialty concerned with illness that has chiefly mental symptoms. The psychiatrist is also concerned with mental causes of physical illness, for we have come to recognize that physical symptoms may have mental causes just as mental symptoms may have physical causes. The psychiatrist, with or without consultation with other physicians, must select from the many different methods of treatment at his disposal those methods that he considers appropriate to the particular patient. His treatment may be medicinal or surgical, physical (as electroshock) or psychological. The systematic application of the methods of psychological medicine to the treatment of illness, particularly as these methods involved gaining an understanding of the emotional state of the patient and aiding him to understand himself, is called psychotherapy. This special form of medical treatment may be highly developed, *but it remains simply one of the possible methods of treatment to be selected for use according to medical criteria for use* when it is indicated. Psychotherapy is a form of medical treatment and does not form the basis for a separate profession.

"Other professional groups such as psychologists, teachers, ministers, lawyers, social workers, and vocational counselors, of course, use psychological understanding in carrying out their professional functions. Members of these professional groups are not thereby practicing medicine. *The application of psychological methods to the treatment of illness is a medical function.* Any physician may utilize the skills of others in his professional work, but he remains responsible, legally and morally, *for the diagnosis and for the treatment of his patient.*

"The medical profession fully endorses

controlling on the courts is plainly entitled to great weight.

My difficulty with the opinion of the majority, as distinguished from the remand for additional evidence, is that it fails to give adequate guidance as to the scope and nature of the inquiry to be conducted by the trial judge on remand. I agree that it is entirely within the discretion of the District Court whether he should conduct the hearing out of the presence of the jury. In this particular case, since this is an exploratory process, there are probably valid practical reasons to hold the hearing out of the presence of the jury although once we resolve the basic problem, that process would not be necessary in future cases.

As I see it, the hearing to be conducted in this case will be somewhat unusual because of the nature of the question and the need for a comprehensive record of testimony. The practical reason for conducting this particular hearing out of the presence of the jury is that the hearing could well take several days. It is not a question which can be resolved simply by examination of the particular psychologists whose testimony is offered. The preliminary hearing on qualifications will be enlarged if the District Judge allows, as he might well do, participation by the several amici curiae, who are highly qualified to be of aid to the court. That would be a dubious process for every future case but entirely appropriate for this case.

---

the appropriate utilization of the skills of psychologists, social workers, and other professional personnel in contributing roles in settings directly supervised by physicians. It further recognizes that these professions are entirely independent and autonomous *when medical questions are not involved;* but when members of these professions contribute *to the diagnosis* and treatment of illness, their professional contributions must be co-ordinated *under medical responsibility.*" (Emphasis added.)

We have said that the conduct of the hearing lies in the sound discretion of the trial judge. But it is not enough to say that it is within the sound discretion of the trial judge and at the same time fail to reflect just what we are driving at.

We must bear in mind that there is a difference between the holdings "that some psychologists are qualified to render expert testimony in the field of mental disorder" (see note 14 majority opinion) and the question of a psychologist's competence to make a diagnosis of *mental disease.* The former proposition is, as we have noted, widely accepted; the latter is not—and it is the latter we are now exploring.

On remand I assume broad areas are to be explored and should be explored in order to give the trial judge, in the first instance, and this court if need be, an evidentiary basis and a record on which to act. As I see it, the remand hearing ought to cover among other things the following:

(a) The scope, nature and extent of the education of a Ph.D. in Psychology and in Clinical Psychology, including time spent in hospitals, with patients, and under what supervision.
   (1) What is the education, training and clinical experience of the proffered witness?
   (2) Define for the record the term "clinical experience."

(b) What, in particular, is the extent and scope of this Clinical Psychologist's clinical education in physiological and medical subjects? How does it compare with that of a psychiatrist?

(c) What is the scope of the work of Clinical Psychologists at St. Elizabeths Hospital?[2]

   (1) Do they make diagnosis of mental diseases on their own independent responsibility or only subject to the supervision of a psychiatrist? The relationship should be developed fully.

   (2) What is the scope of the work and extent of clinical responsibility of the particular Clinical Psychologist with patients *independent* of psychiatrists? That is, what work is done fully by the Clinical Psychologist alone and without regard to any supervision or overseeing by a psychiatrist?

(d) In how many specific cases has the particular Clinical Psychologist made a diagnosis of mental disease, prescribed or supervised treatment of patients without the intervention or approval of a psychiatrist?

(e) In how many cases approximately (whether at St. Elizabeths or elsewhere) has the witness made a diagnosis of the existence or nonexistence of mental disease and communicated that diagnosis directly to the patient or patient's family independent of a psychiatrist?

(f) To what extent has the witness prescribed or supervised treatment of mental patients independent of a psychiatrist?

(g) The opinions of both psychiatrists and clinical psychologists ought to be made part of the record on the following:

---

[2] In this connection an obviously well qualified expert, who might well be called as a witness by the court, if he is not called by any party, is the Superintendent of St. Elizabeths Hospital who has presided over a staff of psychiatrists and clinical psychologists dealing with precisely the issues of criminal responsibility.

(1) In what kinds or categories of mental disease are the physiological and medical factors not of any consequence?

(2) In what categories does a diagnosis of mental disease involve analysis, understanding and synthesis of physical and physiological factors as well as psychological factors?

(3) If diagnosis of mental disease always involves consideration of or evaluation of physical, biological or physiological data, how does a clinical psychologist acquire clinical experience and scientific competence to make such diagnosis?

(4) What is a differential diagnosis in the context of diagnosis of mental disease?

(5) Is the process of diagnosis of mental disease the elimination of various alternative explanations?

(6) In this process what factors must be taken into account?

(7) In the process of eliminating alternative explanations do the medical history of the patient, the physical examination and various medical tests play a part?

(8) Can any mental disease be diagnosed without taking into account pathological data? If so, what mental diseases can be diagnosed independent of and without regard to pathological data?

The cases cited by the majority concerning the optometrist, the toxicologist and other skilled specialists who are not medical doctors are not in any real sense relevant. Indeed they tend to divert us from the central issue. Of course an optometrist or the toxicologist is permitted to give *some* expert testimony within his competence just as a skilled shoemaker might be qualified to testify from long observation and experience as to the effect of wearing certain kinds of shoes, or a farrier to give expert testimony about the effect of certain types of shoeing on horses.

The heart of our problem is not whether a clinical psychologist is qualified to testify as an expert, for of course he is in some areas, but whether he is qualified to give expert testimony in the form of a diagnosis of a mental disease or illness, and to express an opinion on whether a stated mental disease "caused" the patient to commit a given unlawful act or "produced" that act. More rationally the question ought to be whether mental disease so substantially affected him that he was unable to control his conduct.

I agree with the majority that the scope of the training of the psychologist is of critical importance and that many factors other than academic degrees go to the admissibility and weight of the expert testimony. For example, if a general medical practitioner testified on the subject of mental disease, and gave a diagnosis of presence or absence of mental illness in opposition to a trained psychiatrist it would obviously be proper for the trial judge to tell the jury they could take into account the differences in training and experience in weighing the testimony of the one against the other. In the same way it would be proper, if a clinical psychologist is found qualified to testify as to the presence or absence of a mental disease and does so in opposition to a psychiatrist, to tell the jury they could take into account the difference in the education, training and experience of psychologists and psychiatrists and the absence of medical training in the former.

BASTIAN, Circuit Judge, with whom WILBUR K. MILLER, Chief Judge, joins, dissenting.

In the early morning of June 10, 1959, the complaining witness was in her apartment alone, in the process of getting ready to go to work that day, when she heard a knock at her front door and, upon partially opening it, she found herself face to face with the appellant. He showed her a card, saying something about an address. Then he suddenly burst into the apartment, knocked her to the floor, stuffed a gag into her mouth, and informed her he was going to rape her. When she began to fight back at her attacker, kicking and scratching at him as best as she could, he proceeded to punch her into unconsciousness with his fists. When she regained consciousness, she found herself lying on her apartment floor, disheveled, badly beaten, and bleeding profusely. She had been stabbed with a sharp instrument, presumably a knife, a number of times, causing severe loss of blood and necessitating subsequent surgery. As a result of this ordeal she remained hospitalized for approximately six weeks. In the District Court, a jury convicted appellant of housebreaking, assault with intent to commit rape, and assault with a dangerous weapon.

In reversing this conviction, the majority of this court, without adequately discussing the real nature and present medical understanding of mental illness, hold *inter alia* that certain psychologists can qualify to give *expert* opinion concerning the existence *vel non* of a mental disease or defect and its connective relationship, if any, to criminal behavior. We cannot agree. In our opinion it should be an absolute condition precedent to expert testimony as to a medical diagnosis that the witness be a medical doctor.

In the first place, we think it must be concluded beyond doubt that the existence of a mental disease or defect is, first and foremost, a *medical* problem. The ascertainment of such a medical illness in a given individual with reference to kind, quality, degree and influence is, except in extreme cases, a highly unverifiable process, judged by any objective standard, even when undertaken by a *medical* doctor with years of special training in the detection of medical disturbances of the mind. Time and time again, where insanity is raised as a defense at the trial of criminal cases in this jurisdiction, sincere and experienced *psychiatrists* have taken the stand and voiced diametrically opposite opinions as to whether or not the defendant had a mental disease or defect at the time he committed the crime charged against him. And even when these psychiatrists are in some agreement that the defendant had a mental disease or defect at the time of the crime, they frequently differ widely concerning its symptoms, nature, intensity, and causal influence with respect to the offense committed.

Our emphasis of this situation is not to belittle the integrity of the psychiatrists who testify at these trials, nor to disparage the integrity of the psychiatric profession, but merely to illustrate how nebulous and uncertain is the issue of mental illness even to those of the *medical* profession who are experienced and trained in its diagnosis and treatment. If the issue is so debatable among conceded professional medical experts, it is sheer folly, in our opinion, to attribute to a lay psychologist, who admittedly is not a doctor of medicine, such presumptive medical knowledge and diagnostic acuity as to entitle him to wear in a criminal courtroom the badge of an expert witness with respect to the existence of that elusive *medical* condition known as mental disease or defect.

By this we do not mean to suggest

that a psychologist should never be called upon to testify in insanity cases. Ih proper circumstances, testimony concerning the results of psychological tests administered to a defendant should be admissible as a means of enlightening a jury with respect to the specific information contributed by the psychologist to the over-all mass of information ultimately utilized by the medically trained psychiatrist in arriving at an expert opinion concerning the medical diagnosis of mental disease or defect. But to say that a psychologist is qualified to give an expert opinion with reference to a medical diagnosis is, in effect, to say that a non-medical witness can render an expert answer to a medical question on the strength of information insufficient to resolve it.[1] Such an opinion is a conclusion by guesswork, as far as a valid and proper medical determination is concerned.

We are not alone in our views on this precise issue. The American Psychiatric Association, an organization "comprised of those twelve thousand qualified Doctors of Medicine who specialize and practice as psychiatrists," in its amicus curiae brief, urges this court not to allow psychologists to qualify as experts to express opinions. We find in the brief this pertinent observation in regard to the proper medical ascertainment of mental disease or defect:

"The diagnostic synthesis of *all data* collected is properly carried out only by an individual Doctor of Medicine with a broad training, experience, and familiarity with *all* of the areas indicated, and the diagnosis must reflect a comprehensive medical judgment in which the proper weight is given to all of the data available. Further, we know of no mental illness which does not have a biological as well as a psychological component. No facet of the data can be assumed to reflect the total diagnosis until viewed in the context of the total picture. A clinical psychologist, lacking *medical* training and the specialization required of the qualified psychiatrist, is not qualified to make this total *medical* diagnosis or to testify as a *medical* expert thereon." [Emphasis appears in amicus brief.]

The majority of the court ignores the above quoted wise counsel from the only undisputed experts now at work in the area of medical illness of the mind. In doing so, the court, we suggest, is bypassing all objective criteria in reaching the highly questionable and subjective conclusion that lay psychologists, whose opinions are predicated on the basis of test results, may qualify as experts on the medical question of the diagnosis of mental disease or defect, as well as experts concerning the causal relationship between a particular defendant's mental abnormality, as such may be "diagnosed" by these psychologists, and that defendant's criminal activity. In our opinion, the holding of the majority on this issue is wholly untenable. We would affirm the judgment and sentence of the District Court.

---

[1] It is well to remember that a psychologist's opinion in this respect is grounded basically upon his interpretation of the results of certain psychological tests administered to the defendant. As an example of the instability of such test results, we mention that in the instant case the appellant was subjected to the same I.Q. test on three separate occasions, scoring, respectively, 63 (high moron), 74 (borderline defective), and 90 (average).

FRYE v. UNITED STATES.
(Court of Appeals of District of Columbia. Submitted November 7, 1923. Decided December 3, 1923.)
No. 3968.

1. **Criminal law** ⟵ 472—Expert testimony, explaining systolic blood pressure deception test, inadmissible.

The systolic blood pressure deception test, based on the theory that truth is spontaneous and comes without conscious effort, while the utterance of a falsehood requires a conscious effort, which is reflected in the blood pressure, *held* not to have such a scientific recognition among psychological and physiological authorities as would justify the courts in admitting expert testimony on defendant's behalf, deduced from experiments thus far made.

2. **Criminal law** ⟵ 472—Principle must be generally accepted, to render expert testimony admissible.

While the courts will go a long way in admitting expert testimony, deduced from a well-recognized scientific principle or discovery, the thing from which the deduction is made must be sufficiently established to have gained general acceptance in the particular field in which it belongs.

Appeal from the Supreme Court of the District of Columbia.

James Alphonzo Frye was convicted of murder, and he appeals. Affirmed.

Richard V. Mattingly and Foster Wood, both of Washington, D.C., for appellant.

Reprinted with permission 293 F.1013 (D. C. Cir. 1923). Copyright © by West Publishing Co.

Peyton Gordon and J. H. Bilbrey, both of Washington, D.C., for the United States.

Before SMYTH, Chief Justice, VAN ORSDEL, Associate Justice, and MARTIN, Presiding Judge of the United States Court of Customs Appeals.

VAN ORSDEL, Associate Justice. Appellant, defendant below, was convicted of the crime of murder in the second degree, and from the judgment prosecutes this appeal.

A single assignment of error is presented for our consideration. In the course of the trial counsel for defendant offered an expert witness to testify to the result of a deception test made upon defendant. The test is described as the systolic blood pressure deception test. It is asserted that blood pressure is influenced by change in the emotions of the witness, and that the systolic blood pressure rises are brought about by nervous impulses sent to the sympathetic branch of the autonomic nervous system. Scientific experiments, it is claimed, have demonstrated that fear, rage, and pain always produce a rise of systolic blood pressure, and that conscious deception or falsehood, concealment of facts, or guilt of crime, accompanied by fear of detection when the person is under examination, raises the systolic blood pressure in a curve, which corresponds exactly to the struggle going on in the subject's mind, between fear and attempted control of that fear, as the examination touches the vital points in respect of which he is attempting to deceive the examiner.

In other words, the theory seems to be that truth is spontaneous, and comes without conscious effort, while the utterance of a falsehood requires a conscious effort, which is reflected in the blood pressure. The rise thus produced is easily detected and distinguished from the rise produced by mere fear of the examination itself. In the former instance, the pressure rises higher than in the latter, and is more pronounced as the examination proceeds, while in the latter case, if the subject is telling the truth, the pressure registers highest at the beginning of the examination, and gradually diminishes as the examination proceeds.

Prior to the trial defendant was subjected to this deception test, and counsel offered the scientist who conducted the test as an expert to testify to the results obtained. The offer was objected to by counsel for the government, and the court sustained the objection. Counsel for defendant then offered to have the proffered witness conduct a test in the presence of the jury. This also was denied.

Counsel for defendant, in their able presentation of the novel question involved, correctly state in their brief that no cases directly in point have been found. The broad ground, however, upon which they plant their case, is succinctly stated in their brief as follows:

"The rule is that the opinions of experts or skilled witnesses are admissible in evidence in those cases in which the matter of inquiry is such that inexperienced persons are unlikely to prove capable of forming a correct judgment upon it, for the reason that the subject-matter so far partakes of a science, art, or trade as to require a previous habit or experience or study in it, in order to acquire a knowledge of it. When the question involved does not lie within the range of common experience or common knowledge, but requires special experience or special knowledge, then the opinions of witnesses skilled in that particular science, art, or trade to which the question relates are admissible in evidence."

[1, 2] Numerous cases are cited in support of this rule. Just when a scientific principle or discovery crosses the line between the experimental and demonstrable stages is difficult to define.

Somewhere in this twilight zone the evidential force of the principle must be recognized, and while courts will go a long way in admitting expert testimony deduced from a well-recognized scientific principle or discovery, the thing from which the deduction is made must be sufficiently established to have gained general acceptance in the particular field in which it belongs.

We think the systolic blood pressure deception test has not yet gained such standing and scientific recognition among physiological and psychological authorities as would justify the courts in admitting expert testimony deduced from the discovery, development, and experiments thus far made.

The judgment is affirmed.

W. J. ESTELLE, Jr., Director, Texas Department of Corrections, Petitioner,
v.
Ernest Benjamin SMITH.
No. 79-1127.
Argued Oct. 8, 1980.
Decided May 18, 1981.

Texas prisoner sought federal habeas corpus relief. The United States District Court for the Northern District of Texas, Robert W. Porter, J., 445 F.Supp. 647, issued writ, and the state appealed. The Court of Appeals, 602 F.2d 694, affirmed. Certiorari was granted. The Supreme Court, Mr. Chief Justice Burger, held that: (1) where prior to in-custody court-ordered psychiatric examination to determine competency to stand trial defendant had not been warned that he had right to remain silent and that any statement made could be used against him at capital sentencing proceeding,

Reprinted with permission 454 101 S.Ct. 1866, 68 L.Ed.2d. 323 (1979). Copyright © by West Publishing Co.

admission at penalty phase of capital felony trial of psychiatrist's damaging testimony on crucial issue of future dangerousness violated Fifth Amendment privilege against compelled self-incrimination; because of lack of appraisal of rights and a knowing waiver thereof death sentence could not stand, and (2) Sixth Amendment right to counsel was violated as defense counsel was not notified in advance that the psychiatric examination would encompass issue of future dangerousness.

Decision of Court of Appeals affirmed.

Mr. Justice Brennan filed a concurring statement.

Mr. Justice Marshall filed a statement concurring in part.

Mr. Justice Stewart filed an opinion concurring in the judgment, in which Mr. Justice Powell joined.

Mr. Justice Rehnquist filed an opinion concurring in the judgment.

1. Criminal Law   ⟵ 393(1)

Fact that testimony of psychiatrist who was sua sponte appointed by the court to determine defendant's competency to stand trial was used only to determine punishment in capital felony case and not to determine guilt did not render inapplicable the Fifth Amendment privilege against compelled self-incrimination. Vernon's Ann.Tex. C.C.P. arts. 37.071, 46.02; Vernon's Ann.Tex.P.C. art. 1257(b)(2); U.S.C.A. Const. Amend. 5.

2. Witnesses   ⟵ 300

Just as the Fifth Amendment prevents a criminal defendant from being made the deluded instrument of his own conviction, it protects him as well from being made the deluded instrument of his own execution; there is no

basis to distinguish between guilty and penalty phases of a capital murder trial so far as protection of Fifth Amendment privilege is concerned. U.S.C.A.Const. Amend. 5.

3. Criminal Law   ⟵ 986.6(2)

Given gravity of decision to be made at the penalty phase of a capital murder case, the state is not relieved of the obligation to observe fundamental constitutional guarantees. Vernon's Ann. Tex.P.C. art. 1257(b)(2); Vernon's Ann. Tex.C.C.P. art. 37.071; U.S.C.A.Const. Amend. 5.

4. Criminal Law   ⟵ 412(5)
Witnesses   ⟵ 300

Any effort by state of Texas to compel criminal defendant to testify against his will at sentencing phase of capital murder prosecution would contravene the Fifth Amendment; also state's attempt to establish future dangerousness by relying on defendant's pretrial statements to a psychiatrist appointed sua sponte by the court to determine competency to stand trial, with defendant not having been advised that he had right to remain silent and that any statement could be used against him at sentencing proceedings, similarly infringed Fifth Amendment values. Vernon's Ann.Tex.C.C.P. arts. 37.071, 46.02; Vernon's Ann.Tex.P.C. art. 1257; U.S.C.A.Const. Amend. 5.

5. Witnesses   ⟵ 300

Fifth Amendment is not violated where the evidence given by a defendant is neither related to some communicative act nor used for the testimonial content of what was said. U.S.C.A. Const. Amend. 5.

6. Criminal Law ⟸ 393(1)

Where court-appointed psychiatrist's prognosis of defendant's future dangerousness, as admitted at sentencing hearing of Texas capital felony prosecution, rested on statements which defendant made and remarks which he omitted in reciting details of the crime during court-initiated pretrial examination to determine competency to stand trial the Fifth Amendment privilege was directly involved because the state used as evidence against defendant the substance of his disclosure and privilege was not inapplicable on ground that psychiatrist based his adverse diagnosis merely on observation of defendant. Vernon's Ann.Tex.C.C.P. arts. 37.071, 46.02; Vernon's Ann.Tex.P.C. art. 1257; U.S.C.A.Const. Amend. 5.

7. Criminal Law ⟸ 412(5)

Fact that Texas defendant's statements were uttered in context of court-ordered pretrial psychiatric examination did not automatically remove them from reach of Fifth Amendment as regards admission, at penalty phase of capital murder trial, of psychiatrist's adverse prognosis on critical issue of dangerousness; although trial judge sua sponte ordered evaluation for limited, neutral purpose of determining competency to stand trial, results of inquiry were used for broader objective plainly adverse to defendant but if application of psychiatrist's findings had been confined to insuring that defendant understood charges and was capable of assisting counsel, no Fifth Amendment issue would have arisen. Vernon's Ann. Tex.P.C. art. 1257(b)(2); Vernon's Ann. Tex.C.C.P. arts. 37.071(b)(2), 46.02; U.S.C.A.Const. Amend. 5.

8. Criminal Law ⟸ 412.2(3)

Where at capital felony murder case Texas defendant introduced no psychiatric evidence and did not indicate that he might do so and to meet its burden on crucial penalty issue of future dangerousness the state used defendant's statements to psychiatrist who had been sua sponte appointed to trial to determine competency to stand trial and defendant had not been warned of his right to remain silent and that any statement he made could be used against him at capital sentencing proceeding, the Fifth Amendment privilege was implicated. Vernon's Ann.Tex.P.C. art. 1257(b)(2); Vernon's Ann.Tex.C.C.P. arts. 37.071(b)(2), 46.02; U.S.C.A. Const. Amend. 5.

9. Criminal Law ⟸ 412.2(3)

Absent other fully effective procedures, a person in custody must receive certain warnings before any official interrogation, including that he has a right to remain silent and that anything said can and will be used against the individual in court. U.S.C.A.Const. Amends. 5, 14.

10. Witnesses ⟸ 300

Fifth Amendment privilege is as broad as the mischief against which it seeks to guard and the privilege is fulfilled only when a criminal defendant is guaranteed the right to remain silent unless he chooses to speak in the unfettered exercise of his own will, and to suffer no penalty for such silence. U.S.C.A.Const. Amend. 5.

11. Criminal Law ⟸ 698(1)

Texas defendant did not waive his Fifth Amendment claim by failing to make a timely, specific trial objection to court-appointed psychiatrist's adverse testimony on future dangerousness issue at penalty phase of capital murder trial, specifically, claiming that Fifth Amendment was violated because prior to the in-jail examination defendant had not been warned that he had a right to remain silent and that any statement he made could be used against him at a capital sentencing proceeding and, also, state did not present the waiver argument in its petition for certiorari. U.S. Sup.Ct. Rule 40, subd. 1(d)(2), 28 U.S.C.A.; Vernon's Ann.Tex.P.C. art. 1257(b)(2); Vernon's Ann.Tex.C.C.P. arts. 37.071(b)(2), 46.02; U.S.C.A. Const. Amend. 5.

12.   Criminal Law   ⟵ **412(4)**

A criminal defendant who neither initiates a psychiatric evaluation nor attempts to introduce any psychiatric evidence, may not be compelled to respond to a psychiatrist if his statements can be used against him at a capital sentencing proceeding. Vernon's Ann. Tex.P.C. art. 1257(b)(2); Vernon's Ann. Tex.C.C.P. arts. 37.071(b)(2), 46.02; U.S.C.A.Const. Amend. 5.

13.   Criminal Law   ⟵ **412.1(4),
        412.2(3)**

Where prior to court ordered pretrial psychiatric examination to determine competency to stand trial defendant had not been informed of his right to remain silent and possible use of his statements, the state could not rely on defendant's statements of psychiatrist for purpose of establishing future dangerousness issue at death penalty phase and since statements were made while defendant was in custody his statements to psychiatrist, who testified adversely to defendant at penalty phase, could not be said to have been given freely and voluntarily and, hence, death sentence could not stand. Vernon's Ann.Tex.P.C. art. 1257(b)(2); Vernon's Ann.Tex.C.C.P. arts. 37.071(b)(2), 46.02; U.S.C.A.Const. Amend. 5.

14.   Criminal Law   ⟵ **641.12(1)**

Where defendant had been indicted and counsel appointed before he was examined at jail by a psychiatrist sua sponte appointed to determine competency to stand trial and counsel had not been notified of the hearing, defendant's Sixth Amendment right to assistance of counsel was violated when prosecution, at penalty phase of Texas capital murder prosecution, introduced psychiatrist's adverse diagnosis regarding crucial issue of future dangerousness; interview proved to be a "critical stage" of the aggregate proceedings, and waiver was neither shown nor alleged. Vernon's Ann.Tex.P.C. art. 1257(b)(2); Vernon's Ann.Tex.C.C.P. arts. 37.071, 37.071(b)(2), 46.02; U.S.C.A.Const. Amends. 6, 14.

See publication Words and Phrases for other judicial constructions and definitions.

15.   Criminal Law   ⟵ **641.4(2)**

Waivers of assistance of counsel must not only be voluntary but constitute a knowing and intelligent relinquishment or abandonment of a known right or privilege, a matter which depends upon the particular facts and circumstances surrounding each case. U.S.C.A.Const. Amends. 5, 6, 14.

Syllabus*

* The syllabus constitutes no part of the opinion of the Court but has been prepared by the Reporter of Decisions for the conve-

After respondent was indicted in Texas for murder, the State announced its intention to seek the death penalty. At an ensuing psychiatric examination, ordered by the trial court to determine respondent's competency to stand trial and conducted in the jail where he was being held, the examining doctor determined that respondent was competent. Thereafter, respondent was tried by a jury and convicted. A separate sentencing proceeding was then held before the same jury as required by Texas law. At such a proceeding the jury must resolve three critical issues to determine whether or not the death sentence will be imposed. One of these issues involves the future dangerousness of the defendant, i. e., whether there is a probability that he would commit criminal acts of violence that would constitute a continuing threat to society. At the sentencing hearing, the doctor who had conducted the pretrial psychiatric examination was allowed to testify for the State over defense counsels' objection that his name did not appear on the list of witnesses the State planned to use at either the guilt or penalty stages of the proceedings. His testimony was based on the pretrial examination and stated in substance that respondent would be a danger to society. The jury then resolved the issue of future dangerousness, as well as the other two issues, against respondent, and thus under Texas law the death penalty was mandatory. The Texas Court of Criminal Appeals affirmed the conviction and death sentence. After unsuccessfully seeking a writ of habeas corpus in the state courts, respondent petitioned for such relief in Federal District Court. That court vacated the death sentence

because it found constitutional error in admitting the doctor's testimony at the penalty phase. The United States Court of Appeals affirmed.

Held:

1. The admission of the doctor's testimony at the penalty phase violated respondent's Fifth Amendment privilege against compelled self-incrimination, because he was not advised before the pretrial psychiatric examination that he had a right to remain silent and that any statement he made could be used against him at a capital sentencing proceeding. Pp. 1872–1876.

(a) There is no basis for distinguishing between the guilt and penalty phases of respondent's trial so far as the protection of the Fifth Amendment privilege is concerned. The State's attempt to establish respondent's future dangerousness by relying on the unwarned statements he made to the examining doctor infringed the Fifth Amendment just as much as would have any effort to compel respondent to testify against his will at the sentencing hearing. Pp. 1872–1873.

(b) The Fifth Amendment privilege is directly involved here because the State used as evidence against respondent the substance of his disclosures during the pretrial psychiatric examination. The fact that respondent's statements were made in the context of such an examination does not automatically remove them from the reach of that Amendment. Pp. 1873–1875.

(c) The considerations calling for the accused to be warned prior to custodial interrogation apply with no less force to the pretrial psychiatric examination at issue here. An accused who neither initiates a psychiatric evaluation nor attempts to introduce any psychiatric evidence may not be compelled to respond to a psychiatrist if his statements can be used against him at a capital sentencing proceeding. When faced

nience of the reader. See *United States v. Detroit Lumber Co.,* 200 U.S. 321, 337, 26 S.Ct. 282, 287, 50 L.Ed. 499.

while in custody with a court-ordered psychiatric inquiry, respondent's statements to the doctor were not "given freely and voluntarily without any compelling influences" and, as such, could be used as the State did at the penalty phase only if respondent had been apprised of his rights and had knowingly decided to waive them. *Miranda v. Arizona,* 384 U.S. 436, 478, 86 S.Ct. 1602, 1630, 16 L.Ed.2d 694. Since these safeguards of the Fifth Amendment privilege were not afforded respondent, his death sentence cannot stand. Pp. 1875–1876.

2. Respondent's Sixth Amendment right to the assistance of counsel also was violated by the State's introduction of the doctor's testimony at the penalty phase. Such right already had attached when the doctor examined respondent in jail, and that interview proved to be a "critical stage" of the aggregate proceedings against respondent. Defense counsel were not notified in advance that the psychiatric examination would encompass the issue of their client's future dangerousness, and respondent was denied the assistance of his counsel in making the significant decision of whether to submit to the examination and to what end the psychiatrist's findings could be employed. Pp. 1876–1877.

5 Cir., 602 F.2d 694, affirmed.

Anita Ashton, Austin, Tex., for petitioner.

Joel Berger, for respondent.

Chief Justice BURGER, delivered the opinion of the Court.

We granted certiorari to consider whether the prosecution's use of psychiatric testimony at the sentencing phase of respondent's capital murder

trial to establish his future dangerousness violated his constitutional rights. 445 U.S. 926, 100 S.Ct. 1311, 63 L.Ed.2d 758 (1980).

I

A

On December 28, 1973, respondent Ernest Benjamin Smith was indicted for murder arising from his participation in the armed robbery of a grocery store during which a clerk was fatally shot, not by Smith, but by his accomplice. In accordance with Art. 1257(b)(2) of the Texas Penal Code (Vernon 1973) concerning the punishment for murder with malice aforethought, the State of Texas announced its intention to seek the death penalty. Thereafter, a judge of the 195th Judicial District Court of Dallas County, Texas, informally ordered the State's attorney to arrange a psychiatric examination of Smith by Dr. James P. Grigson to determine Smith's competency to stand trial.[1] See n. 5, *infra.*

Dr. Grigson, who interviewed Smith in jail for approximately 90 minutes, concluded that he was competent to stand trial. In a letter to the trial judge,

---

[1] This psychiatric evaluation was ordered even though defense counsel had not put into issue Smith's competency to stand trial or his sanity at the time of the offense. The trial judge later explained: "In all cases where the State has sought the death penalty, I have ordered a mental evaluation of the defendant to determine his competency to stand trial. I have done this for my benefit because I do not intend to be a participant in a case where the defendant receives the death penalty and his mental competency remains in doubt." App. 117. See Tex.Code Crim.Proc., Art. 46.02 (Vernon 1979). No question as to the appropriateness of the trial judge's order for the examination has been raised by Smith.

Dr. Grigson reported his findings: "[I]t is my opinion that Ernest Benjamin Smith, Jr. is aware of the difference between right and wrong and is able to aid an attorney in his defense." App. 6. This letter was filed with the court's papers in the case. Smith was then tried by a jury and convicted of murder.

In Texas, capital cases require bifurcated proceedings—a guilt phase and a penalty phase.[2] If the defendant is found guilty, a separate proceeding before the same jury is held to fix the punishment. At the penalty phase, if the jury affirmatively answers three questions on which the State has the burden of proof beyond a reasonable doubt, the judge must impose the death sentence. See Tex.Code Crim.Proc., Art. 37.071(c) & (e) (Vernon Supp. 1980). One of the three critical issues to be resolved by the jury is "whether there is a probability that the defendant would commit criminal acts of violence that would constitute a continuing threat to society." Art. 37.071(b)(2).[3] In other words, the jury

must assess the defendant's future dangerousness.

At the commencement of Smith's sentencing hearing, the State rested "subject to the right to reopen." App. 11. Defense counsel called three lay witnesses: Smith's stepmother, his aunt, and the man who owned the gun Smith carried during the robbery. Smith's relatives testified as to his good reputation and character.[4] The owner of the pistol testified as to Smith's knowledge that it would not fire because of a mechanical defect. The State then called Dr. Grigson as a witness.

Defense counsel were aware from the trial court's file of the case that Dr. Grigson had submitted a psychiatric report in the form of a letter advising the court that Smith was competent to stand trial.[5] This report termed Smith "a

---

[2] Article 37.071(a) of the Texas Code of Criminal Procedure (Vernon Supp. 1980) provides: "Upon a finding that the defendant is guilty of a capital offense, the court shall conduct a separate sentencing proceeding to determine whether the defendant shall be sentenced to death or life imprisonment. The proceeding shall be conducted in the trial court before the trial jury as soon as practicable. In the proceeding, evidence may be presented as to any matter that the court deems relevant to sentence. This subsection shall not be construed to authorize the introduction of any evidence secured in violation of the Constitution of the United States or of the State of Texas. The state and the defendant or his counsel shall be permitted to present argument for or against sentence of death."

[3] The other two issues are "whether the conduct of the defendant that caused the death of the deceased was committed deliberately and with the reasonable expectation

that the death of the deceased or another would result" and "if raised by the evidence, whether the conduct of the defendant in killing the deceased was unreasonable in response to the provocation, if any, by the deceased." Tex.Code Crim.Proc., Art. 37.071(b)(1) & (3) (Vernon Supp. 1980).

[4] It appears from the record that Smith's only prior criminal conviction was for the possession of marijuana. See App. 64.

[5] Defense counsel discovered the letter at some time after jury selection began in the case on March 11, 1974. The trial judge later explained that Dr. Grigson was "appointed by oral communication," that "a letter of appointment was not prepared," and that "the court records do not reflect [the entry of] a written order." App. 118. The judge also stated:
"As best I recall, I informed John Simmons, the attorney for the defendant, that I had appointed Dr. Grigson to examine the defendant and that a written report was to be mailed to me." *Ibid.* However, defense counsel assert that the discovery of Dr. Grigson's letter served as their first notice that he had examined Smith. *Id.*, at 113, 116.

severe sociopath," but it contained no more specific reference to his future dangerousness. *Id.*, at 6. Before trial, defense counsel had obtained an order requiring the State to disclose the witnesses it planned to use both at the guilt stage, and, if known, at the penalty stage. Subsequently, the trial court had granted a defense motion to bar the testimony during the State's case-in-chief of any witness whose name did not appear on that list. Dr. Grigson's name was not on the witness list, and defense counsel objected when he was called to the stand at the penalty phase.

In a hearing outside the presence of the jury, Dr. Grigson stated: (a) that he had not obtained permission from Smith's attorneys to examine him; (b) that he had discussed his conclusions and diagnosis with the State's attorney; and (c) that the prosecutor had requested him to testify and had told him, approximately five days before the sentencing hearing began, that his testimony probably would be needed within the week. *Id.*, at 14–16. The trial judge denied a defense motion to exclude Dr. Grigson's testimony on the ground that his name was not on the State's list of witnesses. Although no continuance was requested, the court then recessed for one hour following an acknowledgment by defense counsel that an hour was "all right." *Id.*, at 17.

After detailing his professional qualifications by way of foundation, Dr. Grigson testified before the jury on direct examination: (a) that Smith "is a very severe sociopath"; (b) that "he will continue his previous behavior"; (c) that his sociopathic condition will "only

get worse"; (d) that he has no "regard for another human being's property or for their life, regardless of who it may be"; (e) that "[t]here is no treatment, no medicine . . . that in any way at all modifies or changes this behavior"; (f) that he "is going to go ahead and commit other similar or same criminal acts if given the opportunity to do so"; and (g) that he "has no remorse or sorrow for what he has done." *Id.*, at 17–26. Dr. Grigson, whose testimony was based on information derived from his 90-minute "mental status examination" of Smith (*i. e.*, the examination ordered to determine Smith's competency to stand trial), was the State's only witness at the sentencing hearing.

The jury answered the three requisite questions in the affirmative, and, thus, under Texas law the death penalty for Smith was mandatory. The Texas Court of Criminal Appeals affirmed Smith's conviction and death sentence, 540 S.W.2d 693 (Tex.Cr.App.1976), and we denied certiorari, 430 U.S. 922, 97 S.Ct. 1341, 51 L.Ed.2d 601 (1977).

B

After unsuccessfully seeking a writ of habeas corpus in the Texas state courts, Smith petitioned for such relief in the United States District Court for the Northern District of Texas pursuant to 28 U.S.C. § 2254. The District Court vacated Smith's death sentence because it found constitutional error in the admission of Dr. Grigson's testimony at the penalty phase. 445 F.Supp. 647 (1977). The court based its holding on the failure to advise Smith of his right to remain silent at the pretrial psychiatric examination and the failure to notify defense counsel in advance of the penalty phase that Dr. Grigson would testify. The court concluded that the death penalty had been imposed on Smith in violation of his Fifth and Fourteenth

On March 25, 1974, the day the trial began, defense counsel requested the issuance of a subpoena for the Dallas County Sheriff's records of Dr. Grigson's "visitation to . . . Smith." *Id.*, at 8.

Amendment rights to due process and freedom from compelled self-incrimination, his Sixth Amendment right to the effective assistance of counsel, and his Eighth Amendment right to present complete evidence of mitigating circumstances. *Id.*, at 664.

The United States Court of Appeals for the Fifth Circuit affirmed. 602 F.2d 694 (1979). The court held that Smith's death sentence could not stand because the State's "surprise" use of Dr. Grigson as a witness, the consequences of which the court described as "devastating," denied Smith due process in that his attorneys were prevented from effectively challenging the psychiatric testimony. *Id.*, at 699. The court went on to hold that, under the Fifth and Sixth Amendments, "Texas may not use evidence based on a psychiatric examination of the defendant unless the defendant was warned, before the examination, that he had a right to remain silent; was allowed to terminate the examination when he wished; and was assisted by counsel in deciding whether to submit to the examination." *Id.*, at 709. Because Smith was not accorded these rights, his death sentence was set aside. While "leav[ing] to state authorities any questions that arise about the appropriate way to proceed when the state cannot legally execute a defendant whom it has sentenced to death," the court indicated that "the same testimony from Dr. Grigson based on the same examination of Smith" could not be used against Smith at any future resentencing proceeding. *Id.*, at 703, n. 13, 709, n. 20.

II

A

Of the several constitutional issues addressed by the District Court and the Court of Appeals, we turn first to whether the admission of Dr. Grigson's testimony at the penalty phase violated respondent's Fifth Amendment privilege against compelled self-incrimination because respondent was not advised before the pretrial psychiatric examination that he had a right to remain silent and that any statement he made could be used against him at a sentencing proceeding. Our initial inquiry must be whether the Fifth Amendment privilege is applicable in the circumstances of this case.

(1)

[1] The State argues that respondent was not entitled to the protection of the Fifth Amendment because Dr. Grigson's testimony was used only to determine punishment after conviction, not to establish guilt. In the State's view, "incrimination is complete once guilt has been adjudicated," and, therefore, the Fifth Amendment privilege has no relevance to the penalty phase of a capital murder trial. Brief for Petitioner 33–34. We disagree.

[2] The Fifth Amendment, made applicable to the states through the Fourteenth Amendment, commands that "[n]o person . . . shall be compelled in any criminal case to be a witness against himself." The essence of this basic constitutional principle is "the requirement that the State which proposes to convict *and punish* an individual produce the evidence against him by the independent labor of its officers, not by the simple, cruel expedient of forcing it from his own lips." *Culombe v. Connecticut*, 367 U.S. 568, 581–582, 81 S.Ct. 1860, 1867, 6 L.Ed.2d 1037 (1961) (opinion announcing the judgment) (emphasis added). See also *Murphy v. Waterfront Comm'n*, 378 U.S. 52, 55, 84 S.Ct. 1594, 1596–1597, 12 L.Ed.2d 678 (1964); E. Griswold, The Fifth Amendment Today 7 (1955).

The Court has held that "the availability of the [Fifth Amendment] privilege does not turn upon the type of proceeding in which its protection is invoked, but upon the nature of the statement or admission and the exposure which it invites." *In re Gault*, 387 U.S. 1, 49, 87 S.Ct. 1428, 1455, 18 L.Ed.2d 527 (1967). In this case, the ultimate penalty of death was a potential consequence of what respondent told the examining psychiatrist. Just as the Fifth Amendment prevents a criminal defendant from being made " 'the deluded instrument of his own conviction,' " *Culombe v. Connecticut, supra,* at 581, 1867, quoting 2 Hawkins Pleas of the Crown 595 (8th ed. 1824), it protects him as well from being made the "deluded instrument" of his own execution.

[3, 4] We can discern no basis to distinguish between the guilt and penalty phases of respondent's capital murder trial so far as the protection of the Fifth Amendment privilege is concerned.[6] Given the gravity of the decision to be made at the penalty phase, the State is not relieved of the obligation to observe fundamental constitutional guarantees. See *Green v. Georgia*, 442 U.S. 95, 97, 99 S.Ct. 2150, 2152, 60 L.Ed.2d 738 (1979); *Presnell v. Georgia*, 439 U.S. 14, 16, 99 S.Ct. 235, 236, 58

L.Ed.2d 207 (1978); *Gardner v. Florida*, 430 U.S. 349, 357–358, 97 S.Ct. 1197, 1204–1205, 51 L.Ed.2d 393 (1977) (plurality opinion). Any effort by the State to compel respondent to testify against his will at the sentencing hearing clearly would contravene the Fifth Amendment.[7] Yet the State's attempt to establish respondent's future dangerousness by relying on the unwarned statements he made to Dr. Grigson similarly infringes Fifth Amendment values.

(2)

[5] The State also urges that the Fifth Amendment privilege is inapposite here because respondent's communications to Dr. Grigson were nontestimonial in nature. The State seeks support from our cases holding that the Fifth Amendment is not violated where the evidence given by a defendant is neither related to some communicative act nor used for the testimonial content of what was said. See, *e. g., United States v. Dionisio*, 410 U.S. 1, 93 S.Ct. 764, 35 L.Ed.2d 67 (1973) (voice exemplar); *Gilbert v. California*, 388 U.S. 263, 87 S.Ct. 1951, 18 L.Ed.2d 1178 (1967) (handwriting exemplar); *United States v. Wade*, 388 U.S. 218, 87 S.Ct. 1926, 18 L.Ed.2d 1149 (1967) (lineup); *Schmerber v. California*, 384 U.S. 757, 86 S.Ct. 1826, 16 L.Ed.2d 908 (1966) (blood sample).

[6] However, Dr. Grigson's diagnosis, as detailed in his testimony, was not based simply on his observation of respondent. Rather, Dr. Grigson drew his conclusions largely from respondent's account of the crime during their interview, and he placed particular emphasis on what he considered to be respondent's lack of remorse. See App. 27–29, 33–34.[8] Dr. Grigson's prognosis as to

---

[6] Texas law does provide that "[n]o statement made by a defendant during the examination or hearing on his competency to stand trial may be admitted in evidence against the defendant *on the issue of guilt* in any criminal proceeding." Tex.Code Crim.Proc., Art. 46.02(3)(g) (Vernon 1979) (emphasis added). See also 18 U.S.C. § 4244; Fed.Rule Crim. Proc. 12.2(c); *United States v. Alvarez*, 519 F.2d 1036, 1042–1044 (CA3 1975); Note, Requiring a Criminal Defendant to Submit to a Government Psychiatric Examination: An Invasion of the Privilege Against Self-Incrimination, 83 Harv.L.Rev. 648, 649, and cases cited at nn. 8–9 (1970).

[7] The State conceded this at oral argument. Tr. of Oral Arg, 47, 49.

[8] Although the Court of Appeals doubted the applicability of the Fifth Amendment if

future dangerousness rested on statements respondent made, and remarks he omitted, in reciting the details of the crime.[9] The Fifth Amendment privilege,

---

Dr. Grigson's diagnosis had been founded only on respondent's mannerisms, facial expressions, attention span, or speech patterns, 602 F.2d, at 704, the record in this case sheds no light on whether such factors alone would enable a psychiatrist to predict future dangerousness. The American Psychiatric Association suggests, however, that "absent a defendant's willingness to cooperate as to the verbal *content* of his communications, . . . a psychiatric examination in these circumstances would be meaningless." Brief for American Psychiatric Association as *Amicus Curiae* 26 (emphasis in original).

[9] On cross-examination, Dr. Grigson acknowledged that his findings were based on his "discussion" with respondent, App. 32, and he replied to the question "[w]hat . . . was the most important thing that . . . caused you to think that [respondent] is a severe sociopath" as follows:

"He told me that this man named Moon looked as though he was going to reach for a gun, and he pointed his gun toward Mr. Moon's head, pulled the trigger, and it clicked—misfired, at which time he hollered at Howie, apparently his other partner there who had a gun, 'Watch out, Howie. He's got a gun.' Or something of that sort. At which point he told me—now I don't know who shot this man, but he told me that Howie shot him, but then he walked around over this man who had been shot—didn't . . . check to see if he had a gun nor did he check to see if the man was alive or dead. Didn't call an ambulance, but simply found the gun further up underneath the counter and took the gun and the money. This is a very—sort of cold-blooded disregard for another human being's life. I think that his telling me this story and not saying, you know, 'Man I would do anything to have that man back alive. I wish I hadn't just stepped over the body.' Or you know, 'I wish I had checked to see if he was all right' would indicate a concern, guilt, or remorse. But I didn't get any of this." *Id.*, at 27–28.

therefore, is directly involved here because the State used as evidence against respondent the substance of his disclosures during the pretrial psychiatric examination.

[7] The fact that respondent's statements were uttered in the context of a psychiatric examination does not automatically remove them from the reach of the Fifth Amendment. See n.6, *supra.* The state trial judge, *sua sponte,* ordered a psychiatric evaluation of respondent for the limited, neutral purpose of determining his competency to stand trial, but the results of that inquiry were used by the State for a much broader objective that was plainly adverse to respondent. Consequently, the interview with Dr. Grigson cannot be characterized as a routine competency examination restricted to ensuring that respondent understood the charges against him and was capable of assisting in his defense. Indeed, if the application of Dr. Grigson's findings had been confined to serving that function, no Fifth Amendment issue would have arisen.

Nor was the interview analogous to a sanity examination occasioned by a defendant's plea of not guilty by reason of insanity at the time of his offense. When a defendant asserts the insanity defense and introduces supporting psychiatric testimony, his silence may deprive the State of the only effective means it has of controverting his proof on an issue that he interjected into the case. Accordingly, several courts of appeals have held that, under such circumstances, a defendant can be required to submit to a sanity examination conducted by the prosecution's psychiatrist. See, *e. g., United States v. Cohen,* 530 F.2d 43, 47–48 (CA5), cert. denied, 429 U.S. 855, 97 S.Ct. 149, 50 L.Ed.2d 130 (1976); *Karstetter v. Cardwell,* 526 F.2d 1144, 1145 (CA9 1975); *United States v. Bohle,* 445 F.2d 54, 66–67 (CA7 1971); *United States v. Weiser,* 428 F.2d 932, 936

(CA2 1969), cert. denied, 402 U.S. 949, 91 S.Ct. 1606, 29 L.Ed.2d 119 (1971); *United States v. Albright*, 388 F.2d 719, 724–725 (CA4 1968); *Pope v. United States*, 372 F.2d 710, 720–721 (CA8 1967) (en banc), vacated and remanded on other grounds, 392 U.S. 651, 88 S,Ct. 2145, 20 L.Ed.2d 1317 (1968).[10]

[8] Respondent, however, introduced no psychiatric evidence, nor had he indicated that he might do so. Instead, the State offered information obtained from the court-ordered competency examination as affirmative evidence to persuade the jury to return a sentence of death. Respondent's future dangerousness was a critical issue at the sentencing hearing, and one on which the State had the burden of proof beyond a reasonable doubt. See Tex. Code Crim.Proc., Art. 37.071(b) and (c) (Vernon Supp. 1980). To meet its burden, the State used respondent's own statements, unwittingly made without an awareness that he was assisting the State's efforts to obtain the death penalty. In these distinct circumstances, the Court of Appeals correctly concluded that the Fifth Amendment privilege was implicated.

(3)

[9] In *Miranda v. Arizona*, 384 U.S. 436, 467, 86 S.Ct. 1602, 1624, 16 L.Ed.2d 694 (1966), the Court acknowledged that "the Fifth Amendment privilege is available outside of criminal court proceedings and serves to protect persons in all settings in which their freedom of action is curtailed in any significant way

---

[10] On the same theory, the Court of Appeals here carefully left open "the possibility that a defendant who wishes to use psychiatric evidence in his own behalf [on the issue of future dangerousness] can be precluded from using is unless he is [also] willing to be examined by a psychiatrist nominated by the state." 602 F.2d 705, 707.

from being compelled to incriminate themselves." *Miranda* held that "the prosecution may not use statements, whether exculpatory or inculpatory, stemming from custodial interrogation of the defendant unless it demonstrates the use of procedural safeguards effective to secure the privilege against self-incrimination." *Id.*, at 444, 86 S.Ct., at 1612. Thus, absent other fully effective procedures, a person in custody must receive certain warnings before any official interrogation, including that he has a "right to remain silent" and that "anything said can and will be used against the individual in court." *Id.*, at 467–469, 86 S.Ct., at 1624–1625. The purpose of these admonitions is to combat what the Court saw as "inherently compelling pressures" at work on the person and to provide him with an awareness of the Fifth Amendment privilege and the consequences of foregoing it, which is the prerequisite for "an intelligent decision as to its exercise." *Ibid.*

The considerations calling for the accused to be warned prior to custodial interrogation apply with no less force to the pretrial psychiatric examination at issue here. Respondent was in custody at the Dallas County Jail when the examination was ordered and when it was conducted. That respondent was questioned by a psychiatrist designated by the trial court to conduct a neutral competency examination, rather than by a police officer, government informant, or prosecuting attorney, is immaterial. When Dr. Grigson went beyond simply reporting to the court on the issue of competence and testified for the prosecution at the penalty phase on the crucial issue of respondent's future dangerousness, his role changed and became essentially like that of an agent of the State recounting unwarned statements made in a post-arrest custodial setting. During the psychiatric evaluation, respondent assuredly was "faced with a phase of the adversary system" and was "not in the presence of [a] person[ ] acting solely in his interest." *Id.*, at 469, 86 S.Ct., at 1625. Yet he was given no indication that the compulsory examination would be used to gather evidence necessary to decide whether, if convicted, he should be sentenced to death. He was not informed that, accordingly, he had a constitutional right not to answer the questions put to him.

[10, 11]   The Fifth Amendment privilege is "as broad as the mischief against which it seeks to guard," *Counselman v. Hitchcock*, 142 U.S. 547, 562, 12 S.Ct. 195, 198, 35 L.Ed. 1110 (1892), and the privilege is fulfilled only when a criminal defendant is guaranteed the right "to remain silent unless he chooses to speak in the unfettered exercise of his own will, and to suffer no penalty . . . for such silence." [11] *Malloy v. Hogan*, 378 U.S. 1, 8, 84 S.Ct. 1489, 1493–1494, 12 L.Ed.2d 653 (1964). We agree with the Court of Appeals that respondent's Fifth Amendment rights were violated by the admission of Dr. Grigson's testimony at the penalty phase.[12]

---

[11] While recognizing that attempts to coerce a defendant to submit to psychiatric inquiry on his future dangerousness might include the penalty of prosecutorial comment on his refusal to be examined, the Court of Appeals noted that making such a remark and allowing the jury to draw its own conclusions "might clash with [this Court's] insistence that capital sentencing procedures be unusually reliable." 602 F.2d, at 707. See also *Griffin v. California*, 380 U.S. 609, 85 S.Ct. 1229, 14 L.Ed.2d 106 (1965).

[12] For the reasons stated by the Court of Appeals, we reject the State's argument that respondent waived his Fifth Amendment claim by failing to make a timely, specific objection to Dr. Grigson's testimony at trial. See 602 F.2d, at 708, n. 19. In addition, we note that the State did not present the waiver argument in its petition for certiorari. See this Court's Rule 40(1)(d)(2) (1970).

[12, 13]   A criminal defendant, who neither initiates a psychiatric evaluation nor attempts to introduce any psychiatric evidence, may not be compelled to respond to a psychiatrist if his statements can be used against him at a capital sentencing proceeding. Because respondent did not voluntarily consent to the pretrial psychiatric examination after being informed of his right to remain silent and the possible use of his statements, the State could not rely on what he said to Dr. Grigson to establish his future dangerousness. If, upon being adequately warned, respondent had indicated that he would not answer Dr. Grigson's questions, the validly ordered competency examination nevertheless could have proceeded upon the condition that the results would be applied solely for that purpose. In such circumstances, the proper conduct and use of competency and sanity examinations are not frustrated, but the State must make its case on future dangerousness in some other way.

"Volunteered statements . . . are not barred by the Fifth Amendment," but under *Miranda v. Arizona, supra*, we must conclude that, when faced while in custody with a court-ordered psychiatric inquiry, respondent's statements to Dr. Grigson were not "given freely and voluntarily without any compelling influences" and, as such, could be used as the State did at the penalty phase only if respondent had been apprised of his rights and had knowingly decided to waive them. *Id.*, at 478, 86 S.Ct., at 1630. These safeguards of the Fifth Amendment privilege were not afforded respondent and, thus, his death sentence cannot stand.[13]

---

[13] Of course, we do not hold that the same Fifth Amendment concerns are necessarily presented by all types of interviews and examinations that might be ordered or relied upon to inform a sentencing determination.

B

[14, 15]   When respondent was examined by Dr. Grigson, he already had been indicated and an attorney had been appointed to represent him. The Court of Appeals concluded that he had a Sixth Amendment right to the assistance of counsel before submitted to the pretrial psychiatric interview. 602 F.2d, at 708–709. We agree.

The Sixth Amendment, made applicable to the states through the Fourteenth Amendment, provides that "[i]n all criminal prosecutions, the accused shall enjoy the right . . . to have the Assistance of Counsel for his defense." The "vital" need for a lawyer's advice and aid during the pretrial phase was recognized by the Court nearly 50 years ago in *Powell v. Alabama*, 287 U.S. 45, 57, 71, 53 S.Ct. 55, 60, 65, 77 L.Ed. 158 (1932). Since then, we have held that the right to counsel granted by the Sixth Amendment means that a person is entitled to the help of a lawyer "at or after the time that adversary judicial proceedings have been initiated against him . . . whether by way of formal charge, preliminary hearing, indictment, information, or arraignment." *Kirby v. Illinois*, 406 U.S. 682, 688–689, 92 S.Ct. 1877, 1882, 32 L.Ed.2d 411 (1972) (plurality opinion); *Moore v. Illinois*, 434 U.S. 220, 226–229, 98 S.Ct. 458, 463–465, 54 L.Ed.2d 424 (1977). And in *United States v. Wade*, 388 U.S. 218, 226–227, 87 S.Ct. 1926, 1932, 18 L.Ed.2d 1149 (1967), the Court explained:

"It is central to [the Sixth Amendment] principle that in addition to counsel's presence at trial, the accused is guaranteed that he need not stand alone against the State at any stage of the prosecution, formal or informal, in court or out, where counsel's absence might derogate from the accused's right to a fair trial." (Footnote omitted.)

See *United States v. Henry*, 447 U.S. 264, 100 S.Ct. 2183, 65 L.Ed.2d 115 (1980);

Massiah v. United States, 377 U.S. 201, 84 S.Ct. 1199, 12 L.Ed.2d 246 (1964). See also *White v. Maryland*, 373 U.S. 59, 83 S.Ct. 1050, 10 L.Ed.2d 193 (1963); *Hamilton v. Alabama*, 368 U.S. 52, 82 S.Ct. 157, 7 L.Ed.2d 114 (1961).

Here, respondent's Sixth Amendment right to counsel clearly had attached when Dr. Grigson examined him at the Dallas County Jail,[14] and their interview proved to be a "critical stage" of the aggregate proceedings against respondent. See *Coleman v. Alabama*, 399 U.S. 1, 7–10, 90 S.Ct. 1999, 2002–2004, 26 L.Ed.2d 387 (1970) (plurality opinion); *Powell v. Alabama, supra,* 287 U.S., at 57, 53 S.Ct., at 60. Defense counsel, however, were not notified in advance that the psychiatric examination would encompass the issue of their client's future dangerousness,[15] and respondent

---

[14] Because psychiatric examinations of the type at issue here are conducted after adversary proceedings have been instituted, we are not concerned in this case with the limited right to the appointment and presence of counsel recognized as a Fifth Amendment safeguard in *Miranda v. Arizona, supra,* 384 U.S., at 471–473, 86 S.Ct., at 1626–1627. See *Edwards v. Arizona,* —— U.S. ——, 101 S.Ct. 1880, 67 L.Ed.2d —— (1981). Rather, the issue before us is whether a defendant's Sixth Amendment right to the assistance of counsel is abridged when the defendant is not given prior opportunity to consult with counsel about his participation in the psychiatric examination. But cf. n. 15, *infra.*

Respondent does not assert, and the Court of Appeals did not find, any constitutional right to have counsel actually present during the examination. In fact, the Court of Appeals recognized that "an attorney present during the psychiatric interview could contribute little and might seriously disrupt the examination." 602 F.2d at 708. Cf. *Thornton v. Corcoran,* 132 U.S.App.D.C. 232, 242, 248, 407 F.2d 695, 705, 711 (1969) (opinion concurring in part and dissenting in part).

[15] It is not clear that defense counsel were even informed prior to the examination that

was denied the assistance of his attorneys in making the significant decision of whether to submit to the examination and to what end the psychiatrist's findings could be employed.

Because "[a] layman may not be aware of the precise scope, the nuances, and the boundaries of his Fifth Amendment privilege," the assertion of that right "often depends upon legal advise from someone who is trained and skilled in the subject matter." *Maness v. Meyers*, 419 U.S. 449, 466, 95 S.Ct. 584, 595, 42 L.Ed.2d 574 (1975). As the Court of Appeals observed, the decision to be made regarding the proposed psychiatric evaluation is "literally a life or death matter" and is "difficult . . . even for an attorney" because it requires "a knowledge of what other evidence is available, of the particular psychiatrist's biases and predilections, [and] of possible alternative strategies at the sentencing hearing." 602 F.2d, at 708. It follows logically from our precedents that a defendant should not be forced to resolve such an important issue without "the guiding hand of counsel." *Powell v. Alabama, supra,* 287 U.S., at 69, 53 S.Ct., at 64.

Therefore, in addition to Fifth Amendment considerations, the death penalty was improperly imposed on respondent because the psychiatric examination on which Dr. Grigson testified at the penalty phase proceeded in violation of respondent's Sixth Amendment right to the assistance of counsel.[16]

Dr. Grigson had been appointed by the trial judge to determine respondent's competency to stand trial. See n. 5, *supra.*

[16] We do not hold that respondent was precluded from waiving this constitutional right. Waivers of the assistance of counsel, however, "must no only be voluntary, but constitute a knowing and intelligent relinquishment or abandonment of a known right or privilege, a matter which depends . . .

C

Our holding based on the Fifth and Sixth Amendments will not prevent the State in capital cases from proving the defendant's future dangerousness as required by statute. A defendant may request or consent to a psychiatric examination concerning future dangerousness in the hope of escaping the death penalty. In addition, a different situation arises where a defendant intends to introduce psychiatric evidence at the penalty phase. See n. 10, *supra.*

Moreover, under the Texas capital sentencing procedure, the inquiry necessary for the jury's resolution of the future dangerousness issue is in no sense confined to the province of psychiatric experts. Indeed, some in the psychiatric community are of the view that clinical predictions as to whether a person would or would not commit violent acts in the future are "fundamentally of very low reliability" and that psychiatrists possess no special qualifications for making such forecasts. See Report of the America Psychiatric Association Task Force on Clinical Aspects of the Violent Individual 23–30, 33 (1974); A. Stone Mental Health and Law: A System in Transition 27–36 (1975); Brief for American Psychiatric Association as *Amicus Curiae* 11–17.

In *Jurek v. Texas*, 428 U.S. 262, 96 S.Ct. 2950, 49 L.Ed.2d 929 (1976), we held that the Texas capital sentencing statute is not unconstitutional on its face. As to the jury question on future dangerousness, the joint opinion an-

---

'upon the particular facts and circumstances surrounding [each] case. . . .'" *Edwards v. Arizona, supra,* —— U.S., at ——, 101 S.Ct., at 1883–1884, quoting *Johnson v. Zerbst,* 304 U.S. 458, 464, 58 S.Ct. 1019, 1023, 82 L.Ed. 1461 (1938). No such waiver has been shown, or even alleged, here.

nouncing the judgment emphasized that a defendant is free to present whatever mitigating factors he may be able to show, e. g., the range and severity of his past criminal conduct, his age, and the circumstances surrounding the crime for which he is being sentenced. *Id.*, at 272–273, 96 S.Ct., at 2956–2957. The State, of course, can use the same type of evidence in seeking to establish a defendant's propensity to commit other violent acts.

In responding to the argument that foretelling future behavior is impossible, the joint opinion stated:

"[P]rediction of future criminal conduct is an essential element in many of the decisions rendered throughout our criminal justice system. The decision whether to admit a defendant to bail, for instance, must often turn on a judge's prediction of the defendant's future conduct. And any sentencing authority must predict a convicted person's probable future conduct when it engages in the process of determining what punishment to impose. For those sentenced to prison, these same predictions must be made by parole authorities. The task that a Texas jury must perform in answering the statutory question in issue is thus basically no different from the task performed countless times each day throughout the American system of criminal justice." (Footnotes omitted.) *Id.*, at 275–276, 96 S.Ct., at 2957–2958.

While in no sense disapproving the use of psychiatric testimony bearing on the issue of future dangerousness, the holding in *Jurek* was guided by recognition that the inquiry mandated by Texas law does not require resort to medical experts.

III

Respondent's Fifth and Sixth Amendment rights were abridged by the State's introduction of Dr. Grigson's testimony at the penalty phase, and, as the Court of Appeals concluded, his

death sentence must be vacated.[17] Because respondent's underlying conviction has not been challenged and remains undisturbed, the State is free to conduct further proceedings not inconsistent with this opinion. Accordingly, the judgment of the Court of Appeals is

Affirmed.

Justice BRENNAN.

I join the Court's opinion. I also adhere to my position that the death penalty is in all circumstances unconstitutional.

Justice MARSHALL, concurring in part.

I join in all but Part II–C of the opinion of the Court. I adhere to my consistent view that the death penalty is under all circumstances cruel and unusual punishment forbidden by the Eighth and Fourteenth Amendments. I therefore am unable to join the suggestion in Part II–C that the penalty may ever be constitutionally imposed.

Justice STEWART, with whom Justice POWELL joins, concurring in the judgment.

The respondent had been indicted for murder and a lawyer had been appointed to represent him before he was examined by Dr. Grigson at the behest of the State. Yet that examination took place without previous notice to the respondent's counsel. The Sixth and Fourteenth Amendments as applied in such cases as *Massiah v. United States*, 377 U.S. 201, 84 S.Ct. 1199, 12 L.Ed.2d

[17] Because of our disposition of respondent's Fifth and Sixth Amendment claims, we need not reach the question of whether the failure to give advance notice of Dr. Grigson's appearance as a witness for the State deprived respondent of due process.

246, and *Brewer v. Williams*, 430 U.S. 387, 97 S.Ct. 1232, 51 L.Ed.2d 424, made impermissible the introduction of Dr. Grigson's testimony against the respondent at any stage of his trial.

I would for this reason affirm the judgment before us without reaching the other issues discussed by the Court.

Justice REHNQUIST, concurring in the judgment.

I concur in the judgment because, under *Massiah v. United States*, 377 U.S. 201, 84 S.Ct. 1199, 12 L.Ed.2d 246 (1964), respondent's counsel should have been notified prior to Dr. Grigson's examination of respondent. As the Court notes, *ante,* at 1876, respondent had been indicted and an attorney had been appointed to represent him. Counsel was entitled to be made aware of Dr. Grigson's activities involving his client and to advise and prepare his client accordingly. This is by no means to say that respondent had any right to have his counsel present at any examination. In this regard I join the Court's careful delimiting of the Sixth Amendment issue, *ante,* at 1877, n. 14.

Since this is enough to decide the case, I would not go on to consider the Fifth Amendment issues and cannot subscribe to the Court's resolution of them. I am not convinced that any Fifth Amendment rights were implicated by Dr. Grigson's examination of respondent. Although the psychiatrist examined respondent prior to trial, he only testified concerning the examination after respondent stood convicted. As the court in *Hollis v. Smith*, 571 F.2d 685, 690–691 (CA2 1978) analyzed the issue, "The psychiatrist's interrogation of [defendant] on subjects presenting no threat of disclosure of prosecutable crimes, in the belief that the substance of [defendant's] responses or the way in which he gave them might cast light on

the manner of man he was, involved no 'compelled testimonial self-incrimination' even though the consequence might be more severe punishment."

Even if there are Fifth Amendment rights involved in this case, respondent never invoked these rights when confronted with Dr. Grigson's questions. The Fifth Amendment privilege against compulsory self-incrimination is not self-executing. "Although *Miranda's* requirement of specific warnings creates a limited exception to the rule that the privilege must be claimed, the exception does not apply outside the context of the inherently coercive custodial interrogations for which it was designed." *Roberts v. United States*, 445 U.S. 552, 560, 100 S.Ct. 1358, 1364, 63 L.Ed.2d 622 (1980). The *Miranda* requirements were certainly not designed by this Court with psychiatric examinations in mind. Respondent was simply not in the inherently coercive situation considered in *Miranda*. He had already been indicted, and counsel had been appointed to represent him. No claim is raised that respondent's answers to Dr. Grigson's questions were "involuntary" in the normal sense of the word. Unlike the police officers in *Miranda*, Dr. Grigson was not questioning respondent in order to ascertain his guilt or innocence. Particularly since it is not necessary to decide this case, I would not extend the *Miranda* requirements to cover psychiatric examinations such as the one involved here.

[200] DANIEL M'NAGHTEN'S CASE.
May 26, June 19, 1843.

[Mew's Dig. i. 349; iv. 1112. S.C. 8 Scott N.R. 595; 1 C. and K. 130; 4 St. Tr. N.S. 847. The rules laid down in this case have been accepted in the main as an authoritative statement of the law (cf. *Reg.* v. *Townley*, 1863, 3 F. and F. 839;

Reg. v. *Southey,* 1865, 4 F. and F. 864; *Reg.* v. *Leigh,* 1866, 4 F. and F. 919). But they have been adversely criticised both by legal and medical text writers (see 2 Steph. *Hist Crim. Law,* 124–186; Mayne *Ind. Crim. Law* (ed. 1896), 368), have been rejected by many of the American States (see e.g. *Parsons* v. *State,* 1887, 81 Ala. 577), and frequently receive a liberal interpretation in England. On point as to questions to the Judges, see note to *London and Westminster Bank Case,* 2 Cl. and F. 191.]

Murder—Evidence—Insanity.

The House of Lords has a right to require the Judges to answer abstract questions of existing law (see London and Westminster Bank Case, *ante* [2 Cl. and F.], p. 191 [and note thereto].

Notwithstanding a party accused did an act, which was in itself criminal, under the influence of insane delusion, with a view of redressing or revenging some supposed grievance or injury, or of producing some public benefit, he is nevertheless punishable if he knew at the time that he was acting contrary to law.

That if the accused was conscious that the act was one which he ought not to do; and if the act was at the same time contrary to law, he is punishable. In all cases of this kind the jurors ought to be told that every man is presumed to be sane, and to possess a sufficient degree of reason to be responsible for his crimes, until the contrary be proved to their satisfaction: and that to establish a defence on the ground of insanity, it must be clearly proved that at the time of commiting the act the party accused was labouring under such a defect of reason, from disease of the mind, as not to know the nature and quality of the act he was doing, or as not to know that what he was doing was wrong.

That a party labouring under a partial delusion must be considered in the same situation, as to responsibility, as if the facts, in respect to which the delusion exists, were real.

That where an accused person is supposed to be insane, a medical man, who has been present in Court and heard the evidence, may be asked, as a matter of science, whether the facts stated by the witness, supposing them to be true, show a state of mind incapable of distinguishing between right and wrong.

The prisoner had been indicted for that he, on the 20th day of January 1843, at the parish of Saint Martin in the Fields, in the county of Middlesex, and within the jurisdiction of the Central Criminal Court, in and upon one Edward Drummond, feloniously, wilfully, and of his malice aforethought, did make an assault; and that the said Daniel M'Naghten, a certain pistol of the value of 20s., loaded and **[201]** charged with gunpowder and a leaden bullet (which pistol he in his right hand had and held), to, against and upon the said Edward Drummond, feloniously, wilfully, and of his malice aforethought, did shoot and discharge; and that the said Daniel M'Naghten, with the leaden bullet aforesaid, out of the pistol aforesaid, by force of the gunpowder, etc., the said Edward Drummond, in and upon the back of him the said Edward Drummond, feloniously, etc. did strike, penetrate and wound, giving to the said Edward Drummond, in and upon the back of the said Edward Drummond, one mortal wound, etc., of which mortal wound the said E. Drummond languished until the 25th of April and then died; and that by the means aforesaid, he the prisoner did kill and murder the said Edward Drummond. The prisoner pleaded Not guilty.

Evidence having been given of the fact of the shooting of Mr. Drummond, and of his death in consequence thereof, witnesses were called on the part of the prisoner, to prove that he was not, at the time of committing the act, in a sound state of mind. The medical evidence was in substance this: That persons of otherwise sound mind, might be affected by morbid delusions: that the prisoner was in that condition: that a person so labouring under a morbid delusion, might have a moral perception of right and wrong, but that in the case of the prisoner it was a delusion which carried him away beyond the power of his own control, and left him no such perception; and that he was not capable of exercising any control over acts which had connexion with his delusion: that it was of the nature of the disease with which the prisoner was affected, to go on gradually until it had reached a climax, when it burst forth with irresistible [202] intensity: that a man might go on for years quietly, though at the same time under its influence, but would all at once break out into the most extravagant and violent paroxysms.

Some of the witnesses who gave this evidence, had previously examined the prisoner: others had never seen him till he appeared in Court, and they formed their opinions on hearing the evidence given by the other witnesses.

Lord Chief Justice Tindal (in his charge):—The question to be determined is, whether at the time the act in question was committed, the prisoner had or had not the use of his understanding, so as to know that he was doing a wrong or wicked act. If the jurors should be of opinion that the prisoner

was not sensible, at the time he committed it, that he was violating the laws both of God and man, then he would be entitled to a verdict in his favour: but if, on the contrary, they were of opinion that when he committed the act he was in a sound state of mind, then their verdict must be against him.

Verdict, Not guilty, on the ground of insanity.

This verdict, and the question of the nature and extent of the unsoundness of mind which would excuse the commission of a felony of this sort, having been made the subject of debate in the House of Lords (the 6th and 13th March 1843; see Hansard's Debates, vol. 67, pp. 288, 714), it was determined to take the opinion of the Judges on the law governing such cases. Accordingly, on the 26th of May, all the Judges attended their Lordships, but no questions were then put.

On the 19th of June, the Judges again attended the House of Lords; when (no argument having been [203] had) the following questions of law were propounded to them:—

1st. What is the law respecting alleged crimes committed by persons afflicted with insane delusion, in respect of one or more particular subjects or persons: as, for instance, where at the time of the commission of the alleged crime, the accused knew he was acting contrary to law, but did the act complained of with a view, under the influence of insane delusion, of redressing or revenging some supposed grievance or injury, or of producing some supposed public beneft?

2d. What are the proper questions to be submitted to the jury, when a person alleged to be afflicted with insane delusion respecting one or more particular subjects of persons, is charged with the commission of a crime (murder, for example), and insanity is set up as a defence?

3d. In what terms ought the question to be left to the jury, as to the prisoner's state of mind at the time when the act was committed?

4th. If a person under an insane delusion as to existing facts, commits an offence in consequence thereof, is he thereby excused?

5th. Can a medical man conversant with the disease of insanity, who never saw the prisoner previously to the trial, but who was present during the whole trial and the examination of all the witnesses, be asked his opinion as to the state of the prisoner's mind at the time of the commission of the alleged crime, or his opinion whether the prisoner was conscious at the time of doing the act, that he was acting contrary to law, or whether he was labouring under any and what delusion at the time?

[204] Mr. Justice Maule:—I feel great difficulty in answering the questions put by your Lordships on this occasion:—First, because they do not appear to arise out of and are not put with reference to a particular case, or for a particular purpose, which might explain or limit the generality of their terms, so that full answers to them ought to be applicable to every possible state of facts, not inconsistent with those assumed in the questions: this difficulty is the greater, from the practical experience both of the bar and the Court being confined to questions arising out of the facts of particular cases:— Secondly, because I have heard no argument at your Lordships' bar or elsewhere, on the subject of these questions; the want of which I feel the more, the greater are the number and extent of questions which might be raised in argument:—and Thirdly, from a fear of which I cannot divest myself, that as these questions relate to matters of criminal law of great importance and frequent occurrence, the answers to them by the Judges may embarrass the

administration of justice, when they are cited in criminal trials. For these reasons I should have been glad if my learned brethren would have joined me in praying your Lordships to excuse us from answering these questions; but as I do not think they ought to induce me to ask that indulgence for myself individually, I shall proceed to give such answers as I can, after the very short time which I have had to consider the questions, and under the difficulties I have mentioned; fearing that my answers may be as little satisfactory to others as they are to myself.

The first question, as I understand it, is, in effect, What is the law respecting the alleged crime, when at the time of the commission of it, the accused knew he was acting contrary to the law, but did the act [205] with a view, under the influence of insane delusion, of redressing or revenging some supposed grievance or injury, or of producing some supposed public benefit?—If I were to understand this question according to the strict meaning of its terms, it would require, in order to answer it, a solution of all questions of law which could arise on the circumstances stated in the question, either by explicitly stating and answering such questions, or by stating some principles or rules which would suffice for their solution. I am quite unable to do so, and, indeed, doubt whether it be possible to be done; and therefore request to be permitted to answer the question only so far as it comprehends the question, whether a person, circumstanced as stated in the question, is, for that reason only, to be found not guilty of a crime respecting which the question of his guilt has been duly raised in a criminal proceeding? and I am of opinion that he is not. There is no law, that I am aware of, that makes persons in the state described in the question not responsible for their criminal acts. To render a person irresponsible for crime on account of unsound-ness of mind, the unsoundess should, according to the law as it has long been understood and held, be such as rendered him incapable of knowing right from wrong. The terms used in the question cannot be said (with reference only to the usage of language) to be equivalent to a description of this kind and degree of unsoundness of mind. If the state described in the question be one which involves or is necessarily connected with such an unsoundness, this is not a matter of law but of physiology, and not of that obvious and familiar kind as to be inferred without proof.

Second, the questions necessarily to be submitted to the jury, are those questions of fact which are **[206]** raised on the record. In a criminal trial, the question commonly is, whether the accused be guilty or not guilty: but, in order to assist the jury in coming to a right conclusion on this necessary and ultimate question, it is usual and proper to submit such subordinate or intermediate questions, as the course which the trial has taken may have made it convenient to direct their attention to. What those questions are, and the manner of submitting them, is a matter of discretion for the Judge: a discretion to be guided by a consideration of all the circumstances attending the inquiry. In performing this duty, it is sometimes necessary or convenient to inform the jury as to the law; and if, on a trial such as is suggested in the question, he should have occasion to state what kind and degree of insanity would amount to a defence, it should be stated conformably to what I have mentioned in my answer to the first question, as being, in my opinion, the law on this subject.

Third, there are no terms which the Judge is by law required to use. They should not be inconsistent with the law as above stated, but should be such as, in the discretion of the Judge, are

proper to assist the jury in coming to a right conclusion as to the guilt of the accused.

Fourth, the answer which I have given to the first question, is applicable to this.

Fifth, whether a question can be asked, depends, not merely on the questions of fact raised on the record, but on the course of the cause at the time it is proposed to ask it; and the state of an inquiry as to the guilt of a person charged with a crime, and defended on the ground of insanity, may be such, that a question as either of those suggested, is proper to be asked and answered, though the witness has **[207]** never seen the person before the trial, and though he has merely been present and heard the witnesses: these circumstances, of his never having seen the person before, and of his merely been present at the trial, not being necessarily sufficient, as it seems to me, to exclude the lawfulness of a question which is otherwise lawful; though I will not say that an inquiry might not be in such a state, is that these circumstances should have such an effect.

Supposing there is nothing else in the state of the trial to make the questions suggested proper to be asked and answered, except that the witness had been present and heard the evidence; it is to be considered whether that is enough to sustain the question. In principle it is open to this objection, that as the opinion of the witness is founded on those conclusions of fact which he forms from the evidence, and as it does not appear what those conclusions are, it may be that the evidence he gives is on such an assumption of facts, as makes it irrelevant to the inquiry. But such questions have been very frequently asked, and the evidence to which they are directed has been given, and has never, that I am aware of, been successfully objected to. Evidence, most clearly open to this objection, and on the admission of which the event of a most important trial probably turned, was received in the case of *The Queen* v. *M'Naghten,* tried at the Central Criminal Court in March last, before the Lord Chief Justice, Mr. Justice Williams, and Mr. Justice Coleridge, in which counsel of the highest eminence were engaged on both sides; and I think the course and practice of receiving such evidence, confirmed by the very high authority of these Judges, who not only received it, but left it, as I understand, to the jury, without any remark derogating from its [208] weight, ought to be held to warrant its reception, notwithstanding the objection in principle to which it may be open. In cases even where the course of practice in criminal law has been unfavourable to parties accused, and entirely contrary to the most obvious principles of justice and humanity, as well as those of law, it has been held that such practice constituted the law, and could not be altered without the authority of Parliament.

Lord Chief Justice Tindal:—My Lords, Her Majesty's Judges (with the exception of Mr. Justice Maule, who has stated his opinion to your Lordships), in answering the questions proposed to them by your Lordships' House, think it right, in the first place, to state that they have forborne entering into any particular discussion upon these questions, from the extreme and almost insuperable difficulty of applying those answers to cases in which the facts are not brought judicially before them. The facts of each particular case must of necessity present themselves with endless variety, and with every shade of difference in each case; and as it is their duty to declare the law upon each particular case, on facts proved before them, and after hearing argument of counsel thereon, they deem it at once impracticable, and at the same time dangerous to

the administration of justice, if it were practicable, to attempt to make minute applications of the principles involved in the answers given by them to your Lordships' questions.

They have therefore confined their answers to the statement of that which they hold to be the law upon the abstract questions proposed by your Lordships; and as they deem it unnecessary, in this peculiar case, to deliver their opinions seriatim, and as all concur in [209] the same opinion, they desire me to express such their unanimous opinion to your Lordships.

The first question proposed by your Lordships is this: "What is the law respecting alleged crimes committed by persons afflicted with insane delusion in respect of one or more particular subjects or persons: as, for instance, where at the time of the commission of the alleged crime the accused knew he was acting contrary to law, but did the act complained of with a view, under the influence of insane delusion, of redressing or revenging some supposed grievance or injury, or of producing some supposed public benefit?"

In answer to which question, assuming that your Lordships' inquiries are confined to those persons who labour under such partial delusions only, and are not in other respects insane, we are of opinion that, notwithstanding the party accused did the act complained of with a view, under the influence of insane delusion, of redressing or revenging some supposed grievance or injury, or of producing some public benefit, he is nevertheless punishable according to the nature of the crime committed, if he knew at the time of committing such crime that he was acting contrary to law; by which expression we understand your Lordships to mean the law of the land.

Your Lordships are pleased to inquire of us, secondly, "What are the proper questions to be submitted to the jury, where a person alleged to be afflicted with insane delusion respecting one or more particular subjects or persons, is charged with the commission of a crime (murder, for example), and insanity is set up as a defence?" And, thirdly, "In what terms ought the question to be left to the jury as to the prisoner's state of mind at the time when [210] the act was committed?" And as these two questions appear to us to be more conveniently answered together, we have to submit our opinion to be, that the jurors ought to be told in all cases that every man is to be presumed to be sane, and to possess a sufficient degree of reason to be responsible for his crimes, until the contrary be proved to their satisfaction; and that to establish a defence on the ground of insanity, it must be clearly proved that, at the time of the committing of the act, the party accused was labouring under such a defect of reason, from disease of the mind, as not to know the nature and quality of the act he was doing; or, if he did know it, that he did not know he was doing what was wrong. The mode of putting the latter part of the question to the jury on these occasions has generally been, whether the accused at the time of doing the act knew the difference between right and wrong: which mode, though rarely, if ever, leading to any mistake with the jury, is not, as we conceive, so accurate when put generally and in the abstract, as when put with reference to the party's knowledge of right and wrong in respect to the very act with which he is charged. If the question were to be put as to the knowledge of the accused solely and exclusively with reference to the law of the land, it might tend to confound the jury, by inducing them to believe that an actual knowledge of the law of the land was essential in order to lead to a conviction; whereas the law is adminis-

tered upon the principle that every one must be taken conclusively to know it, without proof that he does know it. If the accused was conscious that the act was one which he ought not to do, and if that act was at the same time contrary to the law of the land, he is punishable; and the usual course therefore [211] has been to leave the question to the jury, whether the party accused had a sufficient degree of reason to know that he was doing an act that was wrong: and this course we think is correct, accompanied with such observations and explanations as the circumstances of each particular case may require.

The fourth question which your Lordships have proposed to us is this:—"If a person under an insane delusion as to existing facts, commits an offense in consequence thereof, is he thereby excused?" To which question the answer must of course depend on the nature of the delusion: but, making the same assumption as we did before, namely, that he labours under such partial delusion only, and is not in other respects insane, we think he must be considered in the same situation as to responsibility as if the facts with respect to which the delusion exists were real. For example, if under the influence of his delusion he supposed another man to be in the act of attempting to take away his life, and he kills that man, as he supposes, in self-defense, he would be exempt from punishment. If his delusion was that the deceased had inflicted a serious injury to his character and fortune, and he killed him in revenge for such supposed injury, he would be liable to punishment.

The question lastly proposed by your Lordships is:—"Can a medical man conversant with the disease of insanity, who never saw the prisoner previously to the trial, but who was present during the whole trial and the examination of all the witnesses, be asked his opinion as to the state of the prisoner's mind at the time of the commission of the alleged crime, or his opinion whether the prisoner was conscious at the time of doing the act that he was acting contrary to law, or whether he was labouring under any and **[212]** what delusion at the time?" In answer thereto, we state to your Lordships, that we think the medical man, under the circumstances supposed, cannot in strictness be asked his opinion in the terms above stated, because each of those questions involves the determination of the truth of the facts deposed to, which it is for the jury to decide, and the questions are not mere questions upon a matter of science, in which case such evidence is admissible. But where the facts are admitted or not disputed, and the question becomes substantially one of science only, it may be convenient to allow the question to be put in that general form, though the same cannot be insisted on as a matter of right.

Lord Brougham:—My Lords, the opinions of the learned Judges, and the very able manner in which they have been presented to the House, deserve our best thanks. One of the learned Judges has expressed his regret that these questions were not argued by counsel. Generally speaking, it is most important that in questions put for the consideration of the Judges, they should have all that assistance which is afforded to them by an argument by counsel: but at the same time, there can be no doubt of your Lordships' right to put, in this way, abstract questions of law to the Judges, the answer to which might be necessary to your Lordships in your legislative capacity. There is a precedent for this course, in the memorable instance of Mr. Fox's Bill on the law of libel; where, before passing the Bill, this House called on the Judges to give their opinions on what was the law as it then existed.

Lord Campbell:—My Lords, I cannot avoid express-**[213]**-ing my satisfaction, that the noble and learned Lord on the woolsack carried into effect his desire to put these questions to the Judges. It was most fit that the opinions of the Judges should be asked on these matters, the settling of which is not a mere matter of speculation; for your Lordships may be called on, in your legislative capacity, to change the law; and before doing so, it is proper that you should be satisfied beyond doubt what the law really is. It is desirable to have such questions argued at the bar, but such a course is not always practicable. Your Lordships have been reminded of one precedent for this proceeding, but there is a still more recent instance; the Judges having been summoned in the case of the Canada Reserves, to express their opinions on what was then the law on that subject. The answers given by the Judges are most highly satisfactory, and will be of the greatest use in the administration of justice.

Lord Cottenham:—My Lords, I fully concur with the opinion now expressed, as to the obligations we owe to the Judges. It is true that they cannot be required to say what would be the construction of a Bill, not in existence as a law at the moment at which the question is put to them; but they may be called on to assist your Lordships, in declaring their opinions upon abstract questions of existing law.

Lord Wynford:—My Lords, I never doubted that your Lordships possess the power to call on the Judges to give their opinions upon questions of existing law, proposed to them as these questions have been. I myself recollect, that when I had the honour to hold the office of Lord Chief Justice of the Court of **[214]** Common Pleas, I communicated to the House the opinions of the Judges on questions of this sort, framed with reference to the usury laws. Upon the opinion of the Judges thus delivered to the House by me, a Bill was founded, and afterwards passed into a law.

The Lord Chancellor:—My Lords, I entirely concur in the opinion given by my noble and learned friends, as to our right to have the opinions of the Judges on abstract questions of existing law; and I agree that we owe our thanks to the Judges, for the attention and learning with which they have answered the questions now put to them.

The PEOPLE of the State of Colorado, Plaintiff-Appellant,

v.

Michael Joseph WRIGHT, Defendant-Appellee.

No. 80SA256.

Supreme Court of Colorado, En Banc.

July 26, 1982.

The District Court, El Paso County, Joe A. Cannon, J., entered judgment finding the defendant not guilty by reason of insanity, and the People appealed. The Supreme Court, Lee, J., held that: (1) conclusion of trier of fact that the People had failed to prove sanity beyond a reasonable doubt and that the defendant, though not suffering from an organic brain syndrome, had a comprehension of reality which was too distorted for him to be held legally accountable for his criminal conduct was supported by record, and (2) expert testimony concerning the psychological testing of the defendant, results of those tests, the nature of the condition of minimal brain dysfunction, and its relation to poor impulse control and lack of willpower was admissible as relevant to issue of defendant's sanity despite claim of its unreliability.

Affirmed.

1. Criminal Law ⟜ **311, 331**

Every criminal defendant is presumed sane, but once any evidence of insanity is introduced at trial, burden of proof is on the People to prove sanity beyond a reasonable doubt. C.R.S.1973, 16–8–101, 18–1–802.

2. Criminal Law ⟜ **740**

When evidence of sanity is in dispute, fact finder must resolve conflict in testimony and weigh all relevant evidence to determine whether defendant was legally insane at time of act. C.R.S.1973, 16–8–101, 18–1–802.

3. Criminal Law ⟜ **48**

One who is legally insane at time of commission of act which would otherwise be criminal is not criminally accountable and is excused from punishment. C.R.S.1973, 16–8–101, 18–1–802.

4. Criminal Law ⟜ **494**

Where expert testimony on the issue of sanity is in conflict, the resolution of the conflict and the weight to be given to the testimony is solely the province of the trier of fact. C.R.S.1973, 16–8–101, 18–1–802.

5. Criminal Law ⟜ **740**

The question of sanity in a criminal case is an issue of fact to be determined by the trier of fact. C.R.S.1973, 16–8–101, 18–1–802.

Reprinted with permission 648 P.2d 665 (Colo. 1982). Copyright © by West Publishing Co.

6.   Homicide   ⟸ 237

Conclusion of trier of fact in prosecution for first-degree murder that the People had failed to prove sanity beyond a reasonable doubt and that the defendant, though not suffering from an organic brain syndrome, had a comprehension of reality which was too distorted for him to be held legally accountable for his criminal conduct was supported by record. C.R.S.1973, 16–8–101, 18–1–802.

7.   Criminal Law   ⟸ 354, 456

Traditionally, the scope of evidence admissible on the issue of insanity is broad, and even lay persons are free to testify as to the sanity of the defendant if a proper foundation is presented. C.R.S.1973, 16–8–107(2), 16–8–109.

8.   Criminal Law   ⟸ 488

Expert testimony concerning the psychological testing of the defendant, results of those tests, the nature of the condition of minimal brain dysfunction, and its relation to poor impulse control and lack of willpower was admissible as relevant to issue of defendant's sanity despite claim of its unreliability. C.R.S.1973, 16–8–107(2), 16–8–109.

———————

John Anderson, Special Deputy Dist. Atty., Dennis Faulk, Deputy Dist. Atty., Colorado Springs, for plaintiff-appellant.

J. Gregory Walta, Colorado State Public Defender, Susan L. Fralick, Deputy State Public Defender, Denver, for defendant-appellee.

LEE, Justice.

The defendant, Michael Joseph Wright, was charged with the first degree murder of a child, and he entered a plea of not guilty by reason of insanity. After a trial to the court on the issue of the defendant's sanity, the court entered its order finding the defendant not guilty by reason of insanity. The People bring this appeal of the judgment,[1] arguing that the evidence was insufficient, as a matter of law, to support the trial court's finding of insanity, and that the court improperly considered evidence that the defendant suffered from a minimal brain dysfunction in reaching the conclusion that the defendant was insane. We affirm the judgment.

On the night of July 3, 1979, the defendant was staying in the home of his parents along with his girlfriend, Neva, and her five-month old infant. Neva bathed the infant and put him to bed, then went to bed herself, while the defendant stayed up watching television. In the early morning hours of July 4 the defendant awoke Neva and asked her where the flashlight was, telling her he thought he heard prowlers outside. He took the flashlight and went out of the house for about twenty minutes. He came back in and engaged in sexual relations with Neva before both fell asleep. The next morning Neva realized that her son was not in his crib. She searched the house and asked the defendant if he knew where the child was. He denied any knowledge of his whereabouts but did not seem concerned. Neva first called relatives and then the police. The defendant sat passively in the house while searchers looked for the child.

[1] Section 16–12–102, C.R.S.1973 (1978 Repl. Vol. 8), creates a right of appeal in the prosecution regarding any question of law in a criminal case.

The searchers noted that several holes had been recently dug in the field behind the house. The child's body was found buried a short distance from the house. The defendant was questioned by police and eventually confessed to the killing. He described how he had given the baby a bottle of antifreeze to drink, but the child had spit it out. He then took the child into the yard and buried him alive. He later apparently attempted to save the child, but his efforts were too late as the child had already suffocated. He then reburied the child.

The defendant had a history of problems concerning the child. About a week preceding the homicide he took the child for a walk, but returned to the house with the child soaking wet. He told Neva that he had accidentally dropped the child in the creek when he walked across a log bridge. He later admitted that he had attempted to drown the child, but had saved him in time, fearing the wrath of Neva's father should anything happen to the baby. On another occasion he seized the child and refused to give him to his mother when Neva threatened to leave him after an argument. Police were summoned before he finally relinquished the child. On the afternoon prior to the homicide the defendant became angry when he learned that his sister's boyfriend had opened a savings account for the child without his knowledge.

After his arrest and incarceration awaiting trial, the defendant repeatedly attempted to contact Neva and wrote to her asking if she still wished to have a baby with him. To the examining psychiatrists he explained that he would be let out of jail if he told his lawyer that he would not do bad things anymore. He expressed his belief that he and Neva could be closer with the child out of the way.

I.

[1–3] Every criminal defendant is presumed sane, but once any evidence of insanity is introduced at trial, the burden of proof is on the People to prove sanity beyond a reasonable doubt. *People v. Ware*, 187 Colo. 28, 528 P.2d 224 (1974); *People ex rel. Juhan v. District Court*, 165 Colo. 253, 439 P.2d 741 (1968).[2] When evidence of sanity is in dispute, the fact-finder must resolve the conflict in the testimony, and weigh all relevant evidence to determine whether the defendant was legally insane at the time of the act. One who is legally insane at the time of the commission of the act which would otherwise be criminal, is not criminally accountable and is excused from punishment. *See* section 18–1–802, C.R.S.1973 (1978 Repl.Vol. 8).

Both the prosecution and the defense presented considerable evidence

[2] Legal insanity is defined at section 16–8–101, C.R.S.1973, as follows:

"The applicable test of insanity shall be, and the jury shall be so instructed: 'A person who is so diseased or defective in mind at the time of the commission of the act as to be incapable of distinguishing right from wrong with respect to that act, or being able so to distinguish, has suffered such an impairment of mind by disease or defect as to destroy the willpower and render him incapable of choosing the right and refraining from doing the wrong is not accountable; and this is so howsoever such insanity may be manifested, by irresistible impulse or otherwise. But care should be taken not to confuse such mental disease or defect with moral obliquity, mental depravity, or passion growing out of anger, revenge, hatred, or other motives, and kindred evil conditions, for when the act is induced by any of these causes, the person is accountable to the law.'"

regarding the defendant's mental state at the time of the commission of the crime. The People called three psychiatrists, one neurologist, and one psychologist, all of whom concluded that the defendant was sane.

The defendant's cell-mate testified that the defendant had confided to him that he had tricked the doctors into thinking he was insane. The defendant allegedly wished to appear insane so that he would be sent to the state hospital rather than to prison in the hope that he would get out sooner. The experts presented by the prosecution agreed that they thought the defendant was malingering and trying to appear insane to avoid punishment.

The defense presented testimony of experts to the effect that the defendant suffered from minimal brain dysfunction and that he was insane according to the legal definition. Dr. Cole, an expert in forensic psychiatry, testified that the defendant had a "disease or defect of the mind which [rendered] him incapable of distinguishing right from wrong or adhering to the right at the time of the crime." This opinion was developed by relying on the defendant's history, reports of other experts, and personal interviews with the defendant over approximately four and one-half hours. Dr. Cole related the defendant's belief that he would improve his relationship with the child's mother by disposing of the child. He described how the defendant wrote to the child's mother from prison in the apparent belief that their relationship would be ongoing, asking if she would wish to have another child with him. Dr. Cole testified that the defendant suffered from an organic brain syndrome with a psychosis, and as a result he had poor impulse control. This condition was manifested in the defendant's tendency to overreact to irritating forces by striking out in a rage

rather than inhibiting his anger more reasonably.

In addition, the defense offered the testimony of Dr. Coutts, a psychologist specializing in neuropsychology. Dr. Coutts testified that the defendant suffered from minimal brain dysfunction, a condition that results when neurotransmitters in the brain do not function normally. As he described it, neurotransmitters such as norepinephrine and seratonin activate "switches" in the brain's "inhibitory command post" to "either turn on or shut off whole behavior." When a person suffers from minimal brain dysfunction, his neurochemical responses do not act properly, either preventing inhibitory cells from turning off or allowing too many excitory cells to turn on. Dr. Coutts testified in terms of the decision-making process of the defendant, stating that the defendant's willpower was destroyed and that his mind was impaired by disease or defect so as to render him incapable of refraining from the wrong and choosing the right.

After hearing all testimony on the issue of the defendant's sanity, the court concluded that the prosecution had failed to prove sanity beyond a reasonable doubt. The court did not find that the defendant suffered from an organic brain syndrome. However, the court was of the opinion that the defendant's comprehension of reality was too distorted for him to be held legally accountable for his criminal conduct.

[4–6] Where expert testimony is in conflict, the resolution of the conflict and the weight to be given to the testimony is solely the province of the trier of fact. *People v. Lowe,* 184 Colo. 182, 519 P.2d 344 (1974). The question of sanity in a criminal case is an issue of fact to be determined by the trier of fact, in this case the trial judge. *Henderson v. People,* 156 Colo. 229, 397 P.2d 872 (1965); *People v. Haines,* 37 Colo.App. 302, 549 P.2d 786 (1976); *see also People v. Ware, supra; Gomez v. District Court,* 179 Colo. 299, 500 P.2d 134 (1972). On review of this record, we find no prejudicial error which would warrant our reversal of the trial court's factual determination.

II.

Even though the court did not base its conclusion of legal insanity on a finding that the defendant suffered from an organic brain syndrome, nevertheless, the People argue that the testimony concerning minimal brain dysfunction, also known as organic brain syndrome, should not have been admitted or considered by the trial court in determining whether the defendant suffered from a "mental disease or defect" within the meaning of the statute. The People contend such evidence is unreliable and is not relevant to the issue of sanity.

The People analogize the presence of minimal brain dysfunction to the presence of XYY chromosomal deficiency, which has been rejected as an indication of insanity by other courts. *See, People v. Tanner,* 13 Cal.App.3d 596, 91 Cal.Rptr. 656, 42 A.L.R.3d 1408 (1970). Evidence of XYY chromosomal deficiency has been excluded as irrelevant on the basis that the studies on the subject are inconclusive on the issue of insanity or aggressive behavior as a result of the syndrome, and that not all those who possess the XYY chromosome make-up are involuntarily aggressive. *See People v. Tanner, supra; see also People v. Yukl,* 83 Misc.2d 364, 372 N.Y.S.2d 313 (1975); *Millard v. State,* 8 Md.App. 419, 261 A.2d 227 (1970). We find the People's analogy inapposite.

In this case the expert witnesses, who were qualified without objection, testified that the defendant suffered from a psychosis as well as an organic brain syndrome. Moreover, the prosecution stipulated at trial that the defendant suffered from minimal brain dysfunction. Both defense experts testified that the defendant's minimal brain dysfunction resulted in poor impulse control, and that the defendant was incapable of choosing the right and refraining from doing the wrong.

[7] Traditionally, the scope of evidence admissible on the issue of insanity is broad. Even lay persons are free to testify as to the sanity of a defendant if a proper foundation is presented. *See* section 16–8–109, C.R.S.1973 (1978 Repl.Vol. 8); *People v. Medina,* 185 Colo. 101, 521 P.2d 1257 (1974); *Rupert v. People,* 163 Colo. 219, 429 P.2d 276 (1967). As we stated in *People v. Trujilio,* 150 Colo. 235, 238, 372 P.2d 86, 88 (1962):

"A much wider area of conduct on the part of a defendant can be made the subject of inquiry in a trial relating to his sanity, than would be permissible in a trial upon a plea of not guilty. Any abnormal conduct, whether related to the act forming the basis of the accusation or not, may be relevant and important on the issue of his mental condition. Conversely, evidence of normal conduct, and actions reflecting the usual and ordinary under the circumstances, may be shown to prove sanity."

Section 16–8–107(2), C.R.S.1973 (1978 Repl.Vol. 8), also indicates the scope of admissibility of expert testimony in an insanity trial. That subsection provides:

"(2) In any trial or hearing concerning the defendant's mental condition, physicians and other experts may testify as to their conclusions reached from their examination of hospital records, laboratory reports, x-rays, electroencephalograms, and psychological test results if the material which they examined in reaching their conclusions is produced at the time of the trial or hearing."

[8]   The expert testimony concerning the psychological testing of the defendant, the results of the tests, the nature of the condition of minimal brain dysfunction, its relation to poor impulse control and lack of willpower, was clearly admissible in evidence and relevant to the issue of the defendant's sanity. The People have not demonstrated that the court erred in admitting such evidence.

Judgment is affirmed.

Appendix 2

Current Training in Psychology and the Law

It can be expected that as psychologists become more aware of the potential for the interaction of psychology and the law, more training will become available. As of this writing, the following programs represent all of the joint-degree, Ph.D. specialty programs, Ph.D. minors, internships, and post-doctoral training opportunities currently available.*

PROGRAM DESCRIPTIONS

Institution: The University of Alabama.

Level: Ph.D. specialty.

Subdiscipline: Clinical.

Special Features: All students in the Ph.D. Psychology-Law specialty are also

*Reprinted from the *Newsletter*, Division of Psychology and the Law, 3, (3), Fall, 1983. With permission of Gary B. Melton, Ph.D., Editor.

clinical psychology Ph.D. students. They are required to take 16 hours in Psychology-Law courses. The actual courses include a seminar in Psychology and Law, and a seminar in Clinical-Correctional psychology, among others. Ours is very much an applied program, with students having direct, supervised clinical experience in competency and responsibility assessment, consulting with attorneys and judges, training police, working with the juvenile court. Jointly with the Law School, we publish the journal *Law & Psychology Review,* and one of our students always serves as one of the senior editors. Dissertation topics and internship choices additionally reflect the specific areas of interest individual students have in clinical psychology and the law.

Contact: Stanley L. Brodsky, Department of Psychology, P.O. Box 2968, University, AL 35486 (205/348-5083).

Institution: University of Arizona.

Levels: Joint-degree (JD-Ph.D.); Ph.D. specialty; post-doctoral (research).

Subdisciplines: Primarily clinical; environmental; psycholegal; also will consider applications in social, cognitive, biopsychology.

Special Features: Strong active involvement of law faculty; strong multidisciplinary training opportunities beyond psychology and law, particularly in sociology, criminology, education, and legal philosophy.

Contact: Bruce D. Sales, Department of Psychology, University of Arizona, Tucson, AZ 85721 (602/621-7448).

Institution: Atascadero State Hospital.

Levels: Post-doctoral (clinical); internship.

Subdiscipline: Clinical.

Special Features: Atascadero is a maximum security hospital with a patient population of 1100, including sex offenders, incompetent to stand trial, and not guilty by reason of insanity.

Contact: Robert Haynes, Training Center, P.O. Box A, Atascadero, CA 93423 (805/461-2219).

Institution: California School of Professional Psychology.

Levels: Ph.D. minor; post-doctoral (clinical).

Subdiscipline: Clinical.

Special Features: Aimed at practitioner in clinical/counseling psychology; program is two years—six weekends per year, one day/week internship in second year (can be regular employment, if appropriate); individual and group supervision; covers criminal and civil areas, including personal injury, workers' compensation, and domestic relations; multidisciplinary faculty.

Contact: David D. Stein, 1900 Addison Street, Berkeley, CA 94704 (415/548-5415).

Institution: University of Denver.

Level: Joint-degree (JD-MA; JD-Ph.D.).

Subdiscipline: Developmental (with an experimental component).

Special Features: Students must apply separately to the Department of Psychology and the College of Law. Admitted students then spend their first year at the Law School, followed by active participation in both programs. We welcome students to apply who have interests that overlap law and any of the following areas of psychology: social, cognitive, developmental, or clinical.

Contact: Gail S. Goodman (Psychology) or Murray Blumenthal (Law), University of Denver, University Park, Denver, CO 80208 (303/753-2478). For application materials, write: (Psychology) Andrea Edwards, Graduate Secretary, Department of Psychology, University of Denver, Denver, CO 80208; (Law) Office of Admissions, College of Law, University of Denver, CO 80208.

Institution: Federal Bureau of Prisons.

Level: Internship.

Subdisciplines: Clinical; counseling.

Special Features: Ten service-oriented, full-time, paid trainee positions located in federal correctional institutions across the country.

Contact: Robert D. Levinson, Federal Bureau of Prisons, 320 First Street, NW, Washington, DC 20534 (202/724-3042).

Institution: Hahnemann University, in conjunction with Villanova University School of Law.

Level: Joint-degree (JD-Ph.D.).

Subdiscipline: Clinical.

Special Features: By specializing within one area of law-psychology, students and faculty have the freedom of delving into certain areas in much greater detail than is otherwise possible. For example, one of the five interdisciplinary courses offered is entirely devoted to psycholegal assessment, diagnosis, and testimony.

Contact: Amiram Elwork, MS403, Law-Psychology Graduate Program, Hahnemann University, 230 North Broad Street, Philadelphia, PA 19102 (215/448-7896).

Institution: University of Illinois at Urbana-Champaign.

Level: Ph.D. minor.

Subdisciplines: Clinical; social.

Special Features: Several faculty have psycholegal interests: Golding and

Rappaport in Clinical; Davis and Lind in Social. There is no "program" as such, but students can do research, take courses, and minor in law.

Contact: Julian Rappaport, Department of Psychology, University of Illinois, Champaign, IL 61820 (217/333-8547).

Institution: John Jay College of Criminal Justice.

Level: MA specialty.

Subdiscipline: Clinical.

Special Features: Emphasizes the evaluation and treatment of individuals with psychological problems who come to the attention of the criminal justice system (e.g., adult and juvenile offenders; victims of crime and intrafamilial violence; criminal justice personnel) and the role of the psychologist in the courtroom. The program also provides opportunities for supervised research and practica in forensic settings. Two members of the Psychology faculty are psychologist-lawyers, and the program draws upon the resources of a college of criminal justice.

Contact: James S. Wulach, Department of Psychology, John Jay College of Criminal Justice, 445 W. 59th Street, New York, NY 10019 (212/489-5075).

Institution: University of Maryland School of Law/Johns Hopkins University.

Level: Joint-degree (JD-Ph.D.).

Subdisciplines: Any substantive research area.

Special Features: Rigorous research design, methodology, statistics, and measurement skills; urban setting with easy access to psychological, legal, and medical facilities as well as Washington, D.C.

Contact: Donald N. Bersoff, University of Maryland School of Law, 500 West Baltimore Street, Baltimore, MD 21201 (301/528-5619).

Institution: Napa State Hospital.

Level: Internship.

Subdiscipline: Clinical.

Special Features: Program includes some didactic input as well as observation of evaluations and/or court testimony.

Contact: Kristin Wombacher, Napa State Hospital, Box A, Imola, CA 94558 (707/255-5631).

Institution: University of Nebraska-Lincoln.

Levels: Joint-degree (JD-Ph.D.); Ph.D. specialty; Ph.D. minor; post-doctoral (research).

Subdisciplines: General-experimental (JD-Ph.D. or Ph.D. minor); social-personality-developmental (JD-Ph.D., Ph.D. minor, or post-doctoral); community-clinical (Ph.D. specialty or Ph.D. minor).

Special Features: UNL offers opportunities in all major subfields and at several levels of psycholegal training. Special tracks are available in mental health policy and administration (JD-Ph.D. or post-doctoral, with applied-social/com-munity psychology emphasis) and in research in forensic psychology (Ph.D. specialty program). The program aims to prepare researchers skilled in legal policy analysis. Core faculty (i.e., those whose primary area of emphasis is psycholegal studies) include Gary Melton (child and family policy; mental health law and forensic psychology; land use planning), Roberta Morris (labor law; tax policy; evaluation research), and a law faculty member to be hired. Other faculty who are presently heavily involved in the program include: *Psychology*—John Berman (evaluation research); James Cole (Forensic psychology); David S. Hargrove (mental health policy); Brian Sarata (community psychology; juvenile justice); Theo Sonderegger (neurotoxicology); Ross Thompson (child and family policy); *Law*—Alan Frank (law-related education; family law); Martin Gardner (criminal law; criminal procedure; juvenile and family law); Stephen Kalish (legal profession; legal history). There is a monthly law/psychology colloquium series; there are also opportunities for practica and research in state agencies.

Contact: Gary B. Melton, Department of Psychology, 209 Burnett Hall, UNL, Lincoln, NE 68588-0308 (402/472-3130).

Institution: Northwestern University.

Level: Joint-degree (JD-Ph.D.).

Subdisciplines: Social, clinical, evaluation research.

Contact: Tom Tyler, Department of Psychology, Northwestern University, Evanston, IL 60201 (312/492-5190).

Institution: Patton State Hospital.

Level: Internship.

Subdiscipline: Clinical.

Special Features: Psychological assessment of dangerousness issues secondary to all facets of psychopathology; reports utilized by staff and courts; some sex-offender patients; majority of patients are NGRI or unable to stand trial and sent to the hospital for treatment. Only California penal-code hospital receiving women. The intern acquires considerable knowledge about forensic issues throughout the training year. Intern attends court with supervisor several times during the year on select cases and learns about expert testimony. Psychotherapy, individual and group, with supervisors throughout the year; intern has four rotations during the year throughout all treatment programs.

Contact: Milo Scherer, Psychology Internship Program, Patton State Hospital, 102 East Highland Avenue, Patton, CA 92369 (714/862-8121).

Institution: Saint Elizabeths Hospital.

Levels: Post-doctoral (clinical/research); internship.

Subdiscipline: Clinical.

Special Features: As part of a general APA-approved internship, we offer a 25-hour placement in our Forensic Division. We also offer an advanced specialization in Forensics with some combination of clinical and research activities.

Contact: Elliot R. Blum, Clinical Psychology Training Section, Saint Elizabeths Hospital, Washington, DC 20032 (202/574-7171).

Institution: Saint Louis University.

Level: Ph.D. minor.

Subdisciplines: Clinical; applied-experimental.

Special Features: Clinical—Specialization by way of participation in ongoing research in Psychology-Law Research Center, and own MA and Ph.D. research. Predominant content areas currently: (a) forensic assessment research and development; (b) developmental psychology and law; (c) decisionmaking processes in legal systems. *Applied-experimental*—A structured curriculum for specialization in psychology-law in later years of Applied-Experimental program. Includes a set of interdisciplinary coursework and research, under supervision of any of three faculty members whose research is in psychology-law.

Contact: Thomas Grisso (clinical) or Richard Weiner (applied-experimental), Department of Psychology, Saint Louis University, 221 North Grand Boulevard, Saint Louis, MO 63103 (Grisso—314/658-2272; Weiner—314/658-2273).

Institution: University of Southern California School of Medicine.

Level: Post-doctoral.

Subdiscipline: Clinical.

Special Features: The goal of the program is to upgrade clinical professionals' expertise in dealing with legal issues involving mental health factors of significance. The full-time, one-year program consists of 32 hours/week of lectures, seminars, and supervision. Postdoctoral fellows are assigned one day per week to a field service commitment where they function as forensic psychological consultants to state hospitals, county jails, state or federal prisons, juvenile justice agencies, and other agencies that interrelate with mental health and law. There are extensive opportunities to serve as consultants to the superior, municipal, juvenile, federal criminal, and family law courts, as well as county and federal probation agencies and local and state governmental agencies. Courses are provided in criminal law, civil law, juvenile and family law, mental health law, crime and delinquency. The post-doctoral fellows have a minimum of three supervisors, including psychologists and psychiatrists. The fellows conduct at least one treatment group per week for mentally disordered offenders. Each fellow receives an academic appointment wherein he or she teaches and supervises psychiatry residents in the area of psychiatry and law.

Contact: Linda E. Weinberger, University of Southern California Institute of Psychiatry, Law and Behavioral Sciences, P.O. Box 2945, Los Angeles, CA 90051 (213/226-4942).

Institution: Stanford University.

Levels: Joint-degree (JD-Ph.D.; Ph.D.-MLS); Ph.D. minor; post-doctoral (research).

Subdisciplines: Social; cognitive; personality; psychopathology.

Special Features: Research-oriented, "apprenticeship" program.

Contact: Phoebe Ellsworth or David L. Rosenhan, Department of Psychology, Stanford University, Stanford, CA 94305 (415/497-3361 or 3738).

Institution: University of Virginia.

Levels: Ph.D. specialty; Ph.D. minor; post-doctoral fellows welcome, but no formal program or internal financial support at that level.

Subdisciplines: Community; clinical; specialty in Social Ecology and Development.

Special Features: We grant a Ph.D. in psychology with a major and a minor area. Law and Psychology can be a minor area. Also possible are a major area in Community Psychology with emphasis on psycholegal issues and a major in the specialty area of psychology, law, and children. Faculty members with major interests in psycholegal studies, especially with respect to law and children, include: Psychology—Lois Weithorn, Robert Emery, N. Dickon Reppucci; Law/Institute of Law, Psychiatry, & Public Policy—Elizabeth Scott, John Monahan, Walter Wadlington, Sheila Deitz, Park Deitz; Psychiatry—Andre Derdeyn. Several courses and practica are available.

Contact: N. Dickon Reppucci, University of Virginia, Gilmer Hall, Charlottesville, VA 22901 (804/924-0662).

Institution: University of Virginia Medical Center.

Level: Internship.

Subdiscipline: Clinical.

Special Features: One day/week rotation (six months) embedded within comprehensive medical center internship. Forensic rotation within Forensic psychiatry Clinic of the Institute of Law, Psychiatry, and Public Policy of UVa. Intern becomes involved in forensic evaluations in cases such as: juvenile delinquency; domestic relations (i.e., abuse and neglect; child custody); adult criminal; sexual sterilization. In addition to one day of clinical rotation, intern has opportunity to audit or enroll in any of several law-psychology courses offered by the Institute related to adult criminal forensic psychology; juvenile and family forensic psychology; law and the mental health system; behavioral science and law, etc. Interns also can take a six-day forensic training workshop which has been designed for, and is offered to, community mental health professionals in Virginia.

Contact: Robert Van de Castle, Psychology Residency Program, Behavioral Medicine Center, University of Virginia Medical Center, Blue Ridge Hospital, Charlottesville, VA 22901 (804/924-5314). For information specifically about the forensic rotation, contact: Sheila Deitz, Institute of Law, Psychiatry, & Public Policy, Blue Ridge Hospital-Box 100, Charlottesville, VA 22901 (804/924-5435).

Institution: University of Wisconsin.

Levels: Joint-degree (JD-Ph.D.); Ph.D. minor; post-doctoral (research).

Subdisciplines: Social; clinical.

Special Features: Primary contact person in psychology is Steven Penrod, whose research focuses on legal decision making (jurors and judges), the psychological aspects of the rules of evidence and procedure, and eyewitness reliability. Most of this research is in field settings. Several members of the social area maintain active research on forensic issues (aggression and violence, victims, vandalism . . .), and members of the clinical area have active research programs in corrections and the courts. A further strength of the program is that there are several social scientists on the law school faculty, and faculty in sociology, political science, communication, and social work also conduct law-related empirical research.

Contact: Steven Penrod, Psychology Department, 1202 West Johnson, University of Wisconsin, Madison, WI 53706 (608/262-2076 or 7470).

Institution: Wisconsin Division of Corrections, Bureau of Program Resources.

Level: Internship.

Subdiscipline: Clinical.

Special Features: The program is designed to expose the intern to the full range of psychological problems found among residents of institutions and people under field supervision. The intern can expect a placement in an adult institution, a juvenile institution, and a probation and parole office. There is work with both male and female offenders.

Contact: Eugene Strangman, Box 7925, Madison, WI 53707 (608/266-0492).

Forensic Glossary

Ab Initio. "From the first act." Refers to the validity of statutes and so forth.

Abrogate. To annul or cancel.

Acquit. To set free or judicially discharge.

Actus Reus. The criminal act. "The guilty act." The physical act as opposed to the psychical (mens rea).

Ad Hoc. For a particular or special purpose.

Admissible Evidence. Evidence that can be received by the trier of fact (judge or jury).

Adversary Process. A contest by two opposing parties.

Adverse Party. The person on the opposite side of litigation.

Amicus Curiae. Friend of the court. One who gives information to the court on some matter of law that is in doubt. A brief submitted by one who is not a party to a lawsuit.

A Posteriori. From the most recent point of view. That which can only be known from experience.

Appellant. The party who appeals a decision.

Appellate Court. A court having jurisdiction to review law as a result of a prior determination of the same case.

A Priori. To reason from factual and historical knowledge that certain facts are true.

Attest. To affirm as true.

Bailiff. A court attendant.

Bar. The complete body of attorneys.

Bench. The court; the judges composing the court.

Bill of Particulars. A statement used to inform the defense of the specific occurrences intended to be investigated on the trial and to limit the course of evidence to the particular scope of the inquiry. An amplification of the pleading.

393

BONA. Good or virtuous.

BURDEN OF PROOF. The duty of a party to substantiate allegation so that dismissal can be avoided. To convince the trier of facts as to the truth of a claim. In civil cases proof must be by a *preponderance* of the evidence, while in criminal cases the state's persuasion burden is met only by proof *beyond reasonable doubt.* In some equity matters and more recent Supreme Court decisions, *clear and convincing evidence* is the standard of proof.

CERTIORARI. A means of gaining an appellate review. A discretionary writ with the Supreme Court of the United States that may be issued to any court in the land to review a federal question if at least four of the nine justices vote to hear the case.

CIVIL LAW. Roman law embodied in the Justinian Code.

CIVIL RIGHTS. Rights given, defined, and specified by positive laws enacted by civilized communities. Note the difference from *civil liberties.* Civil rights are positive in nature, and civil liberties are negative. These are immunities from governmental interference.

CLEAR AND CONVINCING. A standard of proof beyond preponderance but below reasonable doubt. Less than the degree required in criminal cases but more than that required in ordinary civil actions.

CLEAR AND PRESENT DANGER. A standard used to determine when one's First Amendment rights may be curtailed or punished. The degree to which a certain act or occurrence is highly likely to bring about substantive evils that the government has a right to prevent.

COLLUSION. The making of an agreement with another for the purposes of fraud.

COMMON LAW. Jurisprudence originating in England and applied to the United States. Contrasts with civil law, the descendant of Roman law.

COMPOS MENTIS. Mentally competent.

CONSPIRACY. The combination of two or more people who propose to commit a criminal or an unlawful act or to commit a lawful act by criminal and unlawful means or who propose by concerted action to accomplish an unlawful purpose.

CONTEMPT OF COURT. Either an act or an omission tending to obstruct or interfere with the orderly administration of justice in the court. To impair the dignity of the court or to impair respect for its authority.

CORPUS DELICTI. The body of the crime. Objective proof that a crime has been committed. *Not* the body of a victim of a homicide. In a murder prosecution, *prima facie* evidence showing that the alleged victim met death by criminal agency. The weight of proof is beyond reasonable doubt.

CORPUS JURIS. The body of law.

COURT MARTIAL.   Military tribunal that has jurisdiction of offenses against laws of the service in which the offender is engaged. Military status is not sufficient. The crime must be service-connected. (General Court Martial—Presided over by a law officer, has not less than five members, tries defendants on all military offenses, and can prescribe any permitted sanction.) (Special Court Martial—Presided over by three members, may try noncapital offenses, but limited in authority as to sanctions that can be prescribed.) (Summary Court Martial—Presided over by a single commissioned officer, and limited in respect to the personnel over whom it can operate and sanctions it may prescribe. The accused may refuse trial by Summary Court Martial, but the charges can then be referred to a higher level.)

CRUEL AND UNUSUAL PUNISHMENT.   Punishment found to be offensive to the ordinary person. The Eighth Amendment provides "excessive bail shall not be required nor excessive fines imposed nor cruel and unusual punishment inflicted." This term cannot be defined with specificity. It broadens as society pays more regard to human decency and dignity. In general, punishment that amounts to torture or is grossly excessive. Unfair, shocking, or disgusting to people's reasonable sensitivity. Beyond any force needed to maintain order in a prison.

CULPABLE.   Deserving of moral blame. Fault rather than guilt.

CUSTODY.   Applied to property. Not ownership but keeping, guarding, caring for, preserving. Implies that the object is within immediate personal care and control of the person in whose custody the object is subjected. When applied to a person, it may mean to require restraint and physical control.

DAMAGES.   Monetary compensation that the law awards to an injured party.

Actual Damages.   Losses that can be readily proved to have been sustained.

Special (Consequential) Damages.   Loss or injury that is indirect or mediate.

Double (or Treble) Damages.   Two or three times the amount of damages that a court or jury would normally find for a party, awarded for certain kinds of injuries pursuant to statutes authorizing same.

Punitive (Exemplary) Damages.   Compensation in excess of actual damages. A kind of punishment to the wrongdoer. Actual damages must come first before these.

Incidental Damages.   Losses reasonably incident to or conduct giving rise to a claim for actual damages, such as expenses.

Nominal Damages.   A trivial sum as recognition that a legal injury was sustained although slight. The amount is usually so small (one dollar) as not to constitute damages.

DE BENE ESSE. Provisionally or conditionally.

DE FACTO. By virtue of the deed. Reality.

DEFAULT JUDGMENT. A judgment entered against a defendant because of the defendant's failure to respond to a plaintiff's action.

DEFENDANT. In civil proceedings it is usually the party responding to the complaint. In criminal proceedings it is the accused.

DEFENSE. Can be denial, or a plea opposing the truth or validity of a plaintiff's case.

Affirmative Defense. One that serves as a basis for proving some new fact.

Equitable Defense. One that is recognized by courts of equity.

DE NOVO HEARING. A new hearing. Usually the judgment of the trial court is suspended, and the reviewing court determines the case as though it originated in the reviewing court.

DEPONENT. A witness. Facts to be given under oath.

DEPOSITION. A method of pretrial discovery. It consists of a statement from the witness under oath taken in question-and-answer form. Similar to an appearance at court, with the adversary present and the opportunity for cross-examination. May be taken by any party of any witness. Can be oral (face to face) or written.

DIRECTED VERDICT. A verdict returned by the jury at the direction of the trial judge. Usually done when the judge feels that the opposing party fails to present a *prima facie* case. May occur when a necessary defense is not presented.

DISCOVERY. Pretrial procedure. Vital information concerning the case is obtained from the adverse party. Disclosure by adverse party of facts, documents, or information in his or her possession.

DOCKET SOUNDING. Meeting between the attorneys and the judges to determine the schedule of cases for a particular period of time.

DURHAM RULE. A test of criminal responsibility adopted by the District of Columbia Court of Appeals (1954). States: "An accused is not criminally responsible if his unlawful act was the product of mental disease or defect" (214 F.2d.862,874-75). First major modification of M'Naghten's Rule. Many times negated by the American Law Institute's Model Penal Code test (§4.01)(1) Cite 471 F.2d.969,971 (1972).

EXCULPATORY. Evidence or statements tending to justify or excuse defendant from fault or guilt.

EXPERT WITNESS. A witness having "special knowledge of the subject about which he is to testify" (26 A.2d 770,773 [1942]) (22 A.2d 28 [1941]). An expert need not have formal training. The court must be satisfied that the testimony will help the triers of fact.

GRANDFATHER CLAUSE.   Certain legal provisions that permit persons engaged in business or profession before the passage of an act regulating that business or profession to receive a license or prerogative without meeting the criteria of new entrants into the field.

GRIEVANCE.   One's charges that something imposes an illegal obligation or burden. A denial of an equitable or legal right or cause of injustice.

HABEAS CORPUS.   Used in the criminal and civil contexts. A procedure for obtaining a judicial determination of the legality of an individual's custody. In the criminal context—bringing the petitioner before the court to decide on the legality of confinement. Related to due process of law.

HEARSAY RULE.   A statement made other than by a witness while testifying at the hearing offered to prove the truth of a matter stated. This is inadmissible evidence. Oral or written statements are nonadmissible. When witnesses are asked what some other person told them, it is inadmissible if the material being described is for the purposes of determining the truth of the matter asserted. If, however, it is elicited merely to show that the words were spoken, it is admissible.

IMPEACHMENT.   To charge a public official with wrongdoing. With reference to the testimony of a witness, to call into question the evidence offered for that purpose. Can also occur by showing that the witness is unworthy of belief. Sometimes by the witness's own statements.

IN CAMERA.   Meaning "in chambers." A room adjacent to the courtroom where the judge performs the duties of his office. Also applies if the judge performs a judicial duty or act while the court is not in session.

INCOMPETENCY.   Inability. A relative term that is employed to mean disqualification, inability, or incapacity. It may be used to show a lack of physical, intellectual, or moral fitness.

INFORMED CONSENT.   Consent given only after a full notice is given as to what is being consented to.

IN LOCO PARENTIS.   In the place of the parent.

INSANITY.   Not responsible mentally to some degree. The ALI Model Penal Code quotes: "A person is not responsible for criminal conduct if at the time of such conduct as a result of mental disease or defect he lacks substantial capacity either to appreciate the criminality or wrongfulness of his conduct or to conform his conduct to the requirements of the law" (Model Penal Code §4.01 [1]).

JUVENILE COURTS.   Judicial systems first established in the late nineteenth century to treat youthful offenders separately from adults. Places the judge in the position of *parens patriae*. Intended to remove the adversary nature of normal proceedings.

LEADING QUESTION.   A question posed by a trial lawyer that is improper on direct examination because it suggests to the witness the answer that the witness should deliver.

MANDAMUS.   An extraordinary writ issued from a court to an official compelling the performance of an act that the law recognizes as a duty. Used when other judicial remedies have failed.

MENS REA.   A guilty mind. A general intent to do a prohibited act.

MENTAL ANGUISH.   Compensable injury embracing all forms of mental, as opposed to physical, injury. Can include distress, grief, anxiety, fright, and bereavement.

MISTRIAL.   A trial that is terminated and declared void prior to the jury's returning a verdict. Usually because of some fundamental error prejudicial to the defendant that cannot be cured by instructions to the jury. Sometimes because of the jury's inability to reach a verdict (hung jury). It does not result in a judgment for any party. It indicates a failure of trial. In criminal prosecution it may prevent retrial under the doctrine of double jeopardy.

M'NAGHTEN'S RULE.   Common-law test of criminal responsibility. Acquittal by reason of insanity. "If as a result of a mental disease or defect the defendant did not understand what he did or that it was wrong, or if he was under a delusion (but not otherwise insane) which if true would have provided a good defense. Thus, if one does not understand what one was doing at all or did not know that it was wrong, he is excused. He is also excused if due to an insane delusion he thought he was acting in self-defense or carrying out the will of God. Often called the right/wrong test."

MOTION.   An application to the court requesting an order or a rule in favor of the applicant.

NEGLIGENCE.   Failure to exercise the degree of care that a person should, with ordinary prudence, exercise under similar circumstances.

NON COMPOS MENTIS.   Not having control over the mind or intellect. Insane.

PLEA.   A special answer relying on one or more things as a cause why a suit should be dismissed, delayed, or barred. Technically it is the defendant's answer by matter of fact to the plaintiff's declaration. In a criminal proceeding, the defendant's attorney will enter a plea at the arraignment of either guilty or not guilty. A plea can be *dilatory* (contests grounds other than the merits of the plaintiff's case, such as improper jurisdiction, wrong defendant, or other procedural defects) or *peremptory* (answers to plaintiff's contention).

PLEA BARGAINING.   A process by which the accused and the prosecutor negotiate a mutually satisfactory disposition of the case.

PRECEDENT.   A previously described case that is used as an authority for the disposition of future cases.

PRIVILEGED COMMUNICATIONS.   Communications that occur in a setting of either legal or other professional confidentiality. Allows those who are presenting to resist legal pressure to disclose contents. A breach of the confidentiality can result in a suit.

PRO BONO PUBLICO.   For the public good or welfare. An attorney or other professional takes a case without compensation for the purpose of advancing a social cause or representing a party who cannot afford it.

PROSECUTION.   Pursuing a lawsuit or a criminal trial. Also the state. The criminal equivalent of litigant in a civil suit.

REASONABLE DOUBT.   Refers to the degree of certainty required of a juror for a legally valid determination of the guilt of a criminal defendant. The judge will generally use this term and instructions to the jury to indicate that innocence is to be presumed unless the guilt is so clearly proved that the jury can see no reasonable doubt. It does *not* require proof so clear that no possibility of error exists.

RECESS.   An adjournment of a trial or a hearing that is temporary and occurs after the commencement of the trial. If there is going to be substantial delay, it is called a *continuance.* A temporary dismissal is called *sine die.*

RETAINER.   Compensation paid in advance to an attorney for services to be performed in a specific case. May be a payment simply to get the attorney to be available. It may be the whole sum to be charged or, more often, a deposit.

STAR CHAMBER.   An ancient court of England. No jury present. Abolished in modern jurisprudence.

STRICT LIABILITY.   Liability without a showing of fault. For example, someone who engages in an activity of an ultrahazardous nature is liable for all injuries caused by the enterprise even without negligence being shown. A recently developed area of strict liability concerns *product liability.*

THIRD-PARTY BENEFICIARIES.   Persons who have enforceable rights created by a contract to which they are not parties and for which they give no consideration.

TORT.   A wrong. A private or civil wrong or injury independent of a contract resulting from a breach of a legal duty.

TRIAL.   The offering of testimony before a competent tribunal according to established procedures.

VENUE.   A neighborhood, and synonomous with "place of trial." It refers to the possible place or places for the trial of a suit. Among several places where jurisdiction could be established.

VERDICT.   The opinion of a jury or a judge sitting as a jury on a question of fact.

VOIR DIRE.   To speak the truth. Examination by the court or by attorneys of prospective jurors to determine their qualification for jury service. To determine if cause exists for a challenge to excuse them.

WAIVER.   An intentional and voluntary giving up or surrender of a known right.

WEIGHT OF THE EVIDENCE.   The relative value of the totality of evidence presented on one side of a judicial dispute in light of the evidence presented by the other side. Refers to the persuasiveness of testimony of witnesses.

WITNESS.   One who gives evidence of a cause before a court and who attests or swears to the facts.

WORK PRODUCT.   Work done by an attorney in the process of representing a client that is ordinarily not subject to discovery. It can generally be defined as writings, statements, or testimony that would substantially invade an attorney's legal impressions or legal theories about pending litigation. An attorney's legal impressions and theories would include his tactics, strategy, opinions, and thoughts.

WRIT.   A mandatory precept issued by an authority in the name of the sovereign or the state for the purpose of compelling a person to do something.

Bibliography

ABA Standing Committee on Association Standards for Criminal Justice. (1983). *First Tentative Draft—Criminal Justice Mental Health Standards.* Washington, DC: American Bar Association, pp. 7-259–7-297.

Abarbanel, A. (1979). Shared parenting after separation and divorce: A study of joint custody. *American Journal of Orthospsychiatry, 50,* 320–329.

Ainsworth, M. (1973). The development of infant–mother attachment. In B. Caldwell & H. Riccioti (Eds.), *Review of Child Development Research* (Vol. 3). Chicago: University of Chicago Press.

American Psychiatric Association. (1980). *Diagnostic and statistical manual of mental disorders* (3rd ed.). Washington, DC: Author.

American Psychological Association. (1974). *Standards for educational and psychological tests.* Washington, DC: Author.

American Psychological Association. (1977). *Standards for providers of psychological services.* Washington, DC: Author.

American Psychological Association. (1981). Ethical principles of psychologists. *American Psychologist, 36*(6), 633–638.

Anastasi, A. (1981). *Psychological Testing* (4th ed.). New York: Macmillan.

Anderson, K. (1982). American prisons. *Time, 11*(120), 38–82.

Anthony, N. C. (1971). Comparison of client's standard, exaggerated, and matching MMPI profiles. *Journal of Consulting and Clinical Psychology, 36,* 100–103.

Bazelon, D. (1974). Psychiatrists and the adversary process. *Scientific American, 230,* 18–23.

Beal, E. W. (1979). Children of divorce: A family systems perspective. *Journal of Social Issues, 35*(4), 140–154.

Belli, M. (1982). The expert witness. *Trial, 17*(7), 35–37.

Belsky, J. (1981). Early human experience: A family perspective. *Developmental Psychology, 17*(1), 3–23.

Bersoff, D. (1981). Testing and the law. *American Psychologist, 36*(10), 1047–1059.

Blau, T. H. (1959). *Private practice in clinical psychology.* New York: Appleton-Century-Crofts.

Blau, T. H. (1982). *The psychologist as expert witness: Compendium.* Tampa, FL: Psychological Seminars, 169–171.

Bockman, R. (1982, December 13). Expert: Leave insanity defense alone. *Tampa Tribune,* pp. B1–2.

Boffey, P. M. (1983, January 20). Psychiatric group urges stiffer rules for insanity pleas. *New York Times,* p. 8.

Bonnie R., & Slobogin, C. (1980). The role of mental health professionals in the criminal process. *Virginia Law Review, 66,* 427–522.

Brody, J. E. (1983, March 29). Bonding at birth: A major theory being questioned. *New York Times, Science Times,* pp. 15, 16.

Buckout, R. (1974). Eyewitness testimony. *Scientific American, 231*(6), 23–31.

Buros, O. (Ed.). (1933–1978). *Mental measurement yearbooks.* (Vol. 1–8). *Tests in print—Educational, psychological and personality tests of 1933 and 1934.* Highland Park, NJ: Gryphon Press.

California State Psychological Association. (1980). Standards for professional services on court panels and other legal consultations. *The California State Psychologist, 14*(2), 21–22.

California State Psychological Association. (1981). Two professionals urge ban on psychiatric testimony. *The California State Psychologist, 15*(5), 1, 16.

Chambers, M. (1983, January 21st). Insanity defense backed by panel. *New York Times.* p. 15.

Clark, H. H. (1974). *Cases and problems in domestic relations.* St. Paul: West Publications.

Clingempeel, W. G., & Reppucci, N. D. (1982). Joint custody after divorce. *Psychological Bulletin, 91*(1), 102–127.

Cofer, C. N., Chance, J. E., & Judson, A. J. (1949). A study of malingering on the MMPI. *Journal of Psychology, 27,* 491–499.

Collins, G. (1982, December 20). Some broken families retain many bonds. *New York Times,* p. 17.

Committee on Pattern Jury Instructions. (1979). *Pattern jury instructions (Criminal cases).* St. Paul, MN: West Publishing Co.

Committee to Develop Joint Technical Standards for Educational and Psychological Testing. (1982). *Standards for educational and psychological testing (Draft).* Washington, DC: American Psychological Association.

Dahlstrom, W. G., Welsh, C. S., & Dahlstrom, L. E. (1975). *An MMPI handbook.* Minneapolis: University of Minnesota Press, p. 164.

Dix, G. (1977). The death penalty, "dangerous," psychiatric testimony and professional ethics. *American Journal of Criminal Law, 5,* 151–214.

Dullea, G. (1983, February 7). Wide changes in family life are altering the family law. *New York Times,* pp. 1, 12.

Executive Committee, Family Law Section, NJSBA. (1983). Mediation committee report. *New Jersey Family Lawyer, 11*(5), 75–80.

Federal Rules of Evidence for United States Courts and Magistrates. (1975). St. Paul, MN: West Publishing Co.

Freed, D. J., & Foster, H. H., Jr. (1981). Divorce in the fifty states: An overview. *Family Law Quarterly, 14,* 229–284.

Fulconer, D. M. (1942). *The adjustive behavior of some recently bereaved spouses.* Doctoral dissertation, Northwestern University.

Gardner, R. A. (1982). *Family evaluation in child custody litigation.* Creekskill, NJ: Creative Therapeutics.

Glaser, G. (1979). Discretion in juvenile justice. In L. Abt & I. R. Stuart (Eds.), *Social psychology and discretionary law.* New York: Van Nostrand Reinhold.

Glick, I. O., Weiss, R. S., & Parkes, C. M. (1974). *The first year of bereavement.* New York: Wiley.

Glick, P. C. (1979). Children of divorced parents in demographic perspective. *Journal of Social Issues, 35*(4), 170–181.

Glueck, S. S. (1925). *Mental disorder and the criminal law.* Boston: Little, Brown.

Goldofski, O. B. (1974). The psychology of testimony. *Vyestnik Prava,* No. 16–18, 185.

Gough, H. G. (1954). Some common misconceptions about neuroticism. *Journal of Consulting Psychology, 18,* 287–292.

Gourvitz, E. H. (1983). Divorce mediation—An alternative to the adversary approach. *New Jersey Family Lawyer, 11*(5), 81–85.

Gozansky, N. (1976). Court-ordered investigations in custody casts. *Willamette Law Journal, 12,* 511–526.

Grand Jury Defense Office. (1982). The witness' appearance before the grand jury. In National Lawyer's Guild (Ed.), *Representation of witness before federal grand juries.* New York: Clark Boardman.

Gregory, C. O., Kalven, H., & Epstein, R. A. (1977). *Cases and materials on torts* (3rd ed.). Boston: Little, Brown.

Greif, J. B. (1979). Fathers, children, and joint custody. *American Journal of Orthopsychiatry, 50,* 311–319.

Haney, C. (1984). Special issue. Death qualification. *Law and Human Behavior, 8,* (1/2), pp. 1–193.

Hetherington, E. M., Cox, M., & Cox, R. (1979). Play and social interaction in children following divorce. *Journal of Social Issues, 35*(4), 26–49.

Holland, T. R., Holt, N., & Beckett, G. E. (1982). Prediction of violent versus nonviolent recidivism from prior violent and nonviolent criminality. *Journal of Abnormal Psychology, 91*(3), 178–182.

Holmes, T. H., & Masuda, M. (1973). Life change and illness susceptibility. In *Separation and Depression* (AAAS Publication No. 94). Washington, DC: **Publisher,** pp. 161–186.

Howell, R. J. (1982). In defense of the insanity plea. *Bulletin of the American Academy of Forensic Psychologists, 3*(1), 1–2.

Institute of Judician Administration (American Bar Association). (1977). *Juvenile justice standards project.* Cambridge, MA: Ballinger.

Isaacson, W. (1982, July 5). Insane on all counts. *Time,* pp. 22–26.

Jaffe, S. (1903). Ein psychologisches experiment in Kriminalistischen seminar der universitaet Berlin. *Beitraege zur Psychologie der Aussage, mit besonderer Bereuecksrchitigung der Rechtspflege, Paedogogik, Psychiatrie und Geschichts forschung, I,* 79.

Jones, A. (1977). Suicide by aircraft: A case report. *Aviation Space, Environmental Medicine, 48,* 454–459.

Kalven, H., & Zeisel, H. (1966). *The American jury.* Boston: Little, Brown.

Kaufman, R., & English, F. W. (1979). *Needs-assessment: Concept and application.* Englewood Cliffs, NJ: Educational Technology Publications.

Kazen, B. A. (1977). *When father wants custody: A lawyer's view.* Austin: State Bar of Texas.

Kerr, N. L., & Bray, R. M. (Eds.). (1982). *The psychology of the courtroom.* New York: Academic Press.

Ladd, J. (1952). Expert testimony. *Vanderbilt Law Review, 5,* 414, 419.

Lamb, M. E. (1977). The development of mother–infant and father–infant attachments in the second year of life. *Developmental Psychology, 13*(6), 637–648.

Leo, J. (1982, July 5). Insane on all counts. *Time,* pp. 22–27.

Leo, J. (1982, July 5). Is the system guilty? *Time,* pp. 26–27.

Lezak, M. D. (1976). *Neuropsychological Assessment.* New York: Oxford University Press, pp. 476–477.

Lichter, D. H. (1981). Note: Diagnosing the dead. *American Criminal Law Review, 18,* 617–635.

Lipsitt, P. D. (1970). *Competency Screening Test.* Boston: Competency to Stand Trial and Mental Illness Project.

Lipsitt, P. D., Lelos, D., & McGarry, A. L. (1971). Competency for trial: A screening instrument. *American Journal of Psychiatry, 128*(1), 137–141.

Litwak, T. R., Gerber, G. L., & Fenster, C. A. (1980). The proper role of psychology in child custody disputes. *Journal of Family Law, 18,* 269–300.

Lobsien, M. (1904). Veber psychologie der aussage, *Zeit schrift feur Paedagogische Psychologie, VI,* 161.

Loftus, E. F. (1979). *Eyewitness testimony.* Cambridge, MA: Harvard University Press.

Loftus, E. F. (1981). Eyewitness testimony: Psychological research and legal thought. In M. Tonry & N. Morris (Eds.), *Crime and justice: An annual review of research* (Vol. 3). Chicago: University of Chicago Press.

Loftus, E. F. (1983). Silence is not golden. *American Psychologist, 38,* 564–572.

Loftus, E. F., & Monahan, J. (1980). Trial by data. *American Psychologist, 35*(3), 270–283.

Louisell, D. W. (1955). The psychologist in today's legal world. *Minnesota Law Review, 39*(3), 235–272.

Lowery, C. R. (1981). Child custody decisions in divorce proceedings: A survey of judges. *Professional Psychology, 4*(12), 492, 498.

Luepnitz, D. A. (1978). Children of divorce: A review of the psychological literature. *Law and Human Behavior, 2*(2), 167–169.

Marx, M. L. (1977). Prison conditions and diminished capacity—A proposed defense. *Santa Clara Law Review, 17,* 855–883.

Maudsley, H. (1898). *Responsibility in mental disease.* New York: D. Appleton & Co.

McCloskey, M., & Egeth, H. E. (1983). Eyewitness identification: What can a psychologist tell a jury? *American Psychologist, 38,* 550–563.

Melton, G. B. (1983). More on insanity reform. *Division of Psychology and Law Newsletter, 3*(2), 6–8.

Millon, T. (1982). *Millon clinical multiaxial inventory.* Minneapolis: Interpretive Scoring Systems.

Molinoff, D. (1977, May 22). Life with father. *New York Times Magazine.*

Monahan, J. (1975). The prevention of violence. In J. Monahan (Ed.), *Community mental health and the criminal justice system.* New York: Pergamon Press.

Monahan, J. (1981). *Predicting violent behavior: An assessment of clinical techniques.* Beverly Hills, CA: Sage.

Morse, S. (1978). Law and mental health professionals: The limits of expertise. *Professional Psychology, 9,* 389–399.

Mullen, J. M., & Dudley, H. K., Jr. (1981). Development of an actuarial model for predicting dangerousness of patients in maximum-security mental hospitals. In J. R. Hays, T. K. Roberts, & K. S. Solway (Eds.), *Violence and the violent individual.* New York: SP Medical and Scientific Books.

Mulvey, E. P. (1982). Family courts: The issue of reasonable goals. *Law and Human Behavior, 6*(1), 49–64.

Munsterberg, Hugo. (1908). *On the witness stand.* New York: Doubleday.

National Conference of Commissioners on Uniform State Laws. (1971). Uniform marriage and divorce act. *Family Law Quarterly, 5,* 205–251.

Norton, John E. (Ed.). (1981). *The anatomy of a personal injury law suit* (2nd ed.). Washington, DC: Association of Trial Lawyers of America.

Nottingham, E. J., & Mattson, R. E. (1981). A validation study of the competency screening test. *Law and Human Behavior, 5*(4), 329–335.

Orthner, D. K., & Lewis, K. (1979). Evidence of single father competence in child-rearing. *Family Law Quarterly, 13,* 27–47.

Perline, M. L. (1980). The legal status of the psychologist in the courtroom. *Mental Disabilities Law Review, 3*(4), 194–200.

Petrella, R. C., & Poythress, N. G., Jr. (1983). The quality of forensic evaluations: An interdisciplinary study. *Journal of Consulting and Clinical Psychology, 51*(1), 76–85.

Petrich, J., & Holmes, T. H. (1977). Life changes and onset of illness. *Medical Clinics of North America, 61*(4), 825–838.

Poythress, N. G. (1980). Coping on the witness stand: Learned responses to "learned treatises." *Professional Psychology,* (1).

Poythress, N. G. (1982). Concerning reform in expert testimony. *Law and Human Behavior, 6,* 39–43.

Press, A. (1983, January 10). Divorce American style. *Newsweek,* pp. 42–48.

Rahe, R. H. (1972). Subjects' recent life changes and their near-future illness reports. *Annals of Clinical Research, 4,* 250–265.

Rey, A. (1941). L'examen psychologique dans las cas d'encephalopathie traumatique. *Archives de psychologie, 28*(112), 286–340.

Robinson, D. N. (1982, June 23). The *Hinckley* decision: Psychiatry in court. *Wall Street Journal,* p. 5.

Robitscher, J. (1980). *The powers of psychiatry.* Boston: Houghton Mifflin.

Roesch, R. (1979). Determining competency to stand trial: An examination of evaluation procedures in an institutional setting. *Journal of Consulting and Clinical Psychology, 47*(3), 542–550.

Roesch, R., & Golding, S. L. (1978). Legal and judicial interpretation of competency to stand trial statutes and procedures. *Criminology, 16,* 420–429.

Rossi, P. H. (Ed.). (1982). *Standards for evaluation practice* (Publication No. 15, New Directions for Program Evaluation: Evaluation Research Society). San Francisco: Jossey-Bass.

Ruback, R. B. (1982). Issues in family law. In J. C. Hanson & L. Abade (Eds.), *Values, ethics, legalities and the family therapist.* London: Aspen Systems.

Rudestam, K. E. (1977). Physical and psychological responses to suicide in the family. *Journal of Consulting Clinical Psychology, 45*(2), 162–170.

Rutter, M. (1971). Parent–child separation: Psychological effects on the children. *Journal of Child Psychology and Psychiatry and Allied Disciplines, 12,* 233–260.

Rutter, M. (1972). Maternal deprivation reconsidered. *Journal of Psychosomatic Research, 16,* 241–250.

Saks, M. J., & Hastie, R. (1978). *Social psychology in court.* New York: Van Nostrand Reinhold.

Sales, B. D. (Ed.). (1981). *The trial process.* New York: Plenum Press.

Sanborn, N., & Sanborn, J. (1976). The psychological autopsy as a therapeutic tool. *Diseases of the Nervous System, 37*(4), 7.

Santruck, J. W., & Warshak, R. A. (1979). Father custody and social development in boys and girls. *Journal of Social Issues, 35*(4), 112–115.

Scanlon, J. C., & Weingarten, K. (1963). The role of statistical data in the functioning of courts. *Buffalo Law Review, 2*(12), 522–527.

Shneidman, E. (1967). Some current developments in suicide prevention. *Bulletin of Suicidology, 33,* 41.

Shneidman, E. (1976) *Suicidology: Contemporary developments.* New York: Grune & Stratton, pp. 351-352, 540-544.

Shneidman, E. S. (1978). *Voices of death.* New York: Bantham Books.

Schoenfeld, L. S., & Lehmann, L. S. (1981). Management of the aggressive patient. In C. E. Walker (Ed.), *Clinical practice of psychology.* New York: Pergamon Press.

Shah, S. (1963). Crime and mental illness: Some problems in defining and labeling deviant behavior. *Mental Hygiene, 53,* 21–33.

Shah, S. (1977, February). Editorial. *APA Monitor,* p. 2.

Shah, S. (1978). Dangerousness. A paradigm for exploring some issues in law and psychology. *American Psychologist, 33*, 224–238.

Slovenko, R. (1973). *Psychiatry and law*. Boston: Little, Brown.

Slovenko, R. (1983, February 14). Pleading insanity is here to stay; insanity plea or not. *New York Times*, p. 18.

Sluggs, D. L. (1979). The use of psychological research by the judiciary. *Law and Human Behavior, 3*(1/2), 135–148.

Smith, G., & Hall, J. (1983, March 30). Study: "Guilty but mentally ill" verdict having no effect on insanity cases. *Atlanta Journal*, p. 25-A.

Span, M., & Cantor, D. W. (1983). Caution: Joint custody. *New Jersey Family Lawyer, 2*(5), 88–96.

Steadman, H. J., & Morrissey, J. P. (1981). The statistical prediction of violent behavior. *Law and Human Behavior, 3*(4), 263–274.

Steinman, S. (1981). The experience of children in a joint custody arrangement. *American Journal of Orthopsychiatry, 51*(3), 403–414.

Strout, R. L. (1982, August 30). The American family: Winds of change. *Tampa Tribune*, p. 11-A.

Suggs, D. L. (1979). The use of psychological research by the judiciary. *Law and Human Behavior, 3*, 135–148.

Taylor, R. E. (1983, January 20). Insanity defense should be narrowed, psychiatrists say. *Wall Street Journal*, p. 18.

Terman, L. M. (1931). Psychology and the law. *Los Angeles Bar Association Bulletin, 6*, 142–153.

Terman, L. M. (1935). Psychology and the law. *Commercial Law Journal, 40*, 639–646.

Tierney, J. (1982). Doctor, is this man dangerous? *Science, 3*(5), 28–31.

Wald, P. M. (1982). Become a real "friend of the court." *APA Monitor, 13*(2), 5.

Wallerstein, J. S., & Kelly, J. B. (1975). The effects of parental divorce: Experiences of the preschool child. *Journal of the American Academy of Child Psychiatry, 14*, 600–616.

Walters, H. A. (1981). Dangerousness. In J. R. Moon (Ed.), *Encyclopedia of Clinical Assessment* (Vol. 2). San Francisco: Jossey-Bass.

Weitzman, L. J., & Dixon, R. B. (1979). Child custody awards. *University of California, Davis Law Review, 12*, 473–521.

Wells, G. L., Leippe, M. R., & Ostrom, T. (1979). Guidelines for empirically assessing the fairness of a lineup. *Law and Human Behavior, 3*, 285–294.

Wenke, E. A., Robison, J. O., & Smith, G. W. (1972). Can violence be predicted? *Crime and Deliquency, 18*, 393–402.

Wigmore, J. H. (1909). Professor Munsterberg and the psychology of testimony. *Illinois Law Review, 3*(7), 399–445.

Wigmore, J. H. 3 *Wigmore on Evidence* (3rd Ed. 1940). 367–368.

Wolinsky, J. (1982). Programs join "distrustful" disciplines. *APA Monitor. 13*(2), 15.

Ziskin, J. (1981a). *Coping with psychiatric and psychological testimony* (3rd ed.). Marina del Ray: Law and Psychology Press.

Ziskin, J. (1981). Use of the MMPI in forensic settings. *Clinical Notes on the MMPI*, No. 9, pp. 1–13.

Ziskin, J., & Coleman, L. (1981). Two professionals urge ban on psychiatric testimony. *The California State Psychologist, 15*(5), 1–13.

Author Index

Abarbanel, A., 112, 153
A.B.A. Standing Committee, 83, 88
Ainsworth, M., 109, 144
Allport, G., 271
American Psychiatric Association, 4, 292
American Psychological Association, 5, 45, 55, 119, 266, 269, 326, 333
Anastasi, A., 55
Anderson, K., 15
Anthony, N.C., 73
Atkinson, R.C., 271
Atkinson, R.L., 271

Bartlett, F.C., 273
Bazelon, D., 4, 334
Beal, E.W., 121, 153
Beck, A.T., 81
Beckett, G.E., 50
Bedwell, M.A., 145
Belli, M., 12
Bem, D., 272
Bersoff, D., 49
Biller, H.B., 154
Blau, T.H., 3, 49, 54, 303
Bockman, R., 89
Bodenheimer, B.M., 145

Boffey, P.M., 89
Boggiano, W., 278
Bonnle, R., 334
Bourne, P.G., 81
Bower, G.H., 271
Bray, R.M., 7, 17
Brody, J.E., 109
Buckhout, R., 12, 270, 271, 273
Buros, O., 44, 49, 167

California State Psychological Association, 6, 329
Cantor, D.W., 112
Caplan, R., 277
Carrell, P.L., 144
Chance, J.E., 73
Clark, H.H., 107
Clarke-Stewart, A., 144
Clifford, B.R., 270
Clingempeel, W.G., 112
Cofer, C.N., 73
Coleman, L., 53
Collins, G., 112, 153
Contrada, R., 277
Cox, M., 111, 121
Cox, R., 111, 121

Subject Index

420 Subject Index